MUSIC OF THE COMMON TONGUE

MUSIC / CULTURE

A series from Wesleyan University Press
Edited by George Lipsitz, Susan McClary, and Robert Walser

Published titles

My Music by Susan D. Crafts, Daniel Cavicchi, Charles Keil, and the Music in Daily Life Project

Running with the Devil: Power, Gender, and Madness in Heavy Metal Music by Robert Walser

Subcultural Sounds: Micromusics of the West by Mark Slobin

Upside Your Head! Rhythm and Blues on Central Avenue by Johnny Otis

Dissonant Identities: The Rock'n'Roll Scene in Austin, Texas by Barry Shank

Black Noise: Rap Music and Black Culture in Contemporary America by Tricia Rose

Club Cultures: Music, Media and Subcultural Capital by Sarah Thornton

Music, Society, Education by Christopher Small

Listening to Salsa: Gender, Latin Popular Music, and Puerto Rican Cultures by Frances R. Aparicio

Any Sound You Can Imagine: Making Music/Consuming Technology by Paul Théberge

Voices in Bali: Energies and Perceptions in Vocal Music and Dance Theater by Edward Herbst

A Thousand Honey Creeks Later: My Life in Music from Basie to Motown—and Beyond by Preston Love

Musicking: The Meanings of Performing and Listening by Christopher Small

Music of the Common Tongue: Survival and Celebration in African American Music by Christopher Small

Singing Archaeology: Philip Glass's 'Akhnaten' by John Richardson

CHRISTOPHER SMALL

MUSIC OF THE COMMON TONGUE

Survival and Celebration in African American Music

WESLEYAN UNIVERSITY PRESS
Middletown, Connecticut

Published by Wesleyan University Press
Middletown, CT 06459
www.wesleyan.edu/wespress

Originally published in Great Britain in 1987
by John Calder (Publishers) Ltd. and in the
United States of America by Riverrun Press Inc.

First Wesleyan University Press edition 1998

Wesleyan University Press is a member of the Green
Press Initiative. The paper used in this book meets
their minimum requirement for recycled paper.

ISBN-13: 978-0-8195-6357-6
CIP data appear at the end of the book
Printed in the United States of America
5 4 3

To Neville Braithwaite,
who taught me what it was all about

and in grateful memory
of Edwin Mason,
who alone knew what I owed him

and of John Stevens,
for his courage and honesty,
no less than for his musicking

CONTENTS

PREFACE TO THE 1998 EDITION

Music of the Common Tongue remains my favorite of my three children, and to see it take its place alongside the other two in this Music/Culture series is a source of great joy to me. It was my second book (always the hardest to write), and it took me six years' hard and often despairing slog, not a minute of which do I now regret. It went out into the world in 1987 defaced by any number of editorial and typographical slip ups, with whatever virtues it possessed concealed by unsuitable cover designs and without the slightest ripple of publicity to help it on its way. Yet it has survived, and now it has been taken up by a sympathetic publisher and is being sent out once more, this time properly dressed and with the worst of its blemishes removed, ready to embark on what I believe will be its proper trajectory. I could not hope for more; to make it entirely as I should have liked it to be would have necessitated resetting the entire long text, a task which would be beyond the already generously allocated resources of its new patron.

In the Introduction to the book I said that I intended it as a tribute, to those known and unknown thousands of musicians (and as always I meant by that word all those who perform and compose, not just those who make their living from doing so) who created that way of doing music 'to which we can only give the awkward name of "Afro-American"'. That phrase, like the rest of the book, was written twelve years or more ago; these days, of course, we do not give anything or anyone the name of 'Afro-American', and I can only apologize to African American readers of this book, and to anyone else who might be offended by it, for what has become in the intervening years a solecism. Like the British spelling and the overlong paragraphs which make the book less reader-friendly than it might otherwise be, its use in this new edition is a consequence of having been unable to reset it. Those readers who notice that it has been corrected on the title page will, I hope, take the desire for the deed in the body of the text.

As I said, I intended a tribute, and an affirmation that 'by any reasonable reckoning of the function of music in human life, the Afro*[sic]*-American tradition is the major music of the west in the twentieth century'; and in order to support that affirmation I needed to engage in a consideration of what *is* the function of music in human life. It was there that the two alternating streams of discussion that give the book its structure had their origin.

But I discovered that those twin streams made it possible to interpret the book in another way, as being *primarily* a discussion of the nature of the music act and of its function in human life, with African American ways of doing music adduced only as an example in point. Fair enough; even though that was not my intention, if that is how readers choose to interpret me I cannot tell them they are wrong. But it also seems to leave room for another interpretation, which was made by so many reviewers when the book was first issued that I must comment on it. Somehow I seem to have given the impression that I think of African American and European classical music as being entirely separate streams, and that like Mowgli's four-legged friends I make a clear-cut distinction which somehow carries a moral or ethical load: African American good, European classical bad. Further (and in spite of what I thought was an explicit denial), I was maintaining that the former was in a state of perfect health while the latter was degenerate, its 'ossification', as one critic put it, 'contrived by a threatened if not wilfully malign Establishment'.

It is true that I devoted a chapter to the 'Decline of a Music'. I see no reason today to modify my opinion on that; the decline has become if anything even more obvious in the ten years since I first remarked on it. But I did not welcome the news then, if news it was, and I do not rejoice over it now. I certainly did not and do not subscribe to any mind-boggling conspiracy theories to explain it, and I continue to listen to performances in the European classical tradition no less than in other traditions and to play as many of the works of that tradition as my modest piano technique will permit. As for the other interpretations of my book, I can only affirm what my historical chapters must surely make abundantly clear: that African American music is the offspring of both Europe and Africa, and that like all offspring it partakes of the nature of both parents even if it is not the same as either.

Apart from that I think my book is perfectly able to look after itself.

I cannot let this opportunity pass of thanking the editorial and production staff of Wesleyan University Press and UPNE for their helpfulness, good humor and efficiency, and above all I want to thank Robert Walser and Susan McClary for their vision and the support they gave, which revived my flagging energies. Had they not listened, one afternoon on a terrace looking over the roofs of Sitges to the sea, to my complaints about the fate of my two books, those books would today be in limbo, while the third would remain a muddled bundle of manuscripts and computer files.

Sitges, Spain C.S.
February 1998

MUSIC OF THE COMMON TONGUE

INTRODUCTION

I have been prompted to write this book by two impulses, one public and general and the other personal and specific, which are inextricably intertwined with each other. The first is a conviction that the time has come, if it is not well overdue, for a recognition, a celebration even, of the central contribution which Africans and people of African descent scattered over the face of the earth have made to the very mainstream of human culture, that is, to the human race's awareness of itself and of the way in which we relate to the world in which we live. That the principal medium through which this contribution has been made is not words but music and dance is itself important and, indeed, part of the message, and there can be very few people living in industrial societies who do not owe something, whether they admit or even realize it or not, to the power of the African vision of the world. A scholar has called African music and dance 'nonverbal formulations of philosophies of beauty and ethics';[1] the way in which, all unacknowledged, those philosophies have passed into the culture of Europeans and Euro-Americans is a story of endurance and ingenuity which forms much of the substance of this book, since the medium of their passing has been that music and dance of African descendents in the Americas, and elsewhere, to which we can only give the awkward name of 'Afro-American'.

The more personal reason I have for writing is in order to acknowledge, and even perhaps to return something of, what I owe to musicians of the Afro-American tradition, both black and white. As a musician and teacher of entirely European descent, trained in the most academic tradition of European music, I have nonetheless believed ever since I started giving thought to such matters that the gift of music was for everyone, as natural and universal a part of human endowment as the gift of speech, and I have sought for ways to make this belief an actuality. In my early years as a school music teacher, in New Zealand, I believed — or rather, assumed — that it was possible for the European classical tradition to satisfy the musical needs of my pupils, and I tried, as I had been trained to do, to inculcate in them a love of the great European masters, and something of the foundations of their art. The fact that my successes were at best patchy challenged me to look further afield, and when during my studies in London I encountered the European and American avant garde, and the claims of its practitioners that a radical rethinking of the whole musical process was taking place, I tried to bring my pupils and, later, my students to participation in, and understanding of, something whose real nature I now realize I myself understood only dimly. But at the time it seemed that here was a fresh start, which would allow all to take part without the prior need for formal training in all the skills of traditional classical composition and performance. A series of educational experiments took place at that time, in which I played a minor part, which were designed to bring school pupils into the culture of the avant garde, not only as listeners but also as performers and even composers. I suppose, looking back, that any practical experience in music is worth while, but the fact remained that while my amiable pupils were willing to go along with my enthusiasm, they showed nothing of that real commitment which might impel them to make a lifelong practice of music. At any rate, I do not know of any of them who continued either to perform or to compose such music after leaving school.

That was in the 1960s, a time of general loosening of bonds and a tremendous outpouring of creative energy in popular music. It is fashionable to sneer today at the sixties, but at their best they were characterized by an awareness of the social and political power of music, even if most of us did not understand the nature of that power. It was at that time that I started to become aware, at first dimly but then with increasing clarity, of the existence of a music that had been all around me but which I had hardly noticed other than as light entertainment or as a rather intrusive noise from juke-boxes. One key moment was when, inquisitive about the nature of what was then the still quite new phenomenon of rock music, I attended the last great Isle of Wight festival in August 1970; another was meeting and talking with the drummer John Stevens in London and taking part in his spontaneous music workshops in Ealing College of Higher Education, where I was teaching in the early 1970s. From these and other beginnings, I started to explore more widely, if initially quite indiscriminately, across the whole spectrum, or at least as much of it as a middle-aged music lecturer could gain access to, of Afro-American music in both its contemporary and its past forms. As I explored further, and made my first hesitant attempts at playing jazz (the experience of finding myself, after thirty years or more as a pianist, once again a fumbling beginner was both chastening and enjoyable), I was struck increasingly with the profound differences, in both the musical and what I can only call the social assumptions of the music, from the tradition in which I had been brought up, as well as by the coherence and consistency of the culture. It seemed, and still seems, to me (it is in fact a major part of the argument of this book) that such seemingly disparate musics as, say, country-and-western, reggae, jazz, punk rock, Broadway popular songs and calypso were all in fact aspects of one brilliant tradition, which resulted from the collision in the Americas, during and after the times of slavery, between two great musical cultures (perhaps one should say, groups of cultures) that of Europe and that of Africa, a tradition which partakes of the nature of both but is not the same as either. I found increasingly that the music of this tradition fulfilled in me not only an emotional but also an intellectual and a social need which European classical music, however much I loved and admired much of it, did not, and if I was honest, never had fulfilled. I decided to try and investigate what it was in the music that could produce so many kinds of satisfaction and joy, while at the same time disturbing, if not disrupting, the comfortable ways in which I had been accustomed to listening to, performing and thinking about music. The desire to do so was strengthened by encountering the warmth, sophistication and humour of those Afro-Caribbean friends whom I had at that time begun to meet, and by the way they seemed to view the world from an angle that was intriguingly different from my own. This book, then, is a thank-offering to the untold numbers of musicians who created the music and an exploration of my own feelings about it. If I say that whatever understanding I now possess of my experience began with that feeling of 'rightness' in the music which was only later confirmed by thinking about it, it may perhaps suggest something of that unity between mind and nature which is one of its lessons.

My training and background in classical music have obliged me in writing this book to attempt a task which most of those who write on Afro-American music do not as a rule attempt: to consider the position of the music in modern western society, especially vis-à-vis the socially dominant European and Euro-American classical tradition. The one major attempt that I know of to fill this curious gap, and to confront the nature of the European classical tradition as it exists today from inside the tradition itself, is a trio of books by Henry Pleasants.[2] But Pleasants was more interested in the classical tradition than in the Afro-American, and in any case his books were published nearly thirty years ago, and thus antedate most of what has been called the Rock Revolution of the 1960s, which changed the popular-music scene radically. Nevertheless, I do acknowledge here my debt to those brave books, even if I am not setting out to emulate them.

What I am setting out to do is simple, even though I find the magnitude of the reversal from the musical values in which I was brought up unnerving; it is to show that, by any reasonable reckoning of the function of music in human life, the Afro-American tradition is the major music of the west in the twentieth century, of far greater human significance than those remnants of the great European classical tradition that are to be heard today in the concert halls and opera houses of the industrial world, east and west.

To this purpose I need to carry on two discussions simultaneously: first, an examination of the various aspects of the Afro-American tradition in both its contemporary and its historical forms, in an attempt to show them all as aspects of the one great and coherent culture, and, second, a study of what seem to me some important aspects of the art of music in general, in an attempt to understand something of what it is that gives Afro-American music its power in the lives of so many people across the whole world in our century. As music does not take place in a social vacuum, but springs from the ways in which people regard themselves and their relationships with their fellows, I cannot carry out such an investigation without looking also at the social components of music, and especially at the encounter between people of African and of European origins as it has taken place over the centuries; I can only ask black readers of this book to pardon my impertinence in my attempts, obviously made from outside, to understand what seem to me important aspects of their culture.

It is not easy to write about the Afro-American tradition as a whole, perhaps because, as a music that does not in the main rely on written or printed notes, it is not only decentralized but it also does not reveal itself in that linear manner which is characteristic of the notation-dependent tradition of European classical music. Blues, jazz, rock, and so on, are not separate musical categories, however much the analytical temper of Europeans would have it so, but are constantly shifting and interacting facets of the great tradition, meeting and flowing into one another, grouping and regrouping with dizzying rapidity, and without regard for the labours of specialists or archivists. In writing this book I have been obliged by the nature of the printed word to follow some of the streams as if they were separate, and I can only ask the patience of the reader as I attempt to make the connections plain. For me, it is this persistently anarchistic resistance to classification of both the musicians and their music that is one of the enduring delights of Afro-American music; I have therefore no wish to tidy it up, but rather hope that I can convey something of this anarchistic delight, which is, I am sure, part of the profoundly pluralistic inheritance that black people carry around with them still, not as a set of beliefs but as a style of thinking, feeling, perceiving — and of playing, listening and dancing.

It may then be thought that I am trying to write two books at once, but my purpose will only have been achieved if I can show that they are in fact one. To this end, I have interspersed chapters from one 'book' with those of the other, so that discussion of one or another aspect of the Afro-American tradition alternates with more general discussion of music as a human social activity. It is through this discussion, notable for its absence in most accounts of classical music, that I shall try to show the primacy of Afro-American music in the west today, and to establish that this is so on several levels, not just in the simple appeal of the music to vast numbers of people, (though this is not without importance, however much the clerics of the classical tradition may protest) but also in its openness to development, its universal accessibility and the ability of its musicians to evade capture by the 'official' values of the industrial state, which has proved the ruination of the classical tradition in the present century.

I am aware that my free use of the words 'classical' and even 'Afro-American' for the two traditions causes problems. It should be clear, of course, that I am not using the former term to signify that period in European music, between about 1770 and 1830, which music specialists know by that name; rather, I am using it in the vulgar sense, to mean the music of the European concert, church and opera tradition since about 1600 (since it is essentially a dramatic tradition, the date of the first real opera, performed in that year, sets its beginning neatly) as performed today by symphony orchestras, concert soloists and chamber ensembles as well as by opera companies, and including the music of the post-world war two avant garde and its offshoots and successors. I shall use it in this way in the knowledge that not only would it have meant little to the masters of the tradition in the past but also that it is used today mostly by those who are not in sympathy with the music; those who do subscribe to its values feel no need for the qualifying adjective, since to them it is, *tout court*, music, and it is other styles of music making that need qualification: 'popular', 'folk', 'ethnic', 'contemporary' (an odd one, that) and so on. We know what to expect when we open the pages of *The Musical Times*, *Music and Musicians* or *Musical America*, or any number of *Histories of Music*. Similarly with classes in Music Appreciation, while Music Departments in schools, colleges and universities, not to mention conservatoires of music, mostly direct their attention entirely towards the one tradition. I am only too aware, however, that the boundaries of what is meant by 'classical music' are maddeningly difficult to define, the more so as I believe the meaning of the music — or, rather, the meaning of performing it — has changed considerably over the past sixty years or so.

It would probably not be necessary to define it at all were it not for the disastrous pulling-away of the classical tradition from the vernacular over the last hundred years. I shall have more to say about that later, but note here that the disaster (and it *has* been disastrous, for both traditions) can be laid more at the doors of classical musicians and of critics, scholars, teachers and those who are responsible for the financial support of classical music than at those of the musicians of the Afro-American tradition who, as we shall see, have always possessed an easy mastery of classical styles; if they have played in the style we know now as Afro-American, it has never been because they could not play in the European manner but because they have preferred to play in that way.

I shall have to leave to a later work a discussion of the very interesting question of the boundaries of classical music, and ask the reader to accept my rough-and-ready definition as sufficient for the present book. At the same time we might keep in mind that what is and what is not regarded as classical is often as much a matter of performance style as of the actual musical content, and also that classical music can be distinguished from vernacular in that it gives more attention to the musical work in itself than to its social meaning.

For music that does not come under the rubric 'classical', I prefer the term 'vernacular' to either 'popular' or 'folk', both of which have become loaded with secondary meanings and are involved in their own demarcation disputes. The basic meaning of the word, of course, has to do with speech, and its use in respect of music does remind us that the ability to take part in a musical performance is as natural and universal a part of the human endowment as is the ability to take part in a conversation. It can subsume both 'folk' and 'popular' (although I shall use both these words on occasion when their meaning is clear) to mean music of the common tongue that is made for *use*, with little pretension to Art and its high social status, but by no means unselfconscious pipings either; like virtually all music everywhere and at all stages of human history, it is made by musicians who, even if they do not verbalize it, are well aware of what they doing and who work hard to do it. An outside observer of music as a whole in western society would conclude that classical and vernacular music represent different and even opposed values, but this has not always been so; indeed, it would seem as if during the greatest period of European music its practitioners did not think of themselves as in any way separate from the vernacular of their day but both drew on it (after all, the Viennese classical style even at its most elevated has its roots firmly in Austrian folk music) and actively contributed to it. They strove to reach the widest possible audience (Mozart was delighted to find that everyone in Prague was whistling the airs from *Figaro*) and if they made music sometimes for the broader and sometimes for a more exclusive audience they did not feel impelled to make any break in their style; Beethoven remains as recognizably Beethoven in his ballroom dances as in his last string quartets.

I was reminded of this not long ago when I heard a fine British jazz quartet on three successive evenings, on the first evening playing to an audience of connoisseurs in a concert hall, on the second blowing up a storm and setting all the teenyboppers, much to *their* surprise, dancing at a local hop, and on the third playing discreetly for the entertainment of the patrons in a pub, all without any dislocation of style or the slightest hint of condescension or of playing anything but their best. It is possible that Afro-American music has developed its own kind of classical music which, unlike today's European or Euro-American classical music, remains in close touch with its vernacular, both feeding on it and feeding back to it. To my knowledge, the last European master of the classical tradition who was able to inhabit that kind of unified musical universe without strain was Erik Satie, who died in 1925; appropriately, he was one of the few major musicians of the tradition who really did die in poverty — and voluntary poverty at that.

One might say, perhaps tautologically, that vernacular music, 'the music of the common tongue', is, like vernacular speech, the normal experience of the human race. Classical musics are comparatively rare; they seem to need for their existence not only a leisured class able to command a quantity of surplus resources but also a situation where that class is to some degree isolated from the majority of the people and possesses the social power to represent its own tastes as superior. Thus classical musics developed not only in Europe but also in India and China, though not, despite the equal richness and sophistication of the culture and the music, in the African kingdoms or in Bali, in both of which the royal courts and their music were accessible to all. If jazz is today acquiring some of the characteristics of a classical music we might be able to discover comparable social factors at work — but that must wait for a later chapter.

There is another pair of terms that I am going to have to use extensively in this book: 'black' and 'white' as applied to people. The absurdity of these terms when used in this way can be seen from the start by anyone who cares to look, in that those who are labelled 'white' may be anything from greyish pink to mid brown in skin tone, while those labelled 'black' may be anything from pale brown to rich dark brown; not only is literal blackness of skin colour rare but also many of those who are labelled 'black' may be lighter in complexion than many who are labelled 'white'. The two terms, when used to mark off two genetically separate human groups, make no sense at all; what they amount to in terms of human relationships is a highly asymmetrical form of classification which assigns all those who bear the slightest visible sign of African descent to the category 'black', and thus automatically to inferior status, even though, to the unprejudiced eye, they may appear more European (or, to put it, pseudo-scientifically, Caucasoid) than African (or Negroid). In societies that are dominated by European values, European appearance is the norm and taken for granted, becoming in this way invisible, while African is the aberration, and thus highly visible, even, as in the Americas, after nearly five hundred years of daily interaction. The asymmetry requires that only those with no visible sign of the 'aberration' can qualify as 'white'. This paradox of racism compounds its absurdity through the fact that while to be 'black' carries considerable social disadvantage throughout Europe and America, to be 'white' does not carry, as any number of unemployed white people can testify, any balancing advantage, other perhaps than the dubious advantage of being able to look down on a fellow human being. In the long run the only people who derive any real benefit from the whole sorry business are those who have an interest in dividing and ruling.

If 'white' means having exclusively European ancestry while 'black' means possessing any mix of European, African and, indeed, any number of other ethnic backgrounds from one hundred per cent of the latter to ninety-nine per cent of the former, then 'black' has any real significance only as a cultural term. It is worn thus, as a badge of pride, by those who have historically been obliged to accept a definition of themselves by reference to European norms — that is, they have been defined as contravening in their very existence the society's norms of Caucasian racial purity. Black culture, and especially black music and dance, have over the past five hundred years or so been tools by means of which people so defined have struggled, and continue to struggle, to assert their own definition of themselves. If this has necessarily entailed compromises and accommodations with the prevailing definition (and, as we shall see, Afro-American music and dance are shot through with, and indeed have their origin in, such accommodations) and an at least outward acceptance of them, nonetheless the self-definition of those who are classed as 'black' has for the most part been affirmative rather than negative, proud rather than humble, self-assertive rather than self-effacing. And thus, while to label such great American musicians as Charles Mingus, Duke Ellington and Jelly Roll Morton as 'black' may be a genetic absurdity, given their very visible genetic makeup, it does, given the ethnocultural situation, make a certain kind of sense, since they, and countless others, found their cultural roots among those who had been similarly defined. It makes it possible to find a liveable sense in a situation that is essentially nonsensical.

One need not assume from this that 'black' culture is monolithic — far from it. One of the distinguishing features of the culture of the people of the African diaspora has always been an openness and an adaptability which, as I hope to show in due course, is a part of the African cultural inheritance. This is why the variety of Afro-American music is so astonishingly wide, representing as it does any number of different accommodations to the dominant white culture, as well as to other cultures. It is, if anything, white culture that through its exclusionist tendency can be said to be impoverished. We can see this in the music of the classical tradition in our own time; by comparison with the musical whirlwind which is Afro-American music the so-called 'new music' which is associated with the names of Schoenberg and Stravinsky and later of Messiaen, Boulez, Stockhausen and Cage is a mere breeze, imprisoned in its luxurious concert halls and quite possibly heralding the end of the tradition in a state of isolation, solipsism and spiritual anorexia. There seems to be a kind of rule in these affairs, that whenever a policy of exclusion is practised, it is the excluders who are the ultimate losers.

If it were a matter of the mere cultural survival of black people, that would be a remarkable enough achievement, given what they have endured for five hundred years. But there is more. Despite their exclusion, black people in the Americas and elsewhere have been during the present century at the heart of an outburst of creative energy surely unparalleled in the known history of the human race. Its vigour has taken it beyond the shores of the Americas and caused it to become acclimatized throughout most of the world, usually over the dead bodies of the guardians of the official musical culture, but its power to seize the imagination and the sensibilities of so many different kinds of people, most of whom have no direct contact with the black experience, is a phenomenon which still lacks a satisfactory 'official' explanation — understandably so, for the only explanation that makes sense would not be good news to those guardians. So it tends either to be taken for granted, like a force of nature, or to be attributed to the pressures of cynical media manipulators. Neither explanation is anything like adequate — even though it is obviously true that commercial forces have played a considerable (though perhaps less than is generally assumed) part in its development and dispersion. Rather, it is a ceaseless and spontaneous activity of countless human beings, all of them living within, responding to and trying to make sense of, certain social, political and economic situations. But the question of why this music has not remained simply the property of an underdog group in the Americas (after all, there are many such underdog musics the world over, but most of them stay firmly within the societies from which they came), but has instead moved out to transform the musical sensibilities of a large part of the human race, is an important one, to which I propose addressing myself in this book.

How, then, do we define Afro-American music? At first sight, the question seems easy enough; we know about jazz, yes, and blues, we are possibly aware of the debt owed to the blues by all those varieties of music that are collectively called rock or pop and which are the most audible kinds of Afro-American music to be heard today. There is also disco perhaps, and there are styles that seem to have remained mostly the province of black artists, such as gospel and reggae and soul, although there are white artists who have made soul, if not gospel, their own. There is also calypso and the steel band, among its more exotic manifestations, and rapping, scratching and hip hop. We should also include styles which, although shot through and through with black idioms, are almost exclusively the domain of white musicians, such as country-and-western in all its considerable variety, and Cajun music from Louisiana — in fact not much vernacular music of our time has escaped its powerful presence. And we have not yet mentioned the beguines, the merengues, the sambas and rumbas, the mento and salsa, the reggae and soca, that come from South and Central America and the Caribbean, or the riotous proliferation of styles that has taken place in the various parts of Africa to which the music has returned. We could continue enumerating for a long time, through the ramifications of rock, for example, and it might be possible to compile a catalogue that had some claim to completeness. Possible but pointless, for by the time it was completed it would be obsolete; the art is in such a state of headlong development and change that cataloguing it is rather like painting the Forth Railway Bridge — the job gets finished just in time to start it all over again.

But the key to all this magnificent confusion lies in any case not in a catalogue at all, however complete, since catalogues enumerate objects and music is not an object, or even a collection of objects, but an activity. Afro-American music making (I should prefer, for reasons which will become clear in Chapter 2, to use the word 'musicking', the present participle of the regrettably non-existent verb 'to music') has resulted, seemingly, in the production of innumerable music-objects — and we have the records and the tapes and the sheet music that we can hold in our hands — but as we examine these objects we find that they are not as stable as we thought, but are mere stages in a process of creative evolution, caught for a moment on disc, tape or paper.

The other trouble with the simple enumeration of various styles of Afro-American music is that many of them are merely the creation of those commercial and marketing interests which have intersected at so many points with the musical process, and were often invented either to give the appearance of something new to a way of musicking that has had a long subterranean history or to evade reference to that racism which has also intersected in a significant way with the music. Categories in any case are *never* watertight, but flow ceaselessly into one another; certainly the musicians who play it, the listeners who listen to it and the dancers who dance to it rarely allow themselves to be neatly pigeonholed but move freely across categories according to their own inclination at the time — as well as according to who is paying. Categories are only convenient abstractions, and useful in discussion if we understand that there is, for example, no such thing as jazz, but only musicians who play in a certain manner and listeners who like to listen to them doing so (for that matter, there is no such thing as music, only musicking). The musician who plays in the manner we call jazz is himself also a listener, and does not confine his listening to other musicians who play in the same or similar ways to himself (he may feel a greater sympathy, of course, with such musicians) but will feel free to listen to, and to use, any kind of musicking from any performer who he feels will help to make his own performance more interesting, more satisfying. That such listening is not random in its focus but depends on a measure of social and cultural empathy is a matter which I shall discuss in due time.

What we call Afro-American music, then, is not a collection

of sound-objects, or a repertory of pieces, or even a group of musical styles narrowly considered, but an approach to the act of music making, a way of playing and of responding to music, which derives from those two great ways of making music which came together in the Americas. It is this way, or rather, it is these ways, since there is no one way, which I mean to celebrate in this book. I make no claim for it as a comprehensive survey of either the history or the present of Afro-American music; that would require whole libraries. Rather, I hope to present what seem to me important aspects of both that history and that present in order to suggest an approach, a conceptual and historical framework, in which listeners, and indeed performers, may place the experience of the music, to find out a little of what it can have to say to us on the important concerns of human life, and how it can help us in constructing an identity that is appropriate to ourselves and our time. At the same time I hope that this book may suggest something of the richness and complexity of both the culture and the history, which have been so fraudulently denied by the majority culture, of black people in the Americas.

In order to keep my study to manageable proportions I have had to confine it to those aspects of the music which originated in the United States, with brief glances only toward Latin America, the Caribbean and Africa. But while this restriction does represent a loss of scope, it does not really affect my argument, which is that Afro-American music is a unified culture through which are explored and celebrated aspects of human experience and identity that are not dealt with in either the European or indeed the African tradition.

Let us now, without more ado, look at what it was that the people from each of the two continents brought with them to America in the way of human social and musical values.

NOTES

1. THOMPSON, Robert Farris: 'An Aesthetic of the Cool: West African Dance', *African Forum*, Vol 2, Part 2, Fall 1966, p. 85.
2. PLEASANTS, Henry: *The Agony of Modern Music*, New York, Simon and Schuster, 1955
   : *Death of a Music?* London, Victor Gollancz, 1961.
   : *Serious Music — And All That Jazz*,, London, Victor Gollancz, 1969.

Chapter 1

AFRICANS, EUROPEANS AND THE MAKING OF MUSIC

The first thing we must understand about the Africans who were taken into slavery in the Americas is that they were by no means members of a primitive society. The societies of the Western Sudan, which, at least up to the beginning of the nineteenth century, was the principal source of black slaves, may have been technologically simple by nineteenth-century European standards (at the time of the first large-scale encounters, in the fifteenth and sixteenth centuries, there was little to choose between them, apart from the strategically crucial technologies of shipbuilding and explosives), but, socially, politically, aesthetically and spiritually they had, and still have, much to teach Europeans, those strange creatures whom, according to Okoye, Africans at first derided 'for their horrible looks, red faces, long hair and long heads', and whom they regarded as 'unsightly because they did not possess a black skin, full lips and broad nostrils'.[1]

It is tempting to cite, as evidence for the 'advanced' nature of West African societies, that series of empires which arose in the Western Sudan from the eighth century A.D. onwards, whose names ring in the ears of Europeans like strange music, as alien as the names of planets in an epic of science fiction: Ghana, Mali, Songhai, and Kanem-Bornu. These were immensely wealthy. A fourteenth-century Emperor of Mali, Mansa Musa, who is said to have ruled over the largest domains on earth apart from the Mongol Empire, made his pilgrimage to Mecca in 1324 (Islam spread early into West Africa, but the Africans transformed it, as they did later the Christianity of the missionaries, into a specifically African syncretism that co-existed, and still co-exists, comfortably with the older polytheistic religions); his largesse with gold was so prodigal that the value of the local currency in Cairo was depressed for some twelve years after his visit. The term 'empire' is, however, only a makeshift, for we do not have a term for that kind of political organization in which power, while seemingly vested in a supreme head of state, actually permeated upwards from the smallest social units, from families and clans through a loose confederation, to the Emperor, whose position depended upon the continuing assent of all; government in all essentials took place through the lineage-based community, which was, and seemingly remains today, the basic social unit across the continent. To the western bureaucrat such a community-based system of government will appear proof of primitivity or backwardness; nonetheless I do not intend trying to appease his prejudices by pretending that the decentralized 'empires' of the Western Sudan much resembled their centralized, top-downwards namesakes of Europe.

Instead, one can only point out that, from all accounts, the continent in the centuries before the disruption caused by the slave trade and, later, colonialism, was an orderly and well-governed place. The fourteenth-century Berber traveller Ibn Battuta reported that 'Of all peoples the Negroes are those who most abhor injustice. The Sultan [of Mali] pardons no-one who is guilty of it. There is complete and general safety throughout the land.'[2] That this was a more or less general condition throughout sub-Saharan Africa is confirmed not only by African and Arab travellers but by Europeans also. A Dutch merchant's description of the city of Benin, in what is now Nigeria, was published in Amsterdam in 1668 and includes the following: 'The king's court is square and lies in the right quarter of the town as you approach it from the Cotton Gate. It is as big as the city of Haarlem and is surrounded by a wall like that surrounding the town itself. It is divided into many splendid palaces and comprises beautiful and long square galleries almost as large as the Amsterdam Exchange. These galleries are raised on high pillars covered from top to bottom with cast copper on which are engraved pictures of their war exploits and battles. Each roof is decorated with turrets bearing birds cast in copper with outstretched wings, cleverly made after the living models. The streets of the town are very straight and wide, each over a hundred and twenty feet wide.'[3] Benin was famous not only for its artistic and architectural achievements but also for the shrewdness and enterprise of its merchants.

Even Henry Morton Stanley, by no means a sympathetic observer of Africa, allowed in 1875 that the King of Uganda was 'a pious Musselman and an intelligent humane king,'[4] while as late as 1906 the anthropologist Leo Frobenius could write of his journey to the Congo: 'And on this flourishing material civilization there was a bloom, like the bloom on a ripe fruit, both tender and lustrous; the gestures, manners and customs of a whole people from the youngest to the eldest, alike in the families of princes and well-to-do and of the slaves, so naturally dignified and refined to the last detail. I know of no northern race who can bear comparison with such a uniform level of education as is to be found among these natives.'[5] Frobenius's further comment is worth noting also: 'Judging from the accounts of navigators from the 15th to the 18th century, there is not a shadow of doubt that Negro Africa of that period, stretching from the south to the edge of the Sahara Deserts, was in the heyday of an uninterrupted efflorescence of the arts, an efflorescence which the European conquistadores callously destroyed as fast as they succeeded in penetrating into the country . . .'[6]

One could continue the list: the great Indian Ocean ports of Kilwa (which Ibn Battuta called 'one of the most beautiful and well-constructed towns in the world'), Mombasa and Mogadishu, centres of intricate networks of trade and cultural exchange that extended as far as Indonesia and even China, which the Portuguese with their superior firepower destroyed in an attempt to take them over; Timbuktu, with its splendid court and army of scholars 'bountifully maintained', wrote the sixteenth-century Spanish traveller Leo Africanus, 'at the king's expense', one of a chain of cities along the southern edge of the Sahara which served as 'ports' for the huge caravans, often twelve thousand strong, that brought European goods across the desert and returned with ivory, salt and gold. The great trading houses of Genoa and Venice knew that they were dealing not with 'primitive' people but with shrewd traders whom they treated with respect and even deference.

But, despite the brilliance of these and other city civilizations, the vast majority of Africans lived, then as now, in village societies, content to work a subsistence economy although, as Davidson says, 'the available evidence suggests that most peoples south of the Sahara had a standard of living far above the minimum subsistence level, and enjoyed a reasonably secure life,'[7] mostly nonliterate (I shall have more to say on literacy later), the basis of social and political life the clan or lineage, the common ancestors. Two characteristics of African social life strike one again and again in commentaries.

The first is an absence of separation between aspects of life which Europeans are inclined to keep apart: the political, the economic, the religious and the aesthetic. Despite an absence of either historical founder or systematic body of doctrine, African religion permeates every aspect of human existence. The Christian theologian Dr John Mbiti, who insists that indigenous African religion, even when overlaid with Islam or Christianity, is a unity (there are, he says, many branches but only one tree),[8] tells us that no African lacks a knowledge of God as originator, as other than human, or of the ethical responsibility of humanity in the world. A human being can become fully human only in society, and the model for society is the family — not only those presently alive but also those departed, as well as those yet to be born, all of whom are perceived as present in the society of their currently living relatives. Thus, humanness is not confined to the living; love and generosity are due no less to the dead, who in their turn watch over the living community, while those yet unborn have a right to full existence, so that the living have a duty to procreate in order to bring them to that condition.

The reciprocal relationship between individual and community finds expression in a system of rites of passage; nature may bring the child into the world but only the community can make him or her fully human. Hence the importance of naming ceremonies, in which the child dies to its mother but is reborn to the wider community, gaining not just one but many mothers, fathers, uncles, aunts, brothers and sisters, on all of whom falls the responsibility for nurture. Similarly, the rites of puberty and of marriage, procreation and death, each of which is a stage in the integration of the individual into the community, not only of the living but also of the dead and the not yet born, are each at the same time an occasion for the renewal of that community, injecting fresh energy and keeping death and disintegration at bay.

Just as the living individual is the link between the departed and the yet unborn, so he or she is also the link between the physical and the natural worlds, linking God to nature through membership of the natural world (not master over, but priest of, nature) and through the unique human moral and ethical consciousness. Thus all human life and activity take place within a religious framework, and no human act is without religious significance. The arts, too, contribute to this unified consciousness. 'In Africa,' says Davidson, 'tribal sculpture was seldom designed to be enjoyed as "art". Rather, each piece was designed to attract specific religious spirits. An ancestor figure . . . was carved as a home for the spirit of a long-dead chieftain — a spirit which might otherwise roam in anger and harm the village. A beautiful doll was often fashioned to give sanctuary to the spirit of a child not yet born. Without the presence of such spirits, a piece of sculpture has little value. For example, if a wood carving began to crack or rot and was no longer a suitable home for a spirit, another figure was made to replace it, and the first piece, no matter how beautiful, was discarded as worthless.'[9] A major function of the sculptures, the masks and the costumes, no less than of the music and the dance, was their use in rituals affirming and celebrating the power of the lineage and of the common ancestors; thus art and religion together served to reinforce the integrity of the community. Works of art were not kept on display, but were more often than not hidden away until the proper time to bring them out for the particular ritual purpose for which they were designed.

It is this striking temporal, physical and social continuity that has permeated every aspect of African life, in the rituals that embodied their skills and knowledge in agriculture, in the working of metals, in the weaving and dyeing of cloths, the building of houses, the design of villages and towns, the making of musical instruments and the complementary arts of costume, masking, musical performance and dance, themselves thought of as a single unity, the great performance art for which we lack a name (unless it be 'celebration'). All of these have been devoted to one end, which Davidson calls the art of social happiness. 'Few others', he says, 'dealt in the raw material of human nature with more subtlety and ease, or so successfully welded the interests of community and the individual. The Africans practised the art of social happiness, and they practised it brilliantly.'[10] One might say that the intelligence of Africans is devoted to learning how to live well in the world rather than to mastering it, and they do not imagine, as does the scientifically-minded European, that the latter is necessary in order to achieve the former.

None of what has been said need imply that Africa has at any time been an earthly paradise, or that Africans are in any way better, more instinctively moral, artistic, religious, or, especially, 'closer to nature' than any other human people. Not only is much of that vast continent decidedly inhospitable to human life, but also Africans have shared the same tendencies to selfishness, quarrelsomeness and murderousness that characterize the rest of our species. The point is that in that continent human beings evolved ways of coping with these frailties and other kinds of potentially destructive impulses in ways that on the one hand preserved the fabric of society and on the other allowed room for individuals to work out their own development to the limit. Social and individual needs have been thought of not as opposed but as complementary and mutually dependent. It was in the rituals, the music and the dance forms that the society has dramatized and released the tensions within it, without being under any illusion that such releases can ever be achieved once and for all, but in full awareness that they must be negotiated anew by each succeeding generation.

The second characteristic of Africans is adaptability, and the ability to choose eclectically from a variety of sources and to profit from the potential richness of a number of perspectives simultaneously. This can be seen in the way in which Africans seem to be able at one and the same time, and without visible strain, to hold, for example, both polytheistic 'pagan' beliefs and practices and those of either Christianity or Islam, to be at the same time 'traditional' and 'Europeanized' in their daily lives, in ways which often puzzle and even infuriate Europeans; the latter can deal with contradiction only by denying or eliminating one side of it — hence the rejection and even persecution of deviants, both sacred and secular, which has been such a persistent and bloody feature of European history — while Africans seem to be able to live happily with both sides. One might say that while the European lives in a world of 'either/or', the African's is a world of 'both/and'.

Even what Europeans call African 'tribalism', which is represented as an archaic and disruptive force in present-day African states, was in all probability created by the nineteenth-century colonial powers with the collusion of a small number of African rulers and intellectuals. Terence Ranger is of the opinion that in pre-colonial Africa 'there rarely existed the closed corporate consensual system which came to be accepted as characteristic of "traditional" Africa. Almost all studies of nineteenth-century Africa have emphasised that, far from there being a single "tribal" identity, most Africans moved in and out of multiple identities, defining themselves at one moment as subject to this chief, at another moment as a member of that cult, at another moment as part of this clan, and at yet another moment as an initiate in that professional guild. The overlapping networks of association and exchange extended over very wide areas. Thus the boundaries of the "tribal" polity, and the hierarchies of authority within them, did *not* define the conceptual horizons of Africans.' Ranger also quotes another writer who contrasts the 'colonial freezing of political dynamics' with the 'precolonial shifting, fluid imbalance of power and influence.'[11]

That this is not 'primitive' or 'prelogical' behaviour can be seen from the emphasis put on multiplicity in African performing arts; John Miller Chernoff, who himself trained for some years as a drummer in the Ewe tradition of Ghana, makes a strong case for a parallel 'between the aesthetic conception of multiple rhythms in music and the religious conception of multiple forces in the world'. He says, 'African affinity for polymetric musical forms indicates that, in the most fundamental sense, the African sensibility is profoundly pluralistic . . . Just as a participant in an African musical event is unlikely to stay within one rhythmic perspective, so do Africans maintain a flexible and complicated orientation towards themselves and their lives . . . The sensibility we have found in musical expression more accurately appears to represent a method of actively tolerating, interpreting and even using the multiple and fragmented aspects of everyday events to build a richer and more diversified personal experience . . . the adaptability and strength of an African's sense of community and personal identity reside in the aesthetic and ethical sensibility which we have seen cultivated in one of its aspects, music. As such the values of an African musical event represent not an integrity from which we are moving away but rather an integrity which, with understanding, we might approach. It is a felicitous orientation in a world of many forms.'[12]

It is music and dance that have been, and remain, the prime manifestation of the African sensibility and worldview. Robert Farris Thompson goes so far as to say: 'The traditional choreographies of tropical Africa constitute, I submit, complex distillations of thinking, comparable to Cartesian in point of influence and importance.'[13] Music itself, as these statements suggest, hardly exists as a separate art from dance, and in many African languages there is no separate word for it, although there are rich vocabularies for forms, styles and techniques.

The question, What are the distinguishing features of African music? may seem absurd when we consider the enormous variety of ways in which music is made and listened to in that vast and culturally diverse continent. It can, however, be said that beneath the diversity of technique and instrumentation, of repertory and style, there is a unity of attitude, of approach to the making of music, which can be called African, and which has proved much more persistent in the Americas than any technical features in themselves. It is not surprising that these underlying features can be related to those social attitudes which I have been discussing.

In the first place, music is not set apart in any way from everyday life but is an integral and essential part of it, and plays an important role in all aspects of social interaction and individual self-realization. Music is closely identified with social events and purposes; without music many of those events simply could not take place at all. Just as we noted earlier that various aspects of social life tend not to be kept apart, so we find that the various functions of music making, allied always with dance, flow into one another; the most apparently frivolous of events may well reveal itself as having a serious moral import, while, conversely, the most serious and vital of rituals is extremely enjoyable for the participants. The musician who leads the occasion does so with the realization that he is responsible not only for the sounds he makes but for the whole event; Chernoff goes so far as to say that 'the music is important only in respect to the overall success of a social occasion', and that the African 'does not focus on the music but on the way the social occasion is picked up by the music'.[14] The social importance of music is reflected in the social importance accorded to professional musicians, even where their actual social status is low, and in the high level of tolerance for the deviant behaviour that seems almost to be expected of them. Alan Merriam says that among the Basongye of Zaire, 'the reaction to the facetious suggestion that these ne'er-do-wells be banished was one of extreme seriousness and even real horror . . . The fact of the matter is that without musicians a village is incomplete; people want to sing and dance, and a number of important village activities simply cannot be carried out without musicians. The villagers are unanimous in stating that musicians are extremely important people; without them, life would be intolerable.'[15]

Secondly, rhythm is to the African musician what harmony is to the European — the central organizing principle of the art. In practically all African music making there is a rhythmic polyphony, with at least two different rhythms proceeding in counterpoint with each other, held together only by the existence of a common beat; even the downbeats will quite likely not coincide in different parts. This emphasis on rhythm implies also the existence among Africans of what has been termed a 'metronome sense' — an ability to hear the music in terms of that common beat even when it is not explicitly sounded. It is assumed that musicians, dancers and listeners alike are able to supply it for themselves, making it possible to create rhythmic structures of a complexity and sophistication unknown in European music. This rhythmic sophistication makes up for what Europeans may think of as a lack of melodic development, so that an instrument capable of a very limited range of pitches, even of only one, will be interesting to an African provided he can extract sufficiently interesting rhythms from it. For this reason, sounds of indeterminate pitch are often as much valued in African musical cultures as are precisely pitched sounds; the drum orchestra, in which each instrument is capable of perhaps two or three not very precise pitches only, is a major African ensemble. As one might expect also, percussive sounds are prominent in African music; even the sounds of voices, flutes and stringed instruments may be given a percussive edge, while musicians like to introduce into their instrumental sound a good deal of indefinitely-pitched 'noise', even with such definite-pitch instruments as the xylophone and *mbira*. Their music is rich in buzzes, thuds, bangs and other non-harmonic sounds, of much the same kinds as apparently used to fascinate the medieval ancestors of modern-day Europeans. Chernoff argues strongly that the multiplicity of rhythmic perspectives which is available to musicians, dancers and listeners reflects the multiple orientation of Africans.

Thirdly, it is assumed that everyone is musical, that all are capable of taking part in some capacity in the communal work of music making. Musicking is in fact thought of as being as basic a form of social interaction as talking. This does not mean that everyone is equally gifted or skilled, or that skills are not highly valued; African societies have always supported various kinds of professional and semi-professional musicians, but the music has never been taken over, as has the European classical tradition in our own time, by professionalism. Musicians are not separated from the rest by their skills, but function as leaders and pacemakers. The balance between leader and followers, between innovation and tradition, between individual and society, is perhaps most strikingly embodied in that ubiquitous feature of African choral singing which is known as call and response, in which solos, often improvised, alternate under strict rhythmic rules with invariant choral responses. But even if not formally involved in the performance, the listeners are never silent and static, but respond with what J.H.K. Nketia calls 'outward, dramatic expression of feeling'. He says: 'Individuals may shout in appreciation when something in the performance strikes them, or indicate at a particular point their satisfaction with what they have heard or seen. In addition, their conduct may indicate that the performance satisfies or makes manifest a social value, or that it satisfies a moral need.'[16]

Fourthly, improvisation is widespread and richly developed. I shall have more to say about improvisation in a later chapter, but here we should note that it does not mean random or even 'free' playing, even assuming that such things are possible for human beings, but is always carried on within the framework of rules or conventions analogous to those of speech — which may of course be thought of as mainly improvisatory too. Nor does improvisation mean totally new creation on the spot, or rule out the existence of a good deal of pre-existing material; such material is indeed the basis of most improvisation, and it is even true that not much original invention need be involved. A master drummer, for example, will not necessarily wish to invent new patterns of rhythm or melody, but will use existing ones with due regard for the social shape of the occasion for which he is playing, and for the ways in which his fellow-musicians and dancers are performing.

This characteristic, taken with the preceding, means that music making does not depend on the existence of a body of pre-existing pieces; songs may be made up on the spot to suit a specific occasion and be as quickly forgotten once it is over. Everyone is a potential composer, and songs are often made up by taking fragments of existing songs, both words and music (the two may be taken together or separately) and welding them into new shapes. On the other hand, formal composition is by no means unknown, for example among the Chopi of Mozambique, where a composer-music director makes those extended multi-movement works called *mgodo* (plural of *ngodo*) for which the Chopi are famous, for chorus, xylophone orchestra and dancers — but even these *mgodo* are ephemeral, existing for perhaps a year or so before being replaced, movement by movement, with a new work. The old *ngodo* is forgotten without regret, even by its composer, as the creative process continues. There are also repertoires of traditional songs which may have been handed down through generations; these are usually associated with the celebration of lineages and ancestral values and serve often to affirm the legitimacy of chiefs and kings. These songs are known and performed mainly by members of a hereditary caste of praise singers known outside Africa by the French term *griots*, whose social function is complex and embraces everything from local historian to social critic and village gossip.

As Nketia says; 'There are restrictive traditions that tend to limit the freedom of performers to make significant changes of their own, such as the court tradition of some societies which demand fidelity to known texts, particularly in historical songs and pieces that legitimize the authority of a reigning chief or his claim to the throne. The latitude for variations as well as for extemporaneous expression gets wider and wider as one moves from such musical types to those which provide a basis for expressions of social values or social interaction. Songs of insult, songs of contest or boasting songs, songs designed in such a way to allow for references relevant to the present moment, all give scope for creativity or for limited improvisation.'[17] A mainly non-literate society, as were most of those of West Africa, was able to remember what it wanted to remember and to forget what it was better to forget, and even the most formal of praise songs would quite likely have undergone changes and adaptations in response to the dynamics of the 'shifting, fluid imbalance of power and influence' of precolonial Africa. In the main, then, fidelity to a received text is not highly valued in African music making.

Lastly, music and dance interpenetrate to an extent that can scarcely be imagined in white society. It is not just a matter of musicians playing while dancers dance, but of musicians dancing as they play and of dancers contributing to the music, and of both responding to one another on equal terms, in doing so contributing to the meaning of the occasion. 'The dance,' says Nketia, 'can be used as a social and artistic medium of communication. It can convey thoughts or matters of personal or social importance through the choice of movements, postures and facial expressions. Through the dance, individuals and social groups can show their reactions to attitudes of hostility or cooperation and friendship held by others towards them. They can offer respect to their superiors, or appreciation and gratitude to well-wishers and benefactors. They can react to the presence of rivals, affirm their status to servants, subjects and others, or express their beliefs through the choice of appropriate dance vocabulary or symbolic gestures.'[18] Likewise, the total bodily involvement of the master drummer as he leads the ensemble, giving the pattern to the other musicians and the dancers, is not merely ornamental but is an essential element of the performance, adding as it does an extra strand to the rhythmic texture, while the sounds made by the dancers as they stamp and leap, often emphasised by bells or rattles tied around ankles and wrists, are not incidental but integral to the great performance art which comprises not only music and dance but also masking, costume and drama.

That the continent of Africa is the home of one of the great civilizations of the human race there can be no doubt; and at the heart of that civilization lie music and dance. Nowhere else is the affirmation and the celebration of identity and of right social relationships through music and dance more highly cultivated. Not only tribes and peoples, but religious cults, occupational groups, age groups and the two sexes, all enact in music and dance those rituals which are the embodiment of selfhood, and an acting-out of those myths which shape and give meaning to life. Music and dance give the individual his or her precious sense of uniqueness, of worth, of place in the scheme of things, and mediate relationships, teach responsibilities and show opportunities. That the human values embodied in the great performance art are wide (one is tempted to say, universal) in their appeal is shown not only in the way in which the art proved its value in the social and psychological, as well as the sheer physical, survival of those Africans, and their descendants, who were enslaved in the New World, but also in the way in which it has gone out to become the dominant music and dance in the west in our time. Like all aspects of West African culture brought by the slaves to the Americas, it was profoundly modified both by their ordeal and by the encounter with European culture, but I intend showing that these values, or something very like them, have survived, even when most of the actual technical features of African music have disappeared, and that they continue to exert a life-giving influence, deeply subversive of the official values of industrial society, within that society today.

To conclude this summary of some of the aspects of African culture, which will reveal their relevance in later chapters, it might be useful to remind ourselves of how Europeans have reacted to their encounter with Africa. The two quotations I give below tell us, the first all unawares, and the second with insight, something about the ways in which Europeans persistently project on to Africa, and on to Africans, their own fears and fantasies. The first is from a curious book of African travels by the distinguished Italian novelist Alberto Moravia, in which he says: 'The "Africa sickness" is a spell with a basis of fear, and this fear is the fear of prehistory, that is, of the irrational forces which in Europe man has succeeded in repelling and dominating during many thousands of years, but which here in Africa are, instead, still intrusive and uncontrolled. It is a fear to which the European finally becomes accustomed, partly because he has his roots elsewhere and his personality is sounder and less unstable than that of the African; it is a fear, in fact, that is painfully agreeable. But the fear of the African, who has no historical background, whose personality is flickering as the light of a candle, is a serious fear, a nameless fright, a perpetual, vague terror. Magic is the expression of this prehistoric fear; it is as foul and gloomy and demented as the "Africa sickness" is aphrodisiac, even is disruptive and destructive. The truth is that magic is the other face of the "Africa sickness"'.[19] This extraordinary statement was first published in English, not in 1874, but in 1974.

The second, published in 1979, comes from Patrick Marnham's *Dispatches from Africa*: 'As the North has penetrated Africa, it has proved less and less capable of learning from the experience; we can only instruct. Even the anthropologists, who originally approached their subject in the spirit of pure enquiry, are increasingly willing to place their knowledge at the disposal of governments or international companies whose objectives are less detached. The North justifies its pedagogy by characterizing the African as ignorant, uneducated, or impoverished. At the same time, it has found in Africa "a refuge from the intellect" or an invitation to indulge in stupidity and dishonesty on its own account. It becomes increasingly difficult for us to explain the prolonged frustration of Northern plans in terms of "backwardness" or "isolation". Much of Africa has had close contact with the North for six hundred years and the African characteristics that have survived such long exposure are not going to be eliminated now.

'African resistance to the North takes many forms. But its constant purpose is surely to reject the alien uniformity which the North strives to impose on the unnerving variety of African life. The North finds this variety unnerving because it challenges the necessity for the progress, control, authority and research with which we order our lives. We fear Africa because when we leave it alone, it works'.[20] We might see the history of Afro-American culture, too, and especially its music, as one of constant struggle to resist the uniformity imposed by industrial society, of which slavery was an early manifestation; it is no wonder, then, that those who run the agencies of authority, control and research in western society fear and reject both the bearers of that culture and their music making.

At the time when the first African slaves were imported into the Americas, slavery was a common enough institution, not only in Africa but also in Europe. There had been African slaves in Portugal since the early fifteenth century, long before Columbus, and in West Africa it is by no means extinct, even today. But the slavery practised in Africa bears little resemblance to the ruthless and voracious institution, with its insatiable appetite for human souls and bodies, which evolved in the Americas. An African slave could become a respected member of his master's household, even of his family, perhaps by marriage, and could accumulate wealth in his own right, becoming perhaps the most trusted adviser of a king or aristocrat. Nor was slavery generally hereditary; as Davidson says, 'Captives . . . became vassals, vassals became free men, free men became chiefs.'[21] Even the Arabs, whose system of slavery was in many ways closer to the American, were exhorted by the Koran to manumit slaves, and, again slavery was not hereditary; a child born of slaves could be a full and free member of the household. Those African kings and other rulers who sold prisoners of war and other, to them, surplus subjects to the white adventurers in their huge ships had not the faintest idea of what they were delivering those unfortunates into — a system which equated human beings at best with livestock, to be bought and sold like cattle, not only themselves but their descendants in perpetuity, deprived of any rights through which it might be recognized that they were human. And of course the social and economic ruin brought to West Africa, as one kingdom after another became caught up in the terrible trade, is well documented.

Black slaves were introduced into the economy and the culture of the Americas very early in the history of European colonization; as early as 1503, a mere eleven years after Columbus, the governor of the Caribbean island of Hispaniola, now Haiti and the Dominican Republic, was writing to the Spanish court to complain that African slaves were escaping and preaching insurrection to the Indians, and asking for an end to the importation of Africans. Queen Isabella granted his request, but the shortage of manpower was so acute that within two years the trade had to be resumed. The consequences for the Americas of the slave trade have been beyond calculation; in all, it seems that not less than twelve and perhaps as many as twenty million Africans reached America (how many were taken but did not reach there we shall never know, but mortality on the terrible sea journey, innocuously named the Middle Passage, probably exceeded twenty per cent) during the three and a half centuries of the trade — surely the greatest forced migration of souls in the whole of human history.

It was not until 1619, the year before the *Mayflower* brought the Pilgrim Fathers to Massachusetts, that the first known group of Africans was imported into the British North American colonies; in that year twenty were disembarked from a Dutch vessel at James Town, in the colony, later to be the state, of Virginia. They were designated as indentured servants, a common enough status in those days, rather than as slaves, and it was not for some time that the slave status of Africans and their descendants became legally established in the British colonies; Massachusetts, interestingly in view of its

Puritan origins, was the first to make slavery legal, in 1641, with Virginia itself and the other southern colonies not following until 1661. The number of black slaves remained small, a matter of thousands only, until the early eighteenth century, when with development of such labour-intensive cash crops as tobacco, and, later cotton, it burgeoned, creating an insatiable demand for more and more workers, not only on the plantations but also increasingly in areas that hitherto had been the province of free artisans and craftsmen, as well as in fields such as domestic service, the care of children, stevedoring and animal husbandry. Contrary to popular belief, it was not just the physical strength of the slaves that was exploited but also their skills and knowledge — for example in the working of wood and metal, in tropical farming, of which they might have been expected to have more experience than their masters —and, as we shall see, in music. By 1800 there were in the United States about a million people classified as black; by 1830 the number had increased to three million and in 1860, the year of the last census to be held under slavery, there were about four and a half million blacks, of whom about three quarters were slaves.

I shall leave to a later chapter an account of the patterns of dependence and mutual influence that evolved between the slaves and their masters; it can be said at this point that it was not just a simple matter of the Africans and their descendants being acculturated into a stratum of American society, but rather a complex process of negotiation which affected masters no less than slaves. Let us consider the possible ways in which the enslaved Africans responded initially to the new situation into which they had been so abruptly and traumatically thrust. One thing is clear: the slaves, from the moment when those first Africans were landed at James Town, were never mere passive victims of the system. When they found themselves delivered to the slavers, marched to the sea (tens of thousands perished on that leg of the journey alone) and transported in a terrible voyage under conditions that, in reading of them, still provoke horror and shame, they may have been stripped of all possessions and of the accustomed support of kin, they may often have found no-one to whom they could speak in their own language or who prayed for relief to the same gods, but they were by no means psychologically helpless; those who survived the journey must have been well equipped to survive in the new conditions under which they found themselves. As we have seen, underlying the diversity of language, of ritual and of social customs were deeper shared values, a shared grammar and syntax of social interaction, and, further, those values were not static but dynamic and adaptable; the natural tendency of Africans has been, and remains, to select what they need from a variety of sources, and to use contradictory and disparate elements to construct meaning from their experiences. Nonetheless, it must have been a daunting task, to reconstruct, in the new conditions, structures of value and belief, and their associated social gestures, which would give meaning to the apparently meaningless nightmare into which they had been thrust. Sydney Mintz and Richard Price put the matter well: 'The Africans who reached the New World did not compose, at the moment, *groups*. In fact, in most cases it might be more accurate to view them as *crowds*, and very heterogeneous crowds at that. Without evading the possible importance of some core of common values and the occurrence of situations where a number of slaves of common origin might indeed be aggregated, the fact is that these were not *communities* of people at first, and they could only become communities by processes of cultural exchange. What the slaves undeniably shared at the outset was their enslavement; all — or nearly all — else had to be *created by them*. In order for the slave communities to take shape, normative patterns of behaviour had to be established, and these patterns could only be created on the basis of particular forms of social interaction . . . Thus the organizational task of enslaved Africans in the New World was that of creating institutions, institutions that would prove responsive to the needs of everyday life under the limiting conditions that slavery imposed upon them'.[22] And they add, 'We can probably date the beginnings of any new Afro-American religion from the moment that one person in need received ritual assistance from another who belonged to a different cultural group'.[23]

The struggle for survival, both physical and psychological, must have been unending. One wonders how long it would have taken the Africans to realize that the cruel and irrational world in which they found themselves, and the seemingly arbitrary events which governed their lives (determining whether they stayed with those they knew and loved or were sundered from them, whether they were submitted to a cruel or a lenient master, even whether they lived or died) were in fact governed by a highly rational god whose name was Mammon, whom their masters worshipped above all others and whose rational calculations were, as they remain today, inimical to the needs of human life. In North America and the Caribbean, to satisfy the demands of the rational god, tribes and even families were deliberately broken up to destroy traditional unities and loyalties and discourage insurrection (in Latin America the opposite policy, of keeping ethnic groups together and playing them off one against another, proved in fact more effective). Apart from the fact that labour was incessant and punishment frequent and brutal on the majority of the slave estates, perhaps the worst feature was the sheer hopelessness of the slave's situation, with nothing to look forward to but a lifetime of labour and beatings, with only the remote possibility of escape (but into a hostile society) to keep hope alive, with all possibility of attaining respect and status within a community, a stable family life and the deference due to the old cut off.

But slavery never took over the minds of the slaves to the point where they had no independent life or personality, however cunningly these had to be concealed. Patiently, persistently, generation after generation, they laboured to create for themselves a psychological living space in whatever restricted areas were allowed to them. Despite prohibitions on learning to read and write, they knew who they were, where they were, what their situation was and what was being done to them. Each generation carefully instructed the next in all that could be remembered of the inherited knowledge. Slavery may have taken away the entire material culture, the social and political institutions, but music, dance and oral poetry, folk tales, and above the essence of the African world view, its spiritual and metaphysical temper, survived. Thomas L. Webber expresses it poetically and precisely: 'The culture of black people under slavery in America can be likened to a deep river. Having as its source a great African well-spring, this ever-moving, ever-changing river had by the 1850s a distinctly American appearance. As it flowed and deepened through its new land it both adapted to the contours of the American landscape and reshaped each bank it touched. It never lost its African undercurrents. For its people it was a healing river. Its waters refreshed them and helped them escape the torturous American environment. To the oppressed slave his culture was like a deep river; to immerse oneself in its water was to commune with one's own cultural identity.'[24]

Of the early music of the black slaves little is known; with a very few exceptions, those whites who left any written record were unable to find in it anything more than a weird and barbarous noise, generally used to accompany what seemed indecent, even lascivious dances. Such perceptive accounts as have come down to us are mainly from the Antilles, where, the blacks being in the majority, more African ways remained than on the North American mainland; nonetheless, they are suggestive of what might have been taking place there also. Thus, one Richard Ligon, an Englishman who may himself have been a professional musician, wrote in 1653 of encountering on Barbados a slave called Macow, 'a very valiant man', according to Ligon, making himself a *balofo*, or African xylophone, which Ligon seems to have thought he had invented for himself; in Martinique in 1694 a French monk saw not only a set of African-style drums but also a four-stringed instrument which was called a *banza*, with a long neck and a body covered with skin. What must have been the same instrument, more or less, was reported also in the English-speaking colonies under the names *banshaw* and *banjil*. The same French monk also reported that some of the slaves on Martinique were proficient on the violin, so that acculturation was clearly under way in both directions by the late seventeenth century.

Of how the process of acculturation began there is practically no record. But if we keep in mind that music and dance were as important as speech to the Africans as a means of communication and self-definition, then we can deduce something about the process from a similar process of linguistic adaptation that was going on at the same time. The slavers' policy in the British territories of splitting up tribal and linguistic groups would have meant that communication, not only with the masters but also among themselves, was for the slaves a problem of prime importance. There is evidence that the language which formed the initial medium of communication was neither English nor any pure African tongue, but a pidgin (trade language) that had earlier evolved in West Africa for the purpose of trade among the various peoples as well as with Europeans; it would have incorporated elements of a number of African languages as well as of English. In America individual African languages would have fallen rapidly into disuse for want of any extensive speech community, to be supplanted by this pidgin, at first limited to the most practical matters, but gradually taking into itself words and constructions from the one language of which everyone had experience, English, while retaining the simplicity of syntax which marks a pidgin and which characterizes, without any loss of either expressiveness or flexibility, both West Indian and black American speech today. The initial pidgin, in fact, rapidly became a creole, or true language of mixed origin, probably in the space of a generation or two.

Remembering, too, that it was not just brute physical labour that was required of the slaves but also skills and even organizational abilities, from blacksmithing to the nurture of the master's children, it becomes even clearer that, however much the masters might have desired it, there were not two separate societies permanently divided from one another, but only one, of which one segment became increasingly dependent on the other, not just for work on the cash crops, but for practically all the skilled manual work that it needed. This dependence was symbolized by the passing of the creole from the mouths of the slaves into those of the masters and their families, a fact upon which shocked visitors from Europe and from the north often commented.

The new creole would have developed in a somewhat different direction in the slave quarters from the way it did in the big house, owing to the slaves' success in preserving some kind of autonomy when out of the masters' sight; different demeanour and modes of address, especially towards members of the extended family (the vulnerability of families to disruption through sale made the development of extended family ties, often to people who were not blood relatives, an essential source of emotional and social stability), while African or African-style words and expressions, often 'translated' into English, became part of the private language of the blacks simply because a different social and emotional situation required a different vocabulary and usage from that used in the presence of the whites.

As far as music was concerned, there would have been fewer outside pressures towards the formation of a creole, since, in the eyes of the masters, music and dance were of little significance in the productive process which was the reason for the slaves' existence, and little attempt was made to control them. Perhaps the most important external pressure was towards the discontinuation of drumming; the masters feared, probably rightly, that the drums would be used as signals for insurrection. Other, less emphatic, ways of marking rhythm had to be found. This had the probable side-effect of hastening the destruction of the old religious rituals, since, as John Storm Roberts puts it, 'when the drums were silent, the old gods came no more.'[25] It is for this reason that drumming is a less central, less autonomous art in North American than in Latin and Caribbean Afro-American music; the art of drumming had virtually to be re-invented in modern times.

Another external pressure towards the absorption of European ways of music making was the reward that could come to the slave from the ability to play a European instrument in the European manner. There is abundant evidence that many slavemasters encouraged their slaves to play, and even supplied them, not only with instruments, but even with instruction, in order that they might provide entertainment and dance music on the often remote plantations; it was a matter of prestige to have slaves who could perform in this way, and skill on fiddle and banjo, as well as on flute, clarinet and even French horn would enhance a slave's saleable value (there is a hint of conspicuous consumption about this, for the slave would have to be withdrawn from productive field or house labour, a luxury which only the wealthier could afford).

For the slave himself, or herself, it could be a great advantage since it would mean relief from other duties in fields or house, and even bring a measure of respect and status; the memorable figure of Fiddler in Alex Haley's *Roots* vividly epitomizes such musicians. As Dena Epstein says, 'These obscure musicians at times achieved what would have been professional status if their earnings had remained in their own hands. Many of them earned a reputation for excellence that extended for miles around. Some had homemade instruments, some store-bought ones, but most were encouraged by their masters to play for the dancing of their fellow-slaves as well as for white visitors or dancing parties.'[26] Nothing, in fact, about the Peculiar Institution, with all its inconsistencies and irrationalities, its gross cruelties and occasional mercies, is quite so peculiar as the variable treatment it accorded to slave musicians. One reads advertisements for runaways who had taken with them nothing but their violin, clarinet, flute or even French horn, while descriptions of festivities at Christmas and other seasons include accounts of bands of '3 fiddles, 1 tenor and 1 bass drum, 2 triangles and 2 tambourines', or a band of two violins and a bass,[27] and, most extraordinary of all, Gilbert Chase mentions one Sy Gilliatt, body servant to the Governor of Virginia in the late eighteenth century, who was also official fiddler to the state balls at Williamsburg: 'He wore an embroidered silk coat and vest of faded lilac, silk stockings and shoes with large buckles. He also wore a powdered brown wig, and his manners were said to have been as courtly as his dress'.[28] This, of course, was not much out of line with the servant status of musicians up to the end of the eighteenth century in Europe; Gilliatt's contemporary Josef Haydn might have been seen in similar livery at the Esterhazy court. And in any case it represents once again the increasing dependence of the society of the masters on what the blacks could provide for them.

But there must have been also pressures from inside the slave society itself towards a creole music no less than to a creole language, and for much the same reasons. The linguistically heterogeneous 'crowds' of Africans who left the slave ships must have been equally heterogeneous musically, even if, as we have noted, they were linked by common attitudes and concepts. Given the strength of the urge to make music and to dance which would if anything have been increased by their predicament, there would have been a strong need to find, or to evolve, a common musical, no less than spoken, language. In this fluid situation, the consequence, not only of the absence of a common idiom, but also of their forcible removal from those social situations in which they were accustomed to make music, the adoption of at least some of the idioms of European music which they encountered would have acted as a stabilizing influence, as well as a means of coming to terms with their present plight. And in any case, European concepts of scale and melody, European instruments and even European concepts of harmony, were not so far removed from them that a fairly rapid rapprochement could not take place. And so a creole music would probably have developed in parallel with the creole language, with the European scales modified by less rigid notions of pitch, its foursquare rhythms enlivened by injections of African additive rhythms and polyrhythms, European choral textures by call and response.

I shall leave to a later chapter a detailed discussion of the forms that the slaves' music making took, and look now briefly at the musical inheritance which the white immigrants brought with them to that New World which, unlike the enslaved Africans, they could approach with at least the hope of building a new life. The great majority of those who came to the British colonies were, naturally enough, from the British Isles, and it is their language, their culture and their music that has left the greatest impression on American culture from that time.

Histories of music tell us that the England the first colonists left behind them was in the last days of what has been called the Golden Age of English church polyphony and the madrigal, while the continent of Europe was seeing the first flowering of opera and of Baroque instrumental music. Many of the early colonists, not only those wealthy and aristocratic people who became the major landowners and ruling class in Virginia and the southern colonies, but also the Pilgrim Fathers who came to New England in the 1620s, whose background was from the emerging English middle class, were, as the first governor of the Massachusetts colony said, 'very expert in music'. Despite the abundance of musical skill and knowledge in England, however, neither the elaborate polyphonic church music nor the madrigal, nor, for that matter, the developing instrumental music, was transplanted into the colonies. This was not just a matter of a lack of established communities or of those surplus resources and leisure that are necessary for the growth of a 'cultivated' tradition, though clearly that had much to do with it; it was also actively discouraged by the Puritans of New England, who insisted for their worship on simple settings of the psalms translated into rhyming verse, as often as not in ballad metre, while in the southern colonies only the most perfunctory of attention was paid by the early settlers to religious observance.

Over half of those who came to North America during the colonial period came as indentured servants, having sold themselves into what amounted to slavery for a limited period in return for their passage; we may assume that those who came in this way were members of the lower orders of English society, and that they brought with them their repertory of songs, ballads and dances, as well as the psalms and hymns that were common to all classes. And even they were not necessarily lacking in musical skills and even in literacy, since both were common among all classes in England at that time; as A.L. Lloyd points out, all of the servants whom Samuel Pepys employed during the nine years when he kept his famous Diary in the 1660s were musical performers and sight readers, while playwrights of the time would often in their plays attribute, even to servants and picaresque characters, the ability to read music. 'It would be interesting,' says Lloyd, 'to know the rate of musical literacy among the lower classes in the decisive folk song period between 1550 and 1850. We might find that at many moments it was a good deal higher than in the present day.'[29]

Lower and upper classes, then, would seem to have shared a considerable repertory of vocal and instrumental music besides the psalms that they sang together in church, and much of that repertory has remained remarkably unchanged for perhaps three hundred years, or even longer, in the remoter reaches of the United States. In the valleys of the

Appalachian Mountains in the early years of this century the English folklorist Cecil Sharp claimed to have found more British ballads and other folksongs than in the whole of England; many of the British ballads are of considerable antiquity, and have survived many centuries of oral transmission with remarkably little change. The ballad, of course, tells a story, and if that story is to make any sense its internal continuity must be preserved, and the fact that such a large repertory of traditional song is narrative in form tells us something of the inherent nature of the way of making music which the white settlers brought with them.

By contrast with this extensive and long-enduring repertory, practically nothing — a few doubtful examples only — of the actual songs which were brought from Africa by the slaves has survived, despite the fact that first-generation Africans were to be found in America right up to the time of Emancipation. That this is so is clearly due in some measure to the disruption caused by the experience of slavery and the necessary adaptations I discussed earlier, but it points also to a difference in attitude between European, and especially northern European, and African musicians, towards their musical material, a difference which has had a significant effect on the course taken by Afro-American music.

The European folk musician usually thinks of him or herself not as a creator of songs, but as a transmitter. As Henry Glassie says, 'the usual folk singer is no more creative than the usual performer of pop or art song; both share in the Western tradition of the performer as repeater, of the performer as distinct from the audience during performance so that the performance amounts to a presentation requiring authority. He is true to his source, taking pride in the fact that the song is being sung as it was when he learned it. With varying degrees of success he attempts to hold the song steady . . . The commonplace folk performer, his audience and fellow performers do not strive for change; they interact in a system of frequent repetition and reinforcement to prevent it.'[30] This agrees with a comment by Cecil Sharp, that 'the traditional singer regards it as a matter of honour to pass on the tradition as nearly as possible as he received it'.[31] Small changes occur over time, owing to lapses of memory and misunderstandings, but both singer and audience have a strong sense of the identity of a song and feel their responsibility to it, to preserve so far as they can its integrity. People do compose new songs, of course, but it is not a common occurrence; Glassie, in his sensitive and sympathetic study of the composer of the anti-integrationist song *Take That Night Train to Selma*, says that 'creative people like Dorrance Weir are uncommon in European-American communities like his.'[32] He points out also that 'The commercial recordings of the twenties and thirties, which are still [1970] played, have done more than influence Southern Mountain music; they have offered acceptable standard texts and melodies — less efficient than the standard texts and melodies of the art musicians because they continue to involve oral-aural channels — and have rendered the repertoires of contemporary Southern Appalachian singers largely predictable.'[33]

The mention of art musicians reminds us, however, that what we find in the European and Euro-American folk tradition appears to be not very different from the attitudes found in the art, or classical, tradition of European and American music, that is to say, an emphasis on the identity and the integrity of a music-object, an assumption that the power of original creation is rare, a clear-cut distinction between those who perform and those who listen (we notice Glassie's use of the word 'authority' for the performer's relation to his audience), and, where and at such times as it is available, the use of written notation for both words and music, as a means of preservation and transmission — though, as we shall see, it is only in the classical tradition that notation has taken over as the medium through which the very act of creation takes place. That these characteristics are found in some degree within the folk tradition as well, may point to a kind of 'set' which lies deep in the minds of Europeans and which may have to do with the scientific-materialist temper of our culture. We have seen, too, that they are alien to the African temper, and the history of Afro-American music can be seen from one point of view as a succession of accommodations between these two opposing sets of values.

It happened that the first white settlers, in the early seventeenth century, came to America at just the time when the modern tradition of classical music first came into being, with its central concept of music as a drama of the individual soul, and its central expressive technique of tonal harmony as the vehicle for that drama. I have written at length in an earlier book on the meaning of tonal harmony,[34] and do not intend repeating it all here, but some observations on tonal harmony, which, as we shall see, passed in various ways into Afro-American music, need to be made. Tonal harmony is essentially the arranging of chords, usually triads and their derivatives, in temporal succession in such a way as to create meaning, the listener being led forward in time, his expectations frustrated and teased, but ultimately satisfied by the final cadence in the home key. The composer's art lies largely in lacing conventional and predictable chord progressions with surprises, either dramatic or witty, which are caused by the insertion into the sequence of a chord which, while unexpected, can be shown to stand in a logical (that is, syntactical) relationship with those which preceded it. This kind of harmonic drama is used both on a small scale, over a span of seconds, and on a large one, which may be a matter of an hour or more. Large-scale planning is central to classical symphonic and chamber music, with its long-range contrasts, even conflicts, of keys; these are generally fought out to a resolution in the final sections, representing a final solution to the emotional and spiritual conflict in the soul of the protagonist. This final solution is equally devoutly wished for by the audience at a symphony concert, as is shown by the storm of applause which breaks over the heads of the performers the moment they come to the end of their drama. That in African societies such a final solution is not regarded as an option is something I have already discussed; resolutions are temporary only and must be negotiated anew with each new life situation, and in any case, in traditional African societies resorting to head-on conflict to resolve an opposition was not a favoured course of action, but an admission of social failure.

Since the European musician's responsibility is to his drama and to its resolution, he can afford, and indeed needs, to structure his musical performance over a long time-span, whether through the devices of tonal harmony or the narrative progression of a ballad, or indeed an opera, knowing that no matter how the audience responds he is going to finish the performance as planned. The African musician's primary responsibility, on the other hand, is to the occasion and to those taking part in it, and he will adapt his performance to enhance the occasion as it develops. He may well plan what he is going to do, but he will certainly not adopt any technical means that are going to commit him to a course of action regardless of its effect on the listeners or on the occasion.

We may, then, sum up the different attitudes underlying European and African music making in these terms. The European tends to think of music primarily in terms of entities, which are composed by one person and performed to listeners by another. These entities, pieces or songs, which the musician regards as his primary reponsibility to reproduce and to hand on as nearly as possible as he received them, are fixed in their over-all identity (some variation within that identity may be possible), and in starting to perform a piece a musician commits himself to finishing it, regardless of the response which it elicits (within limits, of course — the audience may not permit him to finish, although the conduct of conductor and orchestra during the tumultuous 1913 première of Stravinsky's *Rite of Spring* in Paris suggests that it is difficult to stop a really determined musician). It is thus useful for the musician to be able to notate a piece or song, and, to the extent that pieces tend to be treated as permanent objects with an existence over and above any possible performance of them, the tradition as a whole is inclined to be conservative, with new pieces added slowly if at all. Performers and listeners seem to like to play and to hear familiar pieces. The ability to create a new musical entity is thought of as rare, and the ability to perform not very widespread either, while the line between creators and performers, on the one hand, and listeners on the other, is always clear. Composition and performance are separate activities, and the composer dominates the performer as the performer dominates the audience.

The African musician, on the other hand, thinks of music primarily as action, as process, in which all are able to participate. In so far as musical entities exist at all, they are regarded not as sacrosanct, but rather as material for the musicians, whose primary responsibility is to the listeners and to the occasion for which they have come together, to work on. Hence there is as a rule no final form for a piece, rather a constant state of development and change. A new musical entity can come into existence on the instant, and disappear equally instantly once the occasion for it is past. Composition and performance are thus part of a single act which Europeans call improvisation but others call, simply, playing. Notation, if it is used at all, is limited in its utility, since a fully-notated piece defeats the aim of responding to the progress of the occasion. Change is constant and rapid, with new pieces appearing and disappearing with kaleidoscopic speed, though there remains a residuum of pieces and songs that people continue to enjoy playing and singing — but even these will disappear without regret once they have outlived their social usefulness.

When Africans and Europeans encountered one another in the Americas, the first as slaves and the second either as masters or as despised underdogs, in many cases scarcely better off than the slaves, these musical practices underwent profound modification on both sides to give us that kind of music we call Afro-American. It changed, not once and for all, but in a continuous process of accommodation according to the shifting relations of people of African, European and mixed descent, but the two fundamental sets of attitudes have remained remarkably stable and resistant to social, economic and technological change — inevitably, since if music has any meaning at all it must be as the medium through which assumptions about relationships are explored, affirmed and celebrated. Before continuing with the account of the ways in which the two cultures interacted, we need to discuss this more fully.

NOTES

1. OKOYE, Felix N.: *The American Image of Africa: Myth and Reality*, Buffalo, Black Academy Press, 1971, p 72.
2. quoted in DAVIDSON, Basil: *African Kingdoms*, New York, Time-Life Books, 1966, p 82.
3. quoted in OLDEROGGE, Dmitry and FORMAN, Werner: *Negro Art*, London, Paul Hamlyn, 1969, p 43.
4. quoted in DAVIDSON, *op. cit.*, p 172.
5. quoted in CUNARD, Nancy (ed): *Negro: An Anthology*, London, Wishart & Co., 1934, p 602.
6. *ibid.*, p 599.
7. DAVIDSON, *op. cit.*, p 21.
8. MBITI, John: 'African Religion', paper given at Symposium *Africa and the West: The Challenge of African Humanism*, Ohio State University, Columbus, Ohio, 28 May, 1982.
9. DAVIDSON, *op. cit.*, p 153.
10. DAVIDSON, *op. cit.*, p 174
11. RANGER, Terence: 'The Invention of Tradition in Tropical Africa', in HOBSBAWM, Eric and RANGER, Terence (eds): *The Invention of Tradition*, Cambridge, Cambridge University Press, 1983, p 247.
12. CHERNOFF, John Miller: *African Rhythm and African Sensibility*, Chicago, Chicago University Press, 1979, pp 155–6.
13. THOMPSON, Robert Farris: 'An Aesthetic of the Cool: West African Dance', *African Forum*, Vol 2, Part 2, Fall 1966, p 86.
14. CHERNOFF, *op. cit.*, p 67.
15. MERRIAM, Alan: *The Anthropology of Music*, Evanston, Northwestern University Press, 1964, p 136.
16. NKETIA, J.H. Kwabena: *The Music of Africa*, London, Victor Gollancz, 1975, p 32.
17. *ibid.*, p 237.
18. *ibid.*, p 207.
19. MORAVIA, Alberto: *Which Tribe Do You Belong To?*, transl. A. Davidson, London, Panther, 1976, p 17.
20. MARNHAM, Patrick: *Dispatches from Africa*, London, Sphere Books, 1981, pp xi–xii.
21. DAVIDSON, Basil: *Black Mother: Africa and the Slave Trade*, Harmondsworth, Pelican Books, 2nd edition 1980, p 38.
22. MINTZ, Sidney W. and PRICE, Richard: *An Anthropological Approach to the Caribbean Past: A Caribbean Perspective*, ISHI Occasional Papers in Social Change, No 2, Philadelphia, Institute for the Study of Human Issues, 1976, p 10.
23. *ibid.*, p 23.
24. WEBBER, Thomas L.: *Deep Like the Rivers: Education in the Slave Quarter Communities 1831–1865*, New York, Norton, 1978, p 60.
25. Roberts, John Storm: *Black Music of Two Worlds*, London, Allen Lane, 1973, p 39.
26. EPSTEIN, Dena J.: *Sinful Tunes and Spirituals: Black Folk Music to the Civil War*, Urbana, University of Illinois Press, 1977, p 148.
27. *ibid.*, p 156.

28. CHASE, Gilbert: *America's Music*, New York, McGraw-Hill, 2nd edition 1966, p 76.
29. LLOYD, A.L.: *Folk Song in England*, London, Lawrence and Wishart, 1967, p 35.
30. GLASSIE, Henry: '"Take That Night Train to Selma": An Excursion to the Outskirts of Scholarship' in GLASSIE, Henry et al: *Folksongs and Their Makers*, Bowling Green, Bowling Green University Popular Press, n.d. (1970?) p 31.
31. quoted in Lloyd, A.L. *op. cit.*, p 18.
32 GLASSIE, Henry: *op. cit.*, p 30.
33. *ibid.*, p 32.
34. SMALL, Christopher: *Music · Society · Education*, London, John Calder, 1977 and New York, Riverrun Press, 1982.

Chapter 2

ON THE RITUAL PERFORMANCE

In a highly critical article on modern American painting, the journalist Tom Wolfe once wrote: 'Frankly, these days without a theory to go with it, I can't *see* a painting'.[1] He was right in a more general sense than perhaps he knew, since each of us brings to the processes of both artistic creation and the contemplation of art works a number of notions which, although it might be dignifying them too much to call them a *theory* (since for the most part they are unexamined and even held unawares), do nevertheless add up to a set of assumptions and values. Since I intend in this book to examine critically some commonly held assumptions concerning the nature and function of the art of music, it seems only fair to make the reader aware of my own premises, in so far as I myself am aware of them (since it is not possible ever to become consciously aware of *all* the assumptions on which one operates). I must ask the reader therefore to bear with me while I rehearse and enlarge on them; they are simple but they are also, I believe, profound in their implications, not only for our approach to the art of music, but also (since what I might call my pre-assumption is that the way in which we approach music has a bearing on the way in which we approach the business of living) for our very lives themselves. These assumptions are open to either verification or falsification in the best scientific manner by reference to the musical experience which every single one us has had, and it is indeed vital that the reader should bring the evidence of his or her own experience to bear on what I have to say, since that can in itself be a first step towards reclaiming the musicality and the power of musical judgement that belong to all of us.

My first assumption is that *music is not primarily a thing or a collection of things, but an activity in which we engage*. One might say that it is not properly a noun at all, but a verb; the absence of a verb in English, as in most European languages, to express this activity is significant, and may point towards the European attitude to the making of music which I discussed in the previous chapter. Certainly the conceptual gap is interesting. I intend using, in this book, from now on, the verb 'to *music*' (after all, one can say 'to dance' so why not?) and especially its present participle, '*musicking*', to express the act of taking part in a musical performance. In order to narrow the gap that is assumed to exist between performers and listeners in European musicking, I define the word to include not only performing and composing (what is composition but the preparation of material for performance?) but also listening and even dancing to music; all those involved in any way in a musical performance can be thought of as musicking. My coining of this verb should not be put down to perversity, eccentricity or an attempt to be clever; it will simply clarify the discussion that follows. I shall be using it throughout this book without further apology or explanation.

We have seen how European musicians are inclined to consider music as entities; it is in the present-day classical tradition of both performance and composition that we find that this attitude has completely taken over the musical process. Classical musicians and listeners alike today view music as things — treasured symphonies, sonatas, operas, tone poems and concertos handed down to us from a glorious past, as well as those musical works which are offered to audiences by present-day composers. On the one hand, the act of composition is seen as the bringing into existence of one of these sonic objects, a process which does not concern the listener any more than does the making of the radio on which he may be listening to it. On the other hand, the act of performance is seen as rendering a service to those objects, which are assumed to have an existence over and above any possible performance of them; the performer burnishes them and presents them as best he can to an audience whose task is to contemplate them, in stillness and silence. It is never suggested that either performers or listeners have a creative role to play in the proceedings; the music-object is complete before either of them gets to play or hear a note of it. Writings on music in this tradition concentrate their attention on the nature of these objects, on those who created them and on the circumstances of their creation, while the act of performance, on the other hand, receives remarkably little attention; there is not even an entry under 'Performance' in the 1981 edition of *Grove's Dictionary of Music and Musicians*. This may be due to the evanescence of performances, as opposed to the permanence of the musical score, which can be taken out of time and studied at as much leisure as it appears to warrant; performances, on the other hand, can be studied only in real time, as they pass. Further, objects can be duplicated, while every performance is unique, if only because it takes place in a particular place at a particular time.

This state of affairs in all probability did not always exist; Bach clearly regarded his church cantatas simply as something for the choir to sing next Sunday (Evan Parker's phrase 'improvising on paper' sums up the process neatly),[2] while Mozart, for example, seems to have regarded composition as the provision of something to play; it is significant that the occasion for the performance of nearly every work of his is known. And here we have the first statement of what will become an important theme of this book: the idea that the great musical works of the European past, while coming down to us more or less unchanged, have nonetheless had their social function, and thus their meaning, altered by the changing nature of the situation in which they are performed today.

It is, then, the *act* of musicking that is central to the whole art of music the world over. In most of the world's musical cultures this is taken for granted without even having to think about it; it is only the dominance of the classical tradition in the west that obliges us to state it so bluntly. It follows that whatever meaning there is in music is to be found in that act rather than in the actual works themselves, and it is therefore of the musical event rather than of the musical work that we should ask our questions: the really interesting one is not, 'What does this composition mean?' but 'What does it mean when this performance takes place at this time, in this place, with these musicians, before this audience?.' The performance may or may not be of a pre-existing composition; in most of the human race's musicking the acts of composition and performance are simultaneous, while there may not necessarily be an audience at all apart from the performers. The answer to the second question may well be different from that to the first, and, in the case of a written composition, will change considerably during the history of its performance, becoming often quite different from that which its composer envisaged. Consider this: 'The pious Bach, were he to return to us today, would, after recovering from his astonishment at seeing his music performed at all, probably be scandalized to witness the routine annual revival of his *St Matthew Passion*, conducted by a Catholic, Jew or unbeliever, for the aesthetic edification of a miscellaneous population in Carnegie Hall for an admission fee of $3.60, federal tax included. This *Passion*, like the several hundred religious cantatas, was conceived as an integral and inseparable portion of the Divine Service'.[3] Further, he would probably find that most of those present would be quite unable to understand his indignation.

We should notice that, if the act of performance contains the central meaning of music, that does not mean that what is played is without significance; what is played is clearly a part of the act of performance and must be taken into account. The second question thus does not negate the first, but rather subsumes it.

The second assumption is equally simple: *everyone, every normally endowed human being, is born capable of musicking*. The gift of music is as natural and universal as the gift of speech which it so resembles. In many if not most of the world's societies it is assumed that to take part in a musical performance and to dance is as commonplace as to take part in a conversation, and indeed, talking, singing and even dancing may flow into one another as elements of daily social intercourse. John Blacking, in his account of the Venda of South Africa, says of them that they 'learn to understand the sounds of music as they understand speech,'[4] while J.H.K. Nketia says of African communities that 'every member of a community could be involved in one or more of the musical events that take place in community life.'[5] Of the Maori of New Zealand, Elsdon

Best said: 'The Maori folk composed songs on many different occasions when we would never think of doing so. If a woman was accused of indolence, or some other fault, by her husband, she would in many cases retaliate, or ease her mind, by composing and singing a song pertaining to the subject. In the case of a person being insulted or slighted in any way, he was likely to act in a similar way. Songs were composed for the purpose of greeting visitors, of imparting information, of asking for assistance, and many other purposes of an unusual nature from our point of view. Singing entered largely into the social and ceremonial life of the people and in making a speech the Maori breaks readily into song.'[6] Margaret Mead tells us that in the Balinese *gamelan* orchestra the leading metallophone player may be a child so small that he needs a stool to reach the keys, and comments: 'In a continuum within which the distinction between the most gifted and the least gifted is muted by the fact that everyone participates, the distinction between child and adult — as performer, as actor, and musician — is lost except in those cases where the distinction is ritual, as where a special dance form requires a little girl who has not yet reached puberty,'[7] while Colin McPhee says simply that in Bali 'music is above all a popular art'.[8] And finally, the great pioneer musicologist Curt Sachs: 'Every Eskimo must know the art of composition, and in supreme contempt, a jealous Eskimo woman would sneer at her rival, "She can't dance, she can't even sing".'[9] One could multiply such examples, but those will suffice.

Apart from the evidence from other societies, we should note that the entire popular-music industry is based on this assumption, at least as far as the ability to understand the music is concerned; no-one is excluded through being unable to comprehend what the musicians are doing, and no-one seems to need formal instruction in order to do so. But in addition, it is no less certain that everyone has the power to create something of his or her own, in music as much as in speech. The assumption of universal ability to create does not have to mean that everyone is equally gifted, either in speech or in music; we accept without difficulty the idea that some are more gifted with words than others, so that we have poets, orators, writers and bards, and in the same way it is not difficult to imagine that some are more gifted musically than others while still acknowledging a bedrock creativity in all. As with speech, what the individual does in music is couched in a language that has to be learned, but that learning takes place not in a formal situation but in the encounters of everyday life. There are vernaculars of music, no less than of speech, which everyone knows how to use; those who believe themselves incapable of 'speaking the vernacular' in music are that way because they have been taught — too often, alas, in school — that they cannot.

For this assumption of universal musicality is at odds with an unspoken assumption that is fostered in schools and other formal educational institutions, and encouraged by the official arbiters of the arts in our society, of a kind of pyramid of musical ability. At the top of the pyramid, tiny in number and exceptional in the nature and extent of their gifts, are those who are capable of a genuine creative act: the composers, who, it is assumed, require many years of arduous study before they can put those gifts to use. Below them, more numerous, are the performers, also a gifted and admired group, if a little lower in social esteem than the first. They do not for the most part believe themselves capable of a creative act (the two abilities *may* be found in the same person, but never at the same time; a performer who also composes will consider himself bound when working in the former capacity to respect to the letter the text which he has provided in the latter), and indeed are inclined to react with displeasure when called upon by the composer to make any creative gestures during a performance. In the classical tradition are to be found a large number of professional musicians who have never, in the course of their entire careers, made a single composition, or even a public creative gesture, that they can call their own. Mozart, for one, would have been puzzled by this state of affairs, since he regarded it always as part of his brief as a teacher to teach composition as well as instrumental skills, even, as his letters often remind us despairingly, to the least talented of his pupils.

Below this layer of the pyramid are those whose lot it is simply to contemplate and 'appreciate' the music objects created by composers and presented by performers, that large group who call themselves 'listeners' or 'music lovers', and who do not imagine, even though there may be among them many competent amateur musicians, that they might ever take part in a public performance, so completely has the culture been taken over by professionalism. Again, Mozart and his contemporaries might have been surprised at this division, since the audiences to whom they played and for whom they composed expected to take part in the performances; a fully professional orchestral concert was a rarity in Europe up to the middle of the nineteenth century. These 'music lovers' are still in a minority in the society as a whole; the Chairman of the Arts and Recreation Committee of the Greater London Council estimated in 1983 on a potential audience for the London concert halls of about a quarter of a million out of a population of about seven million in the Greater London area[10] — about one in thirty, which is probably an overestimate considering that the catchment area for those halls is actually much larger than just London itself.

Below this again are the remainder of the population, that majority to whom it would appear that classical music has nothing to say, despite the establishment in schools over several generations now of music appreciation classes. Appearances are deceptive, but an image not unlike that of the pyramid exists in the minds of most westerners, and most are fairly sure of the place they occupy in it, even though the boundaries of the layers are not quite as clear-cut as I have suggested. But such is the power of the image, which is instilled through the state education system and other bearers of the official values of our society, that there is a large number of people who, for whatever reason, have not become assimilated into the upper levels of the pyramid and believe themselves to be unmusical, 'tone-deaf' (whatever that might be) or otherwise unfit to take part in any musical activity whatsoever. It is, of course, pernicious nonsense, because every human being is born with the gift of music. It is one of the qualities that make us human, and we are less than fully human to the extent that it remains underdeveloped in us or is allowed to atrophy.

My third assumption is this: *since musicking always takes place in a social context, its meaning has a social as well as an individual dimension*. Or, to be more accurate, the social and the individual meanings of the act of musicking are intertwined, being concerned with the participants' feelings of their own identity, of who they really are. The social dimension arises from the fact that individual identity, who one is, is based on relationships; who one is is how one relates, to oneself, to other people, to the natural and even to the supernatural world, and musicking is concerned with the exploration, the affirmation and the celebration of relationships.

Relationships are built at every stage into the musical act, relationships not only between the sounds created but also between the participants — among the performers, between performers and listeners (assuming that there are listeners), and among the listeners. In an earlier book I attempted to show the ways in which musical forms and techniques (that is, the ways in which people go about making the sounds of music) in a particular culture reflect, and in turn influence, the ways in which the members of that culture view themselves and their relation to the world, and I explored this idea in some detail in the case of western classical music. What I said there I still believe to hold good, but it needs to be extended to the consideration not only of the sounds but also of every aspect of that social event which is a musical performance. We therefore need to devote a little more space to this topic.

All of us derive a good deal of our feelings of who we are from the response which other people make to us; how they react to what we say and do is a major shaping force on our sense of identity (I suspect that Robinson Crusoe's greatest problem alone on his desert island would have been in convincing himself of his own existence). In western society, the most obvious medium through which we explore those responses, and make our own initiatives, thereby establishing our relationships with other people, is speech; but in many other cultures, notably those of Africa, which remain strong in the inheritance of black Americans, music and dance and what we generally call the performance arts are no less important. I believe that they play an important, although generally unrecognized, part in the relationships of Europeans and Euro-Americans as well. But, since speech is a mode of everyday communication to which westerners are more accustomed than they are to music, let us look briefly at some of the aspects of such an everyday matter as a conversation.

Conversation is by its very nature what we might call improvised, that is, it involves a strong element of spontaneous action, either initiatory or as a response to the initiatives of others. But the spontaneity is never total; in the first place we require a mutual acceptance of the rules of the language before any contact can be made. This acceptance will probably be, at least as far as native speakers of the language are concerned, tacit and even unconscious, but is no less necessary for that, since there can be no meanings without rules. Those rules are not only those of the verbal language, its grammar and syntax; when we converse we use also vocal inflection, physical gesture and posture, all of which contribute to the establishment of a relationship with our interlocutors. None of these is invented from scratch; all consist of pre-existing materials — words, tones, gestures, bodily postures and so on — which are organized according to rules and which need to be learned. Further, not even the arrangements we make of these materials need be new; most conversations consist largely of a common stock of phrases and utterances, quotations, clichés and references, which are often merely permutated.

Conversation is seldom if ever wholly about its ostensible topic, but is concerned primarily with the establishment and the exploration of identity. Each participant is affirming who he or she is, exploring the implications of that identity, sometimes trying on an identity to see how it fits, and at the same time sensing and testing the responses of others to that affirmation. Thus identity is not static, but develops and evolves along with the relationships which are at the same time established within the group of interlocutors — relationships not only of liking and disliking, but also of dominance, submission, equality, dependence and so on. These relationships are mediated by the kind of language adopted, not only of words but also of vocal inflection, posture and gesture, as are the degrees of intimacy sought or achieved: lawyers or doctors discussing a case, debaters on a platform, strangers on a train discussing the weather, newly-met lovers talking across the pillow, a long-married couple in the bed they have shared for thirty years, teachers in a staffroom, drinkers in a bar, the monarch 'chatting' with subjects, actors performing the playwright's lines, slave talking to master, master talking to slave — all of these serve to affirm and to reinforce identities and the kinds of relationship that exist between the participants — and the spectators, should there be any. All contain preformed material in various ways and proportions and represent a balance between premeditation and spontaneity — or, rather, the spontaneity is mediated through the preformed elements. None of those encounters would be possible without the existence of an agreed language, not only of word and syntax but also of vocal inflection and bodily gesture.

All of this activity is very important to the individuals concerned; in fact, we might say that it is the most important of all human activities, since it involves the central concern of human life: the quest for who we really are. There are other forms of encounter too, through which we explore various aspects of identity: sports, fighting, even crime — and artistic activity, above all perhaps musicking and dancing, through which relationships and identity (the two are the obverse and reverse of each other) are explored, affirmed and celebrated, on perhaps a more profound level, in that the process is less conscious, than in talking. As Alan Lomax has said: 'The performing arts acquire their quiet and unobtrusive authority in the lives of men precisely because they carry their message about social structure beneath the surface.'[11] It is for that reason that the relationships established during that human encounter which constitutes a musical performance are important indicators, on the one hand, and shapers on the other, of the sense of identity of the participants. Of course, identity is a complex and subtle affair, and it is not static but dynamic; all of us wear a number of identities depending on the social situations in which we find ourselves, and we try on from time to time many more to see how they fit. Some will appear even to be mutually contradictory, though the contradictions, we may assume, must be integrated at a deeper level of the personality.

A musical performance, like a conversation, consists of a mixture of preformed and spontaneously generated material, which is manipulated according to rules, which are the grammar and syntax of the musical style. No performance is completely without spontaneity but none is without preformed elements either; all musicking, like all talking, can be thought of as existing on a spectrum between these two extremes. Again as in talking, the extent to which the performance is governed by the preformed material will determine the relationships that are established between the participants; the more predetermined it is, the lesser will be the intimacy that is sought and attained between them. To show what I mean, let us look at one or two kinds of musical performance, to see what kinds of human relationship are brought into existence through them.

The kind of performance in which preformed elements are at a maximum and spontaneity at a minimum is probably a professional symphony concert as it takes place in a great concert hall in a western city. The building itself is interesting, since it will have been built, and be maintained, at considerable expense, a showpiece set aside entirely for the performance of music, as nearly soundproof as possible and visually isolated from the outside world; its very nature tells that what is to take place there is an occasion set aside from everyday life. Leaving the foyer, where socialization can take place, we enter the performance space itself, which also, before a note has been played, tells us much about the nature of the event which is about to take place. The seats, in their orderly rows, do not facilitate socializing; this is clearly not a place for conversation, or for communication between members of the audience. The rows are curved and the floor raked to centre the lines of sight on the middle of the performers' platform, to which we, the audience, have no access; the social barrier which separates us from the musicians is more insurmountable than the actual physical barrier which is formed by the edge of that platform. As we wait for the appointed hour (classical concerts start dead on time, latecomers being excluded until an interval) the musicians come on to the platform, having entered the hall by a separate entrance and having remained out of our sight up to this point. They are dressed in uniform style, which reduces their individuality, and they ignore the audience, taking their seats casually and tuning their instruments without so much as a gesture to acknowledge our presence. On the conductor's entrance they come to attention, and from then onwards there is no mistaking that he is in charge of the proceedings; as long as he is on the podium no further direct communication takes place between players.

What kind of relationships, then, are being established during this event? Among the audience, during the performance, no communication takes place; each individual sits still and quiet, alone with the music even though that person is among the two thousand or so people who may be present. It is his or her task to contemplate the sounds that are being made by the orchestra, and while of course a good deal of mental work is being done to make sense of the sounds, his or her role is essentially passive; nothing he or she can do, short of rioting, can affect the course of the performance. Communication is in one direction only, to each individual separately. Among the orchestra, relationships are formal, hierarchical and entirely functional, depending only on the job to be done; neither friendships nor dislikes play any part in the musical task to be done. During the performance they have all in any case to be mediated through the conductor, who alone has the power to respond spontaneously to the written notes. Those written notes, those messages from a probably long-dead individual, control the actions of everyone on the platform, but only the conductor has before him the complete picture of what the composer intended; the players see only their individual parts of the whole operation. The modern professional symphony orchestra is in fact a very model of a modern industrial enterprise, devoted like all industrial enterprises to the making of a product, a concert, which is advertised and marketed like any other commodity to the consumers, the audience. The whole enterprise is under the direction of a dominant tycoon-figure, the conductor. The relationship of performers to audience is thus that of producers to consumers, with all the limitations which are placed by that kind of relationship on the possibility of human encounter; the consumers, as with any other industrial product, have no say in its nature, their only choice being either to buy or not to buy it.

The relationships established during a modern professional

symphony concert are therefore those of modern industrial society: the orchestra is a group of individuals who, it seems, can be welded into a productive unit only by the abdication of the individual will to a superior authority; the audience to whom the concert is sold is a group of solitary individuals, whose power to show approval or disapproval can only be exerted after the performance is over. We shall see later that the musical works presented at these events are highly individualistic in nature, being concerned with the emotions and the spiritual progress of an individual soul and they are addressed to the emotions and experience of the audience as individuals; no direct encounter between performers or between listeners is either required or expected. As with many other products of industrial society, we may marvel at the brilliance of the works that are presented in this way and of the way in which they are presented, while noting that the price exacted is a high one in terms of individual autonomy and creativity.

There are, of course, more intimate encounters within the classical tradition; the performance of chamber music may be, within limits, a more convivial affair. A quartet of friends, for example, who sit down in the home of one of them to 'play the thoughts of the absent fifth known to them only through the music'[12] is much more self-directed than the orchestra; the players are able to work out their own response to the notations before them, discussing and arriving at an agreed interpretation, while others who are present may also make suggestions. But the players' actions remain under the control of the composer through his notations; their responses to one another in that human encounter which a musical performance *is* are still mediated through the written notes, which establish and maintain a distance between them and prevent too intimate an engagement — an engagement which they clearly, if not consciously, do not want, or else they would not be taking part in this kind of music making. The musical score provides an immutable given factor to the encounter and accords to it a measure of safety while preventing it from attaining an unwanted intimacy. Thus do styles of musicking evolve in conformity with the favoured styles of encounter of various social groups. The relationships of the string quartet, as with other kinds of classical chamber musicking, may be seen as an exploration, an affirmation and a celebration of the ideal personal relationships of a particular group within western society. The professionalization of chamber-music performing groups, and their removal from the chamber to the concert hall, has of course introduced a further distancing into the encounter, in line with the homogenization of human relationships brought about by the industrial society of today.

We shall see later how non-reliance on a score opens up a new realm of possibilities for relationships, both among players and among listeners and between the two groups of participants, tending to break down the gap between them and to encourage a greater intimacy of encounter. For the moment, it is sufficient to say that in all musical performances, as situations in which human beings encounter one another and try to create meaning from those encounters, it is the relationships that are established between the participants which constitute the most important element of that meaning.

This brings us to the fourth assumption, and the most difficult to expound. *Those relationships which are established in the course of a musical performance are of two kinds: first, those which are created between the sounds* (this is a matter of the forms and the techniques used by the performers — the ways in which they go about the making of the music) *and, secondly, those which are created among the participants*. These two sets of relationships are not necessarily congruent, but there is necessarily some link between them; one might say that the link is flexible but not infinitely so. Both sets of relationships are governed by those rules and conventions of language which, as we have seen, are on the one hand necessary if any meaning, any relationship, is to be created, while, on the other, by structuring the relationships, they prevent a totally intimate engagement between the participants. This is a perpetual paradox of all human relationships and communication, which in most societies is accepted as a necessary and, indeed, creative element of life; it seems to exist in particularly acute form in modern industrial societies of all political complexions, probably as a result of the destruction of old intimacies by the ruthlessly instrumental, functional relationships of industrialism.

Of the two kinds of relationships established in a musical performance, I explored the first, at least from the point of view of western classical music, in my book *Music, Society, Education*. I cannot repeat that exploration here, but, to summarize, I tried to show that the relationships established between sounds — that is, the forms and techniques of the music — in that tradition model the relationships of western society during the period when tonal harmony was dominant, and that the attitude to sounds in that tradition reflects in particular the scientific worldview which has increasingly dominated the west since about 1600. Relationships between sounds in music, in other words, mirror relationships between people.

We shall find comparable mirrorings in the techniques of the music which I shall be examining in this book. But it is the second half of the proposition that I need to discuss more fully here. One of the characteristics of improvised musicking is that any music-object, in so far as it comes into existence at all, is completed only at the moment when the musicians stop playing, so that its existence also ceases at that moment, other than in the memories of the participants. In this case we can assume the ideal instance of complete congruence between the relationships established between the sounds, on the one hand, and those between the participants on the other, since the acts of composition and performance are not separate but are subsumed into a single gesture. If there is any lack of congruence, if, for instance, the players improvise in a way in which the listeners can find no order or meaning, the latter will resolve it by either calling the players to order or by leaving. The situation, in other words, is negotiable.

When a performance takes place of a pre-existing musical work, whose identity is presumed to be independent of any possible performance of it, it is then that a gap begins to occur which can become wider over the subsequent performance history of the piece. For most musical works of the past we can assume that at the time of their first performance there was a congruence (it could be that the initial unfavourable reception given to some of these works, which have since become staples of the classical repertory, may be accounted for by the fact that congruence took a little while to evolve), since it was by catering to the needs of their contemporaries that musicians made a living. The survival of these works in unchanged, or virtually unchanged, form (given today a slighly higher overall level of pitch, more accurate intonation especially in the wind instruments, and the difference in tone produced by wire and nylon rather than by gut strings), obliges us to ask of the musical work the question that I introduced earlier: 'What does it mean when this work is performed in this place, at this time, with these musicians, before this audience?'. If, for example, we consider a symphony by Beethoven, perhaps the Third, the so-called *Eroica*, which was first performed in Vienna in 1804, we can gain a better understanding of this question.

In its time this work was a revolutionary piece, cracking open the traditional eighteenth-century forms of the symphony in a way in which even Beethoven's first two essays in the medium had not, and introducing a breadth and freedom of concept hitherto unknown; to judge from recorded reactions, it excited, puzzled and disturbed its original audiences in about equal proportions. That Beethoven, no stranger to the revolutionary rhetoric of the times, was metaphorically sweeping away the old regime of Europe and celebrating a new society must have been in the minds of his listeners, especially the members of the rising bourgeoisie, themselves bursting with ideas, creativity and libertarianism, with the French Revolution of 1789, which was essentially a bourgeois revolution, already under their belts and looking for new worlds to conquer. Played in a theatre (the purpose-built concert hall is a nineteenth-century invention) by an orchestra largely amateur with a stiffening of professionals, under the direction of the already hard-of-hearing composer, the piece must have contributed to an occasion of a very different kind from those of today, under the concert-hall conditions I described earlier. Today's audience belongs essentially to the same social classes as those of 1804, being overwhelmingly middle-class — a fact which has been confirmed by many social surveys in a number of countries — but today it is on the defensive, its position and values under attack. It is the defender, not the assailant, of the status quo. To a modern audience, the act of performing this symphony, nearly two hundred years and heaven knows how many performances later is no longer disturbing; rather, in its familiarity it has become almost cosy, certainly reassuring, telling us that things are as they have been and will remain so. Beethoven's mighty gesture of attack has become a mighty gesture (for the work remains a work of genius) of defence.

This change of meaning over time affects all art-objects, not just musical works. John Berger has written about paintings: 'It is a commonplace that the significance of a work of art changes as it survives. Usually, however, this knowledge is used to distinguish between 'them' (in the past) and 'us' (now). There is a tendency to picture *them* and their reactions as being embedded in history and to at the same time credit *ourselves* with an over-view, looking across from what we see as the summit of history. The surviving work of art then seems to confirm our superior position. The aim of its survival was us. This is an illusion. There is no exemption from history. The first time I saw [the Grünewald Altarpiece in Colmar] I was anxious to place *it* historically. In terms of medieval religion, the plague, medicine, the Lazar house. Now I have been forced to place *myself* historically.'[13] I take it that what Berger means is that, while the picture has not changed since Grünewald painted it in 1515, the meaning of the act of viewing it has. How much more so this must be when an act of performance has to take place before the work can come to actuality.

The gap that time inexorably opens up between the two meanings, and the way in which that gap can bring about a dangerous distortion of the function of artistic experience, making it an actual impediment to later generations in their task of structuring and making sense of their experience, is something that is understood by Africans. Dennis Duerden, in his study of African art and literature, writes of African attitudes to their sculpture that 'it is better that it should be eaten by ants or decay to be replaced by the most contemporaneous expressions of what the society thinks, that it should slowly disappear, instead of existing as evidence of what society was like historically. In the same way the old men are encouraged to take their memories with them to the ancestors. They may not impose them on their heirs who wish to be free to fulfil their own destinies . . . It seems that the . . . societies not only remember creative events and forget destructive ones but deliberately refuse to adopt symbols which will last long enough to be destructive to the existence of those societies.'[14] He goes on to extend this argument to literacy in general: 'I also suggest that it is this aversion to permanently and universally translateable symbols for the structure of the present . . . that accounts for the African societies' aversion to the use of writing, to symbols becoming recorded signs'.[15] What Europeans, then, consider to be signs of African 'primitiveness' — the lack of fixed cultural symbols such as monuments of architecture and sculpture (he goes so far as to suggest that the famous Benin bronzes, exceptional in African art in their permanence, were the product of a society that had become fixed and rigid in its social forms), of written records and musical scores — are in fact the result of a deliberate social and artistic strategy. To them, it is the creative process that is alive, while created objects are a dangerous legacy which for later generations can stand in the way of self-realization. Tennyson seems to have had a glimmering of the same truth when he made the dying King Arthur say to Sir Bedevere,

> The old order changeth, yielding place to new,
> And God fulfils himself in many ways,
> Lest one good custom should corrupt the world.[16]

The connection, then, between the relationships within the art-work itself and those created by its performance is flexible; the same musical sounds can be made to serve very different social purposes, as we have seen with the *Eroica Symphony*. But although the link may be flexible, it is not infinitely so; sooner or later it will break. It is perfectly possible that some time in the future a performance of a symphony by Beethoven, or anyone else for that matter, may no longer serve to create any desired or even significant social relationships, and in that case it will no longer be performed. And of course for the majority of people, even in western society, it is doubtful if the link ever formed in the first place; if most people do not look to classical performances for social meanings or feelings of identity, but instead to other kinds of musicking, it is not through any inability to comprehend them, but because they do not view human relationships in the same light as do those who use classical performances to support their feelings of identity. Looking further afield, one would not expect Africans to have much use for such performances, with their singleness of rhythmic perspective, their lack of bodily involvement, their separation from their everyday life and experience, as models for their own pluralistic and involved sense of who they are. On the other hand, it is not surprising that Africans today, who on the whole show a remarkable lack of interest in western classical music, in comparison with the industrialized Japanese, the South Koreans and even the Chinese, should find Afro-American styles of musicking useful as a means of coming to terms with themselves in a world dominated by European industrial values.

Again, a person may relate, both as performer and as listener, to more than one kind of musicking, but his or her flexibility will not be endless; identities may be multiple, and musicking is a wonderful way of trying on new ones, but the possibilities for any one individual are not infinite. And, conversely, the same performance may, at one and the same time for different people, serve different senses of identity — but, once again, the number of different identities a performance will support is not infinite, and, in fact, perhaps because participants tend to select themselves, there is a tendency for a performance to draw people together into a common identity.

We can deduce from this that, if as participants we enjoy a performance, we do so first because we feel that our sense of identity, our sense of who we really are, has been strengthened, and feel more intensely and knowingly *ourselves*, and, secondly because we feel that we have been, for the duration of the performance, in the company of like-feeling people, in an ideal society which musicians and listeners have together brought into existence for that duration of time. It is not just a tautology to state that, within a given musical culture, the better the performance, the more it will be enjoyed by the participants; it is important, and comprehensible in the following terms. Given the common concern musicians and listeners have in bringing into existence an ideal society, a set of ideal social relationships, then the more subtly, comprehensively and imaginatively the relationships between the sounds are explored, the more it will strengthen the feeling that those social relationships are valid and important, and will thus intensify the participants' sense of being and well-being.

The key, of course, is in the meaning of the word 'better'. In one musical culture, quality may lie in the accurate and sensitive realization of a difficult score for the benefit of a group of passive listeners; in another it may lie in the extent to which everyone participates, in a church service, a party or a patriotic rally; in a third it may lie in the ingenious rhythmic invention with which the musicians entice everyone present into the dance and support their dancing; in a fourth in the way in which a singer takes command of a group of listeners as she sings for the thousandth time an ancient ballad known to all; while in a fifth it may lie in the way in which a leader and chorus call and respond to each other in mutual encouragement and involvement. Each of these kinds of performance involves a different concept of excellence, and each brings into existence a different kind of society, about which one may make two generalizations: the first is that the more actively involved everyone present is in the performance, and the fewer spectators there are of the musical process, then the more unified that society will be; while the second is that the less dependent the participants are on pre-existing material, including written notations, the more directly and intimately they will be able to respond to one another (though, as we have noticed, there are limits, in that no meanings, or relationships, can be created without some rules; trying to discover how few and minimal rules are necessary has always been an important quest for some musicians).

Thus the participants in a symphony concert are bringing into existence, for the duration of the performance, an ideal industrial society, in which each individual is solitary and autonomous, tidy, disciplined and stable, punctual and reliable, the division of labour is clear, the relationships are impersonal and functional, and the whole is under the control of a charismatic figure armed with clearly defined authority. The music played is drawn from a repertory which, like the ideal industrial culture, is standardized the whole world over and played in a standard manner; it is a repertory of musical works which themselves either celebrate the individualist values of western industrial culture or can be forced into that mould: it consists of abstract dramas of the individual soul through which performers and listeners alike can participate vicariously in the processes of becoming and overcoming, or else of abstract dances, many of them hijacked from more dancing cultures, in which the performance invites us implicitly to do what the concert-hall conventions prohibit us from doing, or else of abstract landscapes, of fantasy Españas, Americas, Hebridean Islands or pastoral Englands of nostalgia or of the tourist imagination. Above all, it is a society in which producers and consumers of the commodity, music, fulfil clearly defined and separate roles. In the ceremony called a symphony concert, which brings this ideal society into existence, the values of performers and listeners, and their sense of who they are, are explored, affirmed and celebrated. It need hardly be said that, for those who do not share these values, neither the concert-hall ritual nor the symphonic drama is likely to be of much interest.

I shall be looking in later chapters at other musical celebrations of identity; I have already raised some questions to which I will propose some tentative answers, in particular 'Why are we moved by music?' and 'What do we mean by beauty in music?' These are, as I am only too aware, questions which have absorbed the attention of aestheticians and philosophers for a long time; if I believe I have anything useful to contribute to them, it is because I am convinced that our important concern should be not music but musicking, and I ask the reader to keep this in mind as we proceed.

To the first question I can propose the answer: We are moved by music because musicking creates the public image of our most inwardly desired relationships, not just *showing them to us* as they might be but actually *bringing them into existence* for the duration of the performance. This will clearly involve our deepest feelings, and thus the act of musicking, taking place over a duration of time, teaches us what we really feel about ourselves and about our relationships to other people and to the world in general, helping us to structure those feelings and therefore to explore and evolve our own identity. Clifford Geertz has said: 'In order to make up our minds we must know how we feel about things; and to know how we feel we need the public images of sentiment that only ritual, myth and art can provide'.[17] And again: 'Human thought is basically both social and public — its natural habitat is the house yard, the marketplace and the town square. Thinking consists not of "happenings in the mind" (though happenings there and elsewhere are necessary for it to occur) but of a traffic in what have been called . . . significant symbols'[18] — or, as Alice might have said, 'How do I know what I feel until I hear what I play?' In musicking, in fact, we are being touched in the deepest parts of who we are.

The musicking that moves us most will be that which most subtly, comprehensively and powerfully articulates the relationships of our ideal society — which may or may not have any real, or even possible, existence beyond the duration of the performance. The ambivalence of the emotions which such musicking arouses in us, posed between joy and melancholy ('I am never merry when I hear sweet music,' said Jessica) can be seen as a response to the realization of that fall from perfection which is present as an element of virtually all cultures and religions. The ambivalence reflects the simultaneous experiencing of the ideal and the impossibility of realizing it — at least in the present, since some musicking *is* about possible earthly societies, and some, as for example when the black slaves sang spirituals and even when modern black Americans continue to do so, about a heavenly and a possible earthly society at the same time. At the same time the musicking can exhilarate us with a vision of that ideal which is not just intimated to us but actually brought into existence for as long as the performance lasts. While it does we *can* believe in its realizability, and the exhilaration and the joy, outlasting the melancholy, can persist long after the performance is over. This is not surprising, for it confirms us in our *feelings*, which, as Geertz says, we must know before we know what we *think,* about what are right and true relationships.

We have seen that there is no agreement on the nature of the the ideal society — what would be heaven for one might be hell for another — which is why we find that the more fragmented a society is, the greater are the number of different kinds of musicking that go on in it, while the deeper the social and political divisions, the less understanding will there be between the various musical cultures. Musicking is not necessarily a unifying force at all; on the contrary, it can articulate and even exacerbate social divisions. On the other hand, identity is a complex and often apparently contradictory business, and musical cultures may take root in unexpected places, as can be seen in the adoption by white London skinheads, a group with a reputation for racial violence, for a brief period in the early 1970s, of reggae, recently arrived from Jamaica, and of some of the style and mannerisms of black youth.

We can also come to understand better the question of musical beauty if we keep the essential nature of music as *act* clearly in mind; there can be no such thing as a beautiful piece of music aside from that act. We can call it beautiful only if it makes possible beautiful performances; certainly there is not much beauty in a score. And, secondly, in order to find a piece beautiful in performance we need, not only to find the society that the performance brings into existence congenial, but also to feel a congruence between the nature of that society and the means adopted to bring it into existence (clearly, we are back to the fourth assumption here).

We see why there can be no absolute standard of beauty, but also why within the classical culture there is general agreement about what are its most beautiful works. We also see why, if we feel the performers are not doing their best, beauty will fly out of the window, no matter how we may love and admire (that is to say, have in the past experienced beautiful performances of) the work being played — and why, conversely, we can always get a glimpse of beauty if the performer, however inept, is doing his honest best; I should go so far as to say that anyone who cannot do so has no conception of what music is all about. I can also find it possible to like a musical work while finding certain performances of it thoroughly objectionable. This is of course not just an 'aesthetic' matter but a political and a moral one, which is what considerations of beauty generally boil down to; certainly I find that there is little genuine beauty to be found in modern concert-hall performances, no matter how technically brilliant or even expressive, of the great works of the past.

Whether those great works can be reclaimed from the concert hall is an open question. Perhaps performances by amateurs, playing for love, may do so, but I am inclined to doubt it. Perhaps only when we learn to love the creative act more than the created object, as the great creators themselves did, shall we be able to arrive at a true understanding of their achievement — and then we need not place such reliance on the objects anyway, being content, like the Africans, to let them slowly disappear, as the old men take their memories to the ancestors. Harry Partch has commented:

> 'It has been said that because more people hear Beethoven in twenty-four hours (on the radio) than heard him in his whole lifetime the people have music . . . We can say, yes, and a citizen doubtless sees more policemen now in twenty-four hours than Beethoven saw in his whole lifetime. The people have more music, and *ipso facto* they are more musical? The people have more laws, and *ipso facto* they are more lawful?
>
> 'Beethoven is a value that may be expected to persist because he has had value for generations of human beings. The point is not the value of Beethoven but whether in our schools of serious [*sic*] music we shall confine ourselves to finer and finer degrees of perfection in the "interpretation" of past treasures, whether we shall go on devouring or unconsciously absorbing vibrating frankfurters to that point of melomaniacal satiety at which our appetite vanishes, or whether a few of us will chuck the music, turn off the radio, and go into the kitchen and cook ourselves a nourishing meal.'[19]

Well, yes, but we should remember that Beethoven's music has had value for a not very large number of generations — perhaps a dozen only since he died in 1827 — few even in terms of the recorded history of European music, and a mere eye-flash in terms of the unknown and unknowable million-year history of human musicking. And, further, all of those dozen or so generations have been part of that quite small sector of the human race which subscribes to certain ideals and assumptions concerning the individual, society and their relation to nature. When these change, as they inevitably will (we have to remind ourselves that we stand, as Berger says, not at the summit of history but perhaps only somewhere near the start of the game), the message of Beethoven's music will quite likely no longer be of any great concern or value; even the very idea of a 'great composer' might arouse nothing more than a patronizing smile. We should remember, too, that Beethoven's music is, even today, of no great interest to the majority of people even within western Christian-scientific-industrial society (that is to say, to those who are not and never have been the beneficiaries of that society), let alone the still overwhelming majority of the human race who have never subscribed to those ideas or those assumptions, even if they have had their practical consequences, from sweatshops to heroin to traffic jams to Agent Orange, wished upon them.

The greatness of Beethoven lies not in any absolute values which performances of his works may embody (every musical performance, of course, embodies some universal human values, just as does every human individual) but in the power, subtlety, authority and comprehensiveness with which such performances explore, affirm and celebrate the values and ideal relationships of European society. Performances of his works today bear witness to the continuing power of those values and relationships in the minds of those whom we can crudely call the middle classes, even if today's performers and audiences take part, no longer for stimulation or for encouragement in the task of turning society upside down, but for reassurance and for encouragement in the task of keeping society as it is. The most powerful evidence for this assertion lies in the amount of money which those, such as the modern state and wealthy business and industrial organizations, who have an interest in keeping society as it is, contribute to the support of classical musicking. In taking part in such performances, especially in the absence of any credible counterbalance from contemporary classical composers (who have nothing more to offer than a technological fix, that is to say, a change in technique which conceals a lack of reconsideration of underlying values) today's classical performers and listeners reveal a dangerously backward-looking cast of mind, even nostalgia (the most dangerous of communal emotional states) and an unwillingness to come to terms with the contemporary world and its pressures for change.

We can now suggest briefly what it is that a person taking part in a musical performance is actually doing. I suggest that he or she is doing three things, which are interdependent and equal in importance, so that any order of enumeration is quite arbitrary:

1. He or she is exploring, affirming and celebrating a sense of identity;
2. He or she is taking part in an ideal society which the participants between them have brought into existence for the duration of the performance;
3. He or she is modelling, in the relationships between the sounds he or she is making, listening to or dancing to, the relationships of that ideal society.

All of this, I must repeat, takes place beneath the surface of consciousness; as Lomax says, it is the power of the performing arts that these messages are transmitted and received in a way that is not necessarily conscious.

Two other points follow: first, no musical tradition or culture is inherently superior to any other. Within a given musical culture there can clearly be some musicking that explores its values better than others, and some musicians who are better at that exploration than others, but if the function of the musical act is to explore and celebrate identity, then the merit of each musical act must be set against the values of its own culture and that alone. Those who maintain, or, more commonly, just assume, as adherents of western classical music tend to do, that their own musicking is in its very nature superior to any other, can only mean, finally, that they believe *themselves*, by virtue of the culture to which they belong, to be inherently superior to all others.

The second point is that it is not necessary to belong to a given social group in order to enjoy its musicking; were this not so, no traffic whatsoever could take place between cultures. What *is* necessary, however, is for the outside participant to feel some empathy with the people whose musicking it is, to feel some comprehension of and sympathy with their values, even if that sympathy is not fully conscious. Further, the musical understanding achieved by the outsider will be commensurate with that understanding and sympathy and no more. This can explain the often crass condescension shown to black American musicians by some white critics who appear genuinely to enjoy their music. Conversely, when some musical interaction does take place between members of two cultures or social groups, it must mean that those of one group feel some empathy with, perhaps even admiration for, those of the other and for their values, that they see something in the lifestyle that appeals, and fills a gap in their own lives — even if, as is often the case, there are considerable surface antagonisms between the two. This empathy has in fact been a major factor in the musical fusion which is the subject of this book.

Finally, the whole of the foregoing can be summed up in different terms: *a musical performance is a ritual in which is acted out the mythology of a social group*. To understand this, we need to consider what is meant by the two words 'ritual' and 'mythology', especially as both have had their meanings so debased in modern usage that it is necessary to explain them. In common usage, to call an action or an event 'ritualistic' is to suggest that it has lost any meaning that it might once have had, and that the participants simply go through accustomed motions; but ritual is in fact an action which dramatizes and re-enacts the shared mythology of a social group. It is as essential a part of human social life as is eating (and indeed a meal is an event which is itself loaded with ritual significance, as Mary Douglas has pointed out).[20] It is an essential part of the human quest for meaning, without which there would be no point in eating, or living, at all.

Ritual, according to the anthropologist Mercea Eliade, celebrates the 'sacred history' of a culture — its creation, the coming of the civilizing heroes, their 'demiurgic activities' and finally their disappearance. 'The sacred history — mythology — is exemplary, paradigmatic; not only does it tell how things came to be but it also lays the foundations for all human behaviour and all our social and cultural institutions.'[21] Myth, in fact, is not to be understood literally as history at all, at least not in the modern sense (though even modern history shades off into myth more often than is appreciated); through its narratives of how things came to be we learn how things are and how they should be. It sets out desirable relationships, between person and person, group and group, and between humanity and the natural and even the supernatural world. Eliade gives also a clue to why in our society we undervalue myth and ritual, even though our lives are shot through and through with them, in that he explicitly confines his examination of ritual and myth to what are called 'primitive' or 'traditional' societies. 'Modern man's originality', he says, 'his newness in comparison with traditional societies, lies precisely in his determination to regard himself as a purely historical being, in his wish to live in a basically desacralized cosmos.'[22] In other words, modern westerners believe themselves to have become divorced from, and even to have outgrown, the beliefs and ideals that shaped the lives of earlier generations, as well as of present-day 'primitive' or 'traditional' societies, to have outgrown, in fact, both myth and ritual. The very use of the former word to signify an erroneous belief is another sign of this state of mind, although the literal truth or otherwise of a myth is actually irrelevant, since it is through its usefulness in shaping our lives and conduct that myth reveals its value; it is only in a moral or a spiritual sense that it can be described as true or false.

Westerners, then, tend to believe themselves to have broken through into a purely secular universe. Eliade himself is doubtful whether this is in fact true; I am certain it is not, that modern westerners are just as much dependent on their mythologies as any members of 'traditional' societies. Nor is there any need to think of myths as relics of a more primitive stage of development, or even as what Max Müller called the 'dark shadow which language throws upon thought and which will never disappear until language becomes entirely commensurate with thought, which it never will.'[23]

Myth, and its cognate activity, ritual, is an essential means by which we grasp the multidimensional nature of reality and give that nature its full significance in our lives; it is interesting that as the researches of physicists become more and more arcane, their language has become more and more that of myth as the only way in which they can apprehend the multivalency of the world in which they move and can resolve its contraditions (it gives one to wonder whether it is not in fact their own minds they are exploring). To the extent that we suppress an awareness of our myths modern westerners are doomed to remain even more in thrall to them than those 'primitives' whom we are pleased to patronize. Our society is shot through and through with myth: a whole mythological system concerning the absolute value and the mysterious efficacy of money which has been embodied in the most practical of ways in the policies and programmes of successive governments; another concerning the power of scientific knowledge and its ability to save us from nature and from ourselves; in Britain the sacred words 'Dunkirk', 'the blitz' and 'El Alamein', which conjure up a whole mythology that I am not sure the British would not be better off without.

To repeat: all musical performances partake of the nature of ritual, the acting-out of desired relationships and thus of identity. It is not difficult to recognize this ritual function in musical cultures that are remote from our own; the western anthropologist will certainly assume such a function when observing the musicking, generally inseparable from dancing, of some remote tribal people, while the western classical music lover may well do the same thing when observing a rock concert, calling it a 'tribal ritual of youth' or some such. It is always less obvious when we come to consider musicking that is closer to us; the same music lover will probably find it hard to accept that his symphony concerts, opera performances and chamber recitals are no less rituals of a particular social group at a particular point in history, preferring to believe in their absolute value and permanent significance. But this permanent significance is apparent only to one who sees the value system of the western middle classes, the official values which serve to validate the industrial state for those who are its beneficiaries, as itself absolute and permanent.

The observant reader will notice that I have said nothing about the effect of economic factors and specific power structures on western musicking today, let alone the effect of twentieth-century media such as records, radio and television. These factors and these media pertain to the next stage of my discussion, and they will appear in due course; what I have set out so far is what I believe are some general meanings of the act of musicking, regardless of economic or technological factors. In so far as musicking is universal to the human race I consider this chapter a necessary ground-clearing operation, which is all too often neglected by those who discuss music as a social institution. It is in fact the ways in which the special conditions under which Africans and Europeans encountered one another in the Americas shaped the musicking of both black and white Americans, and from them that of virtually the whole world, that is the subject of this book. In this exploration I shall be keeping in mind the assumptions set out in this chapter, and I ask the reader to do the same.

NOTES

1. WOLFE, Tom: 'The Painted Word', *Harpers and Queen*, February 1976, p 70.
2. In an aside during the forum *Improvisation: History, Directions, Practice*, Association of Improvising Musicians, London, 31 March, 1984.
3. MUELLER, John H.: *The American Symphony Orchestra: A Social History of Musical Taste*, London, John Calder, 1958, p 15.
4. BLACKING, John: *How Musical Is Man?*, London, Faber & Faber, 1976, p 40.
5. NKETIA, J.H. Kwabena: *The Music of Africa*, London, Victor Gollancz, 1975, p 50.
6. BEST, Elsdon: *The Maori As He Was*, Wellington, Dominion Museum, 1924, p 147.
7. MEAD, Margaret: 'Children and Ritual in Bali', in BELO, Jane (ed): *Traditional Balinese Culture*, New York, Columbia University Press, 1970, p 199.
8. McPHEE, Colin: *Music in Bali*, New Haven, Yale University Press, 1966, p 5.
9. SACHS, Curt: *The Wellsprings of Music*, The Hague, Martinus Nijhoff, 1962, p 137.
10. BANKS, Tony: Letter to the Editor, *The Times*, London, 5 August, 1983.
11. LOMAX, Alan: *Folk Song Style and Culture*, New Brunswick, N.J., Transaction Books, 1968, p 7.

12. DRIVER, Christopher: 'Different Drum', *New Society*, 21 September, 1978, p 639.
13. BERGER, John: *About Looking*, London, Writers and Readers Publishing Cooperative, 1980, p 133.
14. DUERDEN, Dennis: *African Art and Literature: The Invisible Present*, London, Heinemann, 1975, p 18.
15. *ibid.*, p xiv.
16. TENNYSON, Alfred, Lord: 'The Passing of Arthur', in RICKS, Christopher (ed): *The Poems of Tennyson*, London, Longmans, 1969, lines 408–410.
17. GEERTZ, Clifford: *The Interpretation of Cultures*, London, Hutchinson, 1975, p 82.
18. *ibid.*, p 45.
19. PARTCH, Harry: *Genesis of a Music*, 2nd edition, New York, Da Capo Press, 1974, p 58.
20. DOUGLAS, Mary: 'Deciphering a Meal' in *Implicit Meanings*, London, Routledge and Kegan Paul, 1975, pp 249–75.
21. ELIADE, Mercea: *Rites and Symbols of Initiation*, New York, Harper & Row, 1965, p xi.
22. *ibid.*, p ix.
23. quoted in CASSIRER, Ernst: *Language and Myth*, transl. by Suzanne Langer, New York, Dover Books 1953, p 5.

Chapter 3

RITUALS FOR SURVIVAL I: AN EXTATIC DELIGHT IN PSALMODY

A musical performance, then, can be seen as a ritual in which the identity and the values of the members of a social group are explored, affirmed and celebrated. I shall now look at the way in which the musicking of black Americans developed in its religious dimension, keeping in mind that the division of identity into 'sacred' and 'secular' is far from absolute, whether in everyday living or in musicking. Given the centrality of religion as a way of making sense of what was being done to them, it is not surprising that it is in the religious music of the slaves that the encounter with white culture bore its first recorded fruit. Musical interactions do not occur at random, but are indicators always of an empathy, even across a social or cultural barrier, which is not necessarily or even usually conscious. That such empathy exists, at levels deeper than those feelings of fear and guilt which lie at the root of racism, is borne out by the history of the musical interaction that occurred in the United States — and, indeed, wherever such encounters occurred.

We have seen how the slaves constructed communities and a feeling of identity even within the narrow limits allowed by their condition. Such communities were fragile; families and even whole plantations were liable to be brutally disrupted, at the whim of a master or under the pressure of economic circumstance. It was to a large extent the flexibility and the decentralization of the African cultural background that enabled the slaves to create rituals for the celebration of their identity; their musicking, poetry and dancing depended neither on written sources nor on the presence of specialists, and were thus open to endless re-creation not just by a few but by all.

In the early days of slavery in North America, few white people gave much thought to the souls of the slaves; certainly none of the organized churches made any serious attempt at evangelization until early in the eighteenth century. There was for a time even a debate as to whether black people were human at all, and thus whether they had souls to save; it would clearly have been more convenient and less productive of guilt if the answer could have been given in the negative. The attitudes of masters varied; in some households instruction was given in Christian doctrine and church attendance enjoined on the slaves, often in the hope that they would come to believe that their situation was divinely ordained (a catechism to that effect was even taught), while others, generally on the larger plantations, left them to their own devices in this matter. It is doubtful whether any large proportion of slaves was even nominally Christian before 1750. The religious revival of the second half of the eighteenth century that was known as the Great Awakening, which affected whites no less than blacks, was probably the occasion for the baptism of most of the slaves. Their worship was supervised and controlled carefully by white clergymen, at least in the south, although independent black churches did establish themselves in the north in the later years of the century, especially among the Baptists and Methodists. It took a long time before all the planters overcame their resistance to the teaching of Christian doctrine to, and the baptism of, slaves; it was based largely on their fear that the slaves might start applying the doctrine to their own condition — which indeed they did. Even after this resistance was overcome there was further objection to the idea of black preachers, even sometimes as subordinates to white clergy. The blacks usually attended the same churches as the whites, in segregated sections, with the observances carefully supervised to prevent any outbreak of African practices.

The good clergymen who instructed the slaves in Christian doctrine, in snatches of Old and New Testament history and in the psalms (in verse translations, of course) must have been at times amazed at the vehemence of their charges' response to their teachings, and at the same time they must have been more than a little alarmed at the changes they wrought in those doctrines and at the forms their worship took. Two famous letters to friends in London from the Rev Samuel Davies of Virginia in 1755 include the following:

> 'The books were all very acceptable, but none more so than the Psalms and Hymns, which enable them [ie the slaves] to gratify their peculiar taste for psalmody. Sundry of them have lodged all night in my kitchen, and sometimes when I have awaked about two or three o'clock in the morning, a torrent of sacred harmony has poured into my chamber and carried my mind away to heaven. In this seraphic exercise some of them spend almost the whole night. I wish, Sir, you and other benefactors could hear some of these sacred concerts. I am persuaded it would please you more than an Oratorio or a St Cecilia's day . . . I cannot but observe that the Negroes, above all the Human Species that I ever knew, have an Ear for Musick, and a kind of extatic Delight in Psalmody; and there are no Books they learn so soon or take so much pleasure in, as those used in that heavenly Part of divine Worship.'[1]

So, by that date, some at least of the slaves were singing psalms, and it is strongly to be inferred that they were singing them in their own way. These comments are at least consistent with practices described later, and still, in fact, to be heard today — that of vocal improvisation around each single note in turn of a melody, over a beat slowed down almost to immobility, in what has been described as 'a volume of florid sound which ebbs and flows slowly, powerfully and at times majestically in successive surges.'[2]

It is characteristic that, in taking over a repertory of songs, the metrical psalms and their assorted melodies, the slaves should have brought to bear their own ways of singing, transforming the staid and plain hymns, the rhymed expressions of Protestant theology, into expressive fantasies of sound. One can imagine, *pace* the soul of the Rev Davies, that what the slaves seized upon was not so much the repertory of songs in itself, still less the details of the doctrines contained in the verses, as the opportunity it gave them to practise upon both words and music that group vocal improvisation, that affirmation through song of unity in variety that we have seen is the essence of the African sense of community, which transcended the confines of that condition into which they had been thrust, and of the power to structure their community in ways which were otherwise denied to them.

In introducing Christian doctrine into the lives of the slaves, the missionaries were in fact releasing forces which they could not have fully comprehended. For, as has been said, it was not so much a matter of the slaves' conversion *to* Christianity as of a conversion *of* Christianity in accordance with African ways of perceiving the world and with the needs of a ruthlessly oppressed people for a vision that would transcend the hopelessness of the present situation and give them a reason for wanting to survive. The clergymen's assurances that rewards for their suffering (the more passive the acceptance the greater the reward) awaited them in the world to come was, not surprisingly given the African way of thinking, not so much rejected as subsumed into a worldview that saw the past and the future as all of a piece with the present, and the spiritual as part of the natural. Ultimate justice, they believed, may lie in heaven, but it was to be sought also on earth, and the heroes of the Old Testament — Moses, Joshua, Daniel, Ezekiel — were alive and all around them, liberators of the captive Jews with whom the captive blacks could readily identify. Texts like

> Didn't my Lord deliver Daniel?
> So why not every man?

and

> Go down, Moses,
> Down into Egypt's land,
> Tell ol' Pharaoh,
> Let my people go.

were not just apostrophes to historical personages, not just references to some heavenly liberation (they *were* that, but also more) but direct pleas to those whom they knew personally, as their African forebears had known their ancestors — and we must remember that right up to the time of Emancipation in

1865 there were first-generation Africans who would have kept the ancestral feelings alive. The identification worked in the other direction also, in that elements from the ancestral religions, such as spirit possession, dance, trance and chanted sermons, became incorporated into the Christian observances, again to the dismay of the white divines and other religious-minded people; even the vengeful god of the Old Testament became transmuted by the grafting-on of characteristics of the African gods, notably the Yoruba creator-god, Obatala, while Christ often became identified with the Yoruba storm-god Shango. In the Yoruba creation myth the all-too-obvious imperfection of human beings was explained by the story that Obatala got drunk when he was creating us, and his hand slipped — a more forgiving notion, it seems to me, than Christian original sin.

The Christianity of the slaves was in fact very different in its moral direction from that of the whites; it was pieced together from those fragments of orthodox belief that were passed to them, very selectively, by the masters and their church functionaries and from those fragments of African religion that remained functional to their needs — needs for the affirmation of present humanity and community and of the hope for future freedom and justice. The masters might cobble together for them from questionable bits of Christian theology a moral code (God made you in order to serve your masters; obey your master, work hard for him, do not steal from him, and so on) and, with some notable exceptions among whom we may number the Rev Samuel Davies, the clergy might allow themselves, to their eternal shame, to be co-opted into propagating such a farrago, but according to all the evidence the vast majority of the slaves never for a moment accepted it. They remained, over the generations of slavery, aware of who they were and of the grievous offence that was being committed against them, and there was no way the masters' religion of sin and guilt could be foisted upon them. As James Cone points out, the slaves' problem was not sin — that was a luxury only white folk could afford — but the suffering that was being inflicted upon them through what they knew was a monstrous injustice and absurdity. Their problem was to keep from submitting to existential despair, and they solved it, not once and for all, but over and over again every day of their lives, with a faith in a god who was not, could not be, the god of their masters, and in his promise of ultimate justice and freedom, not just in the next world but in this.

It is worth noting that Africans were not the only people who had been enslaved by the new masters of the American continents; in fact, they were imported into America only after attempts to enslave the indigenous 'Indian' populations by the Spanish conquistadores had been frustrated by the fact that the enslaved population simply gave up and died in their chains by the million. Today, the old American civilizations are a memory only, their ruined cities standing as testimony to what was destroyed, their reduced descendants eking out lives as serfs to the great landowners and to mining and drug interests. The factor that enabled the Africans and their descendants in those same circumstances not only to survive as an ethnic and cultural group, not only to retain a proud identity within the societies of North and South America and the Caribbean, but to create a culture which, through its music and dance, has gone out across the world, was not Christianity (the Indians were Christianized too) but the African ability to adapt and to tolerate contradiction, and, above all, the African assurance that the supreme value lies in the preservation of the community; without a community for support the individual is helpless, while with it he or she is invincible. 'Suffering,' says James Cone, 'is not too much to bear if there are brothers and sisters to go down into the valley to pray with you . . . The actual brutalities of slavery were minor in comparison with the loss of community.'[3] In the moral code of the slaves, what was right was what tended to preserve the community, what was wrong that which undermined it. 'The point here' says Thomas Webber, 'is not that quarter members never betrayed each other, or stole from each other, or even killed each other, but rather that most members understood that it was to their mutual advantage to protect each other, and that solidarity was a good which they believed to have moral force.'[4] Thus, it was no offence to steal the masters' property (how could that be theft, the slave asked, not unreasonably, since he was himself the master's property?) but it was to steal from a fellow slave.

And if it was belief in the ultimate justice of God that held the community together, it was musicking and dancing, those twin rituals of affirmation, of exploration and celebration of relationships, with their unique power to weld together into a higher unity the contradictory experiences of sorrow, pain, joy, hope and despair, that was at the centre of their religious expression. It is possible to say it in two ways, both equally true: on the one hand, the African cultural inheritance which located musicking and dancing at the centre of a ritual for the strengthening of community placed in the slaves' hands a tool for survival, while, on the other hand, the survival needs of the enslaved blacks ensured the continuance of African attitudes to and uses for music long after actual African styles had become absorbed into that Creole music which, as we have seen, probably developed in the first generations of slavery.

Unlike the New England colonies, those colonies which became the southern states of the United States were not founded on religious conviction, and for the white settlers life was predominantly secular in tone, with religious observance playing no more than the most conventional of roles. On the other hand, class distinctions were pronounced from the earliest days; apart from the black slaves, there was a despised and repressed class of whites, many of them servants or labourers, even working alongside the slaves on the plantations, or subsistence farmers on poor land for which the great landowners had no use. The upper classes preserved the conventional religious observances, and we have seen that Christianity gradually permeated through the slave population during the eighteenth century, but the established churches left the poor whites very much to their own resources. The transformation of the poor white population of the rural south into a heartland of Christian fundamentalism came about largely through the efforts of the Dissenting sects, notably Methodists, Presbyterians and Baptists, who from the mid-eighteenth century onwards sent itinerant preachers, known as circuit riders, through the countryside to effect conversions. Their preaching fell on fertile ground, since the promise of a good life in the next world was appealing to those who lived such a harsh life and whose background lacked the rich sense of community which the African background furnished for the slaves.

The labours of the circuit riders were part of the wave of religious revivalism known as the Great Awakening. It seems to have come about to a great extent as a result of the tensions between the austere ideals of the early Puritans and the growing materialism and commercialism of the developing colonies, as Christian merchants reaped the profits of the slave trade and connived at the wholesale killing of Native Americans and the destruction of their society and culture. A further wave of revivalism began in the early 1800s, starting in Kentucky and sweeping through into Tennessee, Georgia and the Carolinas. It was this 'Second Awakening' that gave rise to the massive outdoor camp meetings where for the first time black and white met on anything like equal terms, and during which, in all probability, the evangelization of the slaves was more or less completed. There are many accounts of these remarkable events which testify to their highly-charged emotional atmosphere and to their communality, of blacks and whites together testifying, singing, preaching, often right through the nights. That even there, however, communality and equality were not quite all they might have been is suggested from the following modern description:

> 'In both slaveholding and nonslaveholding areas the Negroes were allowed to set up their camp behind the preacher's rostrum. Because of the close proximity, their services often merged with those of the whites, adding no little to the general confusion and excitement. The Negro housing area, with its crazy-quilt tents after the fashion of Joseph's coat, was a picturesque affair. As the camp meeting matured, the Negro camp section was sometimes separated from that of the whites by a plank partition. The barrier was torn down on the final days of the meeting when the two peoples joined together in a song festival and "marching ceremony".'[5]

The atmosphere of those occasions may be judged from the following description of a meeting in 1802:

> 'A speaker arose to give a short parting exhortation, and, wonderful to tell, as if by electric shock, a large number in

> every direction, men, women and children, white and black, fell and cried for mercy . . . a poor black man with his hands raised over the heads of the crowd, shouting "Glory, glory, glory!" and another prostrate on the ground, his aged mother on her knees at his feet'.[6]

The singing of the blacks attracted much comment; one writer spoke of the 'deep, melodious, organ-like music welling from a thousand African throats',[7] while another wrote: 'At every service the negroes were present in large numbers in a special section reserved for them, and made many professions of religion. Their singing was inspiring and was encouraged and enjoyed by the white congregation, who would sometimes remain silent to listen.'[8]

A complaint published in 1819 by one John F. Watson, entitled *Methodist Error, or Friendly Christian Advice to Those Methodists Who Indulge in Extravagant Religious Emotions and Bodily Exercises*, tells us something of the musicking of black people, as well as of the alarm felt by some white clergy at discovering that their way of singing was finding its way into white religious practices also. His description of black song is interesting:

> 'Here ought to be considered, too, a most exceptional error, which has the tolerance, at least, of the rulers of our camp meetings. In the *blacks'* quarter, the colored people get together, and sing for hours together, short songs of disjointed affirmations, pledges or prayers, lengthened out with long repetition *choruses*. These are all sung in the merry chorus-manner of the southern harvest field . . . From this cause I have known in some camp meetings, from 50 to 60 people crowd into one tent, after the public devotions had closed, and there continue the whole night, singing tune after tune (though with occasional episodes of prayer) scarce one of which were in our hymn books. Some of this from their nature (having very long repetition choruses and short scraps of matter) are actually composed as sung, and are indeed almost endless'.[9]

Printed material was not much used in the camp meetings; many if not most, both black and white, were unable to read, and the outdoor conditions in any case did not favour its use.

Such few copies of printed hymns as did circulate consisted of words only; tunes were presumably either well known or catchy enough to be learnt on the spot. There was a considerable amount of improvised hymnody, often with a couplet sung by a leader with a responsorial chorus, which might be a simple 'Glory, Hallelujah!' or 'Roll, Jordan, roll', or an answer to the leader's question: 'O brethren, will you meet me/In Canaan's happy land?' — 'By the grace of God we'll meet you/In Canaan's happy land'. Other hymns of this type were adaptations of Methodist or Presbyterian hymns with the insertion of refrains after each couplet — a procedure which the whites had probably picked up from the call-and-response-singing blacks. There is much argument among scholars about the provenance of spiritual singing, both black and white, in the period that followed these explosive encounters. Some maintain that the dominant influence came from the blacks while others deny that they had any part to play beyond the giving of a particular colouring to what were essentially white melodies and harmonies. None of this controversy would matter were it not for its obvious political implications, for the truth is probably that each group brought to the camp meetings its own characteristic way of singing — and we should recall that the actual notes of the hymns were less important than the hymns *as they were sung* — musicking as opposed to music. No doubt the whites brought their repertory of hymns, which were modified by the conditions of the camp meetings and by the contact with black ways of singing, while the blacks brought that ability to compose on the spot which was so deplored by John F. Watson (after all, he did say of their hymns that 'scarce one . . . were in our hymn books') as well as their heightened rhythmic sense and their penchant for call and response. It was a situation of great creative potential, and no doubt both groups went away the richer for it. The rhythms and responsorial practices entered white hymnody, where they can be found in many collections printed from about 1840 onwards, while the blacks took away many of the white hymns, transforming the melodies and rhythms after their own taste.

The other characteristic manner of hymn-singing that I have mentioned, the slowing-down of the beat and the interpolation of elaborate ornaments in the spaces thus created, is also of disputed provenance. It was certainly to be heard among white congregations in early New England, for there are publications from the early eighteenth century, by cultivated musicians and divines, deploring the practice, and it is even today to be heard among Scottish congregations in the Highlands and Islands, but it has certainly also been a favourite technique of black singers for a long time. The highly decorated and soaring 'surge' style of modern black gospel singers such as Mahalia Jackson and Marion Williams, not to mention that of their soul-singing successors such as Ray Charles and Bobby Womack, bears a strong resemblance to it, and the style has been remarkably tenacious on both sides of the colour line, no doubt partly, at least, because it is extremely enjoyable to do. It is no mere aberration caused by conditions of non-literacy, although that and the lack of schooled musicians may have begun it; singers have obviously enjoyed its intensity and stirring quality and have resisted attempts by schooled musicians to impose 'regular singing' on them. Its survival in white religious folk singing at least into the 1880s is attested by Charles Ives's account of the camp meetings whose singing his father used to lead around that time in rural Connecticut,[10] while many nineteenth-century publications show its popularity among black congregations. William Francis Allen, in his preface to the first published collection of Negro songs, *Slave Songs of the United States* of 1867, says,

> 'There is no singing in *parts*, as we understand it, and yet no two appear to be singing the same thing — the leading singer starts the words of each verse, often improvising, and the others, who "base" him, as it is called, strike in with the refrain, or even join in the solo, when the words are familiar. When the "base" begins, the leader often stops, leaving the rest of his words to be guessed at, or it may be that they are taken up by one of the other singers. And the "basers" themselves seem to follow their own whims, beginning where they please and leaving off when they please, striking an octave above or below (in case they have pitched the tune too low or too high) or hitting some other note that chords, so as to produce the effect of marvellous complication and

> variety. And what makes it all the harder to unravel a thread of melody out of this strange network is that, like birds, they seem not infrequently to strike sounds that cannot be precisely represented by the gamut [ie notation] and abound in slides from one note to another, and turns and cadences not in articulated notes.'[11]

Unlike the song of birds, however, these sounds were not the result of a 'natural' or 'instinctive' way of performance but represent as cultured an approach to choral singing as that of any cathedral choir.

It does seem as if those camp meetings, especially during the early years of the nineteenth century, when blacks and whites worshipped, if not quite together, at least in sight and hearing of one another and in something like a spirit of unity and amity, were the medium through which white and black hymnody passed into each other and back again, possibly many times, with changes which added to the intensity and emotional fervour of the singing. And not only music, but also the black usages, of speaking with tongues, of trance and of dancing, probably passed into white worship at this time; all are to be found, with their own characteristic accent and style, in white fundamentalist sects of the American south today. We should recall, of course, that for many blacks the camp meetings were by no means their first acquaintance with Christian hymnody, nor is it true, as is sometimes claimed, that all black spirituals were adaptations of white hymns. Apart from a dubious tracing of a few songs back to comparable Ghanaian or Dahomeyan songs, we have to keep in mind the nature of black musicking, which favoured, and still favours, improvisation and the constant development of a song according to the creative powers of each individual performer, in contrast to the white tendency to think in terms of fixed entities. As Odum and Johnson, writing in 1925, put it: 'The Negro is going to sing whether he has a formal song or not'.[12] It is these authors who, although writing with that mixture of admiration and condescension that characterizes so much comment of the time by whites on black culture, capture in a vivid passage, clearly based on observation, much of the essence of black musicking. It is in the way here described, one feels, that the spirituals themselves must have come into existence in slavery days:

> 'The Negro's musical nature easily turns these expressions [of emotion] into melody, and a word, phrase or exclamation becomes a song in itself. The song is completed by the imaginative mind, and the sense of fitness is sound. Worshippers often follow the preacher through his sermon in a mental state of song, and when he is finished they burst into song, singing no other than an elaborate sentence which the preacher has used in his sermon. When this is joined to a familiar chorus and tune, a song has originated. Sometimes the song is remembered and sung again; sometimes, like the words of the preacher, it simply becomes a part of the satisfaction of the hour and is forgotten . . . Even more than preaching and praying, shouting gives rise to song among the Negroes; during the exciting times in worship the Negroes sing unheard-of songs which they never recall again. It is indeed a mixed scene of song and action, each contributing largely to the other, while the spectator looks on in wonderment at the astonishing inventiveness of the worshippers. The general motions, the expressions of the face, words and harmonies, rests and rhythms, sense of fitness and even of humor, repetition — these make an occasion that defies limitation to its expression'.[13]

And again: 'Many songs owe their origins to the Negro's keenness at improvisation. Undoubtedly many Negroes have a consciousness of power or ability to create new songs when they wish to . . . From his unlimited store of songs, sayings, stories and experiences he takes a theme and begins his songs. If he does not immediately think of rhyming lines that would be appropriate, he continues to sing the original lines until the song takes further shape in his mind'.[14]

In those passages we see brought together two complementary aspects of Afro-American musicking that are clearly part of the African inheritance, since on the one hand they do not, as we have seen, form an element of the European vernacular, and since on the other they have proved functional in the creation of a ritual for survival and resistance both during and after slavery: the delight in making on the spot a song that is specific to the occasion (what European musicians call improvisation) and the assumption that the ability to create songs is as universal as the ability to create utterances in words. These two assumptions have been central to Afro-American musicking, and for very good reasons: they allow the individual not only to celebrate his or her own individuality, as does the western tradition, but also to affirm and celebrate that vital reciprocal relationship between individual and community that lay at the heart of survival under slavery and in the period of brutal repression that followed. We can understand why scholars have disagreed so profoundly on the source of the slave spirituals, since the essence of Afro-American music lies not so much in created objects, not so much in a repertory of songs or pieces, as in a way of musicking which values the creative power that lies in every person more than it values those objects which, in so far as they exist at all apart from performance, do so only for as long as they continue to serve the communal function, after which they are likely to be abandoned without a second thought. Thus the slaves placed little value on the antiquity of a song and paid little attention to preserving its integrity, while on the other they took, from whatever source came to hand, fragments and even whole songs, welding them into whatever shape suited their purposes at the time. Even the spirituals, which today we regard as the chief glory of the slaves' music, and which must have played an important part in survival, would not have come down to us at all had it not been for the almost fortuitous circumstance of their passing into the consciousness of white audiences and into the literate tradition through the medium of the Fisk Jubilee Singers after the Civil War. For the newly emancipated slaves of that time they were too powerful a reminder of the pains of slavery and they were prepared to let them go.

I dwell on these matters because we can see established in the slave spirituals themes which run through the history of Afro-American music, which constitute its unity, its integrity and its inner consistency; the spirituals are the first music-objects that have come down to us to which we can point as a genuine fusion of African and European traditions, born from nowhere else but the creativity and life-lovingness of the blacks themselves. Often obscured by commercialism and by what sociologists call the hegemony of European high-cultural values, the blacks' delight in improvisation, their insistence on the creative power of every human being and on the functionality of musicking (the responsibility of the musician not only for the sounds he makes but for the progress of the whole social occasion to which he contributes is felt no less by the modern jazz musician than by the West African master drummer) continue to carry their life-giving and subversive message through the increasingly centralized and authoritarian texture of modern industrial society.

In adapting Christianity to their intellectual heritage and present needs, thus laying the foundation for a style of Christianity that is still very much present in the black churches today, the slaves also took its musical styles, introducing into the Protestant hymnody of that time and place forms which left room for the expression at the same time of both individual and communal feeling. Neither their faith nor their music was in any way a retreat from reality, however intolerable; they were means by which the slaves succeeded in preserving a sense of personal worth, of community and hope for the future in the face of a society that denied to them all three.

One of the most remarkable features of the slave spirituals is their affirmative tone; sorrow there may be (it was not for nothing that W.E.B. DuBois called them the 'Sorrow Songs') but of despair there is no sign, nor is there any significant expression of that self-abnegation, sense of sin and worthlessness which is a recurrent feature of European Protestant hymnody; rather, they assert with joy and confidence a faith in ultimate justice and freedom, in this world no less than in the next. And, further, they can in many cases be interpreted as relating to liberty, not just in some unspecified future, but soon; there was built into many of them references to escape, to the north, where some kind of freedom was possible. The meanings are, however, many-layered; when they sang 'Swing low, sweet chariot, coming for to carry me home' (even as I type that line its power and beauty hits me afresh) '. . . If you get there before I do, just tell those others I'm coming too,' there were intertwined into the song meanings of salvation, of reaching heaven, of ultimate freedom and of escape; there was no reason why any of those meanings should have excluded the others, since the meaning of the song was in its performance, not just in its 'text'. So it was with *Steal Away to Jesus*, which was probably composed by the preacher-insurrectionist Nat Turner, while Frederick Douglass, who himself escaped from slavery in his teens to become a leader in the movement for abolition, wrote in his autobiography *My Bondage and My Freedom* of his excitement as he and his comrades prepared for escape:

> 'We were, at times, remarkably buoyant, singing hymns and making joyous exclamations, almost as triumphant in their tone as if we had reached a land of freedom and safety. A keen observer might have detected in our repeated singing of
>
> O Canaan, sweet Canaan,
> I am bound for the land of Canaan
>
> something more than a hope of reaching heaven. We meant to reach the *north* — and the north was our Canaan.'[15]

And the spiritual *Follow the Drinking Gourd* seems meaningless until one learns that the Gourd was the constellation of the Big Dipper, the Plough, the northwards guide for the nonliterate runaway. Harold Courlander tells how legend has attributed the song to a 'peg-legged ex-sailor who wandered around the countryside telling them how to escape to the North.'[16]

The slave spirituals are best known to us today in harmonically 'cleaned-up' and polished versions which we owe primarily to the Fisk Jubilee Singers, a group of black students who between 1871 and 1878 raised money for their newly-founded and desperately under-funded Fisk University in Nashville by singing, among other choral music, spirituals in arrangements that would render them acceptable to the mainly white audiences before whom they appeared. They toured extensively and successfully in the United States and Europe; a Glasgow critic wrote that they 'make us feel how strange it is that these unpretending singers should come over here and teach us the true refinement of music, make us feel its moral and religious power.' It is ironic that the wider fame of these magnificent songs should have come only after they had lost their immediate appeal for the people who had created them. For with the coming of Emancipation in 1865, the close slave communities broke up as mobility became at least legally possible and the agony of slavery became a thing of the past, its memories still, however, too raw to be willingly aroused. The songs had value for the people who created them only so long as they served a social function; when that vanished so did the urge to sing them, and they would no doubt long since have disappeared along with countless other, to us, unknown creations of the slaves had it not been for these 'unpretending singers' and their audiences who took to them much as present-day white audiences have taken to the blues.

There were other kinds of musicking in the slave quarters, but these are poorly documented: work songs, songs of praise, of ridicule and satire (of both white folks and fellow-slaves) songs of longing and of distress at parting, songs of complaint and of flattery. Narrative songs and ballads are few; as we have seen, these go against the grain of black creativity. Where ballads are sung by black singers, such as those of John Henry or Staggerlee, they tend not to be complete narratives but rather commentaries on the story, or an aspect of it, which is presumed known to all. In discussing the role of music in spiritual survival we must not overlook the part played by the cognate art of dance. The habit of dancing never died among black people in America; even after a day of backbreaking labour, field slaves would be observed singing and dancing vigorously, giving rise to a good deal of puzzlement among observers who subscribed to the European idea that to dance is a sign of carefree happiness. Those who opposed slavery could not imagine that such dancing could take place at all and dismissed accounts of it as slaveowners' propaganda, while the slaveowners themselves adduced it as evidence that their slaves were contented and free from care. But the impulse to dance is the same as that which prompts musical performance; dancing, like musicking, was a ritual for survival in those terrible times, and the slaves could for the duration of the dance feel themselves fully realized as individuals and as members of a community. The slaves danced their sorrows no less than their joys; the sorrows would probably have laid on them, even more than did the joys, the impulse to dance.

Descriptions of early dances are almost as vague as those of the music, but mostly they tell us that the dancers moved in a circle with a shuffling step, while two or three couples moved into the centre in a more energetic improvised dance while the rest kept time, to be replaced by others when the first couples tired. The manner of acculturation that took place over the seventeenth and eighteenth centuries is unknown to us, but the slaves would undoubtedly have found the masters' dances easy to imitate; there are many accounts of their fondness for — and their skill in — burlesquing the white dancers. Masters on the whole seemed prepared to allow their slaves to take part in often quite large assemblies, and some of these became almost institutions, what we might today call tourist attractions. The most famous of these was the dance in Place Congo, in New Orleans, where every Sunday afternoon and on feast and saints' days hundreds of slaves would dance before the shocked but fascinated gaze of white citizens and visitors. It was banned by the civic authorities around 1840.

In general the evangelical Christian sects into which most of the slaves were baptized disapproved of dancing, and many slaves resolutely refused to dance at all after being received into the church (it was common also to find converts refusing to take part in secular singing, even in such apparently harmless activities as worksongs). They did, however, engage in a form of religious dance known as the shout, or ring-shout, in which they moved in a circle accompanying themselves with song, handclapping and 'patting juba' (clapping themselves on the thighs), lifting their feet hardly at all from the floor and never crossing them; by one of those sophistries of which the Peculiar Institution was full, the churches apparently conceded that dancing without crossing the feet was not really dancing at all, and so was permissible to the saved. The shout was disapproved by those concerned with black 'improvement' (that is, assimilation into the ways of the whites) after Emancipation, and in time disappeared.

The passing of the Thirteenth Amendment to the US Constitution in the last weeks of the Civil War, which finally outlawed slavery, created for the blacks a new situation which, in comparison with slavery, was not pure gain. Forced to make their way in the mainstream of American society, for which no previous experience or education had prepared them, they learnt fast, as they always had — but they found that, no matter how well they learnt the rules, those rules were constantly changed and conditions stacked against them. Even the mere possibility of movement for its own sake must have been responsible for the breakup of the old slave communities, a process which was hastened by the parcelling-out of land under the system of tenant farming and sharecropping which left the black farmer perpetually in debt. In the initial euphoria the horizons opened up must have seemed limitless, especially with the passing in rapid succession of two further constitutional amendments, the Fourteenth, which affirmed that all people born in the United States or naturalized were to have the rights of full citizens, and the Fifteenth, which stated that no-one was to be deprived of the right to vote by reason of race, colour or previous condition of servitude.

The promise of Emancipation quickly proved false. After a brief period, lasting no more than ten years, of increasing black confidence and participation in civic affairs, and even in state and federal politics, under the umbrella of the Union army which had been stationed in the south to see the provisions of Emancipation carried out, the forces of reaction were released. In 1877 the troops were withdrawn as part of a bargain made by presidential candidate Rutherford B. Hayes in order to secure the support of southern Democrats to his election, and terrorist organizations like the Ku Klux Klan were quick to seize the opportunity that was offered. Then in 1883 the Supreme Court declared the Civil Rights Act of 1875 unconstitutional; under one pretext or another the voting rights of blacks were withdrawn, so that by 1900 their disenfranchisement was to all intents and purposes complete. One history of the United States, not otherwise notably partisan, goes so far as to speak of an 'anti-Negro crusade, comparable in many ways to Adolf Hitler's war against the Jews of Germany in the 1930s,' in which 'whites from different classes were asked to forget their economic differences and unite to preserve their racial purity' and which 'produced rigid forms of social segregation between 1890 and 1910;'[17] this did not begin to relent until the dawning of the modern civil rights movement in the 1940s. Black Americans were consigned, it must have seemed permanently, and with a brutality which seems beyond belief today, to the bottom of the social heap; in the years between 1890 and 1917, for example, over five thousand black men and women were lynched, often after prolonged torture and mutilation — an average of about one every two days. It was a matter, then, of survival, not much less desperate than under slavery. In that situation the black churches, whose number had increased dramatically after Emancipation, continued to form centres of resistance, of education and of community, and, just as important, centres where music and the other arts of performance could be practised, and where men and women could attain to positions of authority, responsibility and respect that were denied to them in the wider world.

No social group, of course, even under such conditions of repression, is monolithic, and any general statement about it can be shown to have notable exceptions. The number of different kinds of accommodation to the situation, and to the values of the majority white society, was endless, varying from complete acceptance, often associated with formal education in one of the black colleges and universities established by the American Missionary Society for the advancement of the ex-slaves (which often proved as much divisive as progressive by creating a small and separate elite) with membership of a profession and a kind of middle-class status, to total rejection of white values, with any number of shades and human idiosyncrasies in between. The varieties of accommodation, as one might expect, were reflected in the churches, and in the kinds of religious observance that were practised. In some middle-class black churches the same formal rituals were carried out as in the white churches, the same hymns, anthems and oratorios sung by the choirs and congregations. Such churches have been a source of bitterness to many; Ben Sidran, for example, says: 'Thus the church, once the bastion for blacks seeking freedom of expression and escape from white man's control, became the stronghold of the very mentality it was established to circumvent. And in focusing too strongly on the notion of life-after-death, the church little by little became the purveyor of conservatism in this life.'[18] It is not for the white outsider to comment on these charges, except to remark that they do not seem true of all the black churches; nonetheless, it is true that from the later years of the nineteenth century not only have a large number of black Americans rejected the churches and Christianity in all its forms, but also they have experienced in their lives, if to a lesser extent than have whites, the splitting-off of life into compartments that has been a feature of industrial society since at least the eighteenth century, and has indeed been essential for the development of the scientific world view which marks the society of our own time — a split between 'work' and 'leisure', between 'home' and 'the world', and, in particular, between 'sacred' and 'secular'. 'To a lesser extent', both because, on the one hand, the majority of black Americans have been only too aware that the affluence of America is not for them even if they do submit to its premises, and so have been less susceptible to its blandishments, and on the other because, possessing a heritage which has always emphasised the unity of human life, they have tended to resist the fragmentation that industrial society demands as the price of that affluence. As Lawrence Levine says:

> 'Having on the one hand been denied full participation in American society and on the other resisted complete acculturation, Negroes had not succumbed to many of society's central projections and dreams. This pattern of denial and resistance increased black separateness and autonomy . . . This truth is important, but care must be taken not to put it too starkly. Social and economic background and aspiration have shaped the attitudes of Negroes as well as of other groups in the society. These intra-group differences produced a kaleidoscope of black behavioral patterns, many of them in agreement with the larger society . . . But for large numbers of Negroes, the bulk of them at the lower end of the social and economic scale, it was possible and necessary to speak openly about a number of realities that American popular culture needed to repress.'[19]

If, then, for black people after Emancipation there opened up at least the theoretical possibility of a completely secular life comparable to that of white Americans, in practice the possibility could not be realized owing not only to their social and economic circumstances but also to their ineradicably religious turn of mind. It would seem as if a completely secular existence is not an option when Africa is in the cultural inheritance. This shows itself in explicit form in the debt acknowledged by what seems like a majority of present-day black American writers, artists, musicians and thinkers to the church, as a formative influence if not as a present resource; it shows itself also implicitly in the real unity of black American music, which at a deep level is *all* religious in content if not in form. It is, to put it crudely, a tool for survival; whether we call it 'sacred' or 'secular' its function is fundamentally the same: to preserve the community and to enable the individual to affirm, to explore and to celebrate his or her place in that community. Between sacred and secular there is in fact not opposition at all, but continuity. 'The affirmation of self in the blues,' writes James Cone, 'is the emphasis that connects them theologically to the spirituals. Like the spirituals, the blues affirms the somebodiness of black people, and they preserve the worth of humanity through ritual and drama'.[20] That being so, it need not surprise us that, as we shall see in a later chapter, a blues performance should take on a religious aspect, or, conversely, that a quite secular enjoyment should be an essential element of music in worship — or, indeed, that sacred and secular musicking should interpenetrate and should feed back and forth, one to the other.

It is tempting to suggest that there is no specific church 'style', but that is an illusion produced by the ubiquity of the church style throughout Afro-American musicking; that musical gestures which developed in the churches should today be a part of the common musical language is an indicator of the latter's pre-eminent role in the creation and transmission of black American culture. The idioms of the churches continue to permeate the culture and consciousness of black Americans, not only their musical idioms but even the individual's style of self-presentation. Tony Heilbut puts it neatly: 'The ghetto mother at a City Council meeting speaks a church rap. Her manner — gutsy, rhetorical, emphatic — takes tone and idiom for granted. This is the only style she knows, and she employs it without selfconsciousness . . . Not that anything about her behaviour is unique to the gospel church; it is simply that the church alone has allowed such free use of common habits of discourse.'[21]

Not all churches, of course. It is principally in the 'Sanctified', 'Holiness' or 'Pentecostal' churches that the older ways of worship have continued; the fact that these ways are to be found not just in remote rural areas but also in city churches where the congregation may well include professional and industrial workers confirms that they are not just antique survivals from a vanished past (a community under pressure has no time for such frivolities) but an autonomous living tradition of worship which satisfies in the present the deep and enduring human need for community and involvement. These churches have as a rule no set order of service, but rely on the inspiration of the moment (that is to say, improvisation) and the interaction of congregation and preacher to bring about a condition of religious ecstasy, the coming of the 'Holy Ghost fire' which, even more than the mere preaching of scripture, is the object of the ceremony. And, when the Holy Ghost descends, sometimes immediately after the ceremony begins, sometimes only after prolonged searching, the intensity of emotion has to be felt to be believed, most especially in the feeling of unity and common purpose between all present. Speech, music and dance are the tools by means of which the Holy Ghost is invoked and brought into the midst of the congregation — not as separate arts but as aspects of the one great performance art of celebration. A gifted black preacher may cover, in his speaking voice, a range of two octaves or more; what he has to say may contain much that is wise and sensible, or, alas, at times, much that is bigoted and intolerant, but the sheer prosaic sense of what he has to say is subsumed into his performance which, starting from plain speech, will grow through stages of excitement in which the sense of his words gives way to more ecstatic musicality, his often reiterated words and phrases being taken up by the congregation and thrown back to him with cries of affirmation and with Amens. Finally, by an all but imperceptible process, the whole congregation are singing, clapping their hands, often in marvellously complex interlocking rhythmic patterns, and moving their bodies each in his or her own idiomatic way. The level of ecstasy thus attained is a matter for each individual, who is free to find God in his or her own way, and there is always space for the talented or confident individual to take up in song the burden of the occasion, but the overwhelming feeling is of a singing, dancing, praying *community*.

What is sung by the congregations may derive in part from Euro-American protestant hymnody back as far as the seventeenth century (the hymns of John Wesley, and especially of Isaac Watts, remain popular) including nineteenth-century revivalist hymns, but there is much also that is the creation of the black churches themselves, such as the hymnal compiled in 1801, probably mainly the work of himself and his congregation, by the Rev Richard Allen, founder of the first independent black Methodist church, or the interdenominational collection called *Gospel Pearls*, which was first published in 1921. Even the old slave spirituals today find an honoured place, not as antiquarian survivals but as living expressions, important elements in the self-definition of a people who, more than a century after the end of slavery in the United States, still do not see themselves as fully liberated from bondage.

No matter what the provenance of the songs, they are seldom if ever sung 'as written', either words or music, even when printed texts are used. Those practices which we saw noted by the editor of *Slave Songs of the United States* are still in evidence today: rhythmic elaboration, pitch bending, handclapping on the off beats, stamping and swaying, call and response and dense improvised harmonic and heterophonic textures, and above all an emotional intensity without parallel in European or Euro-American musicking (to my ears and mind, the excitement generated by a virtuoso performance in the classical concert hall seems shallow and self-absorbed by comparison). It is from this kind of worship that the modern style of singing we know as gospel emerged in the early years of the present century.

The singers who began singing solo or in small groups in the churches were not generally formally trained, nor did they think of their singing as 'art'; it began as a spontaneous outpouring of religious emotion from the individuals within that community which was the congregation, interacting with it, the spontaneity mediated always through the idiom which came most naturally to the singers — that of the folksongs, hymns and hollers which were at around the same time giving rise to that other great Afro-American form, the blues. Their purpose was to testify, in song, to the power of their religious experience, to their very close and personal knowledge of their Jesus and to his ability to carry them through the worst that the society and the conditions of the time could do to them. Thus from the start the key to the singer's power in the church was not the possession of a beautiful voice, though many have in fact been endowed with remarkable vocal qualities, but authority, the authority of one who has lived what he or she sings about, and the ability to communicate the sense of the experience. If you haven't lived it, they say, you can't sing it — though it is acknowledged also that 'out of the mouths of babes and sucklings . . .' and the voices of children are often prized as much as those of their elders.

The authority comes not from the song, but from the singer; a fine song is prized to the extent that it can provide the singer with the material for a fine performance, and the singer is free, indeed expected, to make whatever changes in the song as seem appropriate, either premeditated or on the spur of the moment's inspiration. Aretha Franklin, in one of the greatest of gospel performances on record, took the two verses of the old hymn *Amazing Grace* and extended them over a breath-taking ten-minute span by means of elaborate ornaments and graces, interpolated lines and exclamations, while the congregation to whom — or rather, *with* whom — she was singing, was scarcely less ecstatic, encouraging her with cries, shouts, handclapping, even peals of delighted laughter. That authority needs to be maintained, of course, and cannot be taken for granted; the churches can be very unforgiving towards those who they feel are not practising what they sing. The model for the gospel singer, whether or not he or she lives up to it, is not that of the performing artist so much as of the preacher and religious leader. There is no necessary antithesis between the two roles, as we have seen when considering African ways of musicking; any tension between them arises only when secular considerations of money and fame, extrinsic to the authentic purposes of the musicking, intrude.

What has made gospel music one of the noblest forms of music-making in western society during this century is not mere musical ingenuity, but moral force, and the intensity of the emotions which that force has engendered. Musical ingenuity, not to say brilliance, is there in abundance (as always in Afro-American musicking, it lies more in performance than in composition, although the apparent textual simplicity of many gospel songs may often conceal complex intellectual and emotional cross-references which will be lost on the outsider) but, when the spirit moves the singer, his or her performance exists not for its own sake but, quite simply, in order to save souls and to lead them a fuller, truer life. That this religious and moral power can even be felt by those who cannot share the singers' Christian faith suggests that there is more to those songs and their performance than their overt, consciously intended content, and it behoves us, in considering their meaning, to look at both the overt and the hidden content of a gospel performance.

There is no doubt that modern gospel song differs considerably from the older spirituals, not only in the nature of the texts but also in the style of performance. The history of black America since Emancipation, with the projection of blacks into the mainstream of American life, the growth of education and of literacy, have all brought about major changes in the outlook of black Americans that could not help being reflected in religious belief and observance, bringing them closer to the individualism of the majority white culture. This means that, while gospel singing shares with the older spirituals an affirmation of the immediate and intimate presence of God and the assurance of salvation, the emphasis is different, more on the ways in which the individual can find his or her way through this life and realize the hope of a heaven which remains firmly in the future. As Lawrence Levine puts it: 'The religion of the gospel songs . . . recognized and discussed the troubles, sorrows and burdens of everyday existence but its immediate solutions tended to be a mixture of Christian faith and one variety or another of positive thinking. Touches of American popular culture were increasingly evident: "The best things in life are free", "Just look around and take what God is giving you", "Life can be beautiful".'[22] The captive Children of Israel and the Old Testament heroes play an insignificant part of the imagery, while overt moralizing, individual to individual, is much in evidence.

The manner of performance would seem more in accordance with European ways, the soloists, often virtuosi of their art, and small groups performing to, rather than with, their audience. This impression is given especially by studio records of gospel singers; the recording studio leaves the singer bereft of the response and the support of a congregation, leaving him or her to perform into a void in the manner of European concert artists. It is only when encountering gospel song in church, in fact, that the enduring force of the community can be sensed, interacting with and supporting — and on occasion criticizing — the singers through the various accommodations that have to be made with white individualism. A gospel performance is never just a concert, even when it takes place in a concert hall, but a transaction between individual and community.

To the uninitiated eye and ear, there appears to be in gospel performance, even in church, a greater element of showbiz, of effect for effect's sake, than would seem appropriate for music that is a part of divine worship, but this is to misunderstand the nature of the performance and of the relation that exists between performer and congregation. The apparently secular elements of the performance may include the use of gorgeous and sometimes extravagant costumes, hairdos and wigs, elaborate choreographies that appear to owe more to the theatre and TV than to the church, a system of stardom and superstardom that parallels that in the world of pop and rock music, and the use of pop-style techniques for winning the audience and of lifting them to the edge of frenzy by means that appear to have little to do with actual musical content, as understood in the classical concert or conventional religious observance. Even on record the poetic and musical means employed are frequently disconcerting to those accustomed to conventional religious music making.

But, apart from the fact that in many cases the traffic has been in the opposite direction, that pop performers have used many of the techniques first developed by gospel singers, there is a natural and obvious answer to these doubts; any or all means become holy when used in the service of God and of bringing people to him.

Those whom the style of performance does disturb may take comfort from the fact that modern gospel singers took some time to be accepted in the black churches themselves. The preachers and the elders of the Baptist and Methodist churches in the early 1930s found it hard to accept the bluesy sounds made by gospel artists of the time. The great singer-preacher Willie Mae Ford Smith, in a film made in 1982 about her life and work, recalled that not only did the elders refuse to accept a woman as a preacher in her own right, as she insisted she was, but also refused to hear the way she sang the gospel as anything but blasphemous. 'They said I was bringing the blues into the church . . . "We don't want that coonshine stuff around here, we don't want that ragtime singing in here." "Well," I said, "that's all the stuff I know."'[23] And Thomas A. Dorsey, singer, composer and publisher of gospel songs, perhaps the first major figure of gospel singing, found himself frequently ejected from churches where he and his associate artists tried to perform. Both lived to see their work accepted and themselves revered and loved in the churches that had once rejected them.

It is interesting to consider two or three recorded gospel performances by great singers in order to examine the nature of their art; what we hear on record is, of course, only a part of their performance, and we need to use our minds and imagination to recreate the whole. While this is true of all Afro-American performance on record, it is perhaps more true of gospel than of any other style. My examples are all to be found on the CBS Records double album *The Gospel Sound*, compiled by Tony Heilbut.[24] Let us consider first Marion Williams's performance of the old hymn *The Day Is Past and Gone*, a perennial favorite with gospel singers and congregations alike. The poem is in a tradition which goes back to Isaac Watts, the seventeenth-century English hymnologist, whose religious poetry remains so popular with black congregations that the 'surge' style of singing such as this performance shows is named after him. These verses were in fact written in 1853 by one John Leland, and they find a place also in hymnals such as *The Original Sacred Harp*, which is much used by southern white congregations. The verse consists of two four-line stanzas:

> The day is past and gone / The ev'ning shades appear,
> O may we all remember well / The night of death is near.
>
> We lay our garments by / Upon our beds to rest,
> So death will soon disrobe us all / Of what we here possess.

It is a disturbing image, that of death disrobing us — the word suggests something gentle, even loving, no less than frightening, and the singer delivers the line with a full sense of its strangeness, almost screaming the word 'death' but quietening down to caress the word 'disrobe'. She is accompanied, as is a common practice with gospel singers, by a duo of Hammond organ and piano, her regular accompanists, who follow and even anticipate every nuance of her singing — for this is an improvised performance, in 'surge', or 'Doctor Watts' style, with each syllable drawn out over several improvised, blues-inflected notes, the original outline of the melody being only barely perceptible beneath the elaboration. The Hammond organ, especially when paired with piano, has itself a dubious reputation with classical musicians, who associate it with religious music of the most vulgar and sentimental kind (it has been dubbed by irreverent musicians the 'god box'), and the organist here makes no attempt to conceal its glutinous quality; indeed, she seems almost to revel in it, with sustained chords and whines in the most soupy registers, while the pianist explores a box of old-fashioned virtuoso tricks, with extended arpeggios, trills, double-octave passages and dramatic staccatos — hand-me-downs, as it were, from the nineteenth-century virtuoso tradition.

The singer herself, possessed of a soprano voice that could surely have encompassed anything from Wagner to blues, also exploits without shame every dramatic trick in the book — changes of volume from a whisper to a shout, distortions of the speech rhythms of the verse, abrupt changes of register from falsetto to growl with no attempt to smooth the transition, now crooning and humming as if to herself, now belting out a phrase, and bursting out at the climax, making obvious the strain she and her voice are undergoing, dying away, apparently about to end softly but then, on the final word, spiralling upwards in pentatonic patterns and into falsetto. It is a performance of eerie imaginative power, saved from excess by absolute conviction and subtle musical intelligence as well as a virtuoso vocal technique which, while it owes much to European classical techniques, with extensive use of light, and very beautiful, head tone and vibrato, is not confined to them, but uses also harshly beautiful chest tones without vibrato, as well as growls and falsetto. Nor does she feel obliged to conceal the breaks between vocal registers, or the sense of strain involved in producing her climactic notes. Indeed, she makes a powerful expressive means of both these vocal 'solecisms' (from the classical point of view), the former to bring about sudden dramatic changes of atmosphere, almost from bar to bar, and the latter to express her total commitment and her involvement without reservation in the song and the singing of it — thus issuing an invitation that her church-congregation listeners would have had no hesitation in accepting.

There is another dimension to this performance, as to many other kinds of Afro-American performance, although it reveals itself most clearly in the gospel style. It would be a mistake to think of any of the performances on this record as commonplace or sentimental because they make extensive use of outworn clichés of European classical music. The history of Afro-American music has shown the perpetual ability of black performers to take from European music what they have wanted for their own expressive and ritual purposes and to weld them into something new, to make new meanings that were of use to them in their struggle for spiritual survival. It did not matter at all if those elements were, as far as Europeans were concerned, mere scraps and castoffs, clichés rendered vulgar or meaningless through over-use; black musicians have revealed, over and over again, their ability to revitalize them in a new context — a symbolic act upon whose significance I do not need to enlarge. The emotional power and integrity of this performance by all three participants is testimony enough.

The recycling of castoffs from the dominant culture into powerful new meanings is demonstrated in another performance on the album: *Strange Man*, written and sung by Dorothy Love Coates. She does not possess the majestic voice of Marion Williams, but makes up for it by the fierce integrity and conviction that blazes through her singing. She is accompanied on this record by her own vigorous stride-style piano, with 'god-box' and a rather heavy-handed drummer. Her song tells of two incidents in the ministry of Christ, both taken from St John's Gospel, that of the Samarian woman at the well and that of the woman taken in adultery, and retells them in a clipped journalistic style in commonplace American vernacular speech:

> The stranger was next seen in a city (oh yes he was!)
> Standing off an angry mob,
> Defending a woman that had been caught in the very *act* of adultery,
> For pity and mercy she sought.

(Readers might find it interesting to try and make these words, taken down exactly as the singer sings them, scan, before hearing the natural and effortless way in which she fits them into the musical rhythms.) Again, we have a literary style best described as journalese, and thus despised by the literary establishment, turned into an instrument of power and, above all, immediacy; the author-singer is concerned to bring home the force in her own life of the incidents described, and she adds a final, clinching stanza:

> I met that same man, I met that (Lord!) same man,
> When I turned away from sin,
> He opened up his arms and took me in.
> I felt that same power, Lord! my soul caught on fire,
> I'm just glad he stopped by — in Alabama,
> The Lord stopped by — one Tuesday evening.
> I'm just glad he stopped by, blessed my soul and gone.

The idea that her Lord stopped by one Tuesday evening in Alabama brings one up short, and would no doubt, when sung in its proper church setting, evoke from the congregation a vociferous recognition of the immediacy of the experience.

The matter-of-fact simplicity of the words is matched by the musical performance, in strict time, unlike Marion Williams's performance, and for the most part one note to a syllable, except for a few pentatonic flourishes at the end. Melody and harmonies are those of a blues song, and she sings in a gritty contralto with the words perfectly articulated; the tune in this case is the vehicle for the words, which are a miniature sermon, bringing the familiar gospel stories into striking relation with modern everyday life — in Alabama, one Tuesday evening.

Of all the performances on this album, that which most clearly evokes the atmosphere of the church is that by the Abyssinian Baptist Gospel Choir, conducted by Alex Bradford, himself a fine gospel singer. It is a meditation on the story in St Mark's Gospel of Christ healing the leper, enjoining him to tell nobody — but the leper was so excited that he told everyone he saw. The song takes this idea and applies it to the salvation of the individual; it is called *I Said I Wasn't Gonna Tell Nobody But I Couldn't Keep It To Myself*. In the song the healing of the leper is taken as a metaphor for the healing of the soul by Christian conversion:

> You should have been there / When he saved my soul,
> That Sunday morning / When he put my name on the roll.

A mood that can only be described as ecstatic is established right at the start, by cries from the choir, quickly joined by organ and piano in an up tempo; rhythmically precise hand-clapping on the offbeats provides the only percussion. The style is call and response, with the tenor lead singer (the magnificent Calvin White, clearly revelling in the physical and emotional effort his performance is costing him) taken up by the choir, mostly harmonizing in thirds, joining in with precise timing, even when the lead singer overruns or cuts short his phrases, with that intensity and brilliance of tone that only black choirs seem to be able to achieve. A moment near the end of the recording, when the performance is apparently supposed to come to an end, but cannot because choir and soloist alike are too fired with the music, reminds us that a performance of this kind is not confined by any limits which a composer might intend but depends on the social interplay of the occasion.

The actual song consists of repetitions of a quite small number of verbal and musical phrases; as it is not 'going anywhere' and has no preset limits, the repetitions can be continued as long as everyone present agrees (there are social signals to indicate this) that they should. It is impossible to say on hearing the record whether the ecstasy is real or staged for the recording, nor can we know whether the 'Africanism' of the call-and-response form is traditional or a conscious recreation by people who are aware of their own history; neither of these questions is of much significance, since the fact that the performers wish to record this performance in this way shows what it is that they consider important. In this chorus (and we can only imagine the energetic physical movement, the rocking, the hip rotation and the swaying that is an essential part of it) we have surely a modern version of that 'extatic delight in psalmody' described by the Rev Samuel Davies over two hundred years ago; the sound may be different (how different? one wonders) but the emotional atmosphere is unmistakable, as is the social function of the performance, which is the affirmation and celebration of identity and of community, no less essential now than it was then. It is also, we should remember, the sound of black Americans singing *to themselves*; despite the impact of recordings and of concert circuits, it is essentially a form of musicking that belongs in the black churches, and is at its best and most characteristic there. In contrast to nearly every other form of Afro-American music, white artists have made no significant impact upon it — white gospel singing is a very different affair.

One cannot, of course, pretend that the fame of many artists on record and on the concert circuits (and sometimes even in nightclubs — the Clara Ward Singers appeared for a while in Las Vegas clubs, while a gospel nightclub called the Sweet Chariot had a brief life in New York in the 1960s) has not had its effect on either singers or their singing. Every gospel artist who is offered a recording contract has to make his or her own accommodation to the system of starmaking and to the pressures of secular audience expectations. While these pressures are felt to some extent by every musician who hopes to make a living from his or her art, they are felt in particularly acute form by gospel singers, poised as they are between church and showbiz. Gospel singers are notoriously underpaid, and the temptation to seek wider fame and greater rewards is severe. A recent book on gospel music gives us a melancholy catalogue of gospel singers who have succumbed and gone on to the commercial soul-music circuit: Aretha Franklin, Sam Cooke, Dinah Washington, Ray Charles, The Staple Singers. The implication is that each of these has in some way betrayed his or her origins and in doing so has become smaller in stature, or even a kind of lost soul in the commercial jungle.

This is surely a partial view. In the first place, as I have suggested, it would be dangerous to project an absolute or clear-cut boundary between sacred and secular in black American culture. It is true that the division has widened since Emancipation, and with every move that black people have made towards the main stream of American society (a movement that is in fact more like a zigzag than a consistent evolution, so that it is at least arguable that blacks are little closer now than they were before the civil rights movement got under way), but it remains blurred. It is not just that the ideas of the sacred and of the community interpenetrate, but also that the role of music in defining that community and one's identity within it is very much wider than those accustomed to European concepts of music or of religious observance find it easy to perceive. Even the most 'secular' of blues or soul singers has a sacred function, which I shall discuss in a later chapter.

In any case, it is undeniable that the forms and techniques of gospel musicking have proved a treasure house of musical ideas and materials. They have been raided over and over again, not only by commercial musicians looking for a new gimmick but also by musicians of integrity and skill whose musical origins are in the churches and who feel the intensity and the emotional power of the church in everything they do, even if they may have ceased to be active churchgoers. Thus, not only is the intense melismatic style of Nina Simone, James Brown or Bobby Womack full of echoes of church singing, not only does the whole history of vocal groups, from the doo-wop groups of the 1950s to modern soul and disco, stem from the improvised harmonies of the vocal quartets of the churches, but it is possible to hear even in the intense solos of Charlie Parker an echo of the Sanctified churches of his Kansas City childhood, while it was often said of Bessie Smith that her style and authority had about them much of the preacher. The influences are not one-way, of course; one can hear blues and jazz, and even rock sounds, in modern gospel music, and it is sometimes hard to know who has been listening to whom. But that is the way of the musician in the Afro-American tradition and the ever-renewed source of his or her strength, which as with all living forms of musicking, is not merely musical but also intensely social in nature.

NOTES

1. DAVIES, Rev. Samuel: Letters dated 1755, in SOUTHERN, Eileen (ed): *Readings in Black American Music*, New York, Norton, 1983, pp 27–8.
2. CHASE, Gilbert: *America's Music*, New York, McGraw-Hill, 2nd edition 1966, p 81.
3. CONE, James H.: *The Spirituals and the Blues: An Interpretation*, New York, The Seabury Press, 1972, p 65.
4. WEBBER, Thomas L.: *Deep Like the Rivers: Education in the Slave Quarter Community 1831-1865*, New York, Norton, 1978, p 64.
5. JOHNSON, Charles A.: *The Frontier Camp Meeting — Religion's Harvest Time*, Dallas, Southern Methodist University Press, 1955, p 46.
6. EPSTEIN, Dena J.: *Sinful Tunes and Spirituals: Black Folk Music to the Civil War*, Urbana, University of Illinois Press, 1977, p 198.
7. *ibid.*, p 213.
8. *ibid.*, p 213.
9. WATSON, John F.: *Methodist Error etc*, in SOUTHERN, Eileen, *op. cit.*, p 63.
10. IVES, Charles E.: *Memos*, London, Calder & Boyars, 1973, pp 132–33.
11. ALLEN, William Francis: Preface to *Slave Songs of the United States*, in SOUTHERN, Eileen, *op. cit.*, pp 151–52.
12. ODUM, Howard W. and JOHNSON, Guy B.: *The Negro and His Songs: A Study of Typical Negro Songs in the South*, Raleigh, University of North Carolina Press, 1925, p 36.
13. *ibid.*, pp 31–32.

14. *ibid.*, p 153.
15. DOUGLASS, Frederick: *My Bondage and My Freedom*, in SOUTHERN, Eileen: *op. cit.*, p 87.
16. COURLANDER, Harold: *Negro Folk Music U.S.A.*, New York, Columbia University Press, 1963, p 291.
17. CARROLL, Peter N. and NOBLE, David W.: *The Free and the Unfree: A New History of the United States*, Harmondsworth, Penguin Books, 1977, p 153.
18. SIDRAN, Ben: *Black Talk*, New York, Da Capo Press, 1981, p 22.
19. LEVINE, Lawrence W.: *Black Culture and Black Consciousness: Afro-American Folk Thought from Slavery to Freedom*, New York, Oxford University Press, 1977, p 283.
20. CONE, James H.: *op. cit.*, p 117.
21. HEILBUT, Tony: *The Gospel Sound: Good News in Bad Times*, New York, Simon and Schuster, 1971, p 320.
22. LEVINE, Lawrence W.: *op. cit.*, p 186.
23. in film *Say Amen, Somebody*, shown at London Film Festival 1982.
24. *The Gospel Sound*, CBS 67234, 1972.

Chapter 4

ON CULTURES AND THEIR FUSION

There are in most societies legends and theories concerning the origin of music, of which western 'scientific' theories are in the main the least interesting or illuminating. T.H. Huxley, for example, suggested that music might be a factor in sexual selection, in which the ability to make sweet sounds helps in obtaining a mate; this banal conjecture may look at first sight attractive in view of the proverbial sexual attractiveness of musicians from Orpheus onwards (probably more to do with the musician's presumed personality and lifestyle than with his actual music) but it leaves us where we were, with any number of questions begged, including that of why we should find such sounds attractive. This is especially true since, as Harry Partch was not the first to point out, there is no sound that is enjoyed in one culture that is not thought of as a horrible noise in another (that two or more cultures may find themselves coexisting in a single British or American household is a well-known source of friction). The trouble with virtually all scientific speculation on music, I suspect, lies in the fact that it is the work of people whose habits of thought militate against their having the faintest idea of the real function of music in human life.

Much more interesting and valuable are those myths and legends which tell how music arose, often conveying profound insights into the matter; myth, as we have already noted, is not only descriptive but prescriptive, since in telling how things came to be it tells how things are, or should be. In that sense we could say that scientific theories in general partake also of the nature and function of myth, pretty impoverished myth much of it, if we think in terms of its usefulness in guiding human thought and action. One remarkably consistent feature of these stories of how music came into the lives of human beings is the idea that it happened in response to a desperate need; thus, in Hindu mythology, the god Brahma, after meditating for a hundred thousand years, finally decided to give music to the human race when they begged him for something to relieve their sorrow and hardships. David Reck, who retells the story, comments: 'Music, most people of the world say, originated somewhere other than in man. It came some time in the past from gods or other supernatural beings who, perhaps when man needed it or asked for it, perhaps even at the moment of man's creation, gave music as a gift'.[1] The psychological truth of this would no doubt have been recognized by the black slaves in the Americas who found in musicking a tool for spiritual survival; it must have seemed as if the art were given as a gift in a time of desperate need. It was not just any music; neither the old musical art of Africa nor that of their new masters would do, but an art of their own creating, a music that seemed to be created anew (as indeed the art does seem to be created anew with each new social situation), and it took from the two sides what was needed, no less and no more, to make a new musical art which partook of the nature of both but was not the same as either. It spoke of and to them in their particular predicament, and it came into being, not by deliberately willing it, but as a spontaneous generation which must have seemed like a divine gift of relief in their need.

It must have been by no means the first time that a people has found itself in such a desperate situation during the turbulent history of the human race. We gain a hint of the same feeling when the captive Children of Israel asked how they could sing the Lord's song in a strange land. The era of written history is only a minute fragment of the whole human adventure so far, and that of written music even smaller, and there is no reason to suppose that the humans who painted the caves of Altamira and Lascaux twelve thousand or so years ago, themselves the product of more than a hundred thousand years of recognizably human history, should not have been engaging in equally sophisticated musicking and dancing. The practice, common among present-day classical musicians, of labelling everything prior to about 1750 as 'Early' or even 'Ancient' music would seem to betray a certain narrowness of vision.

With every movement of people, every conquest, every enslavement, every absorption of one human group by another, something of the kind must have taken place, and we might say that we have lost more musical cultures than we presently possess. Only those who treasure the created object over the creative act need deplore this, because what remains, what is more precious than any created object, however magnificent, is the inexhaustible creativity of the human race. But in any case, nothing human is ever quite lost; no culture ever quite disappears but is transformed over and over again, so that every one of us carries within him or herself elements of who knows what cultures and societies, in shards and fragments, passed down from grandmothers to sleepless grandchildren, nursemaids to their charges, older children to younger, in snatches of old songs, garbled tales, odd words, expressions and proverbs, little personal rituals and superstitions. To that extent, we are all Phoenicians, Vandals, Greeks, Egyptians, Africans (who *could* the Ancient Egyptians have been if they were not African?), even perhaps Trojans.

The idea becomes easier to contemplate when we consider what a culture really is, and what its function is in human life. Although the word is a noun, we can be seriously misled if we think of culture as a thing or an entity, not only because it is dynamic rather than static but also because it is not simply a matter of institutions, though institutions can act as repositories and as shaping forces of culture. Raymond Williams has called the word 'culture' 'one of the two or three most complicated words in the English language',[2] and this is not the place for an exhaustive discussion. It is, however, clear that the word has a wider meaning than simply that which is contained in the phrase 'a cultured person' — that is, one who is versed in the high arts and in intellectual works. Rather, I suggest, as a rough-and-ready definition, that culture is a set of attitudes, assumptions and values by means of which a person or a group of people is able to find meaning in, or give meaning to, not only the objects and events of the environment but also to inner experiences, and to construct from them a consistent and usable picture of the world and of relationships within it. In this sense every single human being is cultured, since it is by means of the choices governed by culture that he or she is able to find some order in the seemingly limitless variety of experience. Culture thus mediates also between human potentialities, which although not limitless are very wide indeed, and the realization of that potential in life as it is actually lived. As Clifford Geertz says: 'One of the most significant facts about us may finally be that we all begin with the natural equipment to live a thousand kinds of life but end up in the end having lived only one'.[3] Although it is at least partly external to us, culture is nevertheless part of our essential equipment as human beings, without which we would certainly not be able to function at all in the world, and it must have developed, in evolutionary terms, not after but simultaneously and in parallel with the complex nervous system that produced in our species the need for it. 'Rather than acting to supplement, develop and extend organically-based capacities logically and genetically prior to it,' says Geertz, 'it would seem to be an ingredient in those capacities themselves. A cultureless human being would probably turn out to be not an intrinsically talented though unfulfilled ape, but a wholly mindless and consequently unworkable monstrosity.'[4]

It is not by conscious rational thought that we learn to perform this selective interpretation of the world, since the attitudes and values which govern our selection underlie any process we call rational thought; indeed, the very notion of 'rational thought' may itself be culturally determined. These attitudes and values underlie and govern not only how we think about things but even how we feel about them (the latter being more fundamental than the former). We receive them without as a rule consciously thinking about them from the moment of birth, from elders and authorities; we may modify them, or find them modified for us as we go through life, and we pass them on to our juniors.

This brings us to two important points. The first is that the interiorization of culture, to the point where it becomes a major part of who we are, is a matter in which the emotions play an important role, and the second is that, while no two individuals are identical from a cultural any more than from any other point of view, people do tend to form groups which are joined together by broadly similar sets of these attitudes, assumptions and values which we call a culture.

In the first place, because of the importance of the emotions in the formation of the individual's attitudes and values, as can be seen from the strongly emotional response we make when anyone tries to detach us from our really important values, it is the inseparable trio of myth, ritual and art that are their principal bearers. The latter are, to use Geertz's telling phrase, the 'public images of sentiment' through which a specific kind of order can be imposed on experience. The word 'public' is important here, since, as we have seen, the function of ritual and of art (it is unclear where one ends and the other begins) is to dramatize the myths that shape and justify attitudes and values, explain us to ourselves and assist each of us in the task of discovering who we are in relation to our fellow humans and to the world. Thus the very notion that the human race might ever outgrow the need for myth and ritual is clearly absurd.

And in the second place, the tendency of human beings to form themselves into groups of like-minded, or like-feeling, individuals is often taken for granted, but is interesting. All of us in fact belong simultaneously to a number of groups: families, economic interest groups, political groups, professional or occupational groups, religious and ethnic groups, the two sexes (and assorted sexual orientations), not to mention clubs, societies and workplace associations, all of which overlap one into another but do not necessarily coincide. Each member of a group looks to the others for validation of his or her own sense of self and self-esteem in that part of life with which the group concerns itself; in 'traditional' or village societies those groups tend not only to coincide but also to exist in a single geographical location, while modern groups — associations of scientists, for example, or of world leaders (for we may be sure that the latter form a definite interest group of their own, whatever public noises of antagonism they may make) — may be scattered over the face of the globe. Some groups are powerful and some powerless, some high in social status and some low, but for each individual his or her place in society is a kind of aggregate of the various groups to which he or she belongs. Each group has its own mythology (including of course its mythological heroes) by means of which it justifies its existence, and its rituals by means of which that mythology is acted out and its values interiorized in its members, and by means of which the members tell themselves, one another and the world who they are.

What we call a society is in reality nothing so unified as the term suggests, but a system of interlocking groups. Today most societies are thought of as being naturally coterminous with nation-states, but the latter are in fact of quite recent origin, the oldest of them being not more than a few hundred years old, notwithstanding the efforts made, through the citation of long lineages of monarchs, for example, to make them appear of more ancient date and thus of more natural origin. Despite what political leaders may claim, there is little in terms of attitudes, values or assumptions that can be said to be common to all those groups within a nation-state and that could unite them all. What social cohesion does exist in a nation-state is owed partly to the assiduously fostered notion of 'nationhood' (which has to be evoked sparingly and carefully, and only at moments of carefully prepared crisis), partly to a measure of coercion (the 'rule of law'), partly to a reluctant acquiescence by lower-status groups in the values of the higher-status groups, which are propagated by the education system and by the various official media of information, and partly to a degree of overlap, of genuine coincidence of values, of human understanding and empathy between members of what would sometimes seem the most unlikely of groups.

The cultural relations between the groups in a society are worth discussing. Suppose we have two groups within such a society, one of high status, possessing economic and political power and control over the formal media of cultural transmission, and the other relatively powerless and at the receiving end of those media. It is to be expected that members of the higher-status group will attempt to impose their myths and rituals, their symbols and their art as not only superior but as universally and permanently valid, and that they will use their control of the media to impose upon the lower-status group their own definition of legitimate 'cultural' activity. This will take place not necessarily through any deliberate conspiracy; the simple conviction that their values and their art are superior is sufficient. The power of definition may be used to dismiss the artistic activities (that is, the self-definition) of the inferior group as unworthy of serious consideration, if not downright destructive to the social order. Resistance by the lower-status group to being thus defined is sporadic and unsystematic, understandably since consistency and system are themselves characteristics which are elements of that industrial order which is responsible for the dominance of the upper class in the first place, and it is also hampered by the attractions of social status which the upper-class culture can exert.

Nevertheless, the dominant culture can fall victim to the consequences of its own dominance. In the first place, what would seem to be the ideal conditions for cultural and artistic development — abundant leisure, material resources and access to prolonged periods of training — what Pierre Bourdieu calls 'distance from necessity' — permits the development of an endless cycle of self-reflexivity, a 'play of cultured allusions and analogies, endlessly pointing to other analogies, which . . . weaves around the works a complex web of factitious experiences, each answering and reinforcing all the others, which *creates* the enchantment of artistic contemplation'.[5] This 'aesthetic disposition', as Bourdieu calls it, 'a generalized capacity to neutralize ordinary urgencies and to bracket off practical ends, a durable inclination and aptitude for practice without a practical function, can only be constituted within an experience of the world freed from urgency and through the practice of activities which are an end in themselves, such as scholastic exercises or the contemplation of works of art'.[6] High-status artistic activity, in fact, lacks the life-or-death urgency of lower-class art, such as we have already seen in the case of the enslaved Africans, who had to retain their power of self-definition or perish.

Those same favourable conditions can result also in the growth of conformism and in stultification of the imaginative faculties through over-concern with the maintenance of status, not only in relation to the lower group but also within the dominant group itself. The members of the lower group, on the other hand, have few worries about status, since nothing they can do will place them in the upper group (the fact that some do make the attempt does not invalidate the general statement); they may be afforded only the upper group's leftovers and outworn artistic materials to work on, but they are free to explore then without preconceptions. without worrying about conventions or notions of correctness, to take over the objects and the symbols of the upper group and subvert, deconstruct or reconstruct their meanings, all without the dominant group even noticing what is going on. Indeed, if the lower group are to succeed at all in giving meaning to their experience (another way of saying 'construct a culture') they are bound to do this. Thus, the lower-status culture will always contain within it a much wider variety of self-defining artistic activities, a larger 'gene pool' of identities and styles of relationship than the virtual monoculture which the upper-class culture tends to become — and monocultures, as any biologist knows, court extinction, while variety is the strongest force for survival.

There is another reason why the upper class culture is condemned to endless self-reflexivity. Having proclaimed themselves as superior to all others, its members cannot allow the fertilizing influence of other systems of values and attitudes to penetrate, not, at any rate, on anything like the equal terms that are necessary if anything other than colonization is to take place. Only another 'high' culture can be allowed to penetrate, but high cultures pass each other like ships in the night, perhaps saluting each other in passing but each too isolated in its own assumptions and values to be able to accept from others anything more than a few superficial gestures; any real social empathy such as is needed for genuine fusion seems to be beyond the powers of their members. Each has, in a word, too much to lose.

The one musical phenomenon of recent years which would seem to contradict this assertion — the thoroughgoing penetration of, in particular, the old 'high' musical cultures of the East by European classical music — is in fact no exception. What has taken place in the societies of Japan, South Korea, and to some extent in China and India, has been less a transaction or exchange of values than a wholesale takeover by western industrial values, of which western classical music, as we have already seen, is such a powerful vehicle today. The oriental artists, many of whom show not mere competence but real mastery and creativity in the styles of western classical music, have completely entered into that music, its values and the sense of identity it embodies, leaving their own traditional culture behind. The only trace of that traditional culture that one finds in their compositions is an accent or a dialectical flavour which is used in ways that are not dissimilar to those found in the work of European 'nationalist' composers from the early years of this century such as Bartók or the young Stravinsky. It is interesting that all those Eastern musicians whose backgrounds I have been able to trace come from families in the new industrial middle class of those countries.

In so far as the members of the dominant cultural group are aware at all of lower-class forms and activities, their attitude to them tends to be ambivalent; on the one hand they feel strongly the need to preserve the purity of their own cultural forms from what is seen as pollution by the inferior culture, while on the other they are fascinated with the forms and activities of that culture, especially with what is seen as their freedom and exuberance, as well as a desire to be seen as familiar with, if not master of, those forms — after all, mastery of an inferior culture ought to come easily to the masters of a superior one. That such a desire has repeatedly opened the gates to a trojan horse is something we shall see later, especially when the lower-status culture is Afro-American. We see it at work in the way that upper-class English people borrow words and phrases, for example Cockney rhyming slang, and mimic the accent and cadence of working-class speech. They do it, of course, not because they want actually to be taken for members of the working class, but in order to exhibit their mastery of working-class cultural forms. Similarly, when a famous classical performer appears in public playing ragtime or what is evidently meant to be jazz, his public admires him for his broad-mindedness and accepts it as light relief from the real business of 'serious' music.

The musician of the underdog class has no time for such games, nor can he afford such exclusiveness. To him, musicking is a matter of life and death, being concerned with the very stuff of identity and with resistance to imposed definitions. The games and rituals of upper-class music are of no interest to him, appearing frivolous and lacking in nourishment for his sense of who he is (the observant reader will no doubt notice that this amounts to a reversal of the conventional system of relative values, in which classical musicking is 'serious' and vernacular is 'light'). Nonetheless, if the upper-class audience care to dally with his music, he will go along with it up to a point, if only because there is a living to be made from it. They may patronize him, but they will pay him for his ability to bring a dash of hybrid vigour to their social rituals; this has been a feature of Afro-American musicking since the first slave musicians played for their masters' dancing. At the same time, being based in a position of cultural strength, he will, in Edwin Mason's words, 'invite the stranger group into the trap of reciprocity'[7] to which the masters can only respond with that mixture of fear and fascination which has characterized their side of the encounter from the beginning. This they can deal with only by that process which has been called minstrelization.

On the other hand, while the rituals of modern concert halls may be repugnant to the vernacular musician, that does not mean that he has no access to the musicians whose works are played there. The barrier between classical and vernacular music is opaque only when viewed from the point of view of the dominant group; when viewed from the other side it is often transparent, and to the vernacular musician and his listeners there are not two musics but only one. The musician is free to draw from either in whatever manner he pleases, uninhibited by notions of correctness or good form. To him Bach and Beethoven and other 'great composers' are not dead heroes but colleagues, ancestor figures even, who are alive in the present, and he will treat their work with the same respect and love as he treats that of his own more immediate colleagues — no less and certainly no more. The jazzmen's time-honoured practice of 'jazzing the classics', so unendurable in concert-hall circles, may in fact be seen as a gesture of love and empathy, and perhaps even of sympathy for a fellow-musician whose living music is being otherwise buried beneath the rituals of the concert hall.

So, too, with those Caribbean steelbands who play Bach and Chaikovski with such panache and idiomatic command, having learned the pieces by ear (it cannot be said too often that to play a piece by ear you have to understand it) and who do so without engaging in any of the rituals of modern concert-hall life. In separating the music act from the middle-class ritual in which it has become interred, they have made the performance into a ritual through which at least a part of their identity can be celebrated, cutting out the other identities which the music has been made to serve in the dominant culture. It is, however, a fragile ritual, and easily co-opted by the dominant culture; indeed, to judge from the number of steelbands to be found today in British schools, the process of co-opting steelbands may be well under way.

I am inclined to believe that, through its very nature, upper-class culture is incapable of generating any genuine innovation, being dependent for renewal upon the activities of untold thousands of musicians working in the vernacular, which the upper-class musician then refines and elaborates according to his own criteria. Some of his activities will then be picked up by vernacular musicians, so that the cycle starts all over again. There is nothing wrong with this; certainly the compositions of some of the greatest masters of the classical culture — Mozart, Haydn, Beethoven and especially Schubert are good examples — not only took from the vernacular (indeed, their whole art is rooted in it) but in turn fed back into it; what happens when a classical-music culture cuts itself off from the vernacular I shall discuss in a later chapter. There is of course nothing new under the sun; one of the amazing and, to me, heartening things about human music in general is the extraordinary variety of relationships that can be explored, affirmed and celebrated through what is really a quite narrow spectrum of sounds, and of types of sound-relationship, which come from quite a small number of kinds of source. What is sometimes seen as progress is just another permutation of the materials, so that an advance in one direction is matched by a retreat in another; neither our twentieth-century music, nor the industrial society of which it is a model, would seem to represent a more complete realization of human potential than, say, those cultures of West Africa which were so brutally disrupted, first by the slave trade, and later by varieties of colonial domination which have not yet finished their destructive work. Nor does it seem likely that new musical technologies, however ingenious or expensive, have anything new to contribute to that celebration of human relationships which we have seen to be the real business of music; indeed, like those other modern-day technologies on which they are (consciously and deliberately) modelled, they look like contributing further to the impoverishment of those relationships as fewer and fewer people are empowered to take any active part in the musical process, while the rest are reduced to the role of lookers-on (or listeners-in) at the society of the spectacle thus brought into existence.

Some, especially those who are committed to the idea of human progress and its corollaries, the theoretical perfectability of human nature and the limitlessness of human achievement, may find these thoughts depressing, but I cannot find them anything less than inspiriting, since they leave the human adventure equally open to each succeeding generation, and allow us to raise ourselves up to enjoy the only life that any of us are ever going to live. In any case, to be everything at once, which is clearly impossible, is the only meaning that I can find in the idea of perfectability or limitlessness, and the attempt to be so will only reduce the individual to that 'unworkable monstrosity' of which Geertz speaks. It is surely one function of those patterns of thought and feeling imposed by culture to protect us from the impossible attempt.

What we do need, if we are to realize our human potential, is to avoid becoming so deeply committed to any one set of cultural attitudes or values that it is impossible to adapt should the situation demand it, and, secondly, and no less importantly, to recognize the existence of other and equally valid cultures, and the possibility of learning from them. These two conditions are in reality the same, and are less a matter of intellectual stance than of emotional openness. Just as individuals will learn only from those who can evoke a positive emotional response (a simple fact that both our educational and our penal systems overlook), so in the same way when the characteristics of one cultural group diffuse into another, it is a sign of two things: first, that each of the groups involved is not so completely committed to its own cultural values that it cannot admit the possibility of change, and, secondly, that there is some emotional response from the members of one group for those of the other, a response which may be brought about by a genuine and conscious empathy, a not fully conscious compatability of myth (probably in reality the same thing), an admiration for some aspect of their lifestyle, or even sheer envy. In practice it seems that it is those groups who are at the bottom of the social scale, as a whole rather than just as a few individuals, that are most likely to preserve that uncommittedness, that willingness to look outwards (probably also a consequence of the life-or-death nature of their cultural concerns which we noted earlier) and who can recognize, often across quite wide social barriers, those common concerns which make possible genuine cultural fusion. We shall see that all of these factors were involved in the birth of the hybrid we call Afro-American music.

Other kinds of encounter have, of course, been immensely destructive, especially when delicately-balanced peasant and tribal communities have found themselves in the path of western industrial culture, which admits no empathy with any values other than its own. Professor Alain Daniélou describes the process from his own observations in the East:

> 'It must be recognized that in the industrial civilization customs and traditions tend to disappear to make place for the uniform life which one encounters on all continents. And the necessity to play — or to listen to — music tends to disappear, especially when music is associated with a way of living or social and religious rites which are no longer practised. In this case, how is the shadow-theatre to hold its own against the movies and the folk-dancer against rock-and-roll? Because, in most cases, the industrial civilization obliterates the ancient cultures and takes their place or it forces a hybridization which depersonalizes or deforms the survivors of ancient cultures by making them parodies for tourist consumption.'[8]

Musicking, as an embodiment of the subtle and delicate

structures of social relationships and identities, is naturally disrupted when those relationships are disrupted. Nonetheless, it is also possible to see ways in which it can also function as a tool in the rebuilding of societies, and this can happen in the most unlikely ways. We have to remind ourselves once more that cultures are not things that can be created or destroyed, but sets of learned predispositions to perceive the world in a particular way; it is not accurate, therefore, to speak of the 'death' of a culture, since, as long as the existence continues of those people among whom those predispositions are to be found, so will traces of their culture remain, even if transformed by the need to find new meaning in the world under changed or even disastrous circumstances. We have seen how this happened among the enslaved Africans in North America, and it can still be seen in many places in the contemporary world.

For example, the musicologist Isabel Aretz, writing in the UNESCO quarterly *Cultures*, reports the destruction of the 'authentic' musical culture of those South American peasants who have come to the cities in a search for a better life. For the most part these ex-peasants live crowded into improvised shanty towns on the outskirts of great cities such as Caracas, Rio de Janeiro, Mexico City and Lima, called variously *barrios*, *vecindades* and *favelas*, excluded from the municipal life of the cities, lacking in services such as electricity, paved roads, sewage, sometimes even water, often raided by police and officials, when their shelters are demolished and they themselves moved on. These barrios may constitute as much as half of the real population of a city, and one might expect them to be sinks of poverty, degradation, filth and crime; indeed they are tough and difficult places in which to survive (Oscar Lewis's books on the Sanchez family[9] give a dismaying picture of life there) but chaotic they are not. Peter Lloyd, who has studied the barrios of Lima and other South American cities, says: 'These experiences have given me an image of the city immigrant living in material poverty but enjoying a stable family life, law-abiding and rationally choosing future goals for himself and his family. This view contrasts starkly with the conventional image of the slum population.'[10] And again: 'Those outsiders who have lived and researched in such areas often report strong feelings of corporate identity and well-developed local organizations.'[11] Lloyd points out that this phenomenon, which can be seen in practically all the great cities of what is known as the Third World, from Kano to Calcutta, Nairobi to Manila, is not an isolated matter, but 'stems from the economic development of the industrial nations, which draws ever remoter areas into its field of dependency.'[12] And because these urbanized peasants are being drawn into the industrialized world, albeit at the lowest level, it is inevitable that their culture will be changed drastically with the new range of urban experiences; of particular concern for our investigation is of course their musicking.

Dr Aretz says in *Cultures*:[13] 'they bring with them their own music, but they take on the way of life of their new surroundings, and as an important part of those surroundings they receive the message of the mass media, which usually has a harmful influence on their own cultural background, and, as far as music is concerned, whether "rock" or academic, may turn out to be incomprehensible to them.' She goes on:

> 'It should be a matter of great importance to us who have access to academic culture not to be instrumental in causing the diminution or loss of the culture of other groups of people who are not yet [*sic*] in a position to enjoy our culture . . . In addition to that it is of the greatest concern that those cultures should not be lost, because they represent the real musical reserves of the future, just as forests represent the reserve lungs of the towns . . . so it is important that we should strive to prevent any of the decline of true folk and native music . . . because . . . the music which our culture destines for them, that is to say commercial music, in addition to the fact that it is generally of very poor quality, is an expression of feelings and ways of life that do not correspond historically to the native or the man with a folklore tradition.'

Among the measures Dr Aretz proposes are not only such harmless activities as the collection, filing and studying of the ethnomusic but also its revival, recording and broadcasting, and the introduction of traditional music from nursery school to university, as well as 'to diffuse music on records, well produced and accompanied by pleasing commentaries so that it can be used by the same mass media as now reproduce poor commercial music, and to do everything possible to have singers and musicians include such music in their repertoire or enable the best folk singers to have access to radio, television and live public performance.'

I quote at length from this article because it seems to me to contain a number of unexamined assumptions that are all too common concerning the nature of a culture and of cultural change, as well as a number of quite unwarranted assumptions about popular music. We cannot but agree that radio and TV, especially commercial, have little regard for the cultural development of their listeners and viewers so long as they deliver them in sufficient numbers to the advertisers. We cannot doubt either that Dr Aretz has observed the situation of these urbanized peasants at first hand, but her intepretation of what she sees and her prescription for remedying it (if remedy is needed other than alleviation of the social and economic situation as a whole) seems questionable. Her first assumption is that intervention by cultivated middle-class musicians will have any effect on the survival or otherwise of a way of musicking; but in fact, either it will or will not survive according to the extent to which it continues to embody the identity of those who practise it, and no number of well-produced recordings or radio broadcasts with attractive commentaries will make the slightest difference. The only people who will listen to these will be members of the same middle class, including quite possibly composers looking for new musical resources to exploit. Secondly, it is a mite paternalistic towards the 'natives' to assume that they do not know their own needs in this respect, and even more so to assume that middle-class musicians know those needs any better, and dangerous to assume that people who are capable of making the appallingly difficult transition from village to *barrio*, and of surviving in an extremely hostile environment, would not be able to understand the music of the city. And finally, it seems both insulting and exploitative to regard these 'true folk' musicians as a 'musical reserve' to be used presumably to inject fresh life into an exhausted classical tradition, as Bartók used the music of Hungarian, and Stravinsky of Russian, peasants.

But above all, this musicologist would seem seriously to underestimate the creative power of these erstwhile peasants, the same people whose ancestors presumably created, without the assistance of middle-class musicians, the music which she is now trying to protect from their apparent ignorance and helplessness. We can take as axiomatic the idea that whenever a social group is managing to carve out for itself a new kind of life, however difficult (in fact, the more difficult the more likely it will be) as in these South American *barrios*, there will be new kinds of musicking taking place, which will take as its starting points both the old experience and the new. In those places, grossly materially deprived as they are, and lacking in all the services that should be provided by state and municipal governments, harassed by police and officials and faced by a constant daily struggle for survival, but at the same time unhampered by all the restrictions and inhibitions that inhere in either 'high culture' or in the old peasant culture, what is taking place is an outburst of creative activity that reduces the loss of the traditional ways of musicking to insignificance, if loss it really is; one may be equally sure that there will always be some musicians who, without bothering too much about the preservation of the culture, just continue to play and sing in the old manner. If that is speculation, we have a concrete example in the successive explosions of musicking which have issued from the appalling slums of Trench Town and Back O'Wall in Kingston, Jamaica, to become a powerful social and musical force across the world; each has been an amalgam of traditional Jamaican folk music and that commercial music, beamed in from America, which is so despised by the musicologists.

It must be repeated: if musicking is one way by which human beings order their experience, and explore and celebrate their sense of who they are, then what is to be treasured is not created objects, however splendid they may be, but the creative process itself. We can further see that no canons of correctness or quality laid down by members of a dominant or high-status culture are going to be of the slightest use to lower-class people in their task of self-definition; only those whose musicking it is can decide what is of use to them and what is not. If the history of western music over the last two hundred years or so has anything to teach us, it is that the most vital new developments in the art have come from materially deprived people who have taken whatever lay to hand, without inhibition or second thought, and have made of it something new and expresive, and above all *useful* to them in their struggle for the most basic of human rights: the right to define for oneself who one is. That black Americans are not the only people in western society to have proved richly creative in this way can be seen, both from the variety of folk song which has not only survived but has thriven in European and American working-class societies as a weapon of resistance, and from the ways in which lower-class white people have taken the musicking of black people and made of it something of their own. But the fact remains: it is the musicking of the blacks which has been at the root of all the most potent developments in western musicking today. This in turn suggests that there is in that musicking something more than 'naturalness' or 'primitiveness', something that contributes to the collective experience of all people in industrial societies, which seems to fill what is otherwise a void in their lives.

NOTES

1. RECK, David: *Music of the Whole Earth*, New York, Charles Scribner's Sons, 1977, p 8.
2. WILLIAMS, Raymond: *Keywords: A Vocabulary of Culture and Society*, London, Fontana, 1976, p 76.
3. GERTZ, Clifford: *The Interpretation of Cultures*, London, Hutchinson, 1975, p 45.
4. *ibid*., p 68.
5. BOURDIEU, Pierre: 'The Aristocracy of Culture', *Media, Culture and Society*, Vol. 2, March 1980, p 250.
6. *ibid*., p 251.
7. MASON, Edwin: private communication, 1985.
8. DANIELOU, Alain, in collaboration with BRUNET, Jacques: *The Sitation of Music and Musicians in the Countries of the Orient*, transl. by John Evarts, Florence, Leo S. Olshki, 1971, p 82.

9. LEWIS, Oscar: *The Children of Sanchez*, Harmondsworth, Penguin Books, 1961: *A Death in the Sanchez Family*, Harmondsworth, Penguin Books, 1969.
10. LLOYD, Peter: *Slums of Hope? Shanty Towns of the Third World,* Harmondsworth, Penguin Books, 1979, p. 9.
11. *ibid.,* p. 163.
12. *ibid.*, p 10.
13. ARETZ, Isabel: 'Music in Latin America: The Perpetuation of Tradition', *Cultures*, Vol. 1 No. 3, *Music in a Changing World*, 1974, pp 117-131.

Chapter 5

STYLES OF ENCOUNTER I: A NEED IN WHITE CULTURE

We have seen something of the ways in which the black people who were thrust so abruptly into slavery in North America responded creatively to the new environment in which they found themselves. We have also seen that a response occurred in turn from those white people who encountered the musicking of the blacks at the great camp meetings of the early nineteenth century and took from them elements not only of their musicking but also of their style of worship, making them a part of their own rituals down to the present day. The discussion in the previous chapter suggests that before that response could occur the white people must have felt a kind of empathy which transcended the formidable barriers of slavery and of the presumed genetic inferiority of black people on which slavery was posited. It suggests, too, that those who were able in this way to absorb elements of black culture must have been sufficiently uncommitted to the values of European culture to make such absorption possible. The history of the American south suggests that there was, and still is, a considerable number of such people who, despite the pervasive racism and the continuing inferior position of blacks, have been able to respond directly to black culture, and in particular musicking, in ways that other Americans — and, indeed, Europeans — have not.

That history rests on both the ecology of the southern coastal regions of North America and on the manner of their settlement by British colonists from the beginning of the seventeenth century.Unlike the New England colonies from the time of the *Mayflower* voyage of 1620, with their individualistic Puritan communities based on the family smallholding, the southern colonies were aristocratic and commercial in origin; large tracts of land were granted by King James I and his successors, either to loyal subjects or to joint-stock companies, and those tracts were subdivided on more or less feudal principles.

To overcome the desperate shortage of labour on those large estates, indentured servants and labourers were first brought from Britain; English investors would underwrite the immigrant's fare in return for his or her labour for a set period, after which the immigrant was free. Fifty acres was the standard reward for each immigrant thus sponsored, a device which did enable some people of modest means to acquire land but which meant that the majority went to wealthy people who had put up the money for a large number of fares. In this way ownership of land in the new colonies became concentrated in large units — and still there was a shortage of labour.

Nearly half of those who came to North America from the British Isles during the colonial period came as indentured servants. If they had come in the hope of bettering themselves, few succeeded in doing so; the majority, after working out their time in conditions that often amounted to slavery, remained as servants, labourers, tenant farmers, many of them jobless and rootless. Some acquired land, mostly on poor hill country, and as time went on many moved westward into the valleys of the Appalachian Mountains, and thence into the valleys of the Ohio and Tennessee Rivers; these were the so-called frontiersmen.

The ecology of the region did not favour the growth of towns. By contrast to the large and growing cities of Boston, Philadelphia and New York, the towns of the south were small and insignificant even at the end of the colonial period. In 1782 Thomas Jefferson was able to write about Virginia: 'We have no townships. Our country being much intersected with navigable waters, and trade brought generally to our doors, instead of being obliged to go in quest of it, has probably been one of the causes why we have no towns of any consequence. Williamsburg, which until the year 1780 was the seat of our government, never contained above 1,800 inhabitants; and

Norfolk, the most populous town we ever had, contained but 6,000.'[1] Albert Stoutamire, who quotes this excerpt from Jefferson's *Notes on Virginia*, tells us also that Richmond, at about the time when it became the capital of Virginia in 1780, 'consisted of about 300 houses, most of them crude, wooden structures on streets that were muddy in the rainy season and dusty in the dry season.'[2] It was not the towns but the great estates that formed the centres of life and of culture in those southern colonies which later became states; for those with no access to great houses there was only isolation, or at best the life of small, scattered settlements.

It was into this physical and social environment that Africans were brought from 1619 onwards in an attempt to alleviate the continuing shortage of labour. The poor whites formed a permanent underclass in what became by the late seventeenth century a well-established pattern of class, and there is a good deal of evidence which suggests not only that many of them were little better off than the black slaves but also that they saw themselves as sharing with them much of the same predicament. There was a good deal of association, if not fraternization; not only did black slaves and white indentured servants often work alongside one another in the fields but there were also several uprisings, notably Bacon's Rebellion of 1676, in which frontiersmen, servants and slaves joined together in a hopeless revolt against their exploitation by the landed aristocracy of Virginia. It was not the first, or the last; as Howard Zinn puts it: 'Only one fear was greater than the fear of black rebellion in the new American colonies. That was the fear that discontented whites would join blacks to overthrow the existing order.'[3] The suggestion that, at least in the colonial period, the southern poor whites viewed blacks as being something like fellow-sufferers is reinforced by the quantity of legislation enacted in the colonial assemblies which was designed to prevent association between whites and blacks.

By the time of the Revolution it seemed as if slavery was in decline, as the value of tobacco, the staple crop of the slave plantations, declined; Jefferson and other founders of the Republic were of the opinion that it would quietly wither away as it became less and less competitive with free labour. And, indeed, that is what happened in the north, where it had never in any case been a major institution; humanitarian sentiment coincided with economic interest to bring about its virtual extinction there by 1800. What gave slavery new life in the south was the growing demand for cotton to feed the British mills. It was from the last years of the eighteenth century that the 'Peculiar Institution' took on the form which we recognize from abolitionist literature such as *Uncle Tom's Cabin* and from the memoirs of escaped slaves like Frederick Douglass and Sojourner Truth. What was remarkable was the way in which slavery took over the entire society and culture of the south; as Carl N. Degler says: 'Through the possession of black labour, the small class of slaveholders actually dominated the economic, political and intellectual institutions of the whole white South. And by virtue of this fact the South's civilization was increasingly shaped to fit the needs of the slave system.'[4]

The transformation which wiped out any residual sympathy for the slaves and replaced it, even — or, rather, especially — in the minds of those who were best placed to sympathize with their plight, with hatred and fear is a complex matter. It seems only partly explicable by the deliberate policy adopted by the planters and aristocrats of driving the two groups apart by the constant reiteration, first of the idea that whites were inherently superior to blacks (an attractive idea to those who were despised by everyone else) and secondly of the fear that an end to slavery would release on to the labour market some four million unskilled workers who would depress wages even further than they already were. In both the north and the south the white working class were led to believe that abolitionism was nothing but a plot by the northern industrialists against working people; hence the anti-abolitionist riots which occurred in northern cities before and even during the Civil War, the worst of which, in New York during July 1863, left dead some four hundred blacks. Nevertheless, as Winthrop Jordan says: 'To say, as many have, that racism is merely the rationalizing ideology of the oppressor is to advance a grievous error. To rest the analysis there is to close one's eyes to the complexity of human oppression.'[5] Jordan, however, in his study of the roots of racism in America, does not appeal to any notion of inborn or biological racism but rather suggests a complex network of historical factors which affected in quite specific ways the modes in which the British, as opposed to the Spanish and Portuguese, encountered Africans and led them to view them as inherently, genetically inferior to themselves. This is not the place for an extended discussion, which involves the whole rationale of black American slavery; we need note only that those people of British descent were only too ready to accept the poison which was dripped into their ears, and to give free rein to their fears and fantasies about the blacks.

Not surprisingly, little is known of the early history of the white underdog class in the American south, and we have no way of knowing how they and the first black slaves responded to one another. Could they have witnessed the introduction of the Africans into America, or seen the faces the latter presented to their own people rather than to the masters? The first results of their mutual acculturation did not surface until the camp meetings of the early nineteenth century, and then under highly specific conditions and just at the time when slavery was entering that final, dominant phase which ended in 1865, just a few weeks before the Confederate surrender at Appomattox. What is remarkable is the continuing way in which poor whites and poor blacks, right down to the present day, have continued to interact musically, directly and without the whites' seeming to feel any need to distance themselves from the 'inferior' culture. The continuing existence of this two-way traffic shows clearly enough that they have found enough overlap in their apparently antagonistic senses of who they are, enough in one another's community and values, to admire and even to identify with, to impel them to open themselves to one another's musicking.

White people have always viewed black culture with a mixture of fascination, fear and even envy. Behind the fascination and the envy (and the fear) lies a great deal of misunderstanding and wishful thinking; the perceived irresponsibility, irrepressibility and sexual potency of the blacks are all a source of envy (an ambivalent emotion at best, as many blacks have discovered to their pain) for the white American or Englishman caught up in his own work ethic and industrial discipline. But there is as well a great and genuine subversive and liberating power there, which has enabled black people to endure the generations of oppression and not be sucked up completely into the industrial system of which they were the first victims. And that same subversive power can frighten those whose commitment to the values of the industrial system is such that they cannot admit the validity of any others.

It was probably the slaveowners who were the first Americans to experience that combined fascination and fear which the blacks inspired. We have seen how shocked visitors found, quite early in the history of slavery, that the language of the Great House was taking in much of the vocabulary and general style of the slaves' speech (it is generally agreed today that the southern U.S. accent and idiom derive as much as from black speech as anything else); some of those visitors were even more shocked to find members of the master's household, even his own family, stealing away to take part in the slaves' religious ceremonies in preference to the staider observances of the white churches. The presence of blacks in close proximity, in fact, presented the planter class with two particular problems: first, that of maintaining, if not the reality, at least the appearance of genetic purity, and, secondly, that of preserving the superiority of their culture from what was seen as contamination by the secretly fascinating culture of the blacks.

It was well known, if not publicly admitted, that a good deal of sexual coupling took place on the plantations between whites and blacks, mostly, for obvious reasons, between white men and black women and girls; this presented the problem of what to do about the inevitable offspring of such unions. In theory, their solution was simple (Latin America found other solutions): all those with any visible or otherwise detectable trace of African ancestry were classed as Negro and consigned to the subordinate class. No exceptions were made; any child born of black-white unions was to be a slave unless his or her begetter decreed otherwise — and even to manumit one's own child was hedged with legal difficulties. If the child were freed there was no question of entering the society of the whites (the case of the more free-and-easy society of New Orleans I shall discuss later); the child was black, even if free black, and that was the end of the matter. By this sleight of hand not only was the genetic purity of the whites preserved but also a racial taxonomy established which muddles our thinking to the present day.

The other problem was more difficult. There was no question of acknowledging the equality or even perhaps the validity of black culture; to do so would destroy the very rationale of slavery. And yet the danger of 'pollution' was a very real one, even within the slavemaster's mansion itself. Children were traditionally looked after by slave nurses and spent a good deal of time in the company of black house-servants, so that a certain absorption of black culture was inevitable; Joel Chandler Harris's Uncle Remus was drawn from life. Here again the factor of empathy was vital; it might be simple envy for the supposed irresponsibility and sexual freedom of blacks (the blacks themselves were under pressure to conform to these stereotypes, at least in the presence of the master) or it might be the beginnings of genuine understanding and affection between people, however skewed and distorted by the gross inequality of status and power — but somehow it all had to be channelled off into socially acceptable forms which did not compromise white superiority.

It was, however, not in the south but in the burgeoning cities of the north that such a form was to develop, in the third decade of the nineteenth century. This was a time when the north itself was undergoing an unprecedentedly violent transformation from a mainly agrarian to an urban-industrial society. Not only the older cities of the north-east but also towns which a generation before had been frontier settlements — Pittsburgh, Bethlehem, Gary, Chicago — grew explosively, resulting in the wholesale uprooting of rural communities, the enriching of the rich and the impoverishment of the poor on a scale never before seen, not even in the British industrial revolution of fifty years earlier. Labour for the new industries came pouring into the towns and cities not only as immigrants from Europe but also from the rural areas of the United States. For the new proletariat survival was difficult, and there was not much sympathy to spare for those worse off than themselves; in any case the idea that there was someone worse off, less able to cope, gave a kind of comfort.

Despite the existence of a vocal anti-slavery movement, people in the north generally shared the feeling that blacks were genetically inferior to whites, and racist feelings were as rife there as in the south, as many free and escaped blacks found to their cost. Those feelings were, as we have seen, worked on by the pro-slavery factions, as were the fears that four million blacks would be dumped on to the labour market. It was the need to make sense of this complex of feelings which lay behind the popularity of an extraordinary form of entertainment that flourished during the nineteenth century, known at the time as the Nigger Minstrel Show, or, more pretentiously, Ethiopian Opera, but today generally known as blackface minstrelsy.

This was a farrago in which white actor-singers blacked their faces with burnt cork, dressed outrageously in exaggerated versions of Negro costume and presented in songs and dances, jokes and theatrical sketches a caricature of blacks for the entertainment of white audiences. Just as the music was black music heard and reinterpreted through the ears of white musicians, so the show itself as a whole was a picture of black people as seen and portrayed by whites, and it was therefore a sensitive barometer of white attitudes towards blacks over the course of the nineteenth century. It was enormously popular; indeed, it can claim to have been the dominant theatrical form of nineteenth-century America, and it was virtually the only indigenous form in the first half of the century.

Blacks were not the only figures of fun to be presented on the American stage; practically every immigrant group — Irish, German, Italian, Russian Jewish — at one time or another served its turn as a butt for the humour of those who had arrived earlier and were more versed in the ways of America. But the black was a natural permanent butt; not only was he set apart by the colour of his skin and destined to remain apparently forever on the lowest levels of society, but he was also the bearer of a load of unacknowledged guilt on the part of white people. And, as we have seen, black culture, in particular black music, aroused mingled feelings of attraction and fear which needed to be defused. The strangeness of the blacks to northerners, most of whom had never been near a southern plantation, added to the general appeal of the minstrel show.

The portrayal of blacks by white actors in blackface was not new; it had already had a long history in the theatre on both sides of the Atlantic, in stock parts such as comic servants, and, occasionally, as the Noble Savage, generally sacrificing his life in the last act for the beautiful white girl or for his white master. What was new, in the 1820s, was that performers began to specialize in blackface roles, and to build whole shows around them. The acts, consisting generally of comic patter in dialect, or what passed for dialect, and jokes, with songs and dances, were at first only isolated acts in other forms of entertainment, perhaps between the acts of a play or in a circus. The songs were claimed to be adaptations of Negro melodies picked up by the singers; the most famous of them, Thomas Rice's *Jump Jim Crow*, which for later generations of blacks was to become a synonym for white oppression, was, according to Rice, sung and danced in Louisville in 1828 by an old black stablehand, whose shuffling, crippled step and hunched shoulders he imitated on stage to make a fortune.

The minstrel show as a theatrical form in its own right originated in New York, in February 1843, when four performers who called themselves The Virginia Minstrels presented an entire evening of blackface songs, patter, jokes, dances and sketches, all at a pace which, as Robert Toll says, was 'something new, unusual and compelling'. He goes on to give a vivid description of the performance:

> 'They burst on stage in makeup which gave the impression of huge eyes and gaping mouths. They dressed in ill-fitting clothes and spoke in heavy "nigger" dialects. Once on stage, they could not stay still for an instant. Even while sitting, they contorted their bodies, cocked their heads, rolled their eyes and twisted their outstretched legs. When the music began, they exploded in a frenzy of grotesque and eccentric movements. Whether singing, dancing or joking, whether in a featured role or accompanying a comrade, or just listening, their wild hollering and their bobbing, seeming compulsive movements charged their entire performance with excitement. They sang and danced rousing numbers and cracked earthy jokes.'[6]

It was the Virginia Minstrels who evolved the definitive

form of the minstrel show. In the first part the performers (a minimum of four, though later there were more) sat in a semicircle on stage and exchanged songs, dances, jokes and repartee. The basic musical instruments were fiddle, banjo, bone castanets and tambourine, and each performer's role was clearly defined. The tambourine and bones were played by the two comedians, ('Mr Tambo' and 'Mr Bones') who sat at the ends of the semicircle and became known as the endmen; they had at their disposal a stock of puns, riddles and one-line jokes. There was a singer who could deliver the obligatory sentimental songs of parting and farewell, and the master of ceremonies ('Mister Interlocutor') whose task it was to announce, in fruity and high-flown terms, the various acts. His was a crucial role, and unusual in the theatre of the time; the simplicity and openness of the minstrel-show format meant that the proceedings could be adapted in the course of the performance as the audience's response evolved (it was in fact an improvised performance) and a good interlocutor would be able to sense this development and respond to it in his choice from the troupe's repertoire. The second part, or olio, consisted of a succession of speciality acts played in front of a drop curtain, and might include juggling and acrobatics, as well as novelty musical performances such as musical glasses or musical saw. This was the routine stuff of the variety show, but it climaxed in one of the features of the evening, the 'stump speech', a cod political address delivered in broad dialect, or a caricature of it, abounding in non-sequiturs, malapropisms and comic stumblings, creating and exploiting the image of the stupid incompetent black. The final act was generally a plantation scene, displaying slaves at home, happily singing and dancing under the benevolent eye of the beloved master and his family, without a care in the world; this would conclude with a song-and-dance number, the 'walk-around'.

Much of the material was no doubt culled from first-hand observation of black musicking, dancing and folklore. Many of the minstrels were widely travelled in the south and would have had some opportunity to pick up songs and dances, but we should not imagine that what was presented even aspired to be a true picture of black life, on the plantation or off it. The minstrels were not anthropologists or ethnomusicologists, but entertainers, and they were prepared to present any picture that pleased their audiences. Besides, we have no reason to suppose that the minstrels' view of blacks differed much from that of their audiences, or that they had any greater insight into the social situation that made those audiences flock to see the minstrel shows. The blacks portrayed on the minstrel stage were those which accorded best with the audiences' expectations, and served in turn to reinforce those expectations. The stereotypes changed somewhat over the years, but the message remained essentially the same: that blacks were like children and were happiest and best off on the southern plantations, and that when they were given their freedom and called upon to make their way in the 'adult' world of white America, they were invariably inadequate and unable to cope, often longing to be back in the safe world of the slave plantation where all their needs would be taken care of. True, in the early days of minstrel shows, there were black heroes of a kind: the Brer Rabbit figure who was able through natural wit to outwit a more pretentious opponent; the hunter or frontiersman, strong and autonomous; happy married couples, even sometimes brokenhearted husbands, wives or sweethearts whose partners had been sold away, but characters of this kind disappeared in the 1850s as the United States drifted with increasing speed towards civil war. Favourite characters were the would-be dandy, probably dressed in his 'long-tail blue', believing himself to be cutting a fine figure in his elegant clothes, which were in fact ill-fitting and misshapen, ridiculous, even pathetic, with his endlessly rolling eyes and jerky limbs; or the ancient faithful darkie, patient and enduring on the plantation, loved by master and fellow-slaves alike, dispensing folk wisdom and counselling the young hotheads into acceptance of their lot.

The latter image is of course a deeply sentimental one, and sentimentality is a powerful defence against the recognition of reality. It was an important part of the stock in trade of the minstrel company; prominent among the many composers who provided musical material was Stephen Foster. Foster, having made his reputation as a composer of genteel salon songs, superb of their kind, entered the minstrel business in

1852 with *Old Folks at Home*, an archetypal 'homesick darkie' song; not at the time wishing to be associated publicly with minstrelsy, he sold it to E.P. Christy, of Christy's Minstrels, who published it under his own name — and collected the considerable royalties. Later Foster overcame his scruples (he needed the money) and wrote defiantly to Christy that he was determined 'to pursue the Ethiopian business without fear or shame . . .' His contributions to the minstrel stage are among its most enduring, and many have passed into folksong, so that many today think that they are genuine Negro songs; *Oh Susanna*, *Camptown Races*, *Nelly Bly* and *Old Black Joe* are just a few of them. Between them, Foster and other creators of minstrel songs conjured up a folklore and an image of black people that survives to this day, and continues to bedevil the minds of whites — that of the happy-go-lucky feckless 'darkie' singing and dancing his way through life but by no means to be taken seriously.

It is of course easy to condemn the racial attitudes underlying the minstrel show. But they were no more than a reflection of the prevailing attitudes of the day — and of course minstrelsy was the principal channel through which the majority of white Americans became aware of black musicking and dancing, even if it was filtered through the perceptions of the minstrels. In its very popularity it showed at one and the same time, as Ben Sidran has said, that 'there was a *need* in white culture for what the black culture had to offer,'[7] and that, equally, the majority of white people dared not confront that culture directly but needed to defuse the challenge it posed to their own culture and values by portraying its bearers as ridiculous, or sentimental, or both.

As might be expected, the music of the minstrel show also evaded the challenge posed by black musicking. The actual style of performance has not, of course, come down to us other than in descriptions, but most successful songs were published; they range in style from the entirely European with hardly a trace of black inflection, such as Foster's *Old Folks at Home*, to verse-and-chorus songs, generally in a major key, with a few proto-ragtime inflections (Daniel Kingman draws attention to one of Daniel Emmett's songs, *Nigger on the Wood Pile*, of 1845, which has many rhythmic patterns resembling those in Scott Joplin's *Maple Leaf Rag* of some fifty years later).[8] Some were adaptations of Irish and Scottish fiddle tunes, such as *Turkey in the Straw*; none can actually be traced back directly to black sources, though some do bear traces of black influence, not only in the syncopations of the melodic line but also in those pentatonic shapes, flatted sevenths and verbal repetitions that are favoured in black musicking.

After the Civil War and Emancipation, the nature of the minstrel show changed drastically, owing to two new factors. The first was that white minstrels largely lost interest in the portrayal of black people, and broadened the show to include a high proportion of conventional variety material. Troupes became larger, forty or more, production and costumes lavish and spectacular. Bearing grandiose titles such as 'Haverley's United Mastodon Minstrels' 'Cleveland's Colossals' and 'Keavitt's Giganteans', they toured the country in extravagant pageants, dressed no longer as caricatured blacks but in evening dress or eighteenth-century pantaloons, stockings and wigs, whatever took the director's fancy, and even, from around 1880 onwards, abandoning blackface and with it all the dialogue and business that had been their stock in trade. Eventually, around the turn of the century, white minstrelsy merged with vaudeville and variety, leaving only occasional blackface performers such as Al Jolson and Eddie Cantor, and degenerate revivals, such as could be seen on British television screens in the 1960s (white British viewers mostly could not for the life of them imagine what there was about it that their black compatriots found so offensive).

But the other, more interesting, development which followed Emancipation was the entry of black artists into the minstrel show. There had been a sprinkling of professional black musicians and entertainers on the stage before the Civil War, even whole bands like that of Francis Johnson, which toured northern cities in the 1830s and was also extremely successful in Europe. But the minstrel show was something else, for there we find black artists 'blacking up' and projecting to audiences the same stereotypes as those which white artists had been giving for three decades. Equally surprising perhaps is the fact that they were extremely popular with black and white audiences alike. Black minstrel troupes had begun to appear in northern cities in the mid-1850s, but, naturally enough, they did not venture into the south until after the Civil War; they inherited the form and the content of the white show along with the audiences' expectations, and they were obliged to continue it, burnt cork, 'long tail blue' and all. They did of course have one major advantage over the white artists: their authenticity, having actually lived the life of the plantation and not just observed it. They thus had access to material that was inaccessible to whites, not only songs and dances but also folklore and folkways, and they used this material freely alongside the traditional minstrel material. This authenticity did extract its price, since it added credibility to the stereotypes, in which audiences would accept only very minor modifications. A major innovation was the introduction of the religious music and even the religious rituals of the black community, which were portrayed vividly on stage, initiating a tradition that survives in black dance and folklore companies to this day (Alvin Ailey's *Celebration*, and the Dance Theatre of Harlem's *Dougla* are two that come to mind).

The problem, then as now, for black artists in presenting their culture on stage before white audiences lay in the fact that the more flamboyant, the more vivid and colourful the presentation the more it would be enjoyed by white audiences, unable as they are to enjoy such outlets in their own culture in socially acceptable form — and the more the performances would serve to confirm white assumptions about blacks. The black companies' presentation of, for example, revival meetings, with the gaudily-dressed performers singing, dancing, shouting and laughing apparently without inhibition served once again to introduce the minstrel image, the only image in which it seemed that white people, especially in the south, were prepared to tolerate black people being visible at all. W.C. Handy reported in his autobiography that when black troupes visited small southern towns in the early years of this century they could escape molestation, and possibly worse, when they went into the streets only when dressed in their minstrel costume; those who had the temerity to appear, smartly dressed, as themselves could expect trouble.

Travel was difficult for black artists, finding somewhere to stay a nightmare, for hotels would not have them and the local black population were often too poor to offer anywhere to sleep; better-off black people found the shows anathema, as they did the blues in a later period, representing too closely for comfort the culture from which they had with such difficulty escaped. The larger and more successful companies, usually white-owned, would often provide a railroad car, equipped with food and water and sometimes a hiding-hole for the use of those who offended against the ways of the south (it was on occasion needed, as Handy testifies from his own experience).

It would be easy but fruitless to condemn those often greatly gifted and skilled artists who went on the stage to present these caricatures of their race before white audiences (and, we should not forget, before black audiences also, who apparently enjoyed the jokes no less). Rather, we should look for the reason why they would have done so. First among these of course would have been sheer economics; the minstrel stage was one of the few ways in which a black performance artist could gain employment and earn a living in the theatre. And second, there was the ancient strategy of the downtrodden and abused: to take the abusive label to oneself and wear it as a badge of pride. And, thirdly, there was the chance to define one's culture, to display one's theatrical and musical skills before a white audience, to make them watch and listen. And in their turn, black audiences, who seem to have been mostly lower-class (members of the minute black middle class would mostly not have been seen dead at a minstrel show) were not really much concerned at the kind of figure they were cutting before whites — that was a middle-class worry — but came to laugh at recognizable caricatures of themselves and their foibles, much as English audiences laugh at Tony Hancock and Scottish at Billy Connelly. And, no doubt, the performances of artists like Billy Kersands, a singer, comedian and fine dancer who specialized in outrageous portrayals of stupid black characters (he made great capital out of his very large mouth) and whose popularity forced even southern theatre managers to abandon segregation while he was in the show, must have had a great deal more to say to black than to white audiences — after all, they were descendants of slaves who had been communicating clandestinely for generations.

And so it was that minstrelsy, which had been a way of affirming the inferiority of black people, became for those same people an avenue of advancement and helped in the creation of a language of self-presentation which was not without its importance in the struggle for recognition as people. But, as I have suggested, there was a price; the minstrel image has haunted blacks ever since. We find, in the 1920s, Joe 'King' Oliver, a serious musician if ever there was one, issuing publicity photographs of his band, immaculate in tuxedos, but posturing with their instruments like 'plantation darkies', while his one-time protege Louis Armstrong, one of the greatest musicians ever to have come out of the United States, to his death accepted, at least outwardly, the role of minstrel and entertainer, even clown, often to the embarrassment and even irritation of black colleagues. Of course, jazz would not be jazz without a strong element of playfulness and humour, and self-mockery has always been a strong element of black humour; it is an open question to what extent it was himself and to what extent it was his audiences' expectations Louis was really sending up (calling him 'Louis' feels to me like presumption, but to call him 'Armstrong' feels even more like an insult to his warmth and humanity, so I shall settle for the former).

By the turn of the century the popularity of the black minstrel show was waning, and black minstrelsy becoming restricted to the rural south. It was replaced in the towns and cities by musical comedy, vaudeville and burlesque, all of which had at best limited use for black artists; in each generation only a few 'made it' to more than a local or regional reputation, and most were confined until the 1950s to playing to black audiences. There were vaudeville circuits which flourished more or less invisible to the larger and richer white audience — many of the classic blues artists such as Bessie Smith and Ma Rainey worked on them — and which acted, all unrecognized and unrewarded, as sources of energy and of new styles of musicking and dancing (in the 1920s, for example, the Charleston, in the 1930s, tap dancing, in the 1940s the lindy hop or jitterbug, not to mention blues and various jazz styles) on which many white artists were to become rich and famous.

At the same time, in the early years of this century, blacks were making their presence felt, if to a limited extent, on the musical stage apart from the minstrel show or even vaudeville, not only through the injection of black styles such as ragtime into the popular music of the day, but also through the creative work of writers and musicians such as J. Rosamund Johnson and his brother, the poet James Weldon Johnson, and Noble Sissle and Eubie Blake, as well as through the appearance of black performing artists, at first as speciality acts in otherwise white productions, then later in all-black musical shows, on the Broadway stage itself. The first of these was a mere one-act sketch, *Clorindy, or the Origin of the Cakewalk*, written by the poet Paul Laurence Dunbar and the composer Will Marion Cook; it was presented in New York on a roof garden at midnight, in the summer of 1898, and was an immediate success. Cook's own account of the production, given in Eileen Southern's *Readings in Black American Music*, can still lift the soul:

> 'The Darktown finale was of complicated rhythm and bold harmonies, and very taxing on the voice. My chorus sang like Russians, dancing meanwhile like Negroes, and cakewalking like angels, black angels! When the last note was sounded, the audience stood and cheered for at least ten minutes . . . maybe, when the pearly gates open wide and a multitude of hosts march in, shouting, laughing, singing, emoting, there will be a happiness which slightly resembles that of *Clorindy's* twenty-six participants . . . Gone was the uff-dah of the minstrel! Gone the Massa Linkum stuff! We were artists and we were going a long, long way. We had the world on a string tied to a runnin' red-geared wagon on a down-hill pull. Nothing could stop us, and nothing did for a decade'.[8]

Over that decade Cook wrote the music for three musical shows for the gifted comedy team of Williams and Walker: *In Dahomey*, *In Abyssinia* and *In Bandanaland*, all satirizing for the first time white concepts of black people, while the Johnson brothers and Robert Cole wrote *The Shoo-Fly Regiment*, *The Red Moon* and *Mr Lode of Koal*. This was a new generation of black poets and musicians, whose sophistication was both streetwise and college-educated — a formidable combination. What did stop the 'red-geared wagon', however, was Broadway fashion. There have been successful all-black musical shows in the ensuing years: Blake and Sissle's *Shuffle Along*, of 1921, which brought Josephine Baker, Florence Mills and Paul Robeson to the Broadway stage for the first time, up to *The Wiz* and *The Black Mikado* in the 1970s and *One Mo' Time* in the 1980s, all of which bear witness to the continuing power of black creativity in this medium, but to the average theatregoer the last three remained as much curiosities as had been the earlier shows. Things do not seem to change much.

In the nineteenth century, Irish, Jews, Germans, Italians, all had their turn as comic stereotypes and objects of ridicule; only the blacks retain their continuing fascination for white audiences on the American and British stage. That this should be so is due, in part at least, to the musical and theatrical skills of black performers themselves, but very much more to the unchanging ambivalent attitudes of whites towards their black compatriots who continue today to live lives that are partially hidden from them. The minstrel show articulated with precision these attitudes, being a vehicle for caricature which served to render innocuous the fascinating but dangerous culture of the blacks. It is not just the envy of the white, caught up in the work ethic and puritanism, for the black who is perceived as irresponsible, sexually potent and devoted to the pleasures of the moment, and thus able to enjoy life in a way denied to him or herself — a way, in fact, of indulging fantasies and blaming it on the blacks — though that is certainly a factor. There is also a genuine admiration, even longing, not fully conscious and *never* quite admitted or even articulated, for certain qualities in the black community, of communality, of what one might call emotional honesty — those qualities which blacks themselves call 'soul'. This admiration and longing runs like a thread through the history of black-white relations in America; such feelings must, I am certain, be present before one culture can find it in itself to draw, as white America has drawn on black, on the resources of another.

That they must be present, even in what became the heartland of racial oppression in the deep south, is evidenced by the strong component of black idioms that exists within the indigenous white musical style of that region, what is known today as country or country-and-western. We have seen how the poor white majority, themselves despised and kept in subjugation by the big estate owners, were drawn into a kind of conspiracy to keep the blacks in a position that was even lower than their own. These people were poor, politically and socially conservative, committed to rural values and committed, too, to a brand of fundamentalist Christianity that enforced, and still enforces, a code of conduct of uncompromising straitness. The first Methodist, Baptist and Presbyterian circuit-riding preachers came to the region in the early days of independence, and found a people living mostly in small isolated communities who welcomed them for their emotional brand of religion, for their lack of formality and for their music making. The people gathered together in the great camp meetings, at which the presence of blacks came to be taken for granted, and at which, as we have seen, much musical interaction took place, and they sang the simple songs, memorizing them either from the few songbooks passed from hand to hand or from the preachers' lining-out. In the wake of the evangelists came the Yankee singing-masters, with their shape-note songbooks and their Fasola method of solmization; ousted from the northeastern regions by the growth of 'scientific music' and the tendency towards 'refinement' and to European taste, these remarkable men travelled the frontier regions, teaching their unsophisticated but appropriate, and above all usable, musical skills and establishing a strong tradition of harmonized choral singing that is still very much alive there today. The strained, nasal, vibratoless style of voice production which can be heard from 'Sacred Harp' choirs (so named from one of the most famous songbooks, first published in 1844 and still in print) is also a feature of the style of modern country singers.

The secular music of this isolated people was founded on British folksong brought to America by their forebears, in particular the ballad, with its strong, often bloodthirsty, narrative thread, its melodic and rhythmic simplicity, its intimacy and its impersonal and deliberately non-expressive style of delivery. Of the two most characteristic musical instruments, one, the fiddle, came with the British settlers, while the other, the banjo, shows the mark of the other major influence on this music, the musicking of the blacks. In its original form the banjo had four strings but early in the nineteenth century white musicians who had adopted it added a fifth, a drone, to give it its characteristic melancholy sound.

Poor, rural and deeply conservative as these southern whites may have been, they were by no means isolated completely from outside influences. In the first place, and most importantly, there was the musicking of the blacks, with whom they lived and worked side by side. And regardless of racial discrimination and other factors which kept them apart, there existed a considerable 'common stock' of material — songs and dance tunes — which were the property of both groups impartially, and which needed only a different style of performance to place them in one group or the other. Songs such as *John Henry*, *Frankie and Johnny*, *Staggerlee*, *Moma Don't Allow*, *Careless Love*, and banjo-and-fiddle tunes used for dancing, such as *Turkey in the Straw*, *Sourwood Mountain*, *Old Dan Tucker*, were sung and played by black and white musicians to black and white audiences alike. Many of these tunes were taken into the minstrel shows, whence they gained wide popularity among Americans both black and white.

Apart from this direct contact, there were other ways in which outside influences reached the rural areas of the south. There were the travelling vaudeville shows, often housed in tents, that travelled the length and breadth of the rural south with a wide variety of acts — minstrel singers, dancing girls, conjurers and magicians, circus-style acrobats, Swiss yodellers, Hawaiian string bands, anything that the management reckoned would please an unsophisticated audience. These brought a number of diverse musical styles — Tin Pan Alley tunes as well as yodelling and steel guitars, all of which became important in country music as it developed. More modest but very common, in this area where there were few doctors and few who could afford their fees, were the medicine shows, in which a 'doctor' or 'professor' with his cargo of patent medicines drew a crowd by means of one or two entertainers, often in blackface, who sang, told jokes, played and danced. Since black people were just as likely to be prospective customers as were white, the performers had to be able to appeal on both sides of the colour line simultaneously, a fact which must have been not without significance in the assimilation of black and white styles into each other. Musicians as famous as Jimmie Rodgers, Gene Autry, Bob Wills and Roy Acuff began their professional lives in medicine shows, which thus served the dual function of bringing music to remote areas and of providing employment for musicians and giving them training in the difficult art of engaging a mobile audience and making them good-humoured and receptive to the 'professor's' sales pitch.

But of all the influences which have overlain the original forms of Anglo-Celtic folk music, none has proved more pervasive or more long-lasting than the direct contact which occurred between the races in the south. As Tony Russell points out:

> 'A musician would be open to sounds from every direction: from family and friends, from field and railroad yard, lumber camp and mine; from street singers and travelling-show musicians; from phonograph records and radio; from dances and suppers and camp meetings and carnivals; from fellow prisoners in jails, from fellow workers everywhere. A white youngster could learn a song or a tune not only in the bosom of his family but from their black employees — nanny, Uncle Remus or anyone else. Racial antipathy, of course, hampered the free exchange of musical ideas . . . [but] . . . there were always musicians to whom musical values were more important than racist ones, men who would not care a jot if they, as whites, happened to like black pieces, or vice versa.'[10]

What has in fact taken place here is in fact the opposite of minstrelsy; white people in the American south have been able to respond directly to the musicking of the blacks without seemingly feeling the need to defuse it by ridicule or any other device, and to incorporate elements of it in their own performances. It is a phenomenon that would suggest a greater degree of mutual identification, a more complex intimacy, than the brute facts of southern racism would seem to allow, an admission rather than a denial of the 'need in white culture for what black culture has to offer'. That the admission is made in musical rather than in verbal terms, and is accordingly in all probability not fully conscious, does not lessen its force; certainly it shows a more fully human response than does the distancing imposed by the process of minstrelization, a process which has by no means ended with the demise of minstrelsy itself.

The black influence on white country music has been many-sided; in the first place, it lies in instrumental technique, especially the elaborate finger-picking style of guitar playing, unknown in European folk styles but to be found in West African players of string instruments (and still known to many country guitarists as 'nigger-picking'), while black rhythms permeate the music. Even the blues has passed into the mouths and fingers of white musicians, sharing with the black blues a good deal of poetic and musical material as well as its non-narrative sequence of stanzas, but delivered in the characteristic 'country' vocal style, high, strained and nasal, with much less pitch bending or blue notes, and featuring sometimes a yodelling refrain. The white blues has proved a durable element in country music from its earliest days and has even, especially when sung by the great Jimmie Rogers, proved popular with black audiences.

One curious thing about country music is the low esteem in which it is commonly held by large numbers of musicians and listeners of all kinds — a reflection, it seems, not only of the low social status of the people among whom it originated (after all, poor blacks are even lower in the social scale, and yet black country blues is greatly admired by sophisticated urbanites and intellectuals, but then poor blacks are 'picturesque' while poor whites are just 'sordid' and 'ignorant') but also of the historical position of this group as scapegoats (the *Li'l Abner* cartoon strip says much about the attitude of educated white Americans to their rural southern compatriots). Even today, with its audience numbered in millions, including not only southern migrants to cities trying to hang on to their rural and small-town values, but also long-time city dwellers all over the world who have never ventured south of the Mason-Dixon line, the 'redneck' image remains potent.

The subject matter of country songs reflects the attitudes of white rural southerners and is suffused with nostalgia for the old southern ways. The songs tend to possess a strong narrative thread, a legacy no doubt of the Anglo-Celtic ballad tradition, which is concisely and often eloquently told, frequently pointing a moral, on themes such as loss of love, betrayal and revenge, crime and retribution, the temptations of liquor and evil women, of accidents, disasters and murders, as well as with work. In general they reflect the tensions of people brought up in a strict, not to say severe, moral code and trying to come to terms with the temptations of the flesh and the blandishments of affluent American society; rarely if ever, however, does one come across any real spirit of revolt or even rebellion against either one or the other opposing forces. Not that the songs are necessarily solemn; there are frequent flashes of dry humour and of wild uninhibited fantasy. Some songs deal with current events, usually from a politically conservative point of view (many a populist right-wing candidate for office has found in country music a useful medium of identification with his supporters). But if they reflect the world view of poor, white, rural southern Americans, this does not mean that the performers or the songwriters are poor (many, like Johnny Cash and Dolly Parton, are quite rich, even though they retain the 'country' lifestyle), rural (much of it is today produced in efficient song-factories in and around Nashville) or even white (the black country artist, though rare, is not unknown). It is obvious, too, that the audience is by no means drawn exclusively from that social group; with a devoted and knowledgeable audience of millions in the United States alone (where there were in 1970 over six hundred radio stations playing country music full time) not to mention the rest of the world, country music is a tremendous success story, and one which cannot be unconnected with the revival of 'folk' values in the United States itself in the persona of two recent presidents, Carter and Reagan, and the swing towards right-wing political views which has taken place in the 1980s.

In making this association I do not, of course, attribute any causal force to country music; rather, it is that the music, whose lyrics tend to see situations in terms of 'traditional' simple American values — those of the frontier, in which men were men and women waited at home for them, a myth which has probably no more basis in fact than has that of pastoral

England — which, while it has not hesitated to draw on black musical idioms, has virtually excluded blacks, and which adopts a resolutely demotic and artless stance (an artlessness which, it must be said, conceals these days a good deal of very sophisticated art), seems to articulate a desire for simple solutions to increasingly complex and intractable problems, solutions which are offered more seductively by right-wing populist parties than by their political opponents.

We have to remind ourselves that music is not a thing but an activity, and that meaning is to be found not in 'the music' but in the act of taking part in a musical performance. It is the sense of identity that is affirmed and celebrated in the act of musicking that is significant, and for this reason it does not make sense either to praise or to blame a musical style in itself. One may dislike many of the attitudes that are articulated in a country-music performance, but there is also much to respect and to admire: the weatherbeaten survivorship of a Loretta Lynn or a Jerry Lee Lewis, the warm, intelligent femininity of Dolly Parton, whose sexiness goes to the edge (but never beyond it) of Dogpatch-style self-caricature. Such qualities of these, and many other, performers are to me often moving and memorable, and a reminder that identity, especially as celebrated through musicking, is not a simple matter but is shot through with contradiction and paradox, and that even the apparently simplest of musical performances may evoke the most complex of responses.

It is Elvis Presley who best sums up the contradictions and the paradoxes that are inherent in the white country style of performance — contradictions between the rigidities of old-time fundamentalist religion and the attractions of the world, the flesh and the devil, between the expansive promise of America and the cramped realities of small-town or city life, between the holding-on to the superiority of being white and the attractions of black culture. Before Elvis, country (more commonly called in those days 'hillbilly') singers sang more or less exclusively for a public that was almost as segregated as that for 'race' records; only a small number of artists, mostly 'singing cowboys' such as Gene Autry and Roy Rogers, were known to the wider public, mainly through their films. Elvis was the first singer from that background to make the transition to a mass public, to seize the moment in the early 1950s when black music was breaking out of the ghetto, to add the rebellious tone of rhythm-and-blues to the more passive strains of country music and to make a unique contribution to American vernacular music.

Elvis did *not* sound like a black, of course, but the black influence was clear in his singing, which came from a variety of sources.

> 'We were a religious family,' he said in an interview, 'going around together to sing at camp meetings and revivals. Since I was two years old, all I knew was gospel music, that was music to me. We borrowed the style of our psalm singing from the early Negroes. We used to go to these religious singings all the time. The preachers cut up all over the place, jumping on the piano, moving every which way. The audience liked them. I guess I learned from them. I loved the music. It became such a part of my life it was as natural as dancing, a way to escape from the problems and my way of release' .[11]

Besides, he had grown up in Memphis, a city in its own way as unique as New Orleans, 'where there had long been a relaxed social, as well as musical, interchange between black and white . . . White kids were picking up on black styles — of music, dance, speech and dress.'[12] It was not just that the sounds he made were black-influenced, but his entire manner of stage presentation, with the famous hip swivel that scared Ed Sullivan into showing him on his TV show from the waist upwards only, was derived from black dance. Derived from, but not the same as — his performances were shot through with tensions and restraints to which black singers and dancers are not subject — but enough to thrill or to scandalize his various publics, most of whom did not know where they came from in the first place.

The actual career of Elvis Presley belongs to a later chapter; we note here that his musical roots were, and remained, firmly in the soil of the rural south. As this chapter has tried to show, the synthesis of black and white traditions that one hears in his performances was by no means unique, even if his personal performance style was; it is only an outstanding example of the way in which the two traditions have met, crossed, fused, broken free and fused again, over and over in the American south. That this interaction occurred on the lowest social levels is significant; despite the well-publicized racism of the south there is no hint of condescension, of minstrelization, but a direct encounter between musicians who have recognized in one another's experience and values something that they themselves can value and put to use. At the very least, it should give us cause to wonder.

NOTES

1. quoted in STOUTAMIRE, Albert: *Music of the Old South: Colony to Confederacy*, Rutherford, Fairleigh Dickinson University Press, 1972, p 15.
2. *ibid.*, p 15.
3. ZINN, Howard: *A People's History of the United States*, London, Longman, 1980, p 37.
4. DEGLER, Carl N.: *Out of Our Past: The Forces That Shaped Modern America*, New York, Harper & Row, 2nd edition 1970, p 174.
5. JORDAN, Winthrop D.: *The White Man's Burden: Historical Origins of Racism in the United States*, New York, Oxford University Press, 1974, p ix.
6. TOLL, Robert C.: *Blacking Up: The Minstrel Show in Nineteenth-Century America*, New York, Oxford University Press, 1974, p 36.
7. SIDRAN, Ben: *Black Talk*, New York, Da Capo Press, 1981, p 32.
8. KINGMAN, Daniel: *American Music: A Panorama*, New York, Schirmer Books, 1979, p 295.
9. COOK, Will Marion: 'Clorindy, the Origin of the Cakewalk', in SOUTHERN, Eileen. *Readings in Black American Music*, New York, Norton, 1983, p 232–33.
10. RUSSELL, Tony: *Blacks, Whites and Blues*, London, Studio Vista, 1970, p 10.
11. GURALNICK, Peter: *Lost Highway: Journeys and Arrivals of American Musicians*, Boston, David R. Godine, 1979, pp 120–21.
12. *ibid.*, p 123.

Chapter 6

ON VALUE AND VALUES

The social status enjoyed by a musical culture is inseparably linked to the status of the social group whose world view it incarnates and whose values it celebrates. The account I have given so far of the encounter that occurred in North America between the two great musical traditions will have made it clear that it occurred principally, and in its most fruitful developments, on the lowest levels of American society, among people who, black or white, were united in one respect — their dispossession and their alienation from those who, through their access to power and control of property, were shaping the official, formal values of the emerging American society and nation. We have seen how those who did have a stake in those values found ways to protect themselves from what they saw as pollution by the inferior, intruder culture; from their own point of view they were probably right to do so, since the values that were articulated by the music of that encounter were deeply subversive not only of those of the official United States but also of the entire industrial world. That this situation still holds today is reflected not only in the splitting of the western musical tradition into two opposing streams, but, even more obviously, in the difference in social status that is accorded to them. In this chapter I propose to investigate some of the relationships which exist between musical values and social status as they affect the practice of music in the west today.

It need hardly be said that classical music enjoys a high social status in our society, and that participation in a classical-music performance is an activity that carries the stamp of social approval. It is in fact the official music of the western world; one might say of the industrialized world, since, as we have seen, the development of a western-style classical-music culture and submission to the values of industrialism are processes that go hand in hand. It boasts a long and well-documented history which is traced back to antiquity and it is accorded an intellectual rigour and even a moral value denied to other traditions. It is the music of this tradition that is taught, performed, analysed and researched, in schools, conservatoires and the music faculties of western universities, and it is this which is regarded as the highest achievement of the human race in the art of sound, of which all others are at best approximations, at worst corruptions. Its social pre-eminence is underlined by the frequent and visible presence at classical concerts not only of heads of state and their distinguished guests but also of the leaders of our social and intellectual life. The convergence of values is well illustrated by the story of the famous scientist who, when asked what message should be transmitted by radio into outer space to signal the presence of intelligent life on earth, replied, 'We could transmit Bach, but that would be boasting'. This assumption of superiority is underlined also by the scale and opulence of concert halls, opera houses and other buildings which are given over to the performance of this music, as well as by the frequent appearance of the names of the music's practitioners in lists of those who are honoured by governments for service to their grateful countries.

Given the high status of this music, and the moral and intellectual value that has been attributed to it, it is scarcely surprising, and for the most part taken for granted, that professional composition and performance of classical music (the dominance of professionals is virtually total) is underwritten, even kept alive, by an extensive network of subsidy, not all of it visible to the casual eye. Concerts and concert-giving organizations as well as opera houses and opera companies receive sponsorship from the state and from wealthy organizations, businesses and individuals on a considerable scale; for example, in 1980–81, every time the curtain rose on a performance by the British Royal Opera it was subsidized by the British taxpayer with an average sum of thirty-one thousand pounds.[1] But, further, the life of the professional musician in classical music, tough, demanding and ruthlessly competitive as it unquestionably is, is subsidized at every turn. The aspiring performer or composer is aided by grants, scholarships and competition prizes, at state- or privately-funded schools which pay his teachers' salaries; concert halls and opera houses where he or she will perform are built and maintained by municipalities, radio networks and wealthy organizations, as are the orchestras in which he or she will play or with which he or she will appear as soloist, or which will commission his or her compositions. A composer can be freed from the pressures of having to please an audience in order to earn a living — unlike his seventeenth- and eighteenth-century predecessors — with secure employment in university or conservatoire, often with minimal demands made on his time or energy for teaching, while the young aspirant knows that if he or she should fail to make it as a professional artist there is always a fallback position in teaching, administration, criticism and other ancillary occupations which provide a decent living and an acceptable social position.

The matter of subsidy is interesting in other ways. From the beginnings of civilization, of course, musicians have played for money, and, not surprisingly, their musicking has tended to celebrate the values and the status of those who pay them; indeed, that has been a principal function of professional musicians, West African *griots* and European church and court musicians alike. The musician may well share the values of his patrons without having to give the matter much thought, as did nineteenth-century British music-hall artists, who were generally a part of the working-class society that paid to see and hear them, as did the early stars of blues, and many of the great country-and-western singers, whose identification with their audiences' values and lifestyle was a major element in their appeal. How sincerely Handel admired King George II when he wrote *Zadok the Priest* for his coronation, or Beethoven the Emperor Joseph II when he wrote music for the latter's funeral, is a matter for conjecture (both were ambitious professional musicians who knew on which side their bread was buttered), but we do know that Edward Elgar, whose Coronation Marches, Coronation Odes and other ceremonial music were an important factor in the twentieth-century reinvention of the British concept of monarchy and the broadening of its appeal to the mass of people in an industrial society, was perfectly sincere in his admiration for the monarchy, and for Edward VII in particular, and in what David Cannadine calls his 'genuine love for colour, pageantry, precision and splendour.'[2]

Modern classical musicians, like their illustrious predecessors, receive their financial support from sources close to the centres of power in today's industrial society. In many cases this means the state, either directly, as in the Soviet Union, or indirectly, as in Great Britain through its Arts Council; the latter organization, since its foundation in 1946, has always been presumed to be independent of the government of the day which allots to it a sum of money annually for its operations, even though its senior officials have always been members of that informal and diffuse British power structure which has been dubbed the Establishment. The 1979 and 1983 Thatcher administrations, however, with their unashamed centralizing tendencies, have demonstrated through the nature of their appointments to the Arts Council the spuriousness of the so-called 'arm's-length' policy when the chips are down. In many other countries the sponsorship of classical musicking is in the hands of wealthy organizations, families and individuals; for example, over $100 million of the $250-odd million that the building of New York's Lincoln Center cost was contributed by some two dozen families, probably about half of that sum by the Rockefeller family. Likewise, firms such as Texaco, Eastern Airlines and Ford have sponsored individual productions at the Metropolitan Opera (the New York State and Federal Governments also contribute, but less spectacularly, especially under the Reagan Administration).[3] The classical musician, in fact, remains as much a client of the rich and the powerful as ever he was in the history of the tradition. As I said in a talk in 1984 to the Composers' Guild of Great Britain:

> 'We are often told these days that there is no such thing as a free lunch, and this is no less true of state subsidy than of any other handout; no subsidy, from the state or elsewhere, comes without its price. As I see it, the price that the state exacts for what is after all still quite generous subsidy of classical music is to tie it firmly to its official values; the musician, whether school, college or university teacher, eminent composer, famous conductor or soloist, rank-and-

> file orchestral player, even critic and musicologist, is incorporated into a system by means of which young people are socialized into those values while older people are reassured of their continuing validity even in a world that seems to be coming apart around them. Either that, or he is reduced to playing a kind of Glass Bead Game, an intricate, fascinating and intellectually demanding but quite meaningless activity which, as Hesse suggests, serves no purpose other than to keep some of the best minds of the society in a privileged position and too occupied to question what it is they are doing'.[4]

The classical musician lives in a world which, no matter how fiercely competitive, is fundamentally orderly and tidy, inhabited by people who share the same assumptions about life, in which concerts generally start and end on time, in which hitches are rare and major breakdowns almost unknown. His or her professional life will probably follow an orderly pattern, from selection in school (the way in which certain children are singled out as 'musically talented' is interesting in itself and deserves investigation), through college, conservatoire or university, with examination and certification to mark the completion of each stage, to study with one or more masters and finally to a debut before the public, with the possibility that honours — a decoration, an order, a knighthood, even a peerage, or the title of Honoured Artist (since the Socialist countries are no different in this respect) — will crown a career that has proved especially distinguished. He will find that wherever he goes his calling will be received with respect; he will not be hassled by customs and immigration officers looking for subversive literature or illegal substances, nor will he be required to pay exorbitant insurance premiums on his car. He will find that in dealing with record companies, publishers, managements and the like he will have at least the partial protection of a law of contract and copyright that was drawn up with the neat division of labour characteristic of the classical-music culture in mind. He will find, too, that no matter where he plays he can count on a disciplined audience that knows it must arrive on time, sit still and quiet as he plays, and applaud at the end.

Even the history of the tradition has been tidied up into an orderly sequence of master musicians, the 'great composers' of the past who gave over their lives to the production of musical works for our delectation and spiritual refreshment. That history is regarded as unproblematic, showing a steady development in style from one generation to the next in unbroken succession, as masters of composition passed on their knowledge and skills to their juniors. True, the conventional version of history tells us that there have been revolutions in style every few generations, but hindsight generally reveals these to have taken place within an essential continuity of tradition, and, true, different parts of the European continent and latterly its colonial offspring have developed local accents, but these have always been no more than dialects within the *lingua franca* that is assumed to be generally understood. True, too, some musicians of genius have in each generation developed the common musical language in ways that were not always comprehended by their contemporaries, but these developments have usually found gradual acceptance as they became familiar to later generations. We are invited to admire the integrity, even heroism of those musicians as they maintained the power of their vision in the face of incomprehension without a thought for worldly success; the extraordinarily long time-lag that seems to have been needed for acceptance of the work of twentieth-century masters is taken as evidence of unusual tenacity and integrity on the part of those masters, but it is only a hiccup in an essentially smooth continuity. The classical-music culture of today, in fact, is presented to us as legitimized by a long and consistent history, during the course of which its social and intellectual basis has remained unchanged.

This tidying-up process has also reduced the variety of social meanings which the performance of this music has generated at various times and in various places over its history to a single meaning: that of the concert-hall performance. That manner of performance, as we have seen, affirms and celebrates the values of the industrial state in all its singleness of vision. We are led, then, to ask whether the superior and privileged position of classical music and musicians today is not a matter more of a congruence of values than of any real superiority in the actual process of musicking. Certainly the congruence can be perceived in many ways once one is alert to it.

There is, for example, a curious ritual which takes place in London's Royal Albert Hall every year on the last night of the BBC's summer season of promenade concerts, in which the audience of young people don funny hats and an exuberant manner while the BBC Symphony Orchestra and soloists perform a hodgepodge of 'well-loved classics', many of them harking back to Britain's imperial, and especially naval, past (Elgar's *Sea Pictures*, Henry Wood's *Fantasia on Sea Shanties*, and Parry's *Songs of the Fleet*, all dating from that period of Anglo-German naval rivalry that climaxed in the first world war, are favourites), and patriotic songs, climaxing in *Land of Hope and Glory*, whose music is that of Elgar's first *Pomp and Circumstance March* and whose words disclose a mindless jingoism that one would have imagined to be well and truly buried by now along with the British Empire itself:

> Land of hope and glory, Mother of the free.
> How shall we extol thee, who are born of thee?
> Wider still and wider shall thy bounds be set,
> God, who made thee mighty, make thee mightier yet![5]

The whole proceeding takes place in an atmosphere of warm and indulgent social approval and is televised to huge viewing figures across the British nations; the young audience remain still and quiet in the approved manner during the various items, confining their shenanigans to the spaces between the 'serious' pieces and to those with which it is expected that they will sing along. Those who have protested about the singing of these bellicose patriotic songs have been told, with some impatience, that it was just harmless and healthy fun and didn't mean a thing; the kids were all right. But in the *Sunday Times* during September 1982 appeared a news item that suggested that the event had a deeper meaning. Under the headline THE PROMS' HOPE AND GLORY, it ran:

> 'The euphoria of victory in the Falklands turned what the BBC describe as the "world's most famous musical celebration" into the most patriotic and nostalgic "last night" for years. *Rule Britannia* and *Land of Hope and Glory* and

> *Jerusalem* were sung with tremendous fervour accompanied by the waving of hundreds of Union Jacks and a few Falkland Islands maps . . . And the fun ended with *Auld Lang Syne* and a rendering of *God Save the Queen* which left many weeping eyes both in the hall and in homes up and down the country'.[6]

The link between the performance of classical music and the objectives of the powerful could not have been more nakedly exposed, nor could the extent to which the young music lovers, doubtless in all innocence, have assimilated those objectives as their own.

There are other congruences also. I have suggested that a musical work of the western classical tradition is essentially a drama, in which the individual soul progresses from one spiritual state to another by means of a process of struggle and antithesis, which is finally resolved. In a concert piece, the protagonist remains unspecified; it is often assumed, generally quite without justification, that it is the composer himself (we do not, after all, identify Hamlet with Shakespeare). The very lack of specificity allows each individual listener to identify him or herself with the protagonist, whose relationships, struggles and eventual triumph or defeat we infer from the internal relationships of the musical work itself.

In opera, on the other hand, the drama is external; the characters are given names and a physical and social environment and their actions and relationships are shown to us on the stage as well as in the musical relationships. It is interesting that opera has from its beginnings in the early seventeenth century until the beginning of the present century been the source of most of the technical innovations in western classical music, innovations whose purpose has always been to render the stage situation more dramatic, more explicit; only after the significance of a musical-dramatic gesture was fully understood by audiences in the theatre could it be used to similar effect in the abstract drama of the concert piece. Indeed, our understanding of concert works owes more than we imagine to conventions first established on the stage: the swordplay of cymbals, the rousing call-to-arms of massed brass instruments, the thunderous rumble of the bass drum, the pastoral strains of the oboe. not to mention those abstract dances, triumphal marches, funeral processions, dirges, riotous scenes of celebration and intimate scenes of confession and love — the symphonic repertory teems with such episodes, all of which appeared and were understood by audiences on the operatic stage before they could be comprehended on the abstract stage of the symphonic or concert work.

In the same way, the plots of operas make explicit those attitudes which are implicit in the abstract drama of concert music. Those nineteenth-century operas which form the staple repertory of the modern opera house (indeed, apart from the operas of Mozart, the whole repertory of regularly-performed opera stems from the nineteenth and the early twentieth century) are especially revealing in this respect, not surprisingly in that they were devised for the entertainment and the edification of the nineteenth-century middle class. Like the concert music of the same period, they have consistently presented to their audiences in mythologized form their fantasies, fears and most intimate concerns. Thus we find that the historical and mythological characters of much nineteenth-century opera, for example *Aida* or *Nabucco*, were invested with attitudes and emotions of contemporary nationalism, and the patriotism of the emerging nation-state. The experience of the industrial working class, not unnaturally, finds no voice in these large and glamorous stage works; the only factory I can think of is that tuneful cigarette factory from which Carmen and her gypsy friends emerge to begin the real drama of their lives. Merry peasants, on the other hand, who have just brought in the harvest, sing and dance without a care in the world, other perhaps than the pangs of unrequited love; they populate the stage in many operas — cousins, all unknown to themselves, of the 'plantation darkies' of the contemporary minstrel show — remarkably like those smiling peasants of genre paintings who, as John Berger remarks, 'assert two things: that the poor are happy and that the better-off are a source of hope for the world.'[7]

Notions of male honour and of female virtue — middle-class sex roles, in fact — are hammered home relentlessly in the operas of Verdi, Puccini, Weber, Wagner and dozens of lesser contemporaries; even Brünnhilde finally falls a prize to an ambitious man (that the operas of Wagner, not excepting *The Ring*, are mighty vehicles of middle-class values is a matter which has been discussed fully by both Nietszche and Theodor Adorno). The rare independent and self-possessed women such as Violetta, Aida, Norma, Carmen, Lulu, all come to tragic ends, and even the attempt to achieve independence, made for example by Louise and Katya Kabanova, is doomed to failure and tragedy. Indeed, the only fully realized and successfully independent female character that I can discover in the whole of nineteenth and twentieth century opera is a vixen. And endless comedies of marital intrigue go to show that the most suitable use for female intelligence is in catching and holding a husband; it is not certain whether these moralities were intended to instruct women or to reassure men.

It could of course be said that there is nothing very remarkable about this, that such themes were also the staple of nineteenth-century spoken drama, but nineteenth-century spoken drama does not form the bulk of the repertory of the twentieth-century stage. Opera has always been a powerful vehicle for the transmission of the dominant class's social values, as can be seen from the way it functioned in the seventeenth and early eighteenth centuries to affirm the legitimacy and the nobility of character of absolute rulers (it was they, after all, who used to foot the quite considerable bill). What does deserve comment is that these attitudes should still stand today behind a repertory of stage works which, it is claimed, or just assumed, are some of the highest achievements of western, or indeed human, culture, and which are presented night after night throughout the industrialized world in a ritual that appears to satisfy the dreams and the quest for identity of contemporary middle- and upper-class people, attracting in addition not only the highest social approval but also a level of subsidy that dwarfs that given to other artistic activities. Only the purchase of paintings for national art galleries can match it in scale. One can only conclude that opera as an activity serves to reinforce, or at the very least presents no challenge to, the values which legitimate and maintain the present power structures of the modern state.

It is of course possible to point to a number of modern operas which do, through the stories they tell, offer some challenge to those reigning values; they play as a rule to half-empty houses, and, for the most part, no matter how eminent their composers, become only names in histories of twentieth-century art music. Only a handful of twentieth-century works has entered the repertory of operas that are regularly performed, of which only those of Strauss and Puccini, both essentially composers in the nineteenth-century spirit, have gained real popularity with audiences. Alban Berg's *Wozzeck* does, it is true, appear to challenge the values of the society, in that it enlists our sympathy for a poor devil of a proletarian soldier; the trouble is that the poor devil is so gormless and so obviously defenceless against his tormentors, many of whom are presented as caricatures, that we cannot feel anything but a vague pity, and not much genuine anger at the social forces lined up — one might even say, stacked up — against him. In any case, what finally destroys him is not the hardships of the proletarian soldier's life but our old operatic friend, sexual jealousy; he is Don José in proletarian guise. It is no wonder that *Wozzeck* is becoming something like a repertory piece, despite its relatively unconventional musical language, for it enables audiences to have their cake and eat it too. And its musical language is not that of 'modernism' but of heightened romanticism, and becomes each year more accessible to a general audience.

The heroine of the same composer's *Lulu*, set since the discovery of its final act also to attain a certain popularity, is an updated version of the operatic femme fatale, destined, like her sisters, to come to a bad end. It is probable that Berg did not intend his heroine to be seen in this way; indeed, it seems as if he wanted the opera to stand as a protest against bourgeois society's treatment of women. But the high probability that few of the work's audience will see her in anything but conventional operatic terms highlights an important factor which is shared by concert halls and opera houses today: they impose a set of values on everything that is presented, through the nature of the ritual which is the real content of the performance. The power of that ritual is such that not even the supreme dramatic genius of Mozart can go against the values which a modern opera performance celebrates.

How many opera goers, for example, notice what is *really* going on in *The Marriage of Figaro*, or are even interested? For beneath the comedy, the story concerns the desperate struggle of a servant and his bride to save her from violation by an unprincipled aristocratic lecher, a struggle whose existence they dare not even acknowledge. They conduct their defence with wit and dignity, qualities which are notably lacking in the other characters in the drama; further, to complete the subversion of conventional social roles, it is Susanna the maid who displays the most intelligence and resource, running rings even around her shrewd bridegroom Figaro. The aristocrats are both stupid and frivolous; this is true of even the Countess, despite a certain sympathy won for her by her situation and by her two lovely arias. The bourgeois characters are unpleasant and venal to the point of caricature; only the servants show any real integrity, not to mention genuine love and fidelity. Likewise in *Don Giovanni*: the only emotion that one can take at all seriously, apart from the Don's lust and the other characters' ceaseless desire for revenge, is the love beteen the peasants Masetto and Zerlina, whose aria *Batti, batti* as the two are reconciled is one of the most heartrendingly beautiful moments in the whole of the lyric drama. And as for *Così fan Tutte*, it is perhaps the most ruthless send-up of nascent bourgeois notions of romantic love (to pour such heartbreaking music into farewells that we *know* are not for real is to subvert the entire operatic convention) in the whole history of the European theatre.

That even those three great comedies, *sui generis* in their subversion of both social and theatrical conventions and of the accepted values of today's, no less than Mozart's, audiences, could have become incorporated without apparent effort into the canon of operatic 'masterpieces' is a tribute to the power of the ritual of the modern opera house and to its ability to impose its own values and systems of relationships on whatever is presented there. Nor do recent attempts to dramatize values other than those of modern industrial society fare any better. Luigi Nono, for example, may show us, in *Intolleranza*, the hounding and final destruction of an immigrant; Berthold Brecht and Kurt Weill may show us, in *The Seven Deadly Sins*, the gradual disintegration of a young woman through the pressures of 'getting on', and, in *The Threepenny Opera* and *Mahagonny*, the corruption of capitalist society; Sir Michael Tippett may present us, in *The Midsummer Marriage* with images of community and of mutual love (though his casting of the young mechanic and secretary in the 'Papageno' and 'Papagena' roles, destined to live forever outside the portals of the Temple of Wisdom, shows the continuing class-based limitation of his vision) — all these, and many other attempts to use the operatic stage as a medium for the promulgation of values other than the official values of industrial society, are destined to fail in one of two ways. Assuming they reach the stage in the first place, either they are rejected outright by the audience, as in the first instance, or, like the others, they are accorded a cautious acceptance while their message is quietly put to one side in favour of discussing the conductor's tempi, the producer's and designer's stage pictures and the vocal qualities of the leading soprano.

On the whole those works in what one might call a twentieth-century idiom which have achieved some success in the opera house have been those, such as the operas of Britten, Shostakovich, Stravinsky, Stockhausen, even Tippett (however much he may have struggled to break free of them — and his struggle is not without a certain bleak integrity), which share the values and the assumptions of their middle-class audiences. In fact, like symphony concerts, operatic performances today, whatever they may have been in the past (and we recall that not only does the nature and meaning of the ritual change over time even if the works performed do not, but also each historical period perceives the art works on which its imagination has to work in ways which suit its own mythopoeic needs) are rituals in which are dramatized the mythologies which underlie and legitimate the modern industrial state; therefore the middle and upper classes who are the beneficiaries of that state gain reassurance that their values are the supreme values, as they are believed to have been in the past (hence the importance of asserting the continuity of the tradition) and to remain in the future.

The role played by subsidy is thus ineluctably political; it is here that the most conclusive evidence lies for the coincidence of values between classical musicking and the activities of the state. For those who run the modern state, no matter what their party-political colouring, are concerned primarily with maintaining themselves in power, and only secondly with the welfare of their citizens. Two observations on this are in order. First, not all of those who run the modern state are actually involved in the visible structure of government; as Malatesta put it nearly a hundred years ago, in terms that remain true today: 'Today, government, consisting of property owners and people dependent on them, is entirely at the disposal of the owners, so much so that the richest among them disdain to take part in it.'[8] There is in fact no difference in principle between sponsorship of the arts by the British, American or Soviet governments and that by major corporations such as Texaco, Eastern Airlines and Ford, or by super-rich families like the Rockefellers. They all sponsor the same kind of musical activity. Clearly, neither governments nor big business regard classical music as any kind of challenge to them or to their values.

And, secondly, those who run the contemporary state not infrequently devolve their powers of arts sponsorship on to individuals who may be of impeccable liberal credentials but whose position in society places them near to the sources of power; thus, the first Chairman of the Arts Council of Great Britain, and the man who shaped in a crucial way its nature and its activities, was the economist John Maynard Keynes, whose economic ideas have been powerful for over thirty years in shoring up the institutions of capitalism, while a more recent (1986) incumbent, Sir William Rees-Mogg, was a previous editor of the London *Times*. The links with the power structure may be indirect, even tortuous, but they are real.

We can see the process at work in the music departments of colleges and universities. The majority of university music departments are still stuck in an exclusive concern with the past, but some have taken steps in the direction of 'the new music', while others have committed themselves wholeheartedly to it. This is especially true in the United States; Gilbert Chase in his 1966 history *America's Music* has this to say:

> 'It is a truism that the American university is a traditional haven of the artist; what is significant is the increasingly important role of the university as a creative and disseminating center for the *contemporary* arts providing not only material security for the artist but also a stimulating atmosphere based on awareness of really contemporary values, and an opportunity based on adequate performance resources and the ability to attract limited but receptive audiences. The composer himself — often doubling as performer — has been the most active agent in this development. With backing from the foundations, the universities have proved receptive to his initiatives and have welcomed their new role as patrons of the new as well as guardians of the past. The movement in this direction is nationwide and rapidly growing. Should the present decade accomplish no more than the expansion and consolidation of this trend, its contribution to our musical culture would be of incalculable value.'[9]

Whether or not one can endorse the author's enthusiasm depends, of course, on whether one perceives universities to be those citadels of independence, intellectual freedom, ideological tolerance and exploratory adventurousness which they claim to be. Like all large institutions, universities on the whole tend to be intolerant of genuine innovation, which takes place, if at all, on the fringes, and while no-one in authority is looking (should the innovation become conventional wisdom, credit is naturally claimed retrospectively); their acceptance of musical experimentation presupposes — indeed ensures — that, no matter how outrageous some of it may appear, it will remain socially and ideologically harmless. Tame artists, in fact, make good pets for university establishments as long as they do not attack their masters (not for real at any rate). Campus composers may growl and snarl often most convincingly, but they are careful to keep their claws in (or perhaps they do not notice that their claws have been painlessly extracted). Hesse's story of the Glass Bead Game may be taken as a parable for the activities of many modern university music departments.

It may seem almost improper to link universities, or other institutions of higher learning, with the power structure of the modern state; the legend of academic independence is a powerful one, but universities are indeed an essential part of the education system, whose function is as much to produce the élites of the future as it is to guard the legitimizing past, and the world of vice-chancellors, principals, directors and boards of regents is a part of that loose group of people, whose links with governments may be informal but are nevertheless close, which is called the Establishment. Certainly those who hold power in institutions of higher learning share to a major extent the assumptions and values of those who hold power in government. We may thus not be surprised to find avowedly revolutionary musicians such as John Cage, Mauricio Kagel and Frederic Rzewski finding sponsorship in university music departments; the universities themselves do not consider them to be any challenge to their values, and treat them rather like licensed clowns. And indeed there is nothing in the work of any of these musicians which need cause any member of the Establishment to lose a single night's sleep.

We need not postulate any conspiracy in this. The process of self-identification is less deliberate than that; it is simply that those who hold power in our society tend to view the world in similar terms, and in so far as they feel impelled to give their support to the activities of musicians (and there can be no doubt that there is among many of them a sincere love of music), it is classical music and musicians to whom they look as natural vehicles for those values which they regard as important. They see no need to justify their attitudes; the superiority of classical music is self-evident. Such confidence makes it possible to be indulgent towards other forms of musicking; there is room for a certain amount of Afro-American musicking, as long as it is kept in its place, and even for the creation and performance of a certain number of works whose overt content does run counter to, or at least criticize, the values of modern society. The setting of the concert hall, not excluding college and university auditoria, can be relied upon to neutralize any dissent and assimilate it into the main stream of middle-class musicking. In any case, the naïvety of the political stance of most contemporary concert works is sufficient to render such dissent harmless if not outright laughable. As for any dissent that is too extreme, or too convincing, the separation of function between composer and performer, and the elaboration of the apparatus needed for performance, makes it easy for access to performance outlets to be managed through control of orchestras, concert halls, opera companies and the like. The 'gatekeepers' who regulate the artist's contact with his audience will probably find such work genuinely unfit for performance in those places — as inded it probably will be. The truly dissident artist will be impelled by the nature of his or her vision to work in other styles, media and locations.

The circle of control is complete. The professionalization of music and the insistence on selection, examination and certification within the classical culture has effectively cut off most people from their ability to do anything more than sit and listen to what is presented to them; even their ability, and their right, to hold opinions without reference to the professionals is in doubt. Amateur performers scarcely dare to make an appearance in any public place, and certainly not in the company of professionals, while amateur composers, even if their existence is recognized at all, are usually figures of fun, at best eccentrics. And since the dissolution of the great tradition of improvisation which was a principal glory of the European classical tradition up to the end of the nineteenth century, no performer dares, or is even able to, play anything other than what has been passed to him by a composer. It is a closed situation; and closed situations mean death, if not immediately then in the long run; little professional musicking would survive in the classical tradition if the sources of subsidy were cut off.

It might almost be possible to argue for a definition of classical music, at least in western society, as 'music that gets subsidized'; certainly very little support of this kind is offered to the vernacular artist, who generally has to endure the full rigours of the economic climate. Nevertheless, neither the relatively low status of Afro-American musicking nor its general inability to attract subsidy from the powerful is necessarily all to its disadvantage. It is in fact the very absence of subsidy and of its concomitant ties to the power structure that make Afro-American musicking the best hope for future developments. This is, of course, not to suggest that the Afro-American tradition today is in a state of perfect health, either musical or social, but despite, or even perhaps because of, the money values with which it is saturated, there is an openness about it which contrasts with the closedness of the classical-music culture.

All professional musicians need money, and those who pay them have their own reasons for doing so; states, and wealthy individuals and organizations, which support musicking without the expectation of getting their money back, expect that it will support their values and legitimize their position, while, on the other hand, those who do expect to get their money back — record companies, managers, impresarios and suchlike — are less interested in the content of the musicking, so long as it shows a profit. While this situation, too, has its dangers, it at least allows space for a variety of attitudes and sets of values, which is to my mind preferable to the monolithic content to which the classical-music culture today has been reduced. The values embodied in a vernacular-music performance may also correspond in many respects with those of the state, as one saw, for example, in the presence of Ronald and Nancy Reagan at the twenty-fifth anniversary concert of the American Country Music Association in Washington DC in 1984. Such patronage is of course not accidental but part of a very calculated exercise in image-building and value-assertion, apart from the fact that the Reagans and their entourage had in all probability a liking for country music at least as genuine as that of the British Establishment for classical music. For in the act of participating in a country-music performance, the President and his lady were affirming a community of values with those for whom country music is the natural celebration of identity; as Bill C. Malone says: 'Country music has simultaneously identified with Middle America, the working man, and progressive youth while also reaching out for that affluent middle-class audience which is presumably different from the other three categories.'[10] What better description could we have of the appeal which Ronald Reagan himself hoped to make? We should notice, however, that in this case it is the politicians who are trimming themselves to the values of the music, and not the other way around.

This suggests that country music, like other styles of

musicking which can be identified within the Afro-American tradition, is itself not monolithic, either musically or in terms of values. It is important, as I have observed before, to keep in mind that named categories are convenient subdivisions only, often imposed by people who are outside the practice of the art; in real life they constantly ebb and flow, influencing and penetrating one another. Like vernacular speech, the 'common tongue', vernacular musicking varies, within the use of a common grammar and syntax, almost from one individual to another; there is no selection, no formal training, no examination to be passed or certificate to be gained before the individual is permitted to put the language into practice. Like the spoken vernacular, too, it is open to many kinds of abuse, especially by those who would control our manner of talking or musicking for their own purposes, and it is under constant pressure towards standardization for the benefit of those who would gain money, or power, or both, from us.

We might say that there are two reasons why people pay musicians to play for them; the first is very old and the second is relatively new. The old reason is to celebrate the values which legitimize their position, while the newer reason is in order to make money. In each case the employer will exercise a measure of control over what the musicians play, in the first case to ensure that they will indeed celebrate him (he will probably select, if he can, musicians who share his values, so that there will be no problem in that respect), and in the second to ensure that what they play will appeal to enough people to make it pay. It is easier for the person who pays the piper to call the tune in the first case than in the second. In the first, in the subsidized, or classical, field, not only is what the musician does controlled by the granting or withholding of subsidy, but even more crucially, entry itself into the profession of musician is controlled by examination and certification, through colleges of music and university music departments, in such a way as to ensure that only those who submit to the values of the culture are admitted; the degree of control that is being exerted is thus hardly noticed by the musicians, who believe themselves not only to be doing what they want to do but indeed to be engaging in the only kind of musicking that is worth their time and effort. On the other hand, in the vernacular, or 'commercial', field, anyone who can show that he or she can hold an audience can set up as a musician; the level of formal skill may be anything from elementary to virtuoso (the skills of holding an audience, of course, are themselves considerable and not to be slighted) and the social and political values celebrated anything from individualism to collectivism, statism to anarchism, 'left-wing' to 'right-wing' or any mix of these in coherent or incoherent form (no musical performance, of course, is or can be value-free). The entrepreneur does not mind so long as he makes a profit.

We should notice two other things also. The first is that, since the vernacular musician has to endure the full rigours of the economic climate, with his effort measured on a strictly profit-and-loss basis *which is not of his making*, it is arguable that the degree of commitment required of the vernacular musician is greater, rather than less, than that required of the classical musician. It is perfectly possible, and indeed not rare, for a classical musician to have been selected in school as talented, to have gone through the process of training and to have become a perfectly successful professional without once giving a moment's thought to what he or she is doing or why. The orderly structures and institutions of classical music will be quite enough to propel him or her through life in comfort and without too many disturbing glances outside the profession and its concerns. For the vernacular musician, on the other hand, survival in the chaotic and voracious world in which he or she is obliged to live and move is a matter of daily crises and manoeuvring. Further, while we read continually in the popular press of the exploits of rich rock and pop stars, the rich vernacular musician is in fact very much an exception; for each who makes it to fame and fortune there are hundreds, if not thousands, who think themselves lucky to make enough money from the musicking to pay for their instruments and the indispensable beat-up van.

A BBC radio feature in 1983 estimated that there were about a thousand rock bands (the term of course covers a multitude of persuasions) currently at work in the one British city of Liverpool, of whom at most a dozen or so would ever make a decent living in the pubs and clubs of the city and perhaps three or four would make it to national exposure and the charts. Most musicians, of course, dream of becoming rich and famous but, equally, most know that this is unlikely. In commercial terms, the overwhelming majority are non-starters; the only explanation for their continuing to play (and without doubt most of them are no more than mediocre in terms of musical or performance skill, while some range from elementary to incompetent) lies in the fact that for young people in that devastated city, with unemployment approaching fifty per cent, making music is a way of affirming their identity, perhaps even their very existence, in the face of an uncaring society that would prefer on the whole that they did not exist. Unemployment, as the programme's presenter said, is a great maker of musicians.[11] Similar sentiments were expressed by the British impresario Richard Branson in a recent television programme: 'England leads the world in music because of one thing. The Dole. Instead of having to do work or waste their time playing covers of hits at the Holiday Inn like American bands, they can sit at home and develop their music in peace'.[12]

And, secondly (and this applies to superstars no less than to aspirants), it is virtually axiomatic that whenever a musician makes a great deal of money from his or her musicking, it is only after many more people have made even more money first. The acknowledged rampant commercialism of the rock and pop world stems not so much from the musicians as from those who stand to make money from them. Each musician who enters the field of commercial music (and we should notice that there is no choice for a professional musician in our society other than between commercial and subsidized music — it is a question of which is less distasteful — and at least the commercial field does not compound its commercialism with hypocrisy) has to decide to what extent he or she is going to accede to the demands of the market and plan a career accordingly. An honest musician is obliged to keep constantly on the move to evade the clutches of commercial stereotyping, to make a clearing, however small, in the jungle, where he or she can make something of his or her own; but we should note that even those who do allow themselves to be co-opted all the way by the market do not necessarily make bad music. Certainly the subsidized musician is in no position to stand in judgement.

There are certain points at which the conflict of values between the two musical streams in our society surfaces to reveal the very sharp divisions in it. Two examples must suffice. The first shows that such divisions are not confined to the capitalist sector of the industrial west, and comes from an article by Charles Taylor in the British left-wing weekly *New Statesman*, concerning life in Czechoslovakia today. He says:

> 'Some become dissidents mainly because they feel an irrepressible urge to express themselves more authentically. You find this particularly among young people, a powerful, almost physical need to discover the truth of what they feel. This they can only do through a kind of free experimentation which the official reality can't accommodate . . . The search for expression takes a number of forms: not only direct acts like signing the Charter [Charter 77] but also participation in unofficial classes in history and philosophy, which are barely tolerated and frequently harassed; and perhaps even more important in its impact, participation in clandestine pop music groups . . . Absurd as it may seem, unauthorized pop music really is a threat to Bolshevik regimes. This is because music is the medium through which successive generations of young people in modern urban society work out their own identity through a kind of expressive experimentation. With the dissolution of traditional forms in a society, this kind of experimentation becomes a vital need, because each group of young people, no longer stepping into a millenially-sanctioned identity, has no choice but to work out its own.'[13]

This, we note, is taking place in a country where performance standards in the symphonic, operatic and chamber repertory, and even the avant garde, all generously subsidized, are as high as anywhere in the world. The capitalist sector, of course, has its own ways of dealing with these problems.

The point at which the conflict of values in industrial societies surfaces most sharply is the school system. In schools, as we know, it is classical musicking that is recognized and encouraged, and it is in schools that the primary selection takes place which labels children, according to the criteria of classical music, as either musical or unmusical. Those pupils who accept the values of the school will also be likely to accept the valuation placed upon themselves as well as that placed upon different kinds of musicking; thus we find quite frequently that young adults who are accustomed to listening to, criticizing and even performing in the Afro-American tradition will nonetheless consider themselves unmusical, even 'tone-deaf' (whatever that might be) as a consequence of their experiences in school music. It requires an act of conscious rejection of the school's verdict, and thus of the values of the school, before young people are able to affirm what is assumed in the Afro-American tradition: that everyone is born with the gift of music, no less than with the gift of speech. The very rampant commercialism of which the Afro-American culture is often accused would be less severe if everyone were to believe him or herself capable of active participation in musicking; the schools' dereliction of duty in abandoning the majority of their charges to the mercies of those very commercial arbiters of taste whose influence they so frequently deplore is all the more reprehensible for that reason.

The conflict of values can place a teacher who does want to bring the practice of Afro-American music into the school in a difficult position. Apart from frequent opposition from colleagues and superiors, the fact that examinations, those touchstones of practical worth and intellectual respectability, concern themselves exclusively with classical techniques and history compels the teacher eventually to put those who want to engage themselves seriously in the practice of music to the study of that tradition to the exclusion of the other. And since for the majority of young people it is Afro-American music which remains closest to their own concerns and feelings as they explore their relationships and their sense of identity, the result is a splitting off of all but a minority from the one opportunity they will have of exploring their own musicality and of developing their skills within the context of the school.

The teachers' dilemma is this. On the one hand, their pupils as they perform or listen to music of any kind are finding their way, as humans will if left to themselves, to forms of expression that will assist them in the formulation and articulation of values, the ordering of experience and the definition of identity. On the other, those who opt for Afro-American music are affirming values which may be very different from, and even opposed to, the official values of our society as they are expressed through the schools. Afro-American musicking does not depend on literacy, that essential tool of school, and state, socialization, nor does it require the formal instruction of compliant groups of pupils; its performance involves not stillness, isolation and abstract contemplation but movement, communality and involvement, all of which are out of place, to say the least, in the conventional school classroom. Nor can one imagine any form of examination that would not do violence to the very nature of the music act (how *would* one have awarded comparative marks to, say, Jerry Lee Lewis and Count Basie or to Charlie Parker and Louis Jordan?), not least because of the standardization which examinations by their very nature impose upon the teaching methods themselves. And standardization is death to music.

The value conflict confronts us here head on: how is it that forms of musical expression which are natural and important elements in the formation of the sense of identity of so many young people can have come to represent a threat to the values of the institution that is ostensibly set up to serve them? The only answer to that question which makes any sense lies in the acknowledgement that our school system exists today, not to serve the interests of its pupils at all, but rather to serve the interests of the industrial state, and its masters, in which those pupils will become workers, soldiers, managers, bureaucrats, scientists and political leaders — and members of the seemingly permanent pool of workless. To say this, of course, is not to deny the efforts of many teachers who do genuinely attempt to serve the interests of their pupils as they see them; but the objectives of the state, expressed through examinations, have in the long run to take precedence. It is the classical-music culture which, as we have seen, fits best with those objectives.

We note a further striking coincidence of values; in accepting or rejecting the school's definition of musicality one accepts or rejects much else not only in the school's system of values but also in industrial society as a whole. Such a statement is far too cut-and-dried to match the extraordinary variety of human feelings and actions, of accommodations and compromises with the prevailing values, and of those contradictions which we all carry within us, but it contains enough truth to make it useful. In his perceptive book *Profane Culture*, Paul Willis discusses the way in which bike boys use motor bikes and records of 1950s rock'n'roll to create from 'the plastic ersatz and the detritus of the bourgeoisie' a culture which gives meaning to their lives through values which are opposed to bourgeois notions of time, causality and hierarchy, and yet,

> 'Although they had mastered a technology for their leisure and pioneered embryonic forms — or developed and made explicit working-class themes — of living with technology, they made no attempt to apply these insights to their working situation. They did not make demands, or pioneer changes there for more humanized systems of work — or even see the connection between technology in their leisure and the most massive technology of all: machinery and work. Not only this, but they uncritically accepted the current organization of production and their lowly place within it as well as the legitimacy of a whole range of other institutions — though making, of course, their own local and creative adaptations — which maintain and reproduce society in its present form, and which ultimately outlawed or displaced their own culture.'[14]

Nevertheless, says Willis, 'their profane acid scaled off the pretences and illusions of the bourgeois order and allowed new production in their own cultural fields to penetrate through and show the possibility of the revolutionary in the small, detailed and everyday.'[15]

Afro-American musicking was, as we have seen, first developed by musicians who were in any formal sense unschooled and, in the overwhelming majority, non-literate, as well as of the lowest social status, whether black or white. We have seen that this lowly position was not without its advantages; even today, while there has been a considerable admixture of influences from schooled and literate music, those advantages, along with the social disadvantages, remain.

It is the very openness of Afro-American music today which still, even in its most skilled and elevated forms such as jazz, allows anyone, no matter what their level of skill or formal training (and many Afro-American musicians have, of course, received formal training, often to a high level), to begin playing and to do the best they can with what they have, untrammelled by notions of status or formal correctness. Of course, like speech, all musicking has its rules and conventions, without which no communication, and in all probability not even any thinking, can take place, and these rules must be learnt by the performer and the listener, but, like the rules of speech, they are learnt by doing, and absorbed without conscious thought.

To sum up, one might say that to take part in a classical-music performance is to affirm and celebrate, whether or not one is aware of it, the values and the relationships which underpin and validate the society of the modern industrial state, while a performance in the Afro-American tradition is always *to some degree* subversive, either explicitly or by implication, of those values and relationships. Both of those statements are full of contradictions and overlaps of values, and there is nothing to stop any performer or listener from taking part in performances of both kinds, but nonetheless the tendency is there.

Not all Afro-American musicking is clear-cut in its opposition to the values of classical music and of industrial society; we shall see later how jazz, in particular, has derived much of its creative energy from the fact that it is a field where these two sets of values are debated. But all Afro-American musicking, being the child of the encounter between the two great cultures, partakes of the nature of both while, like all offspring, not being the same as either of its parents. Let us now look at the further development of secular musicking by black Americans.

NOTES

1. NISSEL, Muriel: *Facts About the Arts: A Summary of Available Statistics*, London, Policy Studies Institute, 1983, p 23.
2. CANNADINE, David: 'The Context, Performance and Meaning of Ritual: The British Monarchy and the "Invention of Tradition", c. 1820–1977', in HOBSBAWM, Eric and RANGER, Terence: *The Invention of Tradition*, Cambridge, Cambridge University Press, 1983, p 136.
3. LEVINE, Fay: *The Culture Barons: An Analysis of Power and Money in the Arts*, New York, Thomas Y. Crowell Co., 1976, p 27.
4. SMALL, Christopher: *Treasuring the Creative Act*, Address to the A.G.M. of the Composers' Guild of Great Britain, 5 April, 1984.
5. BENSON, A.C.: *Land of Hope and Glory*, London, Novello, 1902.
6. 'The Proms' Hope and Glory', *Sunday Times*, 12 September, 1982.
7. BERGER, John: *Ways of Seeing*, London, British Broadcasting Corporation and Penguin Books, 1972, p 104.
8. MALATESTA, Enrico: *Anarchy* (1891), transl. by Vernon Richards, London, Freedom Press, 1974, p 20.
9. CHASE, Gilbert: *America's Music*, New York, McGraw-Hill, 2nd edition 1966, p 660.
10. MALONE, Bill C.: 'Honky Tonk: The Music of the Southern Working Class', in FERRIS, William and HART, Mary L. (eds): *Folk Music and Modern Sound*, Jackson, University Press of Mississippi, 1982, p 126.
11. FULWELL, Pete: *Dancing in the Rubble*, feature broadcast on BBC Radio 4, Sunday 16 January, 1983.
12. BRANSON, Richard, on programme *My Britain*, Channel 4 TV, 9 February, 1986.
13. TAYLOR, Charles: 'There is a hidden psychic cost involved in having constantly to play one's part in a systematic lie', *New Statesman*, 6 July, 1979, p 14.
14. WILLIS, Paul: *Profane Culture*, London, Routledge & Kegan Paul, 1978, p 177.
15. *ibid.* p 182.

Chapter 7

RITUALS FOR SURVIVAL II: THE SHEER POWER OF SONG

It has been said that if gospel is the present-day paradigm of Afro-American religious musicking, so blues is of secular. It would be more true to say that blues and gospel are twin modern aspects of that ritual of survival which is the musical act, and that they have not only interpenetrated but also proved an inexhaustible source of inspiration to several generations of musicians both black and white. Further, while we have seen that there is a good deal of quite secular enjoyment in the performance of both spirituals and gospel music, so in blues, and indeed in other 'secular' performance as well, there is a strong element of what can only be called the religious, even if it is not obvious to the casual observer.

But in any case blues is a comparative newcomer to the scene, and its dominance is even more recent. It is hard to say just when the modern form took shape; certainly it could not have been before the last years of the nineteenth century, and even until well into the present one it represented only one of many ways of musicking in which black American musicians and their audiences engaged. Even in the days of slavery there had been a wide variety of musical activity; central to the musical culture may have been the hymns and spirituals, but religious emotions did not prevent the majority of the slaves from engaging in other kinds of musicking as well. Work songs, play songs, songs of love and of parting, songs of commentary on events, of abuse and satire, were mostly spontaneously composed and often lasted only as long as the occasion of their singing — 'as varied', says Levine, 'as narrow, as fleeting, as life itself'.[1] Many contemporary commentators remarked on the slaves' ability to make a song about an occasion, not only to celebrate or to lament but also to tell their masters or other white hearers of their needs and desires, to hint or to beseech.

The words of many of these songs have come down to us through the notations of interested auditors, but the melodies can only be imagined. As with improvised musicking in general, probably little was made up from scratch, the performance evolving through the manipulation of scraps of common-stock material whose provenance would itself be various: long memories of African song, minstrel tunes, hymn tunes, dance tunes, popular songs of the time, all transformed and unified by the singers' synthesising power. Not all of the songs thus made were transient; if it were enjoyed, a song would continue to be sung for as long as it suited the expressive purposes of the singers, but since those purposes themselves were mostly transient, secular songs tended not to last as long as the spirituals, built as the latter were around more abiding concerns. There were exceptions; one ex-slave remembered what she called 'one of the saddest songs we sung en durin' slavery days . . . It always did make me cry:

> Mammy, is Ol' Mass gwin'er sell us tomorrow?
> Yes my chile.
> Whar he gwin'er sell us?
> Way down South in Georgia'.[2]

It was not all song. Instrumental music was also plentiful. There were instruments that had been brought, either physically or in the slaves' minds, from Africa, like the balafo, which Richard Lygon saw the slave Macow building, and the panpipes ('quills'), the musical bow and the banjo as well as other kinds of stringed instruments, but there were also European fiddles, horns, clarinets and guitars which masters often gave to certain slaves and even had them instructed in for performance. These were played mostly for dancing, both for the masters' enjoyment — quadrilles, reels and waltzes, as well as the grand marches that were an important element of any dance occasion — and for the slaves' own dancing. Under those circumstances it was only to be expected that a good deal of traffic in dance tunes and dance styles would take place, especially as the slaves enjoyed parodying the whites' dances (the whites, it seems, tended to think their mockery was a feeble attempt at imitation and laughed indulgently).

We might imagine that a slave musician would feel a certain satisfaction in seeing his masters dancing to his tunes — and perhaps as the evening wore on and inhibitions wore off he might introduce more African-sounding strains to make the dance go with a greater swing. There are indeed hints from contemporary sources that this did occur, and was tacitly approved by the gentry; a dance known as the Congo was popular in polite society in Richmond, Virginia in colonial times, although it is doubtful whether it was quite the same as the famous Dance in Place Congo in New Orleans that was known by that name. It is clear that a complex process of interaction was going on, with the white dances and their music passing into the slaves' culture and becoming Africanized as they did so, while the black elements became part of the white culture, all unacknowledged or else safely distanced by the minstrelizing process.

The minstrel show itself was a medium through which black ways of musicking and dancing passed back and forth between the two groups. To take only one example, the song and dance of the old crippled Louisville stablehand that Thomas Rice observed and 'borrowed' would have been in its original form an improvisation; taken and used in the minstrel show it became fixed in both words and music (seen in print it appears an extraordinarily banal tune, but doubtless the manner of performance counted for much) and became famous with its nonsense verses, such as

> I'm a rorer on de fiddle
> And down in old Virginny
> Dey say I play de skientific
> Like massa Pagganninny

and its chorus of

> Weel about and turn about and do jus so,
> Eb'ry time I weel about I jump Jim Crow

which was taken up by blacks and, according to Levine, was to be heard as late as 1915 in North Carolina as

> Fust upon yo' heel-top, den upon yo' toe
> Ev'ry time I turn about I jump Jim Crow.[3]

This was doubtless only one of dozens of variants which might have been heard across the country from black singers and dancers. Similarly, fiddle tunes and jigs such as *Old Zip Coon* and *Old Dan Tucker*, some of them quite likely Irish or Scottish in original provenance, passed back and forth, the only differences being in manner of performance.

How many of the slave musicians were able to read music is unclear (mention of playing 'by note' is virtually non-existent) but from the seventeenth century onwards, for example in the London collections of Playford and of Thompson, there were plenty of printed sources of dance music available which could satisfy the needs of the colonial society. Many of the black musicians were highly accomplished and were quite probably able to read from those collections as well as from others which from the late eighteenth century onwards were printed in America. How these skills were acquired is something of a mystery. There are hints that some slaves were apprenticed out by their masters for training, and there was a fraternity of music and dancing masters who travelled between the great houses of the south, spending a few days here, a few there, teaching music to the sons and daughters of the family; as in Europe, a smattering of musical skill enhanced the marriageability of a daughter, even if, as was commonly the case, she were to abandon it completely once the objective was achieved. Slavemasters would sometimes arrange to have house servants who showed signs of talent instructed at the same time, and in the towns of the south, music was one of a number of artisan skills in which masters hired out their slaves for profit.

We shall see other examples of encounters with the European literate tradition in Chapter 9; here we need note only that black musicians have always been perfectly at home with literate music, however much they have continued to treasure their oral and improvisatory skills.

Emancipation, while it did not alter the basic social role

played by black musicians, did make substantial changes, among which were the mobility that it made possible and the necessity it imposed upon black people of making a living in a generally hostile society; for musicians, the latter was balanced by the fact that they, like other craftsmen and artisans, were able to be self-employed and to retain whatever money they made. The status of professional musicians was flexible, according to their economic and other circumstances; those who could not, or did not want to, make a living on the farm would take to the town or city streets, or move into the circle of those, often itinerant, musicians who played in the bars and juke joints that sprang up to cater for the social and entertainment needs of the newly freed slaves. On the whole, too, it was black musicians who were preferred by whites for their dance music.

These musicians were — had to be — remarkably versatile; the more kinds of social occasion for which they could make music, clearly the better living they would make. They coined terms for themselves which stuck; a skilled instrumentalist was a 'musicianer', while a singer and songmaker was a 'songster'. Most frequently, of course, they were both, and the terms seem to have alluded not so much to what they could do as to what their speciality was. They were in fact all-round entertainers, not only providing music but also calling the steps for quadrilles and square dances both black and white, telling jokes and making patter, even bringing news and gossip to often remote communities. It would not be stretching things too far to compare their role to that of the griots of West Africa. Paul Oliver says,

> 'Songsters were entertainers, providing music for every kind of social occasion in the decades before phonographs and radio. They were receptive to a wide variety of songs and music; priding themselves on their range, versatility and capacity to pick up a tune, they played not only for the black communities but for whites too, when the opportunities arose. Whatever else the songster had to provide in the way of entertainment, he was always expected to sing and play for dances. This over-riding function bound many forms of black secular song together. Social songs, comic songs, the blues and ballads, minstrel tunes and popular

> ditties all had this in common, and whether it set the time for spirited lindy-hopping or for low-down slow-dragging across a puncheon floor, the music of black secular song could always be made to serve this purpose. It was the regular beat that provided the pulse for the dance and the cross-rhythms of vocal and instrumental that inspired the shuffles, shimmies, hip-shakes and shoulder rolls.'[4]

The closeness of living of blacks and whites in the south, and the understandable overlap in sense of identity which we have already noted, made for much musical interaction, without selfconsciousness or apparent feeling of being infiltrated, between the two groups, which were in so many ways kept apart by the vicious system of racial discrimination. To the black musicianer, of course, everything was grist to his mill, as Oliver makes clear; what was taken by higher-class white culture, on the other hand, was much more selected and, in general, only what could be rendered innocuous. As Roger Abrahams says: 'Negro cultural vitality throughout the American experience, has provided for whites motives of both fascination and dread, a fund of stylized activity on which to draw — and to draw back from. Thus, there have been certain song and dance forms which have been listened to, appreciated and imitated, while there have been other musical expressions regarded by a great majority of whites as too primal, too earthy, to imitate'.[5] Among the latter has been, until comparatively recently, the blues, for while, as we have seen, blues passed easily across the colour line at the lower end of the social spectrum, it became part of the culture of whites generally only by virtue of initially quite conscious acts of rebellion by white musicians against the values of European and Euro-American music.

Even for black musicians blues has never formed the whole of their repertoire. Jeff Todd Titon tells us that the history of two musicians, Carl Martin and Ted Bogan, who

> 'grew up just outside Knoxville, Tennessee, learning the old-fashioned, East Coast string band style, and then decided to improve, is typical of many downhome musicians who migrated to the cities. Wanting a full-time career in music, they rightly observed that the more

versatile they became the more work they would get. At first they travelled through the region, even venturing into Ohio and Michigan, playing for picnics, dances, Rotary Club suppers and the like, for white as well as black audiences. After they learned to read music and acquired "fake books" which contained lyrics, melodies and guitar chords to current popular songs, they could play practically any request. Martin proudly explained, "If you asked me a request today and I didn't know it I'd go get the sheet music tomorrow and learn it so I wouldn't be caught the next time". After 1933 they made their home in Chicago and learned the songs of various ethnic groups — Polish, Italian, German — so they could play at weddings and parties'.[6]

The appearance of specialization by blues musicians is largely a result of record company policies. As Titon says elsewhere, musicians 'did not record their whole repertoires, as a rule, because company officials did not want them to. As late as the early 1940s, when Brownie McGhee asked to record some of the hillbilly songs he regularly performed, he was told that it was not "his kind of music" . . . Record companies wanted blues, for blues sold. If they needed hillbilly music, they might as well turn to hillbillies.'

In its original sense, the word 'blues' refers to feelings of unaccountable and pervasive depression, and in this sense it is of quite old English usage. That such depression should have been common among black Americans in the period after the failure of the great hopes engendered by Emancipation is scarcely surprising, and the first thing we have to understand about the blues as a style of musicking is that it is not just 'about' the blues as a state of mind but, rather, it is a performance which, in articulating and examining that state of mind, enables those taking part in the performance to overcome, or at least to alleviate it. As James Cone has said:

'Like the spirituals, the blues affirms the somebodiness of black people, and they preserve the worth of black humanity through ritual and drama. The blues is the transformation of black life through the sheer power of song. They symbolize the solidarity, the attitudes and the identity of the black community and thus create the

> emotional forms of reference for endurance and for artistic appreciation. In this sense, the blues are that stoic feeling that recognizes the painfulness of the present but refuses to surrender to its historical contradictions'.[8]

The blues, then, represents the continuation of that resistance of black people to spiritual annihilation which was at the centre of all their artistic activity from the first days of slavery.

The second thing that we must understand is that the blues consists essentially of performance, or, to be more exact, a style of performance. I have emphasised throughout this book the necessity, if we are to understand the nature of music, of looking at the performance act rather than at the music object; nowhere is this necessity more obvious than when considering the blues. And, further, as the word 'style' implies, blues consists of a disciplined performance, far more than its apparently spontaneous nature reveals to the casual observer. Albert Murray says: 'One of its most distinctive features . . . is its unique combination of spontaneity, improvisation and control. Sensual abandon is, like over indulgence in alcohol and drugs, only another kind of disintegration. Blues-idiom dance movement, being always a matter of elegance, is necessarily a matter of getting oneself together.'[9] For blues performance, like all Afro-American musicking, is intimately bound up with dance; the conventional image of the aged sharecropper sitting on his front porch bent over a guitar and singing about his woes represents the exception rather than the rule.

The blues style of performance, which pervades almost the whole of the Afro-American tradition as a colour, an emotional tinge, has also given rise to a poetic and musical form, which is to say a definitive way of organizing a performance, of simplicity, clarity and seemingly infinite adaptability. It is essentially an oral form, often improvised and passed on by ear, and thus much of its early history is obscure or lost; by the time the first recordings were made, in 1920, the 'classic' form had already become crystallized. But even today, older and less formally-organized kinds of blues performance persist, especially in the rural south, and most especially in that area of Mississippi State between the Yazoo and Mississippi Rivers that is known as the Delta. Let us start, however, by examining the classic form, as it has been sung, played and danced to since the early years of this century in the black ghettos of American cities, and by professional performers across the United States and, later, the world.

The verses sung by the blues performer consist of a succession of rhyming couplets, with the first line repeated, making three lines to a stanza. Each of these stanzas stands independently, not as part of a narrative sequence as in a ballad; indeed, it is rare for a blues performance to tell a story. Rather, it develops a theme in a rambling and allusive way, which may have to do with the singer's poverty, disease, imprisonment, loneliness, lover's infidelity, even bedbugs or the boll weevil (twin entomological associates of black poverty). Other common topics are sexual invitation, sexual satisfaction or the lack of it, often expressed in cunning *doubles-entendres,* or in so direct a manner as to call forth frequent accusations of obscenity. All these and similar topics arise directly from the experience of black Americans during those years of hope, betrayal and oppression that followed Emancipation (there are blues dealing directly with that subject too, but, not unnaturally, they were never sung before whites and so went unrecorded and unheard outside the black communities). Simply reading the poetry of the blues transcribed, in the absence of performance, often gives the impression that the artist was more or less destitute, had no stable family life and had to keep on the move, could count on the help and fidelity of no-one, had no faith in the consolations of religion, and was at the mercy of the slightest breeze of fate (which might however, from time to time blow the artist raunchy episodes of sexuality). But although the verses concern themselves with bad times and depression (many of them even apostrophize the depressed feelings themselves, sometimes as 'Mr Blues'), the tone is anything but depressing, and certainly lacks anything resembling self-pity or sentimentality; instead they are pervaded with a tough-minded, if fatalistic, will to survive and a wry, often self-mocking, humour which is often illuminated by striking images, metaphors and flashes of wit.

The form in which the blues performance is cast relates to

the orality and the improvised nature of the art; the repeated first line can give the singer time to think of a punch-line, while the absence of narrative thread gives a freedom to the improvising artist, allowing him or her not only to insert lines and even whole stanzas from any number of sources but also to shape the performance, in the time-honoured African and Afro-American way, as the social situation develops between singer and listeners. For this reason, too, we find a good deal of common-stock material which can be drawn on by all singers, making the art accessible to all; the greatly gifted artist can invent new material, still drawing on the common stock and thus remaining in touch with his listeners' expectations, while the less endowed can permutate existing material to make something that embodies his or her feelings.

When printed on the page the verses often seem to make nonsense of scansion, but this is a consequence of writing them down; the singer uses considerable rhythmic ingenuity to make them fit into the number of beats available, without even appearing to consider consciously the 'correct' number of syllables. And of course the ability to make an apparently 'wrong' move in an improvisation come out right, confounding in a witty or dramatic way the expectations of listeners, is a persistent feature of improvised art which black musicians from country blues singers to sophisticated professionals like Charlie Parker have never failed to exploit.

In discussing the musical framework in which the blues performer operates, we are obliged to use musical terminology derived from the European literate tradition which never was part of the thinking of those among whom the style originated. Further, the performer feels those procedures, not as a fixed framework in which he has to work, but rather as a support around which the creative act can take place; he does not feel obliged to observe more than approximately the number of bars and the precise chord sequence. These, however, are *our* difficulties, not *his*, and I mention them here only to remind us of the need for caution in any description of the way in which that artistic process known as the blues operates.

The classic blues performance allies each stanza to twelve bars (four to each of the three lines) of music, each sung line occupying the first two bars of each four, with a reply from the accompanying instrument filling up the remainder. The harmonic scheme which underpins and propels the melody is simple, being based on the three primary triads of European classical harmony, with one harmonic cycle (tonic — subdominant — tonic — dominant — tonic) to a stanza and unvarying from stanza to stanza, almost banal in its simplicity.

Much, most of it speculative without much hard evidence to go on, has been written about the survival in the blues of elements of African music. There does not seem to be much in the way of specific techniques to which one can point; rather, it is a matter, as I suggested earlier, of attitudes towards the act of performance. I shall discuss later the performer's relation to the listeners, which is close and intimate, but we can note here that the relationship between the performer and his instrument is also interesting. The instrument is too much like a second voice to allow us to call it merely accompaniment; this second voice seems to work in a way which reminds us more of African call-and-response procedures than of European concepts of melody and accompaniment, while the way the instrument imitates the vocal sounds suggests a concept of polyphony which may have descended from West African techniqes.

On the other hand, it is obvious that the harmonic scheme within which the blues musician plays is wholly European in origin; African musicians simply do not think in this way. The European ear can, it is true, hear quite clearly what we might call a harmonic progression of triads when Shona musicians of Zimbabwe play the *mbira dzavadzimu*, and, as in blues, the progressions are cyclic — but any attempt to discover an historical connection between Zimbabwe and modern black America would seem merely foolish. The use of harmonic progressions in blues differs from that in European classical music in the way the simple cycle of chords repeats itself endlessly for as long as the performance lasts, without variation, change of key, or any of that sense of rising to a climax and resolution to which we are accustomed in harmonic music. An essential element in harmonic music is surprise, which creates drama, the unexpected chord which is shown to be in a logical or syntactical relationship with those preceding it. But in blues performance, since what we expect to happen, harmonically speaking, always does happen, it is clear that blues harmony is lacking in all those features which makes harmonic music harmonically interesting. The interest of blues lies elsewhere than in the harmony; for the musician who is playing and singing blues, harmony is only a kind of underpinning for what really interests him, which is the melodic and rhythmic invention, as well as the inflections of vocal and instrumental sounds.

This conclusion accords with our knowledge that most early musicians who played and sang blues, the musicianers and songsters of whom I wrote earlier, were in the formal sense unschooled, having picked up their vocal, instrumental and improvisatory skills (which were often considerable) where they could, mostly from other musicians whom they would imitate before striking out on their own to the limits of their own skills and inventiveness. They would certainly not have had in their minds the harmonic terminology of classical music, let alone the harmonic scheme which is often set out diagrammatically in books on blues; those are after-the-fact rationalizations by schooled musicians and of use only to them. Many of the old musicians in fact got by perfectly well by simply strumming one chord on a guitar which had been tuned, as likely as not, not in the 'regular' manner but to a major or minor triad or seventh chord. How and when the particular sequence of chords which all of us know so well, even if we cannot put a name to them, came to crystallize is not clear, since they were already in use when the first recordings were made, but it probably derives from the harmonies of hymn tunes; in any case, one can only marvel at the satisfying simplicity and clarity which has kept it alive for perhaps close on a century and looks like continuing to do so for the foreseeable future.

Apart from its origins, then, the harmony of the blues performance is simple and unproblematic. The complexity and the mystery emerge only when we consider it in relation to the melody against which it is played. While the harmony is tonal, the melody is modal, which is to say it is not based simply on either the major or the minor diatonic scale of classical practice (here we are again using terminology that would have been alien to those who sang and played). While the harmony is conceived in relation to the diatonic major scale the singer sings certain notes of that scale, notably the third and seventh degrees, slightly flat — according to the criteria of classical music, which have no claim to absolute validity. The degree of flatting is not always such that the tones coincide with those of the minor scale; while the seventh degree approximates to the minor seventh, the third is unstable and hovers between the major and minor third (on fixed-pitch instruments such as the piano the major and minor thirds played together sometimes do duty for it). How this should have come about is something on which opinions differ, and need not concern us here, though it must have had something to do with the encounter between European and African concepts of melody. The important thing from our point of view is not only that there is a clash between tonal harmony and modal melody, but also that the distinction between major and minor modes is lost. This distinction, which has such significant dramatic function in classical music, where major equals bright, relaxed and happy while minor equals tense, clouded and sad, does not apply to the ambiguous emotional atmosphere of blues. In addition, the use of flatted, or 'blue' thirds in melody against major thirds in harmony favours the formation of chords of the seventh, which very early, and certainly by the time of the first blues recordings, were functioning as consonances in their own right, so that it was even possible to end a performance with a dominant-seventh chord built on the tonic (the old 'good-evening-friends' formula, for example). This emphasis on seventh chords rather than triads was an important factor in the development of harmony in blues, and, later, jazz, while the clash between major and blue thirds and sevenths accustomed the ears of musicians and their listeners to sharper dissonances, all of which were used cheerfully as if they were consonances. It is the tension between melody and harmony which is the source of much of the musical energy of both blues and jazz.

So much for theory. The important point to be grasped is that harmony in Afro-American music serves both a different and a lesser role than in European classical music, and its derivatives. The differences from classical procedures are twofold: first, the musician does his thinking on his feet rather than in his study (his performance is a series of exciting and daring *acts* rather than an exciting and daring *thing*) and, secondly, he tends, as we have seen, not to adopt any musical means which will commit him to proceed in a preordained way regardless of the effect on the listeners or on the event for which they have come together. Hence, the large-scale harmonic planning which is a principal glory of the European classical tradition is only an impediment to the improvising musician.

Blues is primarily a vocal art; the human voice is always paramount and the paradigm of blues sound is vocal, even when it is transferred to instruments. It is usually solo vocal, accompanied in its early stages by a single instrument, usually a guitar or piano played by the singer, or else by a small instrumental group. The blues singer is usually far less restricted in terms of pitch inflection than a classical singer, feeling free to approach a tone from above or below, to tail off in pitch towards the end of a note, to use any number of different kinds of vibrato, as well as falsetto, grunts, yodels, yells, complex colourings of tone, and abrupt shifts of register, which are featured prominently instead of being smoothed over as with the classical singer. The blues singer has all these ways of singing in common with the gospel singer; the difference between them lies in the relative lack of emotional involvement which the blues singer projects by comparison with the gospel singer. It is only in more recent years that some of the vocal techniques of gospel singers have also become part of the armoury of blues singers. Blues musicians cultivate an individual sound, so that even if they play or sing only a single phrase, Robert Johnson, Muddy Waters, Louis Armstrong, Bessie Smith or Charlie Parker are instantly recognizable. This is not because of primitive or unsophisticated technique, since all of these were highly cultured virtuosi, well in command of what they were doing, but because of a stylistic feature to be found throughout the Afro-American tradition; it is the paradoxical consequence of the musician having been steeped in the idiom, which is the musical expression of the community, to which his or her primary loyalty is given. 'Unlike that of his western contemporaries,' as Charles Keil has said, 'his [the bluesman's] first obligation is to his public rather than to a private muse.'[10]

Not only individual but also regional differences between singers have been noted. In the south of the United States, for example, three separate regional styles, each with its own manner of voice production, guitar playing and harmonic development, have been defined by scholars; collectively those styles, which probably originated in rural areas, later being picked up by songsters and musicianers, are known as country, or downhome, blues. They must have been carried around the south by those musicianers and songsters, who were frequently wanderers, often blind (music was one of the few occupations in which a blind black man could earn a living), who crisscrossed their areas, singing, playing and moving on. The impression one gets is of men who stand slightly aside from the community, articulating and putting into order communal feelings, themselves forming a fraternity of travellers, who might fall in with one another, travel together for a while, then go their separate ways, but always listening to, learning from and influencing one another. Some of them might join with travelling medicine shows, or the tent vaudeville shows that crossed and recrossed the south on their circuits, performing not only blues but also popular songs, ballads and anything else that might please an audience, but giving a blues colouring to other material as well.

It was through these songsters that the blues entered a second phase of its existence, as female singers in the travelling shows, whose basic repertory consisted of popular songs, and whose business it was to project an image of glamour and elegance, heard the blues and took them into their repertory. The most famous of these were Gertrude 'Ma' Rainey and Bessie Smith, but there were many others, often of great distinction, and their blues singing was infused with the techniques of the popular singer and with some of the fizz and synthetic sparkle of showbiz. With a few exceptions, among whom was the magnificent Minnie Douglas McCoy ('Memphis Minnie'), of whom it was said that she sang and played guitar like a man, they relied for accompaniment and support on the show's band. This had two results; first that the blues form became fixed in the three-line, twelve-bar form so familiar today, which gave a firm basis for group improvisation, and secondly, that many of the instrumentalists, who were later to become well known as jazz performers, absorbed into their blood the techniques and the spirit of the blues. It was in 1920, in New York, that Mamie Smith made the first recordings of black music by a black artist, and the success of her recordings encouraged further records, so that it was these 'classic' female blues singers who, through their records and through their appearances on the theatre circuits, were the first to impinge on the awareness of a wider public. Their art mostly did not survive the depression years; by the late 1930s most of the theatres in which they sang were closed and the circuits disbanded.

Billie Holiday is not generally remembered as a blues singer, despite the catchphrase 'Lady sings the blues', but in New York in late 1956 she did record on video a performance that shows her to have been possibly the last of the great classic blues singers. Surrounded by some of the finest jazz players of the time, including Lester Young, Coleman Hawkins and Gerry Mulligan, she sings her own blues *Fine and Mellow* in a way which demonstrates not only her mastery of the idiom and the total authority of one who has lived what she sings about, but also the power that a blues performance has to draw those taking part (we are told the performance was recorded unrehearsed) into an intimate and loving relationship. Indeed, such is the obvious mutual affection and respect between the performers, audible in every note and visible in every gesture, that one might feel an intruder were it not that the performers themselves, through their very act of performance, invite us to enter the society they have created. There is, in particular, no trace in this performance of the tragic and self-destructive figure of popular representation; we see only a woman in perfect and effortless command of herself, who is maturing into physical beauty and vocal powers beyond anything in her earlier life; one wonders to what extent the forces which were to destroy her less than three years later were inside her, as we have been led to believe, and to what extent they were in the environment she was forced to inhabit. In any case, we have, preserved in that grainy monochrome video, a performance which explores, affirms and celebrates, subtly, comprehensively and with authority, a society which is held together by mutual love and respect, heartbreaking and heartening in its human fragility and strength.

The third phase of the blues originated in the mass migration of black people to the north in the years after 1915, when the first world war cut off the flow of immigrants from Europe and at the same time created an enormous demand for labour in the factories of the northern cities. The black populations of cities like Chicago, Detroit, Gary, Cincinnati and Cleveland, as well as New York, increased anything up to five- and even seven-fold between 1910 and 1925. The immigrants from the south were crowded into tenements and shacks in the worst parts of those cities, often without proper sanitation or other civic services, while the bitter cold of the northern winters contrasted brutally with the milder climate of the south, even if the racial climate was less extreme (less extreme, but by no means mild or even temperate, for the forms of racism of the north, where contacts between the races were less frequent than in the south, led to the creation of a ghetto mentality on both sides of the racial divide). Nevertheless, although confined to ghettos, able to obtain only the more insecure or menial forms of employment, subject from time to time to devastating outbreaks of racial violence, blacks organized tirelessly and fought for the improvement of their conditions against a political system that was stacked against them and which manipulated shamelessly the ethnic tensions of the big cities. They still felt that on the whole they were better off than in the south; money, at least until the Great Crash of 1929, was more plentiful and it was possible to maintain a measure of dignity and independence. But it was not easy, and the sense of identity and community was fragile; there can be no doubt that the churches played an important part in keeping disintegration at bay by providing a focus for that identity, but more secular forms of coming-together, often strongly disapproved by the churches, were no less functional.

One of the principal forms of community entertainment was the rent party, in which each guest paid a small admittance fee and either brought his or her own liquor or bought it from the host (the passing in 1920 of the Eighteenth Amendment to the Constitution made the liquor trade more rather than less profitable). The money went to paying rent, as well as to paying the indispensable musician, usually a pianist, whose music was not just for listening to but for dancing; the pianists, themselves often immigrants from the south, had early learnt how to adapt the blues sequences to their instrument, with heavy walking or rolling basses and endless variations in the right hand. It was Pine Top Smith who is said to have first coined the term 'boogie-woogie' for this style (we should note that he used it as a verb, to refer to a way of dancing to the music) and it was his record *Pine Top's Boogie Woogie* that sparked off the craze for this style. Other pianists followed; among those who became famous in the style were his friends Albert Ammons and Meade 'Lux' Lewis (Pine Top himself had the misfortune to be caught in the crossfire of a gangsters' shootout in the club where he was playing and was killed). The piano was also used for a quieter, more introspective blues, made famous most of all by Leroy Carr, who worked with the guitarist Scrapper Blackwell, in a memorable duo that was a powerful influence on the urban blues of the 1930s. They all sang, of course, as well as played.

The rapid expansion of the black populations of the large cities, and their accession to a modest degree of prosperity, brought with it the opening of hundreds of night spots — clubs, theatres and dance halls — where people went to dance and to consume bootleg liquor. The criminalization of the act of drinking alcoholic liquor seem to have brought together people from various social classes, linked together, no doubt, by the fact that there were all breaking the law; as the jazzman Mezz Mezzrow wrote later: 'It struck me funny how the top and bottom crusts in society were always getting together during the Prohibition era.'[11] This state of affairs in turn meant that opportunities for employment for musicians both black and white were enlarged in order to satisfy the demand for more and more dance music. The white socialites and gangsters danced to the music of the big white bands into whose performances traces of jazz were creeping, or to the black jazz bands, in whose repertoires blues featured to various degrees, but for those blacks who could afford a night out, it was blues clubs. The small blues bands expanded into larger combinations, always with their shouting singers (they had to shout, in those days before amplification, just to make themselves heard). This variety of urban blues had the rawness, the harshness that one might expect in the harsh urban environment which the musicians and their audiences inhabited. They sang and played in a way not unlike country blues singers of the south, not surprisingly since many of them had come from there, either directly or via the cities of Atlanta, St Louis or Kansas City. The instrumental sound might have had a greater sophistication, but the singers remained, as they had always been, rough and earthy. More and more, in playing for dancers who were out for a good time, they placed a heavier emphasis on noisy and exhilarating reed and brass sections and on rhythm sections able to pound out a heavy and emphatic dancing beat.

It was this generation of black musicians, too, in the late 1930s and early 1940s, who learned the potential of the amplified guitar, first developed as a way of making the small-voiced instrument function more effectively in a noisy environment; they soon realized that when you apply amplification what you get is not just a louder guitar but an altogether different kind of instrument, with a hugely lengthened decay time, making it to all intents and purposes another horn, but with a sharp and percussive onset sound. Likewise, they played the horns themselves, notably the saxophones, with an increased, even crude, intensity never heard before.

The occasional black blues artist did find wider fame; Louis Jordan with his Tympany Five attained massive popular successes in the mid-1940s with their crisp, infectious rhythms and lyrics whose 'black' content made no concessions to white tastes. I still remember from my teens the impact made by *Caldonia* and *Is You Is Or Is You Ain't My Baby*. Neither I nor my contemporaries had the slightest idea of the provenance of all that vigour, excitement and sheer fun, but we loved it, and tried to dance to it in ways for which our staid Saturday-afternoon classes in foxtrot and quickstep had been no preparation. We could not have known, either, that what was making us dance was the first breath of a gale which would overturn the bland world of adult dance music in which we had grown up. Similarly, T-Bone Walker perfected a dazzling guitar style and an exuberant stage act to match, which was to be influential on the next generation of musicians, notably Bo Diddley and, unexpectedly, Elvis Presley. Along with a number of southerners, notably Professor Longhair, Amos Milburn and Roy Milton, these musicians were bringing into being a style of musicking that still today has lost little of its power to stir the blood and the feet, some of the most exhilarating and unabashedly *physical* musicking ever to have been played, or heard, in the west.

It was still blues, or intimately blues-based, quintessentially a music made by black Americans, which began, in the early 1950s, to 'cross over' into the musical consciousness of large numbers of white Americans. For reasons into which I shall go later, the record companies which at that time began to exploit it for the wider, mainly white, 'crossover' market rechristened it rhythm-and-blues, a not inappropriate name, perhaps, but one which was meant to neutralize the significance of its origins in the black community. I shall consider the career of rhythm-and-blues later. Let us stop for a moment now to consider the meaning of this way of musicking called the blues, keeping in mind always that musical meaning resides in the act of performance and in the kinds of relationship that are established among the participants by that act.

Common to all blues performances, whether by labourers or sharecroppers in the rural south gathered over cans of beer and exchanging comments and stories between songs, or by highly professional artists like Bessie Smith, B.B. King or Muddy Waters singing to a paying audience in a club or theatre, is the cultivation of a close and personal relationship with the listeners, who, by their audible and visible responses help to shape the course of the performance. Here, for instance, is an account by Michael Haralambos of the start of a performance by Albert King in a large black blues club in Chicago in 1968: '"We're here until three," shouts Albert after the opening number, an up-tempo instrumental. "We're with you," shout back several members of the audience. Albert peers from the brightly-lit stage. "There's some missing," he says. "We're all here," shout back two or three people from one table. "Yeah," shout back several others, reinforcing this response. Albert begins by setting the tone of the evening, the mutual support and empathy of performer and audience enmeshed in the ritual of a modern urban blues performance.'[12]

Albert King, like other professional blues singers, is not a poor man, nor does he make any attempt to project an image of poverty — quite the reverse, with his expensive suits, his excellent backing band and his confident, even a touch arrogant, stage demeanour. This is not new; the classic blues singers of the twenties projected images of style and glamour (Bessie Smith was not dubbed 'The Empress of the Blues' for nothing) even when they sang of bedbugs and of faithless lovers. Nor is the audience there in order to take part in a lament for their lot; they are there for a good night out, to dance and enjoy themselves. As with all participants in all musical performances, that enjoyment comes from the affirmation and celebration of an identity, and from the feeling of having that identity reinforced by those in whose company one is experiencing the performance. Unlike the symphony concert, in which the separateness of the individual's identity is reinforced by his or her isolation from all the others in the hall, the blues performance emphasises the communal basis of that identity. It is a realistic ritual; the singer sings about the realities of black people's experience, about the possibility of the disintegration and destruction of the individual and of the community, and does not attempt to dodge the issues, but the style of the performance tells the audience that he is not just playing the blues, but playing *with* the blues. The audience, for their part, do not just sit and listen; their shouts of encouragement and affirmation, and, above all, their dancing, all serve to reinforce the experience. 'The blues-idiom dancer,' says Albert Murray, 'like the solo instrumentalist, turns disjunctures into continuities. He is not disconcerted by intrusions, lapses, shifts in rhythm, intensifications of tempo for instance, but is inspired by them to higher and richer levels of improvisation . . . But then, impromptu heroism such as is required only of the most agile of storybook protagonists, is precisely what the blues idiom has evolved to condition Negroes to as *normal procedure*! Nor is any other attitude towards experience more appropriate to the ever-shifting circumstances of all Americans or more consistent with the predicament of man in the contemporary world at large. Indeed, the blues idiom represents a major American innovation of universal significance and potential . . . It is the product of a sensibility that is completely compatible with the *human* imperatives of modern times and modern life.'[13] A grand claim, but one that is justified by the way in which blues has been at the heart of the outward movement of Afro-American music across the whole world. The least that can be said is that it speaks to the experience not only of black Americans; after all, 'We are all,' as the hero's black lover tells him in a novel I once read, 'somebody's nigger.'

The singer's role, then, is deceptive; in identifying and exploring disintegration and other potentially destructive aspects of black American life he or she is performing an integrative function, drawing on the common experience in a ritual which brings the community closer together. Even the familiarity of so much of the verbal and musical material, drawn as it is from a common stock, is a part of that common experience and has its function in the ritual. And if we remember that the blues arose in a period of intense repression, even terrorism, by means of which black Americans were consigned, it must have seemed permanently, to the lowest ranks of American society, then we can see that the basic function of the ritual has not changed so very much from slavery days, when it was necessary to know that 'suffering was not too much to bear if there were brothers and sisters to go down into the valley with you.' The singer's role takes on many of the attributes of the priest's; as Charles Keil said: 'Bluesmen and preachers both provide models and orientations; both give public expression to privately held emotions, both promote catharsis; both increase feelings of solidarity, boost morale and strengthen the consensus.'[14]

The sense of identity is built not only into the performer-audience relationship, or even into the performer's stage demeanour, but into the very relationships between the sounds he or she makes — the way in which he or she goes about the making of music — in other words, the musical techniques themselves. The description I have given of the blues form and technique makes it clear that there is a tension between the harmony, which is built on bits and pieces of common European harmonic practice reinterpreted to serve the improvising performer's needs, and the melody. But there are more subtle ambiguities as well; the constantly changing pitch of a note, which is itself rarely arrived at directly but in a roundabout fashion, from above or below; the constant inflection of tone colour; the play that is made around the rock-steady beat, the singer being now in front of it, now behind it, now seeming to lose it, only to regain it with often breathtakingly casual virtuosity — all these devices are in antithesis to the European tradition's need for clarity, clearly audible order and precision. I shall have more to say later on the significance of blues harmony, but here we note that all these techniques of performance point to a relationship with the dominant white culture that is not only ambivalent but even slightly derisive.

It is at this point that we can see the connection between blues and gospel singing, which lies not so much in the musical techniques (though, as we have seen, there is a good deal of overlap) as in its ritual function. That similarity of function was not always recognized in the black churches, in many of which the blues was regarded, quite simply, as the Devil's music, while the bars, juke joints and clubs where it was played, sung and danced to were denounced as places of folly, lust and damnation. It was this disapproval of the irreverent secularity and frank sensuality of the blues that made acceptance difficult for those early gospel singers who borrowed much in their performance style from blues singers.

There is in the blues very little hint of genuine rebellion against the social conditions under which black Americans had to live in the early part of the present century; it has been suggested that, by helping to make the unbearable bearable it contributed to their continuing oppression, or at least to their acquiescence in that oppression. That has always seemed to me an insensitive and unimaginative suggestion, which takes no account of the real hopelessness of any form of overt rebellion in those years. What was needed, no less perhaps than in the days of slavery, was a tool for preserving the integrity of the self and of the community, and in that, it seems, blues was and, despite changes, remains effective. For despite the often lugubrious character of the poetry, whose dry humour can often escape the casual listener, a blues performance is at bottom a joyous and life-enhancing experience. Albert Murray asserts that 'the spirit of the blues moves in the opposite direction from ashes and sackcloth, self-pity, self-hatred or suicide. As a matter of fact, the dirtiest, meanest and most low-down blues are not only not depressing, they function like an instantaneous aphrodisiac!'[15]

The blues has never existed in isolation from other aspects of Afro-American musicking; its sound, its melodic mode, its tone colours, its attitude to pitch and to rhythms provide an emotional feeling, a nuance, which suffuses the whole musical culture and unites such varied musicians as Louis Armstrong, Billie Holiday, the Count Basie Orchestra, not to mention Elvis Presley, The Rolling Stones and Bruce Springsteen. We should note, however, that, while its influence has been all-persuasive, it has been part of the main stream of American vernacular culture only marginally and briefly. From its origins it has been the musicking of an underdog minority in American society, and the majority of white Americans — and Europeans for that matter — up to about 1940 and even later would most probably have been scarcely aware of its existence. It circulated mostly on records on the so-called 'race' labels which were obtainable only with difficulty by those who lived outside the black ghettos, and was tied too closely to the experience of an oppressed and patient people to be easily assimilated at that time by those who were outside that experience. It was only through those elements of blues that were subsumed into jazz that blues became available in a way that related to the experience of the white American — and European — majority.

The role of the blues performer as seer, preacher and ritual representative of the people has not only survived the changes that have taken place since the 1940s, with the growth of the black civil rights movement and the changing attitudes of black Americans, but seems even to have been enhanced. Black Americans' interest in the traditional blues has declined sharply; as Big Bill Broonzy, one of the old-time bluesmen, is reported to have said, 'Young people have forgotten how to cry the blues — now they talk and get lawyers.'[16] Interestingly enough, it is white audiences, on the club-and-college circuit in the United States and more generally in Europe, that provide a living for the dwindling band of survivors. In 1969, Paul Oliver was able to write that 'by the mid-sixties, incredibly, European blues enthusiasts had heard more blues singers in person than most of their American counterparts had done.'[17] Why white audiences in Europe and America should have so embraced the blues at a time when interest in it among black Americans was fading is a matter for speculation, but it probably has to do with a more general questioning of received European values and an admiration which is partly genuine, partly condescending, for black culture. But it had unexpected consequences, when young British musicians in the late 1950s started playing blues on their own account.

The style that was christened rhythm-and-blues, which is in essence a speeded-up, highly danceable form of band blues, was one outcome of these changes; another was that many artists around 1960 began wedding the techniques of the gospel singer to those of the blues singer to create a style that spoke more directly to the new aspirations of black Americans. The term 'soul', which emerged in the mid-1960s, was in itself a sign of the confidence of black people in their own culture (not new, but newly exposed for all to see), since it signifies those qualities of warmth, communality and emotional honesty which black people believe themselves to possess, not without reason, to the envy of whites. The three major performers who can be said to have shaped soul music were Ray Charles, Aretha Franklin and James Brown, all three of them graduates of church choirs, who wedded the techniques and often the forms of blues to those of the gospel singer and preacher, with cries, shouts and sobs, as well as the use of gospel-style backing vocal groups, and the call-and-response practices of gospel singers.

It was Ray Charles who, in 1954, took a gospel song, *My Jesus Is All The World To Me* and gave it new lyrics as *I Got a Woman*. Other singers followed suit, including those whose 'defection' from gospel I discussed earlier. But the suggestion that I made at that point may now be more clearly understood: that the distinction between the two modes of self-identification is not very great, and need not represent in any sense a betrayal of the purposes of gospel music. Michael Haralambos, for example, tells us that James Brown 'misses few opportunities to tell his fans that he knows what it's like to be black and poor "This is one cat that knows the meaning of misery. I've been up and I've been down and I know what DOWN is — it's bad," he writes in his column in *Soul*, a bi-weekly tabloid. James Brown personifies the belief that, like the blues singer, the soul singer has experienced what he is singing about. The experience of poverty and hardship and of being black is seen as an essential apprenticeship for the soul singer, and, conversely, this experience is seen to be reflected in the music itself.'[18] Brown's songs, with titles like *Say It Loud — I'm Black and I'm Proud* and *Get on the Good Foot* emphasise conventional morality and positive thinking in a secular parallel to much gospel song. Aretha Franklin also did much to shape the development of soul, singing more about personal relationships than Brown, but still emphasising moral and emotional strength and honesty. As we noted earlier, she has never quite left gospel singing, and would seem to see little conflict between the 'sacred' and the 'secular' aspects of her singing.

'By the late 1970s,' writes Robert W. Stephens, 'soul had become a catch-all term to describe all black popular music. Social conditions and the political astuteness of the black community during the 1960s had begun to effect economic change. It manifested itself in better living conditions for some, better education for others, and better job opportunities for still a few more.'[19] These changes meant, for black Americans, a movement towards the main stream of American economic life and, in particular, the adoption of many of the aspirations and ways of thinking of the majority society — a situation that has involved loss as well as gain. The tension between the aspiration towards a greater share in the economic cake and the desire, perhaps even the need, to retain an identity has resulted in sharp dichotomies within black society in the United States, taking their most extreme form in the disagreement between those who would assimilate completely into majority America and those who advocate completely separate development. To the outside observer, neither of these courses would seem to be a practical possibility, even if either were desirable. It is a cruel dilemma; the price of full assimilation into affluent America, even if the white majority would permit such a thing, would be a denial of five centuries of black history and of the ordeal and the achievements of generations such as have been suggested in this book, as well as acquiescence in an industrial philosophy to which black American culture has been, and remains antipathetic (white British have no reason to feel superior to white Americans in this, since such a dilemma is so far not even on offer to most black British). Perhaps the only real option open to both black Americans and black British is to hang on as the whole ramshackle structure of industrial society shakes itself to pieces — a situation in which their hard-won survival skills (of which music and dance are important components) would give them a distinct advantage.

The social changes, and the developing identity of black people over the last thirty years or so, have been closely mirrored in the changing musical rituals by means of which that identity has been explored and celebrated. We have to remember, once again, that black society is no more monolithic than is white; for many, the hard-won economic and social gains of the last thirty years have been largely reversed under the Reagan administration, and in any case there are still places in the United States, the Delta Region of Mississippi State for example, where many blacks have hardly felt any effect of the changes in the first place; they might well be singing the blues recorded half a century ago by Lonnie Johnson:

> People ravin' 'bout hard times, I don't know why they should,
> If some people was like me, they didn't have no money
> when times was good.[20]

Nonetheless, there can be few black Americans, whatever their present economic position, who have not felt the invigorating wind of protest that began with isolated acts like that of Mrs Rosa Parks on a Montgomery, Alabama, bus in 1955, and grew through the sit-ins and the freedom marches of the early 1960s, the Washington march of 1963 and the black power movement, to the point where today a large number of black people hold municipal, state and even federal office. Or of the spectacular success of black-owned record companies such as Motown of Detroit and Stax of Memphis, in which black artists have been for the first time allowed both the freedom and the resources to develop their own style of performance, or of black artists who since the 1950s have attained to superstar wealth and fame. How much has really changed, especially in terms of real economic power, which is what always counts in the long run, is a matter for debate, and the brutality with which many gains have been reversed in recent years shows the fragility of black social advances; but what is probably irreversible is the refusal of black Americans to acquiesce in their being defined by others in accordance with other people's norms, and the positive assertion of the validity of their own self-definition, which is to say their own culture. But that the fight for self-definition is by no means yet won, can be seen from the history of soul music since the 1960s.

Michael Haralambos, writing in the early 1970s, details the development of soul music in parallel with that of the civil rights movement

> 'the scattered soul records from 1954 to 1960 correspond to the black struggle in those years which was intermittent and sporadic and never reached the proportions of a mass movement. The convergence of style towards soul music from 1960 to 1964 corresponds with the protest movements of the early 60s when the civil rights struggle became a mass movement. The establishment of soul music as the dominant style of black musical expression in the mid-60s correlates with the rise and development of the Black Power Movement.'[21]

Haralambos points to the use of gospel song in the civil rights movement of the early 1960s, when Mahalia Jackson, for example, sang to the 1963 Washington marchers, while demonstrators, marchers and sitters-in sang gospel songs and spirituals to affirm their defiance and to celebrate their new-found political determination. This was of course in accordance with the considerable role played by the black churches in the civil rights movement, but it suggests also a narrowing of the gap between the sacred and the secular which was an essential element in the more general affirmation of black identity. It is on this note that Haralambos ends his book:

> 'In soul music the antithesis of the styles of life that blues and gospel traditionally represented is denied. The divisions in black society that blues and gospel formerly symbolized have in music been eliminated. Reflected in soul music is the spirit and ideal, if not the reality, of black unity.'[22]

It is an attractive idea, that a soul performance brings into existence while it lasts a society in which those dissensions which have divided black people in the United States from one another have been brought to an end, and perhaps at the time when Haralambos's book was published, in the early 1970s, it might have seemed possible that a performance by James Brown or Aretha Franklin might bring about, for a moment, in a spirit of unanimity, an affirmation and a celebration of themselves in which both the sacred and the secular aspects of life were reconciled and harmonized. But even then there was musical dissension; as we have seen, the move from gospel to soul by many singers, not least by Aretha herself, was seen in some of the churches as a defection. Even the Staple Singers' 1965 soul album *Freedom Highway*, celebrating the march from Selma to Montgomery and 'dedicated to all the freedom marchers' was not universally approved.

But a more potent disruptive force that brought pressure on this unity and harmony was the crossover success of black music in general, and soul in particular, which occurred around the beginning of the 1970s. This in turn led to a greater emphasis on money values and to all the other hazards to which vernacular musicians, especially successful ones, are subject. As Robert Stephens says, 'Together, high technology and minimal black-executive input have had a deleterious effect on the continued development of soul. What was once a tradition defined by blacks and recorded on many independent labels is now directly affected by the taste of larger audiences, cost-benefit analysis and increasing dominance by the larger record companies.'[23] It is ironic that this success was due in no small measure to the efforts of Motown and Stax records, the former having launched such major stars as Diana Ross and the Supremes, Smokey Robinson and the Miracles, Martha and the Vandellas, Marvin Gaye and the young Stevie Wonder, the later Otis Redding, Wilson Pickett, Booker T and the MGs, as well as, latterly, Lionel Ritchie and the Jacksons.

Commercialism is of course one of the facts of life with which any professional musician has to live and make his or her own accommodation, and there is no reason why the musicking that takes place in a commercial environment should be poor in either concept or execution; those musicians whose names I have listed are artists of considerable achievement, to say the least, and their musicking has contributed in no small way to the self-definition of contemporary people, white no less than black. But whatever moment of synthesis there might have been, as Haralambos suggests, in the early 1970s passed quickly; the sensibility of contemporary soul music is secular — or, at least, as much so as any black music can be. As Stephens says: 'It is evident that the soul tradition conceived and developed in the 1960s no longer exists. Rather, other styles have emerged which reflect the reinterpretation of the black music aesthetic and which offer instrumental and vocal diversity. In its earliest form, soul spoke to more than purely musical ends. When examined in the context of its cultural parameters, early soul reveals the themes of unity, ethnic consciousness, self-acceptance and awareness. From this philosophical model evolved a secular tradition rooted in past practices, but modified to fit current conditions. The aesthetic governing the essence, evolution and legacy of soul was culture-specific; it celebrated blackness defined on its own terms.'[24]

Among other developments from soul are disco, which might be described as soul without soul, in which the performing musicians are reduced to the status of puppets manipulated by the producer — a mechanical music for a dehumanized age, though still, like the age itself perhaps, not without its excitements. And the way in which young black disc jockeys have taken disco and re-humanized it is the remarkable story of rap, which will have to wait for a later chapter.

But underlying all these developments remains the blues, still present, if not as a form then as a nuance, an emotional tinge, an instrumental and vocal colour and an approach to performance. Nor has the form itself by any means disappeared; it may no longer be a central medium for the affirmation of black Americans' identity (though there is a new generation of black musicians, such as Son Seals and the brilliant Taj Mahal, who continue to speak through it), but the older generation of musicians such as B.B. King and Bobby Bland still perform to sizeable audiences, these days as much white as black. And still today, any jazz musician worth his salt can play a mean blues. But, more importantly, it is blues that is the basis for the explosion of popular music since the early 1950s; not only rock'n'roll (rhythm-and-blues under yet another name) but the whole of what is known as rock is founded upon it. The line which runs from the musicianers and songsters to The Police, The Clash, David Bowie, and even Duran Duran and Boy George, may not always be clear but it is there, and strong.

NOTES

1. LEVINE, Lawrence W.: *Black Culture and Black Consciousness: Afro-American Folk Thought from Slavery to Freedom*, New York, Oxford University Press, 1977, p 19.
2. *ibid.*, p 15.
3. *ibid.*, p 22.
4. OLIVER, Paul: *Songsters and Saints: Vocal Traditions on Race Records*, Cambridge, Cambridge University Press, 1984, p 22.
5. ABRAHAMS, Roger D.: 'Rapping and Capping: Black Talk as Art' in SZWED, John F. (ed): *Black Americans*, Washington DC, Voice of America Forum Lectures, 1970, p 144.
6. TITON, Jeff Todd: *Early Downhome Blues: A Musical and Cultural Analysis* Urbana, University of Illinois Press, 1977, p 53.
7. *ibid.*, p 55.
8. CONE, James H.: *The Spirituals and the Blues*, New York, The Seabury Press, 1972, p 117.
9. MURRAY, Albert: *Stomping the Blues*, London, Quartet Books, 1978, p 50.
10. KEIL, Charles: *Urban Blues*, Chicago, University of Chicago Press, 1966, p 155.
11. quoted in CARROLL, Peter N. and NOBLE, David W.: *The Free and the Unfree: A New History of the United States*, Harmondsworth, Penguin Books, 1977, p 320.
12. HARALAMBOS, Michael: *Right On!: From Blues to Soul in Black America*, London, Eddison Press, 1974, p 54.

13. MURRAY, Albert: *The Omni-Americans: New Perspectives on Black Experience and American Culture*, New York, Outerbridge & Dienstfrey, 1970, p 60.
14. KEIL, Charles: *op. cit.*, p 164.
15. MURRAY, Albert: *op. cit.,*, p 147.
16. quoted in HARALAMBOS, Michael, *op. cit.*, p 82.
17. OLIVER, Paul: *The Story of the Blues*, London, Barrie & Jenkins, 1969, p 166.
18. HARALAMBOS, Michael, *op. cit.*, p 104.
19. STEPHENS, Robert W.: 'Soul: A Historical Reconstruction of Continuity and Change in Black Popular Music', *The Black Perspective in Music*, Volume 12, no 1, Spring 1984, p 37.
20. quoted in OLIVER, Paul: *The Meaning of the Blues*, New York, Collier Books, 1960, p 59.
21. HARALAMBOS, Michael: *op. cit.*, p 154.
22. *ibid.*, p 155.
23. STEPHENS, Robert W.: *op. cit.*, p 38.
24. *ibid.*, p 41.

Chapter 8

ON LITERACY AND NON-LITERACY

Let us now consider further a matter which has already made some appearances in this book: the question of literacy and what it means to be literate — and, indeed, what it means not to be literate. It is a topic which is beset by any number of unexamined assumptions, not least concerning the automatic and unqualified benefits conferred by the ability to read and to write; I believe, and shall argue, that, like all technologies (and literacy is, to use Jack Goody's term, a technology of the intellect) it exacts a price for the benefits it brings. The best-known, and certainly the most controversial, study of literacy in recent years was that of Marshall McLuhan, who drew attention to the alteration in human consciousness that takes place when a culture becomes literate; his attention was focussed on a particular kind of literacy, that which uses a phonetic alphabet, as opposed to that, such as Chinese ideograms and Arabic numerals, in which each written shape corresponds to an object or an idea. In alphabetic literacy, each written shape represents a sound, and the sounds are assembled to form words and utterances. McLuhan maintained that such literacy has been responsible for the breaking up of the intimate tribal experience, for the apparently inbuilt western bias towards logical, sequential thinking and for its 'technique of transformation and control by making all situations uniform and continuous'.[1] One does not have to go along with this, or with his assertion that with literacy the 'hyperaesthetic and delicate and all-inclusive' auditory sense is replaced by the 'cool and neutral eye' or that 'phonetic [ie alphabetic] culture endows men with the means of repressing their feelings and emotions when engaged in action'[2] to agree that there is a marked change in consciousness when a person learns to read and write, and, not least, when he learns to read and to write music.

McLuhan was not the first to worry over the effects of writing; Plato in *Phaedrus* has Socrates point out that writing is a reminder only, not an improver of memories, and that it can make knowledge rigid and inflexible: 'Any work is a matter of reproach to its author . . . if he regards it as containing important truth of permanent validity,'[3] and, by implication, that it makes it appear as if knowledge existed outside of and independently of the knower. He maintains that knowledge can best be passed on by oral means, with a dialectic of question and answer of which the written word is incapable: 'The writer's words seem to talk to you as though they were intelligent, but if you ask them about anything they say, from a desire to be instructed, they go on telling you the same thing forever.'[4] In traditional African societies even though literacy was more widespread than is generally supposed, it was, according to Dennis Duerden, fear of that rigidity from which it seems to be inseparable that made them resist the idea of general literacy, and in particular the use of written records. 'The society's memory must be controlled by a natural process of dying and rebirth . . . Structures must be subject to continual change. Harmony in the society is not achieved by stability of structures. Rather it is ensured that no structure will last too long, and it is therefore important that the memory of a particular structure should not persist in the society when it starts to destroy the equilibrium achieved by competing groups.'[5]

It is worth considering what it is like not to be literate in a culture where literacy is not considered the norm. In the first place, all communication takes place face to face; all knowledge, apart from what one can perceive for oneself, comes from what one is told, directly from another human being, and is thus filtered through memory, with all the changes that such filtering implies. The knowledge may not necessarily be verbal, but may be in the form of musicking, dancing, or of visually representing, such as painting, sculpting or masking (I use the verbs rather than the nouns to remind us that it is the artistic act rather than the art-object that communicates). Memory, on the other hand, is greatly cultivated, often to a level that members of a literate culture find hard to credit; the feats of non-literate Yugoslav bards in remembering and reciting days-long epics have been amply recorded, while Elsdon Best tells of the New Zealand Maori: 'An old man of the Tuhoe tribe recited to the writer no less than 406 songs from memory, while another old fellow recited from memory the genealogy of his clan, a task that necessitated the repetition of over 1400 personal names.'[6] Such feats of memory are no doubt facilitated by the fact that the unit of speech is not the word, or even perhaps the sentence — both of these are concepts that belong to writing — but the utterance, whether statement, question or exclamation; it is only with the coming of writing that these are broken down into smaller units.

If the chief characteristic of the written word is permanence, then we may say that one of the central features of a non-literate culture is changeability. Everything, including the past, is subject to change since there is no permanent record against which to check it. Of the past, only what happened within living memory can be recalled with any pretence to reliability (even then, human memory being what it is, there may be doubts), while what happened before any person now living was born is turned into the stuff of myth, outside of historical time, or at any rate out of historical sequence; a non-literate Europe might well tell stories of the mighty battles between Napoleon and Julius Caesar, while the great bard Richard Wagner sang his songs in praise of the heroes. Secondly, much, if not most, of what happened in the past becomes forgotten, its memory slowly fading with the memory of those who took part, since nothing can be recalled more than what an individual can retain in his mind. This, as Duerden says, can be an advantage for peace and for social happiness, since not only do people tend to remember what he calls 'creative events', that is, events which will be of use in preserving the harmony of the society, while forgetting 'destructive events', but they also 'deliberately refuse to adopt symbols which will last long enough to be destructive of the existence of those societies.'[7] But, in addition, this 'structural amnesia',[8] this constant process of elimination of unwanted memories, enables all individuals to participate fully in the culture, since its total content, being no more than any one individual can carry in his head (though, of course, different people will carry different things), is available to all in a way a literate culture is not.

It is this 'structural amnesia' that gives to the outside observer the impression that non-literate societies are static and unchanging, because there is no unchanging standard against which to calibrate them. But it is likely that non-literate societies actually change much more, rather than less, rapidly than literate ones, even if the process of change is not always recognized. David McAllester says that a colleague of his, discussing an Australian Aboriginal people, told him, '"Every time I go to Hermannsburg I find the Aranda have invented a different culture from the one they had when I was there before,"' and he comments: 'He went on to say that it was the same for the language they spoke, and that all this change was not the function of the European ideas taking over, it was change for practical reasons or for the sheer pleasure of it . . . New gods and ancestors are coming up all the time. Just as the ethnographer starts to write down what he sees (and this goes for the musicologist too) the clear outlines of the culture as it was a moment ago begin to get wavery.'[9]

We also notice that this amnesia does not mean that the society is out of touch with its past; on the contrary, as we have seen with African societies, the relation is organic and intimate, but the past is retained only so far as it is able to serve the present. History is pursued, if at all, not for its own sake but in order to give meaning to the present, to legitimize or to criticize it. It is common, for example, for members of non-literate societies to learn extensive genealogies; these are not merely a matter of family pride but tools for the maintenance of social order. As power relationships shift, as they did frequently in West Africa with the 'precolonial competitive, shifting, fluid imbalance of power and influence', it is common for genealogies to be revised to legitimize the new set of power relationships. This is done not dishonestly or even necessarily deliberately, but simply in order to preserve social equilibrium, which is regarded as a more important consideration than any historical accuracy. Similarly, myths, which, as we have seen, are prescriptive as well as descriptive, and their associated deities, may change their character or even disappear (as we can see in the history of Greek mythology, for example) with every shift of power, and with them the 'timeless' rituals with which they are associated.

Finally, a non-literate society and culture is likely to be much less centralized than a literate society. Without the ability to read and write the growth of bureaucracies is inhibited, and even when large kingdoms and empires do develop, as in pre-Columbian South America and in the medieval Sudanese empires, their organization tends to be very loose, with a great deal of local or regional independence, and with even towns and villages being more or less autonomous, paying little more than lip service to the central authority. Lévi-Strauss is interesting on this matter; having pointed out that what is probably the greatest scientific achievement of human history, the Neolithic Agricultural Revolution, took place without benefit of literacy, he maintains that the principal function of reading and writing in history has been for the tightening of central control:

> 'It seems to have favoured the exploitation of human beings rather than their enlightenment . . . Although writing may not have been enough to consolidate knowledge, it was perhaps indispensable for the strengthening of domination. If we look at the situation nearer home, we see that the systematic development of compulsory education goes hand in hand with the extension of military service and proletarianization. The fight against illiteracy is there connected with an increase of governmental authority over the citizens. Everyone must be able to read, so that the government can say: Ignorance of the law is no excuse.'[10]

But it is not only politically that a lack of centralization can be found in non-literate cultures; also absent are metropolitan standards of taste and fashion. Rather than a metropolitan centre which dictates taste to the 'provincials', there tends to be an interlocking network of communities which watch and listen to one another, now one, now another becoming a temporary centre as patterns of political, artistic, commercial and religious activity and dominance change.

Further, since in non-literate societies communication

takes place face to face, this clearly means that the individual is completely dependent upon the community and upon its intricate and subtle network of relationships for his or her very survival. For the most practical of reasons, then, non-literate societies are close-knit societies, through which information spreads rapidly and which respond rapidly and in unified fashion to events. This may point to a further reason why the powerful prefer us to be literate, since reading is by contrast a solitary activity — McLuhan pointed out the temporal coincidence of widespread literacy and the invention of the concept of privacy — so that individuals receive messages from remote sources in a solitary condition, and a solitary individual is likely to be more docile than a group. This may be less important today as television takes over much of the earlier control function of print; a nation of nuclear families watching a political address each in its own living room will inevitably have a higher flashpoint than an assembly. But in any case both widespread literacy and television are a boon to centralizing governments.

It will be clear from the above that there are advantages as well as disadvantages in living in a non-literate society; to be non-literate in a society where literacy is the norm may, of course, carry considerable practical difficulties, but even so some advantages persist. One is reminded of the visitor to Las Vegas who, on being shown the city and its sky-signs by night, remarked on how much more beautiful they would be if one could not read. But there are in practice very few societies where literacy is completely unknown. As Goody says: 'At least during the past two thousand years, the vast majority of the peoples of the world (most of Eurasia and much of Africa) have lived . . . in cultures which were influenced in some degree by the circulation of the written word, by the presence of groups of individuals who could read and write. They lived on the margins of literacy, although this is a fact that many observers have tended to ignore.'[11] The point is that, even if they were well aware of writing, and may have appreciated its quasi-magical powers, the great majority of the members of those societies were not dependent on the written word, which impinged only slightly, if at all, on their lives. For them the traditions of the society came orally and were stored in memory, or not at all.

Conversely, it is by no means true that members of ostensibly fully literate societies such as our own are divorced from the oral tradition. In the first place, for even the fully literate (who probably compose less than a majority of the population) the principal mode by means of which the culture is transmitted remains oral, through family, peers and elders; a surprising proportion of that oral culture is in fact opposed in its values and relationships to the official literate (that is to say, scientific-rationalist) values of our society. It is full of archaic visions of life, superstitious no doubt and even logically absurd, often traceable back, had we the means, to heaven knows what remote ancestral experience, and clinging on with the tenacity of a spider, but nonetheless an essential, if undervalued, part of our very humanity.

Nor is our written history necessarily so much more reliable than that of non-literate culture; the human tendency to mythologize does not disappear when we write down our version of events. In some ways in fact deceptions and obfuscation are even easier through the written word because of the sheer weight of authority which it carries, a fact which Henry VII, first of the Tudor kings, exploited as his chroniclers blackguarded Richard III, the last of the displaced Plantagenet dynasty, to create a myth which has proved remarkably resistant to the power of demonstrable historical fact. We have seen how the great figures of western classical music have become in the minds of most music lovers very akin to mythological figures, despite the abundance of documentation, while, in another field, we have seen the resonances of such recently mythologized words as 'Dunkirk', 'blitz' and 'El Alamein' and 'The Falklands' in the collective British mind. Military and musical historians may know, or think they know, the 'real' truth about such matters, but the great majority 'know' otherwise, and it is their 'truth' which matters politically — and which is manipulated by politicians.

For most of the world's people, then, as neither total literacy nor total non-literacy is the norm, it might be more helpful to speak of a state of reliance or non-reliance on writing. The modern industrial state would certainly fall apart were all its inhabitants suddenly to develop dyslexia, as, indeed, would the classical-music culture. On the other hand, it does seem easier to avoid the literate culture than the oral, even in our society, as can be seen from the surprisingly large number of non-literate people, many of them living apparently perfectly successful lives, which a survey taken in Britain a few years ago proved to exist.

In most of the world's musical cultures non-literacy is the norm. This may or may not mean that improvised performance is also the norm; I shall discuss improvisation fully in a later chapter, but here we notice that notation is by no means a prerequisite for full and formal composition. Both the Balinese and the Chopi of Mozambique, to name but two, compose and rehearse pieces for a long period before bringing them to performance with every detail worked out, and yet the entire repertory is carried in the musicians' heads. In both these cultures, however, there are two interesting features: first, rehearsals do not take place in private but go on before the eyes and ears of the whole community, all of whom are free to offer suggestions not only *how* to play but also *what* to play (this is in line with the low value placed upon privacy in general), and, secondly, change does take place in a composition over a period of time, so that there is no such thing as a final and definitive version of any piece. Curt Sachs tells us:

> 'There is in primitive [*sic*] and oriental music no silent composing with paper and pencil. Dreamily humming and strumming, composers create their melodies, and, even after polishing ragged passages, they do not pen a definitive version. On playing in public they are not bound to any authentic form — there is none. Producing and reproducing fuse into a delightful unit; the well-wrought, mentally definitive form and the indefinitive momentary impulse reach a perfect balance. Any notation would spoil this equilibrium in the undue interest of finality; it would destroy the possibilities of free-flowing melody in favour of a stagnant impersonality.'[12]

A composition, in fact, is a living organism; any performance of it shows it not in final form but only at a particular stage in its development. To such non-literate composers the final written form of a western classical composition is dead, the score its sarcophagus, while the non-literate composition remains as full of an infinitude of possibilities as does any other living creature. If a musician wishes to learn and to play such a piece he has to listen carefully and to understand it; as John Coltrane once said of the way Thelonious Monk taught him his tunes: 'He would rather a guy would learn without reading because you feel it better and quicker that way.'[13] The receiving musician will of course hear the piece in his or her own way, and, without necessarily even meaning to do so, may well give it a new twist, even a new character, but this is the way in which the work of creation is kept on the move.

Notation must have originated as an adjunct to memory, to remind the musicians of what had been played, or perhaps as a second-best for learning a piece when personal contact with its creator was not possible. As it has developed over the centuries the use of notation has undoubtedly proved of value, which can perhaps be summed up by saying that it makes it possible to play without first understanding. To play a piece 'by ear' it is necessary to understand it, but with notated music one simply follows the coded instructions; understanding, it is assumed, will follow with repeated playings-over. Thus those who have never heard the piece played have the opportunity to learn it, not only perhaps half a world away from where it was previously performed but also several centuries away in time. Through notation it also becomes possible to gain access quickly to a wide repertory — though as I write this I remember the Maori elder with his repertory of over four hundred songs. And, apart from modern professionals for whom time is money, who really *needs* to be in a hurry to learn a piece? It is in the learning that enjoyment principally lies.

But although the notated score may be necessary for such performance, it is not sufficient, since there does not appear to be any notation system which by itself can convey the entire essence of a piece of music; the performer needs to obtain a good deal of information from non-literate sources as well. These precise notations of pitch (precise, that is, assuming an agreed tuning of the scale), of duration relationships, and those less precise ones of dynamics and tempo, if followed precisely and literally would result in a performance that was dismissed as lifeless and unidiomatic. It is from oral-aural sources that performers learn how to interpret not quite precisely those two-to-one durational relationships, how to inflect the pitches and move around them, how to make small but vital changes in tempo and articulation; they learn this from teachers and from other musicians in that historical continuum we call the performance tradition. The limits of distortion to which performers are expected to subject the written notation are variable, being all but infinite in the Afro-American tradition but very narrow in the classical. The limits can also change over time; for one generation what is thought of as a tasteful and expressive realization of the classical composer's text might for another be regarded as over-the-top, even tasteless — a further indication that even the most literate of performers are much more dependent on oral traditions than is generally realized, and that non-literate traditions change faster than literate ones. Since about 1945 the European classical tradition has been intolerant of any liberties whatever with the composer's notations (this accords with the great amount of time and energy which gets spent these days in discovering exactly what those notations were, down to the last semi-quaver, the last ornament and grace), but at no time since about the end of the last century has it been permissable to add or subtract a single note of the composer's text or to make any substitutions within it. So tied to the notation has the performing musician become in the classical tradition that it might almost be possible to define classical music today by reference to this dependence.

We saw earlier, however, that the precise limit of classical music is extremely difficult to define, and thus it is not surprising that the limit of literate musicking proves equally difficult to define. You might, for example, teach me a simple song by Schubert, say *Heidenröslein*, by singing it to me from the printed text and accompanying yourself on the piano, remaining faithful in every detail to that text. I might learn that song from you 'by ear', by imitating every nuance of your performance, and then, as I sing it over and over I might make small changes which are not only my 'interpretation' of it (which in the classical tradition is legitimate, up to a point) but even adding melodic and rhythmic material of my own (which is not legitimate). Being unable to read music, I would have no way of knowing at what point my changes had passed the limit of the acceptable — acceptable, that is, to present-day performers and critics. Where Schubert himself might have drawn the line is a matter for conjecture; as we shall see later, a composer of the early seventeenth century such as Monteverdi would actually have expected the performers to take an active creative hand, while, conversely, a performing musician of the time would have considered a notated text that told him in every detail what he was to play an insult to his skills.

One is tempted to surmise that the boundary between classical and vernacular music is as much a matter of attitude to the text as it is of the nature of that text itself, or even of degree of dependence on the text in order to be able to perform (since while a notated text, as we have seen, is not a sufficient condition for a classical performance, it is a necessary one). It might be more appropriate to speak of notation-dependent and notation-independent performance were the terms not so clumsy and ugly. In any case, musicians who are dependent on notation are inclined to underestimate the power of the human ear and memory and to wonder incredulously at, for example, the accurate, poised and idiomatic performances by the Trinidadian steel band, The Gay Desperadoes (the 'Despers' to their fans), of popular pieces from what is generally considered the classical (and thus by definition literate) repertory — such pieces as Bach's *Toccata and Fugue in D minor* (the idiom in this case being more that of the Stokowski transcriptions than of the purist organists of today), Sibelius's *Finlandia* and Delibes' *Naïla Waltz*, the last with an exhilarating command of the nuances of waltz rhythm — all without the musicians needing a sight of a score or parts. Or at the non-literate performance of the *Hallelujah Chorus*, by the mainly black London Community Gospel Choir, whose precision, brilliance of tone and emotional intensity have to be heard to be believed — again, learnt by rote, and perhaps all the better for not having had to be mediated through the written notes, as John Coltrane noted. Both Coltrane and Thelonious Monk were, of course, perfectly capable of reading and writing music when it was of use to them; in the same way, we cannot assume that the members of the choir, or of the steel band, because they choose to carry out an extended performance without recourse to written music, are unable to read. It is simply that for a number of reasons they find they can perform more satisfyingly without it.

In addition to the ability to 'feel it better and quicker', there is a very important difference betwen notation-dependent and notation-independent musicking; when the performer is not tied to the written notes, he or she has the power not only of interpretation (which, admittedly, classical performers insist is creativity of a kind) but also of original creation within the framework of the idiom and of the given material. The performer may not always choose to exercise the power but it is always there, and through it the nature of musical performance is changed crucially. For, however much it may be denied by the propagandists of the classical tradition, even the greatest of notated musical masterpieces — the Passions of Bach, the symphonies of Beethoven, the operas of Mozart — are not infinite in their interpretative possibilities, but are ultimately as finite as the individual minds that brought them into being. The world inhabited by the performer in the notation-dependent tradition, however much he might try to conceal the fact from himself and from his audiences, is a closed one, which can be opened up once more to infinite possibilities of the communal intelligence only by freeing himself from dependence on notation.

Non-literate performance, then, is not necessarily a sign that the performer is unable to read music but is in many if not most cases a matter of choice, a choice that is not necessarily conscious and deliberate but simply arises from the performer's relationship with what he is playing and with those with whom and for whom he is playing. The skills of reading and writing traditional western notation are not difficult to acquire, especially for anyone who plays an instrument and moves in a musical environment, and it can be said in general that musicians are as literate as they feel they need to be. There is no reaon to consider non-literate performance either inferior or superior to literate; the two are just different modes which are suited to different kinds of musicking, and thus to the celebration of different sets of social and musical values (we may esteem those values differently, but that is another matter).

Two obvious points follow: first, many musicians have been and are capable of working in both literate and non-literate modes; as we shall see, the great masters of the European past were equally at home in both. One might go so far as to maintain that the present-day western classical musician, who almost uniquely among the world's musicians is capable of working in the literate mode only, is seriously deprived in terms of both musical skill and musical experience. And, second, there has always been a great deal of interplay between the two modes. Afro-American musicking has been no exception to this; certainly it is not possible to make any neat equation of black equals non-literate and white equals literate. The most one can say in this regard is that black musicians have historically *tended* not to rely on notation, and also, somewhat more tentatively, that an increase in dependence on notation indicates a tendency towards the aesthetic and the values — and the implicit higher social status — of European classical music. We shall see something of the way in which this operated in the history of Afro-American music in the next chapter. (Another point to mention is that even the conventional vocal categories of soprano, alto, tenor and bass are really no more than conveniences for the purposes of literate composition; when a singer is free to invent his or her own part there is no need to confine the voice in this way, and we find many fine singers in the Afro-American tradition, both male and female, whose treble is as striking and as expressive as their baritone.)

There can be no doubt that any divide which exists in western musical culture between literate and non-literate musicking is as much social as it is aesthetic; the former does have a higher social status, but, again, it is a matter more of mode of performance than of musical material itself, since, as we have seen, the same composition can cross and recross the literacy line. Apart from the instances mentioned, we need only consider those thousands of folksong and folkdance arrangements made by musicians famous and obscure for the benefit of middle-class performers who are, it seems, incapable of either singing or playing them without a score to read from — with in addition the implication that these humble tunes are being somehow dignified and honoured by bringing them into the drawing-rooms and concert halls of middle-class music lovers. If within the Afro-American tradition it is possible to find every shade of dependency upon notation from complete dependence to complete independence, and if, when notation is used, one finds that the written text is generally not master but servant, it is because the Afro-American musician does not regard the music object as central; it is the performance that counts, and the score is to be used when it is useful, and discarded when not, as a means to that end. It is a means of dissemination of the material, to be treated as strictly or as freely as the performer requires, not as a means of fixing it for all time. Musicians in that tradition, in fact, use notation in two ways which we may call 'springboard' and 'mnemonic'.

In the first case, the performer uses the notated music as no more than a guide upon which he or she will build a performance, and does not regard him or herself as in any way tied to it. The degree of divergence from the text will vary greatly from performer to performer, and even perhaps from performance to performance; one performer may do no more than add a few graces, while another may completely reconstruct the melody from the basic harmonic progressions, as Charlie Parker rebuilt *How High The Moon* as *Ornithology*, or as John Coltrane remade Richard Rodgers' innocuous little waltz *My Favorite Things* (jazz musicians in particular seem to take delight in seizing upon the most unlikely-looking material, even of the most banal quality, as raw material for their art).

This practice is reflected in the nature of much printed material — the commercial sheet music available for sale in music shops, for example, written for voice with piano accompaniment with guitar tablature. In these as a rule the harmonies and instrumental textures are simplified to the point of banality, the rhythms reduced to four-to-a-bar with only the most elementary of syncopations notated. The amateur singer-pianist who, having heard a song performed on the radio and bought a sheet copy, puts it on the music-rack of his piano and plays it as written will be disappointed and frustrated at the result. But to play it as written is to misunderstand the function of the notation, which is to give the performer the material on which to work; melody, harmony, instrumental textures and rhythm must all be worked over if the song is to function as a performance. The experienced performer will do this automatically, without sometimes even noticing that he or she is doing it, and the result will be unlikely to sound much like either the notated version or the record that prompted the purchase in the first place. In order to make something of the song the performer needs first of all to make it his or her own, and will most likely soon discard the sheet music as of no further use, other than as a *aide-mémoire* should memory slip.

I have given this rather ponderous description of a common enough practice in order to make explicit what may not at first sight be clear: that the appearance of the notated music may resemble that of any classical song, but its function is very different. It is a springboard for the imagination, not a set of instructions for performance. In fact, if the melody is well known, the only help the player may need is with the harmonic progressions, whose notation is often reduced to a chart; here, for example, is the chart for a well-known and perennially popular 32-bar tune:

G^{m7}	C^7	F^7	$B^{\flat 7}$	$E^{m7\flat 5}$	A^7	Dm	Dm
Repeat first 8							
$E^{m7\flat 5}$	A^7	Dm	Dm	G^{m7}	C^7	F^7	$B^{\flat 7}$
$E^{m7\flat 5}$	A^7	Dm	Dm	$E^{m7\flat 5}$	A^7	Dm	Dm

This chart contains all the information needed for one or more musicians who know the tune to build a performance of *Autumn Leaves*. All that is needed is to set a tempo, and off they can go.

The second use of notation, as mnemonic, overlaps with the first, but does emphasise one characteristic of the creative act in the Afro-American tradition: it takes place generally not on paper or in the silence and isolation of the musician's study, but in sounds and actions. If writing down takes place it does so after the creative event, and functions as a reminder of what has already been done rather than as a set of instructions for future action. When written notation forms the medium through which the creative act takes place, then only what can be written down can be composed at all — a restriction against which European and American composers of classical music must have been chafing for years and which has resulted in a remarkable proliferation of new notational symbols as they strive to extend the range of melodic, rhythmic and timbral material that can be brought under their control. In the absence of an agreed performance tradition, the composer's instructions to the performers need to be very detailed; but even whole conferences of composers have failed to produce an agreed or consistent set of graphic symbols to cover every possible sound, so that every composition that uses non-traditional sounds needs to be prefaced with an explanation of the symbols used, sometimes covering several pages. For the Afro-American musician, on the other hand, the notations can be quite vague and sketchy, just enough to remind him or her of what was done when the piece was first made; it need make no claim to being an authoritative text, and, like the oriental musician described by Curt Sachs, the musician is free to let the composition go on developing. Not only is there no need for the notation to transmit as much information as for classical music; it would be a positive impediment to the performance if it were to do so.

There are occasions in Afro-American musicking where a fully-notated score is used; but such scores, significantly called 'arrangements' rather than 'compositions' or 'pieces', still differ considerably in function from those used in the classical tradition. They have been used since the days of the Fletcher Henderson and Paul Whiteman Orchestras of the 1920s to guide the performance of big jazz and dance bands. Written arrangements are not necessary, as is sometimes said, in order to prevent the sound of a large group from degenerating into chaos — great bands like that of Count Basie were able to get along well without them — but they have proved of value in order to get the smooth 'streamlined' sound of bands such as that of Glenn Miller or the subtle orchestral effects of Duke Ellington, not to mention the sound of show bands required to play the same thing night after night in the pit of a theatre or for floor shows (as the Ellington orchestra did in the Cotton Club in Harlem in the 1920s). These arrangements differ from classical scores in two ways: first, in that they make no pretence to being a final, definitive version of the piece, as can be seen from the fact that a well-known tune may inspire dozens, if not hundreds, of different arrangements over the years of its existence (some of these 'standards' have been around for anything up to eighty years and are still going strong), appearing in as many different guises — different harmonies, different variations on the melody, different instrumental combinations, even different kinds of emotional atmosphere. And secondly, there is generally space left in the arrangement for improvised solos by individual performers; at its best an arrangement will be written, not for a generalized ensemble like 'the symphony orchestra' or 'the string quartet' but for a particular group, and built around the individual characters of the musicians who will be playing it. This was one of the great strengths of the Duke Ellington Orchestra, for example; having selected his players for their individual qualities and disciplined them into a coherent ensemble, Ellington was able to call on what he knew they did best, and (not unimportantly) enjoyed doing, calling for suggestions from the instrumentalists as the arrangement was being put together. This is exemplified in his calling a trumpet showpiece, not *Concerto for Trumpet* but *Concerto for Cootie*, after Cootie Williams, around whose playing the piece was built.

The reader will notice that I have been obliged to call *Concerto for Cootie*, a 'piece', and it is true that over his long career Ellington did compose a number of pieces which he did think of as being in more or less final form, some of them ambitious in size and scope such as *Black, Brown and Beige*, *Liberian Suite* and the three *Sacred Concerts*, and these pieces must be regarded as an edging-away from jazz as it is commonly understood, to become more like classical concert pieces with jazz inflections. But then, as I suggested in the Introduction, what is classical and what is not may depend as much on what is done with it as on what it actually is — and these pieces lack the impersonality and abstraction of classical concert pieces, being built around the abilities and the styles of specific musicians, as those who have tried to revive them away from the Ellington Orchestra have found to their cost. And we may note that Ellington was not averse to recycling the principal melody of *Concerto for Cootie* as a popular song — *Do Nothing Till You Hear From Me*.

In the main, however, the Afro-American musician is not dependent on notation, and treasures his independence, his ability to 'hear better and quicker' by ear rather than by note. I have earlier suggested several of the many ways in which a non-literate culture differs from a literate, and the Afro-American musical tradition shows many of these same characteristics. I suggested that a non-literate culture probably changes more quickly than a literate one, and this is as true of Afro-American music as it is of the language and the customs of the Australian Aranda. I have remarked on the staggering proliferation of styles within the culture, but also on the fact that, as soon as we examine them at all closely, our neat taxonomies of those styles break down into mere approximations and tendencies, useful only so long as we keep in mind that each flows into the others, and that the whole culture keeps reinventing itself as rapidly as that of the Aranda; certainly it has seen more changes in the last thirty years than the classical tradition has seen in the whole of this century.

The process of change is helped by another characteristic of non-literate cultures, the direct oral-aural assimilation of information, which not only gives the musician the ability to absorb from a wide variety of sources while preserving his autonomy, but also helps to keep the culture decentralized, a network of listening individuals and groups all working on equal terms with one another. Unlike the notation-dependent musician, who in reading from his score can receive messages from only one musician at a time (it would be unthinkable for a pianist to incorporate a little Stravinsky into the Chopin prelude he is playing), he is able to draw simultaneously on any number of sources; anything that catches the ear can be incorporated, whether it be melodic material, harmonies, whole solo or ensemble passages, tricks or rhythm, instrumental and vocal inflection, even stage demeanour — a performance may turn out to be a multi-layered fabric of any number of fragments from other musicians in any number of traditions, not excepting the classical. How successfully these are fused depends, of course, on the talent of the musician. Non-literate musicians tend to be very aware of the sources of their influences, not surprisingly since they are transmitted directly, without the intervention of written notes; indeed, a score, as we have seen, would be incapable of transmitting those nuances of performance which are vital elements of style in Afro-American musicking.

We have seen how non-literate cultures resist the development of centres of culture: they acknowledge no metropolitan tastemakers or arbiters, whose dominance would relegate non-metropolitans to the status of 'provincial', while at the same time imposing a uniformity upon the whole culture (one hears the same symphonies, the same quartets, in Reykjavik, Dunedin and Seoul, as in Paris, New York and London if perhaps not so expertly played); they remain networks of interaction whose centres, in so far as they exist at all, are small and temporary. The culture of the itinerant musicianers of the American south, and of the southwestern 'territory' jazz bands, were two examples of this decentralization, at least until the coming of records and radio.

Afro-American music came to maturity alongside the record industry, the history of which latter has been inseparable from it since its earliest days. It is customary to date the association of jazz with recording from 1917, when the Original Dixieland Jass [*sic*] Band made its first discs, and that of blues from 1920 with the records made by Mamie Smith, but ragtime pieces and the kind of instrumental and orchestral novelty numbers that formed part of the ancestry of jazz were being recorded and distributed widely as early as the 1890s. Records do form a medium by means of which a performance can be preserved and carried to the hearing of others who have never seen the performer face to face; they are documents of a kind, though different from scores in that it is performances that they preserve rather than pieces. In so far as they send performances out across the country and even the world, they have a decentralizing function, but in so far as they attract musicians to centres of recording activity, they also act in the opposite direction. Although in the early days of recording, especially of blues and country music, record companies were prepared to send their recordists out to meet the performers, this practice soon became the exception, and recording tended to be centralized in a limited number of cities, of which New York in particular was already the music publishing centre, thus emphasising their dominance. It should be noted, however, that there did remain a number of recording companies in the smaller towns and cities which up to the onset of the Depression, and again after the second world war, managed to function independently of the large corporations, and these were to play an important part in musical developments.

In any case, it is arguable that recording has played a somewhat different part in the Afro-American tradition from the classical. In the first place, since for the classical musician the musical work exists apart from and independently of any possible performance of it, gramophone records provide only one exemplar, one attempt to measure up to the ideal entity; the transmission of the work itself takes place, not from performer to performer, with or without the medium of records, but from the composer to each performer individually through the medium of the score (though of course much of the oral performance tradition is today transmitted through records). In the Afro-American tradition, on the other hand, the record is a means, and frequently the only means, through which the music is propagated. A number of jazzmen's memoirs, especially those of early white musicians who came to the music without direct contact with black culture or black musicians, contain reminiscences like the following, from the trumpeter Jimmy McPartland:

> 'What we used to do was put the record on — one of the [New Orleans] Rhythm Kings', naturally — play a few bars, then get all our notes. We'd have to tune our instruments up to the record machine, to the pitch, and go ahead with a few notes. Then stop. A few more bars of the record, each guy would pick out his notes, and boom! we would go on and play it.'[14]

But even for those who were soaked in black American culture, records have played an important part not only in dissemination but in widening the choices available. As Harold Courlander points out:

> 'Records and radio introduced into the development of Negro musical tradition a new element which ought to be called "feedback". A traditional type of folksong was picked up by a recording artist and sung in a new way. If the record became popular, a new generation of singers began to utilize some of the personalized contributions of the recording artist. In time, this new version, or elements of it, became, once more, folk music . . . One result of this activity is that we may hear cowboy tunes that are reminiscent of Negro blues; blues that sound like songs of the Golden West; hillbilly tunes and instrumental combinations that gallop through mountainized versions of *John Henry* or *John the Revellator*, with jugs, jews-harps and washtubs; jazzlike treatments of old religious songs; Calypsoish skiffle bands in New Orleans and Mobile; and gospel songs with a suggestion of *Moon Over Indiana* in them. This sort of thing is, of course, not essentially new. Musical acculturation between deep sea sailors and Negro stevedores, between Negro churches and white churches, and between Negro and white railroad workers has been going on for a long time. But the pace and acceleration of cross-fertilizations in recent years has probably never been equalled.'[15]

That was published in 1963, and the process has accelerated and widened even further since then.

Albert Murray points out that black Americans have traditionally not been as concerned with the preservation of their past as have Europeans, a characteristic that he traces back to Africa; he is careful to make it clear that it indicates not a lack of awareness of the past, but rather a 'concept of time and continuity, or of permanence and change . . . [which is] . . . different, and certainly the concept of history, heritage and documentation was different.'[16] Accordingly, as he says:

> 'At the advent of the phonograph . . . the typical US Negro musician, not unlike his African ancestor, was clearly more

> interested in playing and enjoying music than in *recording* it for posterity. As a matter of fact, many Afro-Americans in general still tend to regard phonograph recordings more as current duplications (soon to be discarded as out of date) which enable them to reach more people simultaneously than as permanent documents. Euro-Americans, on the other hand, started record collections and archives, which eventually came to include the music of Afro-Americans.'[17]

The musician in the Afro-American tradition today still tends to resist the permanence and the idea of music-as-thing which pervades the classical tradition; to what extent this represents a survival of the African attitude noted earlier by Duerden, the deliberate refusal 'to adopt symbols that will last long enough to be destructive to the existence of their societies', is anyone's guess. But it appears true that the disc which can be held in the hand, is bought and sold like any other commodity and exists, at least potentially, permanently, is still, from the point of view of Afro-American musicians and their audience, including the vast contemporary audience for rock and pop music, only a way of disseminating the performance more widely; if anyone wants to put it in an archive, that is their business, but for them it is disposable, to be thrown away when its usefulness is finished, to make room for new creations.

Thus we return to the starting point of this chapter; that the preservation of music objects through writing down and other media is not necessarily the unequivocal benefit that we have been led to believe it is; not only does the very ephemerality of the performance in Afro-American musicking help to keep in motion the living process of musicking, unlike the virtual stagnation which is all too perceptible in the notation-dependent classical tradition today, but also the musicians' non-dependence on notation permits a much more open situation in terms of both musical techniques (in particular, rhythm) and of potential for continuing development and for the assimilation of multiple influences. Literacy is a good servant but a bad master, and if Afro-American musicians have in the main succeeded in avoiding becoming bound to their past it is largely because of their ability to keep the written notes in their place, as classical musicians in our time seem fatally unable to do. The reasons for this state of affairs lie deeper, as I have suggested in an earlier chapter; we shall return to this discussion later.

NOTES

1. McLUHAN, Marshall: *Understanding Media: The Extensions of Man*, London, Sphere Books, 1964, p 95.
2. *ibid.*, p 96.
3. quoted in DUERDEN, Dennis: *African Arts and Literature: The Invisible Present*, London, Heinemann, 1975, p 23.
4. *ibid.*, p 28.
5. *ibid.*, p 22.
6. BEST, Elsdon: *The Maori as He Was*, Wellington, Dominion Museum, 1923, p 8.
7. DUERDEN, Dennis: *op. cit.*, p 18.
8. GOODY, Jack (ed): *Literacy in Traditional Societies*, Cambridge, Cambridge University Press, 1968, p 57.
9. McALLESTER, David P.: 'The Astonished Ethnomuse', *Ethnomusicology*, Vol XXIII, No 2, May 1979, p 187.
10. LEVI-STRAUSS, Claude: *Tristes Tropiques*, transl. by John and Doreen Weightman, Harmondsworth, Penguin Books, 1976, pp 392–93.
11. GOODY, Jack (ed): *op. cit.*, p 4.
12. SACHS, Curt: *The Wellsprings of Music*, The Hague, Martinus Nijhof, 1962, p 28.
13. quoted in CARR, Ian: *Miles Davis: A Critical Biography*, London, Quartet Books, 1982, p 114.
14. quoted in COLLIER, James Lincoln: *The Making of Jazz: A Comprehensive History*, London, Granada Publishing, 1978, p 126.
15. COURLANDER, Harold: *Negro Folk Music, U.S.A.*, New York, Columbia University Press, 1963, p 10.
16. MURRAY, Albert: *The Omni-Americans: New Perspectives on Black Experience and American Culture*, New York, Outerbridge & Dienstfrey, 1970, p 184.
17. *ibid.*, p 185.

Chapter 9

STYLES OF ENCOUNTER II: ADJUSTING TO WHITE CULTURE

In all musical performances in which notation has been available to aid memory, musicians have always been as literate as they have felt they needed to be. As we have seen, notation is not automatically of use to a musician; it depends on what he wants to play and how he wants to play it. We have seen, too, how while high-status European classical musicians have become completely dependent on notation, the majority of Afro-American musicians have tended not to become so, and to treasure the independence and the creative role which non-literate musicking allows to the performer. Nonetheless, where black musicians did encounter the European classical tradition they have not hesitated to make use of it, and to enter the literate tradition in various ways and in varying degrees.

For the black slaves, making music within their own community, status was not a consideration, nor for the most part would it have been among the poor whites with whom they lived in close proximity in the southern colonies and states. For them, musicking was a tool for survival, for keeping alive their sense of who they were and their feelings of belonging to a community. Similarly, later, with blues and with 'hillbilly' music; these were affirmations of identity by poor and oppressed people at the bottom of American society, strategies for making the unbearable bearable, 'that stoic feeling' as James Cone said, 'that recognizes the painfulness of the present but refuses to surrender to its historical contradictions.'[1] These people had little use for notation in their musicking.

It was a different matter when the slaves came into contact

with the literate tradition of European music, as did those who played for dances and other occasions on the plantations and in the drawing rooms of American colonial homes. These musicians, as we have seen, must have constituted an important two-way channel of communication, if not acculturation, as they played for the dancing of both masters and fellow slaves and brought elements of each style of music, and of dance, from one group to the other. How literate these musicians were is not clear, but they probably followed the rule I have proposed, and were as literate as they needed to be, in order to play, for example, from the printed collections of dance tunes which were commonly to be found in the great houses of the plantations and in the towns, not to mention those European songs and salon pieces they were also called upon to perform.

One group of people who played an important role not only in the acculturation of blacks and whites to one another but also in the formation of black American culture itself were the free blacks, who by 1860 numbered about a quarter of a million in the south and rather fewer in the north. Their position was always precarious; not only were they feared and distrusted by the slavemasters as potential fomenters of revolt, or, more simply, as embodiments of black autonomy and independence, but also they were liable to be seized and taken into slavery if they were unable to prove their status. Many, however, even in the slave states, prospered and even came to own considerable amounts of property. Others attained eminence, as did Frederick Douglass, Martin R. Delany and Sojourner Truth, as writers and editors in the campaign for the abolition of slavery, while some entered the professions. Many became clergymen; the comment by Manning Marable, about the post-Emancipation period, applies also to free blacks in the times of slavery: 'Black faith was crucially important for Black social protest movements in the U.S. . . . Racial segregation and the imposition of racist constraints in electoral politics meant that the majority of politically conscious, aggressive Black males often went into the clergy as a means of expressing their activism . . . The Church itself became a major institutional power-base from which racial inequality could be attacked'.[2]

Well before Emancipation the movement for black equality had begun, and it was blacks themselves who were the most active campaigners, often finding themselves having to confront the racism, conscious or unconscious, of those white men and women who were the official leaders of the abolitionist movement; then as now, it was quite possible for white people to be against slavery while continuing to believe in the genetic inferiority of black people. A vital aspect of that struggle was, and still is, cultural, the fight for the legitimation of black culture, not only in the perceptions of whites but even in those of blacks themselves. For those who have been the victims of cultural putdowns it seems that there is a need to pass through several stages in their evolution towards cultural autonomy. The first seems to be a need to show, both to themselves and to the members of the dominant culture, that they are capable of practising the forms of that culture in an acceptable way, and finally that they are masters of them. It is not only black Americans who have had to go through that evolution; black British and indeed all colonized peoples seem to have followed it in one way or another — we shall see later how Jamaicans in their own country did so in a very interesting way. Only when that stage has been worked through, usually ending with the discovery that nothing they can do will prove acceptable to the guardians of the dominant culture, can the attempt be abandoned, or, rather, superseded by the repudiation of that culture's ideals and the acceptance of their own. It is when the colonized come to affirm and celebrate their own culture (that is, themselves) as anyone's equal that the cultural struggle can be said to have begun in earnest. Such a process has taken place innumerable times even in recorded history; Charles Keil draws many parallels between the development of blues and of polka music during the present century as representing emergent identities of this kind among black and Polish Americans respectively.[3] There is a major difference, of course; the polkas have remained more or less within the Polish-American community, while blues is at the centre of a musical culture which has taken over the world. It is therefore of importance to our discussion that we look not only at the ways in which black Americans entered into the literate tradition but also at the nature of the

European literate tradition as it evolved in North America.

We have seen that among those who came to the British North American colonies in the seventeenth century, even those members of the lower orders of society who came as indentured servants, musical literacy was not uncommon. In the harsh conditions of early settlement, it understandably declined; even after the colonies were well established in the eighteenth century, congregations continued to prefer singing by heart rather than by note, resulting in often remarkable musical effects, but the development of that peculiarly American institution, the singing-school, kept a kind of literacy alive through the use of Fasola* and, later, shape-note notation. As the rough-and-ready communities of the early days gave way to stable villages, towns and even cities (the first census, taken in 1789, showed that of some four million people in the US, Philadelphia had a population of 42,000, New York of 33,000, Boston 18,000, and Baltimore 13,000) a more formal and 'cultivated' musical life began to emerge, largely modelled on what was still the metropolitan centre to which white Americans looked.

Not only did they follow closely musical events in London, even during and after the Revolutionary War, but they also modelled their musical institutions on the London style; in particular, the pleasure gardens which were a feature of London social and musical life had their counterparts in New York and other cities from the 1760s onwards, until well into the nineteenth century. These must have been agreeable places, to which admission could be gained for a modest charge, where the finest musicians of the day were pleased to appear and some of the best musicking could be heard by all regardless of social class, not as a solemn ritual but as part of an enjoyable social scene which included eating, drinking, promenading and, occasionally, watching fireworks. They catered for a public that was not at all selected in terms of class, and this single public enjoyed a single repertory which was known to all — folk music, songs, operatic and orchestral music alike. From the pleasure gardens the music found its way into the homes of Americans. As secular music publishing got under way in America in the 1770s (only church music had been published there up to that time) American taste began to

* A simple method of sight reading for singers.

diverge from the English, showing a tendency to the serious, even the tragic and sentimental. American musicians seized the opportunity created by publication to compose an enormous number of songs, piano pieces and the like, most of it intended for use in the home by amateurs; this made good commercial sense, since, despite the growth of public performance in the larger towns, mainly by combinations of amateurs and professionals, and, from 1735, of opera (mostly ballad operas rather than the grander works of the European stage), the vast majority of Americans lived in villages and rural areas, and their musicking took place within the home or the community. Many of the items in this repertory must have found their way into the hands of slave musicians in the great houses, as well as into the homes of the more prosperous of the free blacks.

In innumerable collections of songs, piano music and concerted music of all kinds published in the early nineteenth century, some of them still in circulation, we may well find songs by Stephen Foster, folk song arrangements (Thomas Moore's Irish Melodies were enduringly popular) and the productions of hundreds of now forgotten musicians rubbing shoulders with songs by Schubert and Mozart and some of the most florid arias of Bellini and Rossini. Charles Hamm comments that such collections 'were purchased by amateur musicians who considered all these songs to be part of a single repertory and performed in American homes by the same singers and accompanists who loved all this music . . . Who is to say that these people did not have sufficient musical background to comprehend these songs fully? Perhaps they understood them better than modern-day American audiences, who hear them sung in large concert halls in a language most of them do not understand.'[4]

As the nineteenth century progressed, however, the single repertory split into two, of high and low status, in a way with which we are today all too familiar. Perhaps the first 'popular' composer of any significance, who aimed deliberately at a mass taste, was Henry Russell, an Englishman who toured the United States extensively and successfully between 1833 and 1841, singing his own songs and leaving us such enduring weepers as *Woodman, Spare That Tree*, *The Old Bell*, and *The Old*

Armchair, as well as such rousing numbers as *A Life On the Ocean Wave*. Russell, and his host of imitators and successors, were despised and ridiculed by the growing musical middle class (who were encouraged in their more exclusive musical tastes by a large number of, especially German, immigrant musicians who had come to the United States after the European social disturbances of the mid-century). But, in collaboration with the burgeoning music-publishing business, they prospered nevertheless and established a musical genre which still survives in corners; songs with a simple melodic line, often with a touch of Italian-opera brilliance or Irish softness, with words that express directly (a cynic might say, exploit) a single, strong and unambiguous emotion or situation, with a piano accompaniment suited to performers of modest technical accomplishment. Such songs, printed and often selling in millions (one of the most popular songs of all time, Charles K. Harris' *After the Ball*, published in 1892, sold over ten million copies), gained their currency through the medium of sheet copies and collections, and were to be found in piles in every home that boasted a piano. Apart from those that were drawn from the minstrel shows, these songs, fascinating as they were, form no part of our study here; they did, however, as Nicholas Tawa says, 'supply a great majority of these [white] Americans with a structure for living and answers to the riddles of their existence even as [they] recreated them.'[5] They thus formed an important element of the musical environment in which those black musicians who worked in white society moved; as we shall see, there were also black composers who worked successfully within the genre.

Another important element of that musical environment was the piano itself. The ubiquity of the piano in nineteenth-century America is a subject of its own; Arthur Loesser tells us that in a single year, 1860, one piano was manufactured in the United States for every 1500 Americans.[6] Even more than to contemporary Europeans, the piano was to Americans the emblem of middle-class prosperity, respectability and culture, and it was thus strongly linked with the tradition of literate musicking. In the United States in particular, playing the piano was regarded as not a suitable occupation for men — at least, not for white, middle-class American men; it was suitable for women, especially for young girls in the marriage market, for visiting European virtuosi — and for blacks. This market was met by a huge volume of sheet music and albums — dance music, marches, battle pieces, descriptive pieces and variations on popular songs; one composer of piano music, Charles Grobe, reached his Opus 1500, while the 1867 catalogue of the publishing house of Oliver Ditson listed no less than 33,000 pieces of music for piano.[7] Pianos were to be found, not only in the growing towns and cities, but as America moved west, in the frontier settlements as well, and in lumber and turpentine camps and mining towns. A piano or organ (that is to say an 'American organ' or harmonium) was one of the first items sent for after the bare needs of survival had been met; how they were carted into such often inaccessible places must be a story of endurance and persistence in itself. In such places the names of Chopin and Beethoven, or even of Charles Grobe, were more or less unknown, and sheet music rare because the formally trained literate pianist was very much an exception. A species of itinerant piano players grew up, very much in demand in remote camps and settlements, often idiosyncratic in technique and used to playing loudly on any out-of-tune, beaten-up instrument that happened to be around; usually their performance was a matter of belting out popular songs, often with embellishments, the melody in the right hand and the bass notes on the strong beats, while the rest of the chords were filled out on the offbeats in the middle of the keyboard — what became known as 'stride' style. A large number, perhaps a majority, of these piano players were black musicianers and songsters, following the tide westwards; they were also in demand in the burgeoning river cities of the midwest — St Louis, Kansas City, Sedalia, Nashville, Cincinnati among many others — as well as in the Atlantic seaboard cities. Before we look further at the art of this remarkable tribe of men, and occasionally, women, in whom the literate and non-literate traditions were to fuse and create an enduring art, we need to examine some other strains in the literate tradition in the United States.

Symphonic music came late to the United States, and it has had remarkably little contact with vernacular music; up to the beginning of the present century classical music was a mere province of the European tradition, with its own colonial identity problem. It has been possible to detect from the mid-nineteenth century a distinct hostility among ordinary Americans to imported European culture, but surprisingly, opera did not, at least up the mid-nineteenth century, suffer in anything like the same degree from this hostility; the English ballad operas of the eighteenth century had found a ready response among all social classes, and even Italian opera, provided it was properly Englished, was popular entertainment in the first half of the nineteenth. Rossini's *Cinderella* is still, in terms of number of performances, one of the most popular works ever to have been given on the American stage. It was in this period, too, that certain operatic excerpts and especially overtures, such as those of *Poet and Peasant*, *Semiramide*, and, above all, *William Tell*, established themselves in any number of arrangements as part of the vernacular culture that was splitting itself off from the 'highbrow' culture of the urban middle class. After about 1850 opera became increasingly part of the identity of that class and its vernacular popularity a victim of the increasing class tensions of the time. But it is curious that, while opera as a whole was no longer popular entertainment in the second half of the century, certain excerpts retained their hold on popular imagination, not only staying in print in large numbers of copies but also crossing the literacy line and becoming a kind of folksong, to have considerable influence on the styles of popular music, from Stephen Foster to the present.

In the latter half of the nineteenth century the place of opera on the American popular stage was taken by operetta, which was closer to the ballad operas of a century earlier in having the action carried mostly by spoken dialogue. The first operettas were imported, from France (Offenbach), England (Gilbert and Sullivan) and Vienna (Johann Strauss), each bearing the imprint of its national style. The first generation of American operetta composers, Victor Herbert, Sigmund Romberg and Rudolf Friml, were all European born and trained, and their work contained no hint of 'American' (i.e. black) inflection; it was into that environment that *Clorindy*, *In Dahomey* and the other all-black shows exploded in the first decade of the present century, demonstrating not only the vigour and the beauty of their black singers and dancers but also a whole new set of indigenous resources for the musical theatre, only hinted at previously in the minstrel shows. This was also the decade of ragtime, and of the first published blues songs, all of which were taken up by the white composers of musicals, so that when H. Wiley Hitchcock, in his history of American music, writes that in the 1920s musicals became 'more brash and brassy, lively and spicy, colloquial and earthy; they incorporated more identifiably American elements of dance and music; and they mirrored faithfully the optimism and hedonism, the motoric energy and the devil-may-care attitudes of the postwar boom era,'[8] he is speaking, essentially, of the incorporation of black idioms, black earthiness and black energy into the idiom of the American popular stage.

The modern musical is a curious hybrid of European operetta and American vaudeville and minstrelsy, with the black influences well assimilated if not actually concealed, a musically fertile but dramatically perpetually unsatisfactory form despite the 'revolutionary' new musicals that seem to appear about once every fifteen years. *Showboat* (1927), *Oklahoma!* (1943), *West Side Story* (1957) and *A Chorus Line* (1977), all in their time hailed as heralding a new seriousness and dramatic depth, have each with the passing of the years revealed a soft-centredness, even a sentimentality, which suggests an origin not so much in the urge to explore and to celebrate identity as in businessmen's calculation and market research. I do not recall any musical, other than the zaniest and most irresponsible, in which I did not feel I was being manipulated by a story line which was designed to feed urban middle-class fantasies. This is what lies behind a comment by John Lahr: 'Musicals are America's right-wing political theatre because they reinforce the dreams that support the status quo.'[9]

It is not only the storylines of musicals that celebrate the values (the 'dreams' of which Lahr writes) that legitimize and underpin the modern industrial state, not even only their assimilation, without acknowledgement, of black cultural forms (especially dance), but also the mechanical perfection of their scenic effects, of their song and dance routines and even of their jokes. Whatever elements of Afro-American idiom may still be present, there can be no other musical form from which the spontaneous creativity and improvisation that are the lifeblood of the Afro-American tradition have been so thoroughly banished. Nothing in a modern musical is left to chance or to the inspiration of the moment; once a few 'out-of-town tryouts' have established the show in all its details, nothing can be changed, and it will be exactly the same show whether it is presented on Broadway, in London's West End or in a remote town in Australia. To attend any one of perhaps thousands of identical performances of a musical is to be caught up in a ritual which, even more clearly than does a symphony concert, celebrates the corporate industrial state; it does not even make a pretence of acknowledging the autonomy of the individual.

The other literate musical body which we should notice here is the wind band, of which Hitchcock says: 'By the early twentieth century hardly an American hamlet was without its village band; hardly a public procession passed without the sound of the brasses, woodwinds, drums and cymbals of a band.'[10] These are not of course the all-brass affairs of the British tradition, but have extensive woodwind sections as well, as well as much and varied percussion. Their performances are usually from notation, and their repertory consists not only of marches and outdoor music but also dance music, selections and pot-pourris from opera and operetta, overtures and specially written concert pieces, usually of a programmatic or impressionist kind. They have for this reason been an important medium by means of which literate music making has become widely disseminated, since most wind bands are composed of amateurs and there is about them little of the social exclusiveness of the symphony orchestra.

Finally, literate music making has always been strongly cultivated in the Protestant churches. The role played by those churches in the propagation of literacy in general is too big a matter to consider here; it has to do with the belief in the need for each person to confront the godhead personally, and thus for him to be able to read the sacred text of the Bible for himself, but it has also to do with the wider matter of the Protestant commitment to the subduing of the emotional, sensuous and instinctual processes of human life and to the rigorous maintenance of the religious life on the conscious and the rational level. I mentioned earlier the decline of literacy in the early days of the American colonies and the efforts made by men of the churches to promote what they called 'regular singing', through methods such as fasola and shape-note notation which were as ingenious as they were apparently effective. Their success can be seen not only in the elaborate anthems and choral singing of the large churches in middle-class areas but also in the large number of hymnals in circulation, and very much in use, today in the poorer regions of the south, often printed in shape-notes, with names like *The Virginia Harmony*, *The Kentucky Harmony*, *The Missouri Harmony*, *The Western Lyre*, and, most famous of all, *The Southern Harmony* and *The Sacred Harp*, the last-named having been first published in 1844.

The pressures on black musicians to adopt literate ways of music making were twofold. The first was that urge to perform within the forms of the dominant culture which we have seen to be a characteristic of the early stages of the fight for cultural autonomy by an underdog or colonized group. In this case it can be seen as part of the more general movement for what was termed 'Negro improvement' which was under way before Emancipation under the leadership of white educators. Its aims were the eventual complete assimilation of blacks into the main stream of American life and the elimination of all trace of 'primitive' and 'ignorant' African ways and of the culture of slavery. It must have been an attractive idea at the time, and, not surprisingly, had the support also of a number of black intellectuals. Here, for example, is James Monroe Trotter, one of the first black officers in the Boston Post Office and an amateur musician, writing in the preface to a collection he made of music by black composers, published in 1878:

> '. . . I shall here make mention by name of none but persons of scientific musical culture; of none but can read the printed musical page, and can give its contents life and expression . . . The singer or player 'by ear' merely,

> however well favored by nature, will not be mentioned. This course will be followed, not because persons of the latter class are regarded contemptuously — not by any means; but because it is intended that the list given here shall be, as far as it goes, a true record of what pertains to the higher reach and progress of a race, which, always considered as *naturally* musical, has yet, owing to the blighting influences of the foul system of slavery, been hitherto been prevented from obtaining, as generally as might be, a *scientific* knowledge of music.'[11]

(Trotter was of course using the word 'scientific' here in accordance with the general usage of his day, to mean simply 'learned' or 'knowledgeable'.)

The second pressure was much more immediate, and concerned the musician's ability to earn a living; one who could read was clearly going to make a better living, other things being equal, than one who could not, especially in a society in which music was of the few occupations in which blacks had any advantage over whites. There is evidence, for example, of a considerable fraternity of black singing masters and music teachers in the northern towns and cities from the late eighteenth century. One Newport Gardiner, for example, African by birth, had been lucky enough to win a lottery prize with which he bought his freedom; he studied in Newport, Rhode Island, with the eminent musician Andrew Law and became well known in the area as a music teacher as well as composer of a large quantity of both sacred and secular music. He was only one of many whose careers went mostly unrecorded.

The black churches also encouraged the formal practice of music and musical literacy. We have already noticed the hymnal which was published in 1801 by the Rev Richard Allen, a formidable and articulate man who was founder of the African Methodist Episcopal Church in Philadelphia; it went through several editions and in 1818 was issued with melodies, many of which must have been written by himself or members of his congregation. Again, it was one of several such hymnals. Eileen Southern says of the black separatist churches in general:

'. . . the church played the important role of patron. It sponsored singing schools of children and adults and offered showcases for the display of talent within the black community through its promotion of concerts and artist recitals. It fostered the development of talent among the young, even to the extent of raising money for necessary musical study. Perhaps most important of all, it provided a place where blacks could experiment with composing all kinds of religious music, from the lowly spiritual to formal anthems and similar set pieces.'[12]

The black churches even sponsored sacred music concerts in which the major works of the European oratorio tradition as well as large-scale choral works by black composers were performed. In the early years of the nineteenth century they must, as Southern suggests, have been a major medium by means of which blacks, both slave and free, were acculturated into literate musicking, and in particular into the classical tradition. Not that literate musicking ever took over completely in most black churches; many accounts tell with how much more love and conviction the congregations sang when it was their own hymns and spirituals they sang, free from the restraints of 'regular singing'. The modern efflorescence of gospel song in black churches gives us ample evidence of the survival of the black styles through several generations of 'improvement'.

Another important medium of acculturation was the army bands into which black musicians were recruited from colonial times onwards. Initially comprising only fifes, drums and, occasionally, trumpets, these bands were enlarged into full military bands by a Congressional order of 1792, and the names of many musicians known to have been black are recorded in their archives. As Southern points out, the number of civilian bands consisting entirely of black musicians which appeared after the War of 1812 suggests strongly that many of them acquired their skills — and even in all probability their instruments — in the army during that war. It was at that time that the first black American musician to win international fame came to public notice as leader of the all-black Band of the Third Company of Washington Guards in Philadelphia. This was Francis Johnson (1792–1844), whose successive bands excelled alike at parades, dances and concert performances; he spent some time in London, where his band's accomplishments gained them a command performance before Queen Victoria, and, on his return to Philadelphia he promoted and conducted a series of promenade concerts that were from all accounts both musically superb and fashionably successful. He was a successful composer, especially of dance and programmatic music; he was, however, only the best-known of many fine black composers and band leaders who enjoyed local or national fame in the years before the Civil War. Indeed, it seems that at that time black musicians enjoyed a virtual monopoly in the provision of dance and other functional music for white urban society. It is interesting to note that the musicians in most of these bands were able to double on both wind and string instruments, using the latter when needed for indoor performance and more polite occasions generally; this versatility would no doubt have increased the demand for their services.

But even with these accomplished musicians whose skills in the literate tradition were clearly outstanding, we can detect an attitude towards the notated score that sets them apart from white colleagues. Of Johnson himself, for example, it was said that he had 'a remarkable taste for distorting a sentimental, simple and beautiful song into a reel, jig or country-dance;'[13] as Southern points out, his compositions as notated and published do not seem at all remarkable in relation to the conventions of the day, so that it must have been in the provision of material for a brilliant performance that the brilliance of his compositions lay, as well as in the rhythmic inflections which his band brought to the music as it was played. One wonders how similar his way of working could have been to that of Duke Ellington a hundred years later.

It was in the peculiar circumstances of New Orleans that not only band music (the citizens of that city were famously devoted to band music for all possible social and civic occasions), but all kinds of concerted music, both literate and non-literate, flourished among black people. The ample opportunities for contact between the various traditions of European and Afro-American musicking were of course to bring forth in the first decade of the twentieth century the style we know as jazz, but even before the Civil War there was a large number of black musicians in the city who were able to play in whatever style was required of them. Henry Kmen[14] even reports a Negro Philharmonic Society which flourished there in the 1830s, with its own symphony orchestra of members, which engaged visiting European artists to play with or for them, and even employed white musicians in the orchestra when needed to make up any deficiencies in instrumentation.

On the North American mainland, such an organization could exist only in New Orleans; elsewhere it was wind bands, ranging in strength from half a dozen to thirty or more musicians, that represented the literate tradition; doubtless, like Johnson's, they frequently took considerable liberties with the notated texts. They played not only for white social occasions — parades, society dances and balls, assemblies and the like — but also within the black community, often accompanying church choirs at concerts and even for services. They must have served as training grounds for generations of musicians, who learned not only reading and instrumental skills but also composition, arranging and direction, which they were to apply in a variety of contexts.

The Civil War itself provided a powerful stimulus to those activities; large numbers, out of all proportion to the total number of black troops, served as musicians in the Union Army. After the war, many of these musicians found employment also in the bands of the minstrel shows which, as we have seen, gradually became all-black institutions which gave black artists the opportunity to show their musical and theatrical skills. Music directors, we are told, often had difficulty in sorting out literate from non-literate musicians, so well did they all know the traditional repertory of the minstrel show.

There has always been a small but significant number of black musicians who have acculturated completely into the European classical tradition, as composers, singers (especially, of course, in opera) and instrumentalists (the latter almost always as soloists — even today it is difficult for a black musician to find employment in symphony orchestras).

Despite the considerable achievements of these musicians, not least in their struggle with racial stereotypes, they must remain outside the scope of this book. There were , however, many black musicians who worked in the field of the popular song, many of them hugely successful. Such were Gussie Davis, composer of comic and religious, but above all of sentimental vaudeville songs such as *The Fatal Wedding*, and *In The Baggage Coach Ahead* (the latter an early million-seller) and, most successful of all, James Bland (*Dem Golden Slippers* and *Carry Me Back To Old Virginny* are two of his most enduring songs). It must be remembered that these, like countless now forgotten colleagues, were highly skilled musicians of all work — conductors, instrumentalists, pianists, arrangers, even actors and dancers when the need arose. It is instructive to consider the repertories which all these remarkable musicians encompassed.

Eileen Southern tells us that the repertory of Francis Johnson's band during its London seasons included 'arias from operas by Bellini, Rossini and Hartmann, instrumental pieces by Mozart and de Beriot, and arrangements of English and American patriotic songs', and, conversely, that his own compositions 'found their way into collections along with pieces of Beethoven, Braham, Bergmuller, Czerny and arrangements of Bellini, Donizetti and Weber.'[15] Again, in his introduction to W.C. Handy's *Blues: An Anthology*, Abbe Niles tells us that in the 1890s 'All minstrel bands were expected to play the *William Tell* and *Poet and Peasant* overtures, and some selections from *The Mikado* and *The Bohemian Girl*, plus a medley like *Plantation Echoes*, interspersed with solos for piccolo, trombone or trumpet. In the theater, the soloist would probably offer the latest tune from Broadway, from Paul Dresser or Charles K. Harris. Mahara's [the Mahara Minstrel Company] star performer, Billy Young, had a repertory that ranged from a selection from Shakespeare to a Chauncey Oleott song — depending on the audience — but his specialities were the tear-jerking songs of Gussie L. Davis such as *Fatal Wedding* or *Picture 84*.'[16] Of the 'coon songs' which were the staples of the black minstrel show, Niles comments: 'These were dutifully undertaken by the musicians, who were obliging or subtle enough to put them over with gusto and get their laughs. But their private opinions of such burlesques were something else again.'[17]

And, from Blesh and Janis's *They All Played Ragtime*, there is this account of the repertoires of ragtime pianists around the turn of the century: 'On the instrumental side, neither individual ragtime players nor groups restricted themselves to ragtime. Light classical overtures were played straight with precise spacing and beautiful counterpoint, and marches were either rendered 'legitimately' or syncopated in the way Buddy Bolden's ragtime band was currently playing them at tough old Masonic Hall in New Orleans. And there were the concert waltzes, slow and dreamy in the age-old fashion of those pieces, tantalizing in their syncopations of three-quarter time, later merging into the hesitation waltz, but a lost art today. The ragtimers' repertory, finally, included descriptive overtures.'[18]

It seems, in fact, that for black musicians there were not two repertoires but only one. Black American musicians have approached the European classical tradition, like any other way of musicking, with respect and love but not with subservience, according it no specially privileged status but simply its legitimate place among the material of their musical experience and performance. Their matter-of-fact musicianship and versatility would appear closer to the true spirit of Mozart or Liszt than does that of today's superstar classical composer or performer; further, if today the classical tradition finds itself cut off from its true sources of nourishment and confined to a gilded ghetto, it is not the fault of the musicians of the Afro-American tradition. Here, for example, are Blesh and Janis once more, this time talking about Thomas 'Fats' Waller: 'The time he and the Cathedral organist played alone in the loft of Notre Dame in Paris is one such memory. When the reporters asked him about it, Waller would only say, "First Mr Dupré played the God-box and then I played the God-box". There are persistent rumours of grand organ recordings made for Victor that are said to begin with superb recordings of Bach chorales and go into dazzling transformations in African ragtime rhythms.'[19]

It could be that these musicians were faithful to an older tradition of musicking akin to that of the eighteenth-century pleasure gardens, a tradition which continued in Europe into the nineteenth century with the public concerts of virtuosi such as Paganini, Liszt, Thalberg and, in America, Gottschalk. The public repertories of those musicians consisted for the most part of operatic fantasies, variations on well-known melodies, programmatic pieces and dance studies, and their concerts were as much social as they were purely musical occasions. As Henry Raynor tells us: 'It was possible to smoke, eat and drink between the items and the seats were arranged so that the audience could move at ease about the auditorium. Liszt would go to the piano and play for a time; then he would descend into the auditorium and talk to friends lucky enough to be presented to him. Then he would play a little more, interspersing the entire programme with socializing descents into the auditorium.'[20] There is clearly a somewhat different kind of social event, a different ritual, taking place here from a modern piano recital. Such 'serious' works as the sonatas of Beethoven and Mozart and the preludes and fugues of J.S. Bach were not played in public concerts; they were intended by their creators, not for public exhibition, but for the enjoyment of connoisseurs in their homes.

Those artists were figures of popular fame not unlike today's rock stars, and they inspired comparable responses in their audiences; they were the 'Philistines' against whom Robert Schumann and his highminded friends did battle in the interest, as they saw it, of 'serious' music making. The reason for this new and, I believe, ultimately destructive solemnity in public music making is suggested by Arthur Loesser in a passage which I suggest should be read against my earlier comments on musicking as social ritual:

> 'During the middle of the nineteenth century, in truth, the *bourgeoisie* was slowly achieving a sophistication of artistic leadership. The showier purchasable habits of the rich could mostly be copied plausibly by people not nearly so rich, thus destroying their distinction . . . Special groups of educated music lovers now became assertive, especially in German cities; they were worthy people of bourgeois background, imbued with intellectual rather than with pecuniary snobbery . . . art pietists, worshippers of the audible God, grown bolder and more influential with

> Germany's remarkable economic and political rise, and breaking into outright arrogance after 1871. They were increasingly able to impose their standards of taste on larger circles of people and partly through the prestige of thousands of emigrated German musicians, they even succeeded in persuading some of the rich and powerful of other nations to climb out with them on their not always comfortable little penthouse porch. Furthermore, they imposed a ceremonious solemnity, a kind of churchly decorum, upon the concert hall, replacing the 'club' atmosphere of earlier German concerts or the 'show' atmosphere of the Paris-heated virtuoso exhibitions.'[21]

It was of course in particular to the United States that those thousands of German musicians emigrated in the nineteenth century; their arrival, coinciding with the growth of a white middle class with aspirations to European culture, completed the takeover of 'cultured' public music-making that had been started by educators such as Lowell Mason earlier in the century. As has so often happened, the older, more informal habits of public musicking passed into the hands of a socially inferior group, and it is quite possible that Liszt, Thalberg and Gottschalk would have felt themselves more at home in the world of W.C. Handy, Scott Joplin and Fats Waller than in that of the modern concert pianist.

Handy, who did more perhaps than any other single individual to bring the distinctive sounds of the blues to the attention of a white audience (and is thus about as much entitled to the sobriquet 'Father of the Blues' as is Haydn to that of 'Father of the Symphony') did not grow up in the blues tradition. In his youth in Alabama in the 1880s, he received a thorough formal training in classical music from a remarkable itinerant musician who had settled by chance in Handy's home town of Florence, and, according to Abbe Niles, 'eternally drilled his classes in singing by the sol fa system until they could perform unaccompanied choruses from Wagner, Verdi and Bizet'[22] (this at a time when Wagner, even in Germany, was a controversial modernist!) Handy became in time an all-round musician, cornettist, singer, composer, arranger, conductor and publisher, who was for a time music director of the famous Mahara's Colored Minstrels. It was during southern tours in the 1890s that he first became aware of the wealth of black folk music, in particular that form which we cannot be sure was yet called blues. Finding himself in Memphis in 1912, and called upon to compose a campaign song for a local politician, he dug into his recollections of the form and produced what was called first *Mr Crump Don't Allow* and later *Memphis Blues*. It may not have been the first song in blues form to have been written down and published, but it was the first to make much of an impact; its publication was a tremendous success. For the purpose of notation Handy evolved what is now the conventional usage of making the flatted third or sharped second, depending on context, represent the ambiguous blues third; as the published versions were for voice and piano accompaniment this was sufficient anyway, since there is no way that the 'true' blue third (if there is such a thing) can be found on the keyboard.

Defrauded by the publisher of his share of profits on the song, he entered the publishing business on his own account with the firm of Pace and Handy, first of Memphis and later of New York. The firm prospered, and Handy saw to it that his subsequent songs, including the famous *St Louis Blues*, remained firmly in his own hands. These two were the first of a stream of successful blues publications, of both traditional material and of his own compositions in blues form, which were to prove deeply influential on succeeding generations, up to and even after the issuing of the first blues recordings by a black artist in 1920. It was Handy who, by systematizing the blues inflections and harmonies, and devising ways of notating them, made them available to popular-song composers. The device of beginning a song with a blue third followed by a major third, as in *St Louis Blues* (*"Oh, I* hate to see . . .' and *'Got the* Saint *Lou-is* blues . . .') became a cliché of popular song, most memorably perhaps in Harold Arlen's *Stormy Weather*. Moreover, it was through the medium of Handy's published versions that many black musicians made their first encounter with blues; even so great a performer as Willie 'The Lion' Smith confessed that that was how he had first encountered the style and the culture (Smith had grown up in New York, which was never a centre of blues culture).

It was Handy's *Blues: An Anthology*, in particular, published in 1926 and still in print today, which disseminated the essentials of the style, its notes if not its performance style, fixing the forms and introducing the idioms into popular song. Looking through the piano arrangements in that volume, they seem today somewhat tame and conventional both in harmony and in rhythm; they are of course schematic, a springboard for the performer's own creation (one interesting feature, however, is the use of Latin rhythms in some blues, for example the habanera accompaniment to *St Louis Blues*). The act of writing did tend to 'freeze' specific blues and to diminish the improvised traffic between one blues and another; 'composed' blues, from *Memphis Blues* onwards, had a much sharper and more individual profile, a permanence of form and content which sets them apart from the older, oral blues. Published blues became objects rather than processes, and writing them down shifted them towards the world of commercial popular song, a process that was helped by the fact that the same publishers and distributors were involved in the dissemination of both. It is fair to say that notating the blues changed its character and took away that fluidity which is characteristic of oral blues; this was the price that had to be paid for the wider availability of the style, especially to musicians who were not otherwise in contact with the culture.

Whereas blues is quintessentially a vocal art, even though it passed into the hands of instrumentalists, ragtime was from its beginning instrumental. The race of itinerant pianists I mentioned earlier is described by Blesh and Janis: 'There existed in Sedalia and throughout the country a large class of Negro — and some white — pianists, many of them gifted and all of them close to the sources of folk music. Drifting from one open town to the next, following the fairs, the races and the excursions, these men formed a real folk academy. After the tonks and the houses closed, they would meet in some hospitable back-room rendezvous and play on into the morning. Ideas were freely exchanged, and rags, true to one meaning of the word, were patched together from the bits of melody and scraps of harmony that all contributed. Among the tribe were men of great potentialities who created complete and beautiful rags and songs, yet the feeling of proprietorship scarcely existed; commercial rivalry had not yet entered this Eden . . . This was all to be changed in time, but during the formative years a player had but two aims: the making of music and the achievement of a personal playing style. Under such circumstances ragtime developed naturally and rapidly.'[23]

The ragtime style, with its rhythmically complex, flowing melodies in the right hand over a simple one-two left hand, must have been around for a long time; not only is it documented in descriptions of the cakewalk dances back in the 1870s, but also, in the compositions of Louis Moreau Gottschalk, from about 1860, one can hear clear pre-echoes of both the melodic style and the rhythms of ragtime. In its brief trajectory (it surfaced in the 1890s, became the basis of a world-wide dance craze around 1900 and was in eclipse by 1920) ragtime underwent a complete evolution, from non-literate 'folk' style to fully literate published compositions to, finally, a completely commercial music.

The early centres of activity were not so much the great cities of the east or New Orleans in the south, as in the midwest, especially along the great river systems which flow into the Mississippi; its roots were in the jigs, coon songs and dances of the minstrel shows, as well as in the music of the wind bands that were ubiquitous throughout the United States but especially popular in the midwest. Ragtime can be seen as a fusion of the rhythmically complex melodic lines of the former with the oom-pah bass of march music. As Blesh and Janis suggest, early ragtime, like blues, was non-literate, and trasmitted orally from one performer to another, with all the fluidity of form and content that belong to non-literate musicking. As its popularity increased and the music spread across the country, writing down and publication ensued quickly. The first rag was published in 1897, about the same time as the first recordings and piano rolls were made of the music. It is interesting that, whereas the writing down of blues remained secondary to its oral transmission, ragtime rapidly became essentially a literate music with very little room for improvisation.

With notation and publication came a number of significant changes within the music itself. Notation tends to produce standardization, and we find in the first place that ragtime became standardized into the same form as the march, with separate, repeated strains and a trio section usually in the subdominant key. Nearly all published ragtime pieces are in this form. But a second, more subtle change was also more profound. Descriptions of ragtime melodies usually tell us they are 'syncopated', that is to say, that they have strong accents on what are naturally weak beats and, conversely, they have rests or tied notes on what are naturally strong beats. But this 'syncopation' is in fact a misnomer brought about by the nature of the traditional western notation that is perforce used to notate the pieces. Ragtime is not in fact a syncopated music at all, but something much more interesting; it is a polyrhythmic music, in which the right-hand melodies are built on a different set of rhythmic concepts from the left-hand basses.

Whereas European musical practice tends to divide the units of duration into two and multiples of two, so that a bar of eight divides into either two groups of four or four groups of two, ragtime melody divides the eight semiquavers of the two-four bar into groups of two threes and a two — one-two-three, one-two-three, one-two (actually it is even more complex than that, for the composer often likes to make elegant play with the difference between the two rhythmic approaches, so that while one bar may divide up one-two-three-four, one-two-three-four, the next may divide up one-two-three, one-two-three, one-two). These 'additive' rhythms, which are opposed to the 'divisive' or 'multiplicative' rhythms of traditional European music, and their polyrhythmic relationship with the one-two bass, bespeak the survival, not of African rhythms, as is sometimes said (and is implied, wrongly, in Blesh and Janis's account of Fats Waller's organ playing), but of African *attitudes to rhythm*, of the liking for multiple patterns going on at the same time and for additive as well as divisive patterns. These patterns are concealed by the way in which they have been notated. This can best be explained by examining the effect of the imposition of European notation on certain West African rhythms.

A ubiquitous rhythmic pattern of West African drum orchestras is that of the timekeeping double bell, or *gangogui*.

Unlike a European timekeeper, the drummer in a brass band for example, the player does not give out a steady stream of equal beats, but himself plays a quite complex pattern which nevertheless serves to keep all the other players in time. The pattern is based on a cycle of twelve beats, divided up as follows (it is very fast indeed, around 200–240 to the minute:

> ONE-(two), ONE-(two)-THREE, ONE-(two), ONE-(two), ONE-(two)-THREE

As played by an African musician the sound is smooth and without accent, other than the marking-off of the first beat of the cycle by playing it on the larger bell while the rest is played on the smaller, and it races ahead like an express train, giving a powerful impetus to all the other layers of the music. I first encountered it written down, however, on the back of a record sleeve, in traditional European notation, thus:

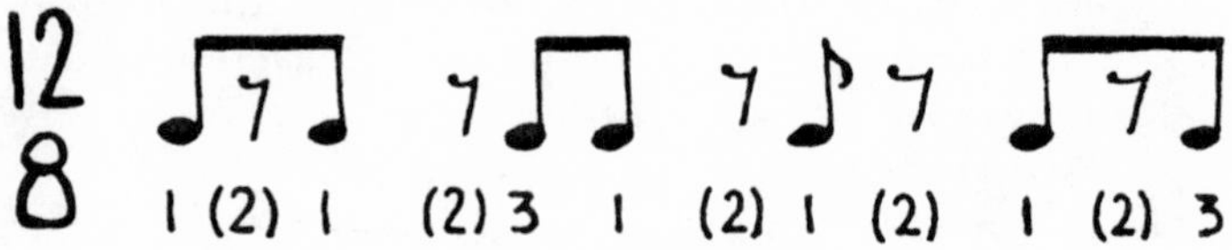

12/8

1 (2) 1 (2) 3 1 (2) 1 (2) 1 (2) 3

In this rendition, although it preserves exactly the placing of the sounds in the time continuum, the natural additive rhythms are turned into displaced accents, or syncopations, which force the person reading them to feel them as bumps; instead of an express train we have an ancient freight train jolting over the points. It is not surprising that I was unable to associate what I read with what I heard on the record; for African musicians that is not their problem, since they do not require notation anyway.

Now the one-two-three, one-two-three, one-two of ragtime melody is a version of a rhythmic pattern which is virtually universal in Afro-American musicking from Buenos Aires to Maine; it is known in Latin countries as clavé (I shall have more to say of it later) and it seems to represent the black musician's neat 'truce' with the rhythmic concepts of European musicking. The twelve-beat cycle of West Africa became transformed in the process of acculturation into the eight-beat four-four or two-four bar of Europe, but the unequal, or additive, subdivision of the eight remains; actually, two threes and a two, in various orderings, are the only ways in which it is possible to make an unequal subdivision of eight beats, so it is not surprising that it is ubiquitous. It is this additive rhythm which is to be found in the melodies of ragtime. There are also other apparent syncopations which arise from the equally natural tendency of Afro-American musicians to place important notes slightly ahead of the beat, a practice which ragtime composers systematized by anticipating the beat by the durational interval of a semiquaver. To call either of these practices 'syncopation' is to impose European concepts on a musical practice that has its roots elsewhere.

Notating the rhythms of ragtime (and to devise a way of notating them at all is an intellectual feat on the part of the ragtimers which has passed without comment) imposed on the smooth additive rhythms of the melodies, and their delightful polyrhythmic play with the bass, a series of bumps and jolts that is alien to the style but which one hears all too often faithfully reproduced by performers. To play ragtime stylishly it is necessary to re-translate the symbols into the original additive rhythms which their composers heard and played; for the classically-trained pianist it is deeply rewarding to make the effort, to submit oneself to the rhythms and eventually feel the melodies flowing as they should.

The complexities of the ragtimers' relationship with the literate European tradition do not end there. We have already noted that they were perfectly familiar with classical music, which they did not appear to feel was in any way alien to them; in particular, the harmonic idioms of classical music, its chord progressions, voice leading and bass-lines, are in ragtime pieces all treated with scrupulous correctness. The harmonies do not have the extreme complexity of those of their contemporaries Strauss, Mahler and Schoenberg, but resemble rather the simpler, more open harmonies of those nineteenth-century Italian operas which formed an important part of the repertory (one might almost say, the mental furniture) of most vernacular musicians of the time. Most of all, unlike blues musicians (and of course blues also formed part of the repertory of the ragtime pianists) they retained something also of the European function of harmony in the creation of surprise and even drama, even if of a fairly mild variety — for example, the descent onto a flatted-sixth chord in the fifth bar of Scott Joplin's *Maple Leaf Rag*. But harmony, being concerned with the succession of chords in time, has also a rhythmic dimension, and tends to reinforce the regularity of phrase and accent, the balancing of antecedent and consequent phrases, which has characterized European music from the earliest days of harmonic music. The ragtime composer, then, has not only to conceive his melodies against the background of the one-two of the bass but also to make them conform to the regular chord progressions and the harmonic rhythm, bringing them to rest in such ways as to coincide with the cadences; this introduces further tensions into the music, but also gives the composer the chance to demonstrate his ingenuity in the ways in which he deals with them. It is in fact the elegant and airy way in which he plays with these tensions and problems that accounts for the fascinating difficulties of playing ragtime.

Confirmation of these features of ragtime comes, in a negative way, from the work of two contemporary musicians of the classical tradition who attempted to write in the ragtime style, namely Debussy and Stravinsky; both, being who they were, made interesting compositions but neither came within earshot of it. Debussy's *Golliwog's Cakewalk*, on the one hand, uses throughout only a single simple syncopated figure, revealing a poverty of rhythmic invention that would have caused ridicule among the ragtimers. Stravinsky, on the other hand, in his *Ragtime* and *Piano-Rag Music* (the former published with a drawing by Picasso on the cover, of what looks like a pair of nigger-minstrel musicians, showing a complete incomprehension of the music), apparently misled by the visual syncopations in the written scores he had studied, and doubtless wishing to show his mastery of this simple vernacular music, piles syncopation upon syncopation until the underlying beat almost disappears, submerging in lumpish and inelegant cleverness the clarity and grace which marks the best ragtime melody, while the relation between his melody and its bass remains stubbornly monorhythmic.

Scott Joplin, probably the greatest and certainly the best-known figure of ragtime, seems, like so many artists, not to have noticed that his art belonged in a pigeonhole, and strove constantly to expand its range while at the same time seeking its acceptance by middle-class music lovers as a serious form of expression. In his hands, ragtime became something akin to European concert music; his later pieces, like the dance pieces of Chopin, are not so much music for dancing as abstractions of dance music which create in the mind of the listener, without causing him to move a muscle, images of dance and of its gestures. It is possible to feel very ambivalent about Joplin's ambitions for his music; in these pieces and in his two operatic ventures, *A Guest of Honor* and *Treemonisha*, one can perceive something of that siren call towards the respectability and the social status of classical music which has affected many vernacular musicians whose mastery of their own style was already complete. On the other hand, those pieces, like the 'serious' works of Mozart and Haydn, in no way deny the validity of the vernacular tradition from which they spring, but rather celebrate and treasure it. And no doubt, feeling nothing of the fatal discontinuity which today divides the western tradition against itself, he would be surprised at our surprise that, with only fairly elementary formal training and never having seen an opera in his life, he should have ventured to create not one but two works in this medium. *A Guest of Honor* is lost, but in *Treemonisha* Joplin is clearly addressing, not a middle-class white audience but his own people, with a message which is loud and clear: abandon your traditional ways, your superstitions and beliefs, and educate yourselves to become part of the world which is dominated by white values.

It is in fact the message of 'Improvement'; however questionable such a message may seem today, however questionable may seem the use of the operatic medium to convey it, the piece stands as a testimony to one man's greatness of spirit and intellectual audacity in what he undertook, and almost brought off.

Ben Sidran has observed that 'Black culture in America has been shaped by the amount of psychic energy it has spent adjusting to white culture.'[24] While it is possible to see this process of adjustment at work in all the black musicking described in this chapter, it is perhaps ragtime which shows it most clearly. It is an elegant and poised art, in some ways the most complete and subtle in the whole history of Afro-American music, which affirms with clarity and precision a particular kind of accommodation to European culture at a particular point in the history of that relationship, and the emerging black affirmation of identity. It was the first black music which had the nerve to affirm that identity, not just as a strategy for survival within the black community, but in a way which also signalled to white Americans the presence and the identity of black people. As a declaration of independence, however, it proved insufficient, too tied to European ways of musicking, especially in its reliance on notation, and thus its finitude and denial of a creative role to the performer, to satisfy for long the need for an affirmation of black American identity. And, perhaps even more important, it was too easy for classically-trained, non-improvising musicians to take it over; the creation in recent years of a ballet, that most European and abstract of dance forms, on the ragtime pieces of Joplin by the British Royal Ballet would suggest that his assimilation by the classical-music establishment is well under way.

Many writers have attributed the rapid eclipse of ragtime after about 1914 to a development that was taking place at the same time as the art became more 'classical' — it also became commercialized. But one wonders how crucial a factor this was in a ragtime's decline; other black musics have survived commercial takeovers and have even thriven on them for as long as those who first evolved the style retained enough interest in it to continue contributing their creative energy to it. Ragtime may have dried up simply because those black musicians who were its powerhouse moved on to other, more open, forms of musicking, notably jazz, which was better fitted to act as a medium for the growing black urge to affirm an identity, not just to themselves but to the world at large.

It is nonetheless true that the evolution of ragtime coincides with the development of American music publishing as big business — the growth of Tin Pan Alley — and that ragtime did become for a time the biggest money-spinner of all. As publishers' hacks ground out rags by the dozen, their quality and interest diminished as reliance was placed on a bag of rhythmic tricks and melodic clichés. There came into being the genre of the ragtime song, in verse-chorus form, with a lightly syncopated melody over a simple one-two accompaniment. The histories of ragtime, vaudeville (which had replaced the minstrel show in popularity from about 1880 onwards), and of Tin Pan Alley, were all more or less contemporaneous. Charles Hamm says of these songs: 'Ragtime songs differ from other Tin Pan Alley songs more in spirit than in musical style; they are brash, spirited, slightly syncopated, breezy, almost always humorous — characteristics they share with many of the songs of George M. Cohan. And, almost without exception, they were written and performed by whites. A pattern was established with the ragtime song that was to recur time and time again in the twentieth century: white popular music skimmed off superficial stylistic elements of a type of music originating among black musicians, and used these to give a somewhat different, exotic flavor to white music.'[25]

It was in this way that both the rhythmic inflections of ragtime and the melodic inflections of blues passed into American popular song; in fact, virtually all the features of American popular song which we are able to recognize as specifically 'American' come from the black influence, either directly, from blues and ragtime, and, later jazz, or indirectly through minstrelsy. Certainly those songs which were composed up to about the first decade of the present century — such hugely popular songs as *After the Ball*, *Bird in a Gilded Cage, Good Old Summertime, Daisy Bell, Sweet Adeline, Meet Me In St Louis* and hundreds of others — could, apart from the American references in the lyrics, have been composed as well in Europe as in America. A surprising number of them are in waltz time; virtually all use a simple harmonic language, harking back to the Italian operas of the nineteenth century, and show in their melodic lines occasional traces of Italian floridity. All are verse-chorus songs, which as we have seen is a European form; it is interesting that as black idioms started to creep in over the years the verse slowly atrophied so that in most popular songs up to the 1950s it is the chorus that is the most memorable part of the song, with the verse reduced to a mere ad libitum scene-setting appendage.

It was ragtime rhythms that first found their way into the armoury of Tin Pan Alley songwriters; the young Irving Berlin, for example, wrote many 'ragtime' songs before his first great success of 1911, *Alexander's Ragtime Band*, a song that despite its undoubted pep and catchiness contains no trace of ragtime rhythms. But it was the melodic inflections of blues allied with a harmonic sophistication that was strictly European (nearly all the Tin Pan Alley writers were white and a surprising number of them of Jewish immigrant stock), that was responsible for the characteristic style of the American popular song from about 1920 to the re-emergence of a strongly black idiom with the rhythm-and-blues of the early 1950s. It was remarkably strict in form; after a perfunctory, usually four-line, verse, there was a chorus which in the vast majority of songs consisted of an eight-bar strain repeated, a contrasting eight-bar strain (the 'bridge' or 'release' or simply 'middle eight') followed by a reprise of the first strain. Within that restricted compass of thirty-two bars the lyricist and composer (increasingly writing lyrics became a separate specialization, so that composers such as Cole Porter who wrote their own lyrics were exceptions) presented a tiny drama, generally of love either requited or unrequited, in tone comic, pathetic or ironic, often indulging in high-flown conceits concerning a love that would outlast the Rockies or that had survived ridicule comparable to that which had supposedly greeted Columbus, the Wright Bothers and Marconi. Some lyrics, such as those of Ira Gershwin or Lorenz Hart, were tiny masterpieces of precision and wit, but the situations they depicted were lacking in context or the specifics of a relationship, and dominated by European notions of romantic love; one element that was never taken from either blues or ragtime songs was black sexual realism. The lack of context was deliberate; it was intended that the listener should supply his or her own. The hints of high life and the sly allusions to European high culture were never strong enough to prevent anyone who was listening from applying the song's mood to his or her own situation. The lyrics were, in fact, not only highly literate; they were quite self-consciously 'literary' with their roots deep in the European tradition of romantic poetry.

Musically, the popular song from the 1920s to the 1950s was much closer to classical music than to black music. Black elements which, as we have seen, were absorbed in the teens of this century from ragtime and from blues as well as through the black Broadway musicals, were now also assimilated through jazz, but they remained what they had always been — a gloss on what were essentially European closed forms (though jazz musicians were to take up those forms in their improvisations and turn them once more into open forms). The degree of jazz inflection in both melody and rhythm was widely variable; a song like Gershwin's *I Got Rhythm* of 1930 was full of the accents of ragtime and, to a lesser extent, blues, while not a trace of either is to be found in Jerome Kern's *All the Things You Are*, written as late as 1939. Melodies could be quite open and diatonic or heavily chromatic; harmonies tended to be quite complex, both in the chords themselves, with seventh, ninth and eleventh chords as well as chromatically altered chords, and in the progressions — most songwriters liked to indulge in at least one striking key change in the course of the song. Each song tended to be a small drama, the onward thrust of the harmonies leading to a climax and resolution in a way that not even the earlier Tin Pan Alley tunes had done; one is not surprised to learn that many of the so-called Broadway masters such as Gershwin, Richard Rodgers, Jerome Kern and Cole Porter were classically trained.

When these songs were recorded, the arranger made of them an equally strict closed three-minute form, extending the tune by repetition of sections in a traditional European way with varied orchestration, and, generally, one sung chorus, to fill the ten-inch, 78-rpm record. But despite the popularity of records (sales of records overtook those of sheet music sometime in the 1920s), sheet music remained the principal medium through which a song was transmitted to performers. Sales of not only voice-and-piano versions but also of a variety of arrangements for everything from small combos to big bands, with written parts, some obbligato, some ad libitum, were still big business; it took the coming of rhythm-and-blues in the 1950s to undermine that market and signal the demise of Tin Pan Alley. It was taken for granted that every home that had a piano would have its pile of sheet music for the home pianist to play the latest hits, and each sheet copy would have in large letters, usually with a blurred photograph, the name not of the composer — his was in small letters at the bottom — but of the artist who had recorded it; then, as now, it was performing artists, not composers, who sold songs among the wider public. Up to about 1950 records and sheet music remained in a symbiotic relationship, with the record making the song known but the sheet copies making it available to those who wanted to perform it. It was thus essentially a literate music, made by whites for whites; black idioms, if they were present at all, were, in Charles Hamm's words, 'several quite superficial aspects of "negro" music . . . skimmed off by songwriters of the 1910s, '20s and '30s to add a touch of exotic seasoning to their products.'[26]

There were large numbers of Americans to whom these songs made no appeal, especially poor whites and blacks, who both had their own ways of musicking, in particular what was known as 'hillbilly' and blues. Their music was orally transmitted, often through records, and thus for the most part of little interest to publishers; what was the sense in trying to sell written music to people who could not read it? But even a non-literate person could and did play the gramophone, and hence there was a proportionately greater impact made by recording on non-literate musics such as blues and country music, in which the medium of dissemination was records. This impact was to carry over into the era of rhythm-and-blues.

It is impossible to say how many of these thirty-two-bar songs were composed, published and recorded in the years between 1920 and 1955. They were the mainstay of stage and film musicals, and the most successful of them sold records and sheet copies alike in millions. They suggested a world which was essentially adult, glamorous, sophisticated and moneyed, with sentiments that were free-floating, ready to attach themselves to any listener and cover him or her with stardust, lifting the hearer, for the duration of the song, into a world of glamour and opulence, as represented not only by the lyrics but also by the rich harmonies and lush orchestrations; these, not coincidentally, made frequent allusions to the gestures of European classical music, with dramatic introductions and codas, and used soaring strings, warm wodges of horn sounds and cascading harp glissandi.

These songs retain their appeal; many people, especially in difficult times, remain as susceptible today to the allure of the appurtenances of wealth as they did then. But, like the European classical tradition whose progeny they are more than black America's, they are living on the past; very little of any great popular appeal has been added since about 1950. New arrangements, new recordings, even new orchestras and singers, but not new songs — or, at least, there is nothing that has achieved anything like the earlier popularity with a wide audience.

What displaced these songs from their pre-eminent position in vernacular music was the music of those despised non-literate musicians whom the publishers and the major record companies had found it possible to ignore. How that happened is a matter for a much later chapter, but we notice that from that point musicians of the main stream of Afro-American musicking have become almost aggressively non-notation-dependent. Nonetheless, such musicians have continued to rub along with the literate tradition and to interpret it in their own way, to use its resources when they want them and ignore them when they do not. The coming of microchip technology may well make considerable differences to the function of notation, but it is difficult to imagine how it might disturb the perennial desire of musicians to establish relationships within their idiom that are direct and unmediated by notation.

NOTES

1. CONE, James H.: *The Spirituals and the Blues*, New York, The Seabury Press, 1972, p 117.
2. MARABLE, Manning: *Black American Politics: From the Washington Marches to Jesse Jackson*, London, Verso Books, 1985, p 35.
3. KEIL, Charles: 'People's Music Comparatively: Style and Stereotype, Class and Hegemony', *Dialectical Anthropology*, Vol 10, 1985, p 125.
4. HAMM, Charles: *Yesterdays: Popular Song in America*, New York, Norton, 1979, p 194.
5. TAWA, Nicholas: *A Music for the Millions: Antebellum Democratic Attitudes and the Birth of American Popular Music*, New York, Pendragon Press, 1984, p vii.
6. LOESSER, Arthur: *Men, Women and Pianos: A Social History*, New York, Simon and Schuster, 1954, p 511.
7. *ibid.*, p 506.
8. HITCHCOCK, H. Wiley: *Music in the United States: A Historical Introduction*, Englewood Cliffs, Prentice-Hall, 2nd edition 1974, p 186.
9. LAHR, John: 'Jean Seberg', *New Society*, Vol 66, No 1096, 17 November, 1983, p 280.
10. HITCHCOCK, H. Wiley: *op. cit.*, p 116.
11. TROTTER, James Monroe: 'Music and Some Highly Musical People', in SOUTHERN, Eileen (ed): *Readings in Black American Music*, New York, Norton, 1983, p 144.
12. SOUTHERN, Eileen: *The Music of Black Americans*, New York, Norton, 2nd edition 1983, p 82.
13. *ibid.*, p 108.
14. KMEN, Henry A.: *Music in New Orleans: The Formative Years 1791–1841*, Baton Rouge, Louisiana State University Press, 1966, p 234.
15. SOUTHERN, Eileen, *op. cit.*, p 113.
16. NILES, Abbe: 'The Story of the Blues' in HANDY, W.C. (ed): *Blues: An Anthology*, New York, Collier Books, 3rd edition 1972, p 24.
17. *ibid.*, p 25.
18. BLESH, Rudi and JANIS, Harriet: *They All Played Ragtime: The True Story of an American Music*, London, Sidgwick & Jackson, 1958, p 59.
19. *ibid.*, p 208.
20. RAYNOR, Henry: *Music and Society Since 1815*, London, Barrie & Jenkins, 1976, p 62.
21. LOESSER, Arthur: *op. cit.*, p 424.
22. NILES, Abbe: *op. cit.*, p 24.
23. BLESH, Rudi and JANIS, Harriet: *op. cit.*, p 17.
24. SIDRAN, Ben: *Black Talk*, New York, Da Capo Press, 1981, p 31.
25. HAMM, Charles: *op. cit.*, p 321.
26. *ibid.* p 358.

Chapter 10

ON IMPROVISATION

I have remarked on the dependence of the modern classical performer on written or printed texts. Virtually never will concert performers of our time attempt in public anything other than the realization of a score which has been rehearsed as thoroughly as time will allow. It is not only that the training of musicians has almost certainly left them unequipped to engage in any kind of on-the-spot invention but it has also left them without the slightest idea that such an activity is either possible or desirable; I have known competent instrumentalists, and even singers, who have been rendered completely mute when they are denied access to a score or asked to perform 'by ear'. Performers are imbued from childhood with the notion that their task is to realize a written musical text, down to the last semiquaver, as faithfully as is in their power; they understand that the musical work they are performing is not theirs, having been created by a higher order of musicality than their own, and that they are required merely to burnish it and present it to their hearers for their edification and admiration. It does not seem to occur to most performers in the classical tradition that they might have a creative role to play in respect to the musical works they perform; even in the comparatively rare case of composers who are sufficiently skilled as performers to appear in their own work, they will regard themselves, in their latter capacity, as bound to reproduce faithfully what they have provided in their former capacity. Memorizing the notes does not diminish their dominant role in the performance, since they are simply transferred from the pages of the score to the performer's head, where their control is if anything even more absolute.

The completeness of the rule of the written notes can be seen most clearly in the performance of a solo concerto from the time of Haydn, Mozart or Beethoven. It was the custom of those masters and their contemporaries to leave, at a point near the end of the first movement, a space where the soloist was expected to show his or her own inventiveness, ingenuity and technical brilliance by improvising an extended passage, known as a cadenza, based on the musical material of the movement that was nearing its conclusion. Today no soloist ventures to do such a thing, but instead plays a fully composed, notated and rehearsed cadenza which has been written perhaps by him or herself in careful imitation of the style of the rest of the piece, or, more probably, by an eminent performer of the past or even by the master himself, should he have provided one. Mozart, who wrote his piano concertos for himself or one of his pupils to play, did leave some written-out cadenzas, but we need not imagine that he ever played them as written, as a modern virtuoso will feel obliged to do; he was far too inspired an improvisor ever to have relied on such a pedestrian procedure. More likely he intended his cadenzas as models, to show pupils and others the sort of thing they might do. Beethoven, on the other hand, was more prescriptive; he wrote cadenzas for all his concertos as he meant them to be played, showing in this way his dissatisfaction with the performers of his day. It was not, as is sometimes said, that the art of improvisation was falling into decay; it was just that he did not like the way performers improvised. With him any pretence that the cadenza was improvised ended with his fifth and last piano concerto, the 'Emperor', for which he not only provided an extended written-out cadenza but wrote an orchestral accompaniment for it as well, leaving no chance for the soloist to improvise even if he wanted to. Beethoven had by this time by reason of his deafness been obliged to retire from public performance, thus increasing the separation of composer from performer which was starting to become apparent in his day. The increasing distrust of performers by composers can be traced through concertos of the nineteenth century from Schumann and Mendelssohn to Chaikovski, all of whom wrote out their cadenzas as they were to be played, thus reducing them to a functionless appendage; twentieth-century composers of concertos have for the most part not even bothered with that pretence.

In the western classical tradition, the art of improvisation is today to all intents and purposes dead, and resists all efforts to revive it. The resistance, surprisingly, comes largely from performers themselves, who mostly have little idea of what improvisation is or what it entails (the late Cornelius Cardew once said that before trying it he had thought it would be 'something like composing, but accelerated a thousand times',[1] a feat of which he believed himself to be incapable), and do not show any desire to make a contribution to the substance of those music-objects which it is their life's work to perform. It is not hard to see why they should feel that way. The professional performer has invested a great deal of time, energy and emotional capital in learning to interpret the work of others; he or she has learnt to seek out and to realize in sound every nuance of a given text, having assimilated at the same time the whole weight of a non-literate performance tradition which conditions him or her to interpret it in a particular way. In improvising, these very considerable skills are thrown into the melting pot, and the performer may be forgiven for thinking the whole investment will be lost if he or she attempts to work without the aid of a score. Besides, both performers and listeners in the classical tradition have learnt to think of music as a collection of sound-objects bequeathed to us from the past, objects that are stable over a long period and subject to the test of time in assessing their quality and value; this idea is negated in improvisation, which is all process and leaves us without a sound-object at all. And, lastly, since the world of classical musicking, like the rest of our society, is permeated through and through with the industrial ethic, and its associated division of labour, it is only natural that performers should feel that it is the composer's job to compose and theirs to play; if the composer's name is on the score and he collects the plaudits and the performing rights fees, then he is in honour bound to be absolutely specific about what he wants the performers to do.

The expectations of listeners in the classical culture have also contributed to the decline of improvised musicking. They, too, want a stable sound-object that they can hear over and over again and become familiar with; music is a commodity which is bought and paid for and the purchasers want to be sure that they are getting their money's worth. What they are buying is stability and reassurance, and the tension and the possibility of failure which are part of an improvised performance have no place in modern concert life.

There are a few survivals in classical musicking of the once-great tradition of improvisation, most notably among organists. This seems to be a consequence of the organist's occupational association with church services, in which pauses of unpredictable length — waiting for a dilatory bride, or during communion — have to be filled with music. It is a traditional part of a recital by a virtuoso organist that he or she be given just before the performance a theme (a sealed envelope is sometimes used to heighten the drama) on which a sonata movement, a fugue or a set of variations is composed on the instant. It may not be coincidental that the one environment in which classical music remains functional (that is to say, it serves a direct social function over that of sheer aesthetic enjoyment) is also that in which the ancient art survives. It survives, too, in a limited way, among keyboard players of baroque music, and I shall have more to say about that in a moment.

It is true that in the last thirty years or so composers of the European and American avant garde, for example Karlheinz Stockhausen and John Cage, have in some of their pieces asked from the performers something which resembles improvisation. In all cases of which I am aware, however, it is the composer's name which is on the score; the piece remains his, even when the score consists of nothing more than a few sentences, and the performers remain the instruments of his will, even if the way in which they implement it retains some flexibility. The composer has to remain in charge, otherwise he would forfeit the title, and with it the socially elevated position, in which he has invested so much time and energy. The desire to give freedom of action to the performers may be quite genuine (even if it is not in fact the composer's to give), but it seems that it cannot extend to the decisive step of acknowledging that the essence of music lies in performance, not in composition, and of handing over responsibility to those who are actually performing.

The subservience of the performer to the composer and to the score is a comparatively recent phenomenon. At least until the end of the eighteenth century the ability to extemporize was an essential element of the skills of any musician worthy of the name. We should remember that those whom we call the 'great composers' of the past, at least up to the time of Beethoven, saw themselves not just as composers but as working musicians whose duties centred around performance; when they composed it was to give themselves and their patrons something to play, for those patrons were themselves not mere listeners but active performers and even sometimes competent composers. And of course if the composer were also on a particular occasion (nearly all pieces were written for a specific occasion) to be the performer he might feel no obligation to write his ideas down at all. Many of these musicians were valued in their own time as much for their unwritten as for their written compositions, and such evidence as we have (it is tantalizingly scanty) suggests that their improvised performances were even more daring, exciting and memorable than the compositions that have come down to us (anyone who has engaged in improvising will agree that their free flights of instrumental invention can become tethered and even mundane if they attempt to write them down after the event). Here for example is a contemporary of Mozart writing about his improvisation: 'It was to me like the gift of new senses of sight and hearing. The bold flights of his imagination into the highest regions, and again, down into the very depths of the abyss, caused the greatest masters of music to be lost in amazement and delight,' while another wrote: 'If I were to dare to pray to the Almighty to grant me one more earthly joy it would be that I might once again hear Mozart improvise.' I also leave the reader to ponder the implications of one breathtakingly casual remark by the teenaged genius himself concerning his performances of one of his early piano concertos: 'Whenever I play this concerto I play whatever occurs to me at the moment.'[2] One could cite similar accounts of the improvisation of other masters such as J.S. Bach, Beethoven, Hummel and Liszt, but it is clear that they represent only the peaks of achievement in what was regarded as a necessary skill for any competent musician.

Even Mozart, however, like his contemporaries of the late eighteenth century, notated exactly what others were to perform. If we look further back, to the early years of orchestral music and opera in the early seventeenth century, we find that the skills of composers and performers were less differentiated from each other; the performing musicians functioned as partners in the musical act and not as mere executants of the composer's instructions. In the operas of the early seventeenth century, singers and players were presented only with notations which showed the composer's melody line and bassline, along with a kind of numerical shorthand known as figured bass to indicate the harmonic progressions. Even the melodic line was not expected to be sung as written; there are surviving notations in Monteverdi's own hand which give a melody and, in parallel, an almost unrecognizably ornamented version of it, showing the sort of thing he expected the singer to do. From this, not only the singer but also each orchestral musician invented his own part, with due regard for what colleagues were doing as well as for the over-all effect. A treatise of 1640 has this advice for the player: 'If the player is good, he does not have to insist so much upon making a display of his own art as of accommodating himself to the others . . . They will show their art in knowing how to repeat promptly and well what another has done before, and in giving room to the others and fit opportunity for them to repeat what they have done; and in this way, with a varied and no less artful manner, though in a manner neither too difficult nor requiring such deep knowledge, they will make known to the others their true worth'.[3] There are even in the scores of early operas instructions such as 'The Chorus of Tempests is repeated here; let them play,' with no notations given or even a suggestion of what instruments might be concerned; clearly the orchestral musicians were expected to work things out for themselves during rehearsals, which were customarily thorough and extensive. It might be added that the orchestra for a major performance might well consist of forty or more players; nothing was skimped, either musically or scenically, in those early opera performances, and we can be sure that whatever, from the modern point of view, was omitted from the composer's instructions to his players it is not to be taken as evidence of carelessness but was in accordance with the best professional practice of the day.

Here we have the reason why it is today found necessary, if a performance is to be given of an opera by Monteverdi, Cavalli, Cesti or the other masters of that first brilliant explosion of the new art form, to make a notated 'realization' of the original score, with all the musicians' actions prescribed in the modern manner, down to the last detail, since the training of modern classical musicians who make up the virtuoso orchestras of today not only does not prepare them for, but indeed actively discourages them from, engaging in the kind of improvisation which was everyday practice in the seventeenth and eighteenth centuries.

In the concerted instrumental music of the period, the figured bass was played not only by a bass instrument following the composer's bassline but also by a keyboard player, who would delight in improvising an elaborate part over the given bass and harmonies. Some modern keyboard players have trained themselves to play this continuo part; that such players remain limited in number is shown by the continuing healthy market in editions of baroque music with the keyboard part realized by an editor for those who cannot, or dare not, attempt to make their own as the composer expected them to do. Even more interesting for our discussion is the fact that any such improvised continuo is circumscribed by the need to work in a style that has been extinct as a contemporary creative medium since about 1750. We should speak more of historical reconstruction than of creation, since the player's task is not to bring about a new experience, as would have taken place when the piece was first performed, but to recreate an old one. It is significant that an eminent modern baroque harpsichordist and conductor, when asked in an interview how he would view a performance that was more memorable for the continuo player's improvisation than for the composer's music, replied, 'That would be an absolute artistic crime.'[4]

It is a thought that would almost certainly have puzzled and distressed Mozart, that most present-day performing musicians spend their entire careers, from before adolescence to retirement, without ever acknowledging a single musical idea or gesture as their own. One wonders why it was that the art of improvisation became thus lost in the western classical tradition, and the domination of the art by notation so complete in our own time. Some clues are given, so far as I can tell all unawares but perhaps the more honestly for that, by the English composer Jonathan Harvey in his book *The Music of Stockhausen*, in a chapter where he discusses those works of the composer which do leave room for an element of improvisation. He says: 'Only to the extent that functional harmony (even in the *very* broadest sense) does not matter any more are group improvisations successful, for it is strictly impossible to improvise *cogent* harmony in a group. Simultaneous intervals or controlled densities do still matter and those works such as [Stockhausen's] *Adieu* and *Stimmung* in which the harmony is not improvised are therefore the most successful. But even that must (logically) be considered inferior (for all the liberation of performers etc) to music with all the "best improvisation" thought out and written down in the leisure of the composer's workshop, and then well performed. That is why Baroque improvisation — for example as in a Corelli violin sonata where the violinist ornaments his lines furiously and the harpsichordist realizes his figures with all the imagination the tempo will allow him — for all its brilliance — was eventually and progressively superseded by the exact notation of all the cleverest ideas of the harpsichordist, with other middle parts added, to create an even more complex interplay of independent life in individual parts under an overriding harmonic order.'[5] (italics in original)

The historical correctness of this view is not in question; what is interesting about it is the implicit set of values, accepted apparently without question, in which the perfection of the music-object, which the performers present ready-made to the listeners, is considered to be of more importance than the music act, in which performers and listeners are involved together. Assuming this order of priorities, it is clearly worth while to curtail the performer's freedom of action (the dismissive tone of that 'etc' is too obvious to be missed) in order that the quality of the music-object can be improved, and the author, rightly in my opinion, gives as the principal factor in the eclipse of improvisation in the classical tradition the urge towards an ever more fully worked-out and complex interplay within the created object. The fact that this process requires the gross simplification of the relations, not only between performers and creative act but also between performers and listeners, passes, as it passes in countless histories of western music, without comment. What is gained in the 'cleverness' of the created object is lost in the engagement of the performer, on the one hand with the musical material and the process of its elaboration, which has become none of his business, and, on the other with his listeners' responses to his playing; once the music-object becomes fixed in all its details and the centre of attention in the performance, then clearly the listeners have no role other than to contemplate it, in stillness and in silence. And, further, it is not just that the performers' liberty etc is curtailed but also that in having no creative role to play each becomes a non-person, whose personality and idiosyncrasies, instead of being something human to treasure, are just a nuisance to the composer in the realization of his ideas; the performer whom the composer likes best is one who, assuming him or her to be equipped technically to realize the composer's ideas, submits wholly to them. The eagerness with which many composers in the 1950s seized hold of tape composition shows how strong was the desire to 'eliminate the middleman' in the musical transaction.

When a musician improvises, the act of creation is experienced at first hand, with the active participation of all those present, listeners as well as performers, while in fully-composed music the act is already in in the past, complete before the first sound is heard; it is abstracted, distanced from performers and listeners alike. That this abstraction and distancing have made possible the creation of magnificent sound-structures which have fascinated, and continue to fascinate, generations of players and listeners should not blind us to the price we pay for them, or give us leave to assume the inherent inferiority of other ways of musicking, as does clearly the author of the above passage. It is not just that Mozart, J.S. Bach, Beethoven and Liszt, as well as numberless other musicians great and forgotten, would protest at such an assumption, but we also have evidence that many of their most felicitous ideas grew out of improvisation, which strongly suggests that the existence of a thriving tradition of notated music depends not only on a thriving tradition of improvisation but also on an intimate connection between the two. That such a tradition is not only dead but even derided by classical musicians would seem to have serious implications for the health of their art.

I shall have more to say later concerning the above quotation, but first I wish to examine the concept of improvisation itself, to try to arrive at an understanding of what the word means. It is in fact extremely difficult to pin down any agreed understanding, either of what it is, or indeed of what it is not. The best definition I have been able to find comes from H.C. Colles's article in the 1954 edition of *Grove's Dictionary*, where it appears under the heading of 'Extemporization', and is defined as 'the art of thinking and performing music simultaneously.'[6] Even this, however, for all that it pays tribute to the instantaneity of the art, takes no cognizance of one of its most important characteristics: that it involves a great deal of prior thought, knowledge and agreed convention. Never do the performers start completely from scratch, even if the prior work is done without the participants giving it conscious thought or even necessarily being aware that it is taking place. Improvisation occurs always within a set of rules, or, rather, conventions, which are agreed, either explicitly or implicity, by all the participants before playing begins. Most commonly, the musicians have an idea before they start of how they are going to play, what conventions they are going to adopt, and quite possibly an over-all plan, which may be modified as they go along through factors such as audience response. In this respect an improvised performance is not unlike a conversation — which is also, as we have noted, an improvised art. Both musical performances and conversations are occasions for exploration, affirmation and celebration of identity and of relationships, and both depend on the existence of a commonly agreed language.

Improvisation, then, is never total uncontrolled invention — indeed, it is doubtful if the human mind is capable of such a thing — and most commonly these rules, or conventions, as well as a good deal of predetermined material, are provided by the idiom in which the players operate. In many musical cultures, such as the high-classical culture of India and the drum cultures of West Africa, the players do not consciously choose their idiom, any more than they choose the community into which they are born, of which in many ways the idiom is the ritual embodiment, but are acculturated naturally into it from infancy in much the same way as they enter their language community. This was once true also of improvisation in the western classical tradition. But in the west today improvisation flourishes only within the Afro-American tradition, where performers are free to choose within a number of styles and modes, and many are indeed to be found operating in different styles at different times and on different kinds of occasion. The various styles of improvisation will not be separated, but flow into and feed one another, producing an interaction of idioms, which is to say, of communities, that is absent in the virtual monoculture that is classical music today. Let us look now at some other modes of improvisation that have been found in the classical tradition in the past.

After the demise, around 1750, of the Baroque art of group improvisation, it was solo improvisation exclusively that was practised in classical music. There are important differences between solo and group improvisation; in the first place, the solo improvisor can engage in the wildest and most unfettered flights of the musical imagination, the most surprising harmonic changes, the most original formal devices, the most dramatic contrasts of texture, tempo and tone colour, without being bothered by the basic problem of group improvisation, which is that of ensuring among all the performers a common understanding of what is going on.

And secondly, it is clear that classical solo improvisors not only adhered to the melodic, harmonic and rhythmic conventions of their day but also worked within its conventional forms — fugue, sonata, variations and so on. Here we see one of the most striking differences between the improvisation practised by the classical masters and that which we find in the modern Afro-American tradition: the former were making compositions on the spot. Bach improvised, we are told, a piece 'in extemporized fugal form' on a theme given him by Frederick the Great; Beethoven's pupil Carl Czerny tells us that the master, working extempore from a single theme, composed a sonata movement, a free fantasia and a set of variations; and we have from Mozart a pair of fantasies, in D minor K397 and in C minor K475, which according to tradition started life as improvisations, but which bear all the signs of eighteenth-century compositional techniques: careful preparation when introducing a new theme or an important key change, adherence to acceptable key relations and a sense of over-all formal balance, with a return to the tonic key in time to establish it as firmly as in any carefully-composed sonata movement. We cannot, of course, know just how closely these pieces resemble the original improvisations, but they are pointers to what the latter might have been like. In fact, as Colles has it, 'what impressed listeners in that classic age most profoundly was the ability of the masters to extemporize in fugue and sonata, which the written art had evolved. Their triumph was to show that they could do without premeditation at the keyboard what they did in their studies on paper.'[7] There was, as the comments which I quoted earlier suggest, certainly more to it than that; it must have been not just a party trick but a genuine increase in excitement and daring over the written-down compositions. But we shall never know for sure.

In any case, the intention was to create on the spot a rounded composition that conformed to the conventions of the day. I know of no evidence to allow us to decide whether the performance was affected in any way by audience response, which is an important shaping force in other kinds of improvisation; none of the accounts makes any direct reference to it. A description by Ferdinand Ries of a performance by Beethoven of his Quintet for piano and wind in E flat, Op 16, is instructive, however: 'In the last allegro there is, in several places, a pause before the theme begins again. In one of these, Beethoven suddenly began to improvise, taking the Rondo as a theme, entertaining himself and the others for quite a long while. This, however, did not at all entertain the accompanying musicians; they became quite indignant and

Herr Ramm actually furious. It was truly comical to see these gentlemen waiting every moment for their entrance, put their instruments continuously to their mouths, and then quietly put them down again. Finally Beethoven was satisfied and led into the rondo once more. The whole company was delighted.'[8]

Except, no doubt, for the four wind players; the story emphasises once again the essentially soloistic nature of improvisation within the classical tradition. Participation for the wind players was impossible, however much they might have wanted to join in, for the pianist's imaginative flights, no doubt into remote and unexpected harmonic fields, would have excluded them. It is interesting that tonal harmony, that field upon which is acted out those dramas of the individual soul which are compositions in the classical tradition, should also through its very nature be the factor which makes direct group interaction impossible and confines improvisation to those displays of individual virtuosity which we have seen described.

On the other hand, jazz musicians and other musicians in the Afro-American tradition do improvise together within a framework of tonal harmony; we shall see in a moment how this has become possible, through a change which they have wrought in the meaning of harmony. First, however, let us look at improvisation outside the western tradition, especially in Africa, which has of course been the major formative influence on the music which is the subject of this book.

A study of African improvisation brings home once more the very important truth about the art, that it is never total on-the-spot invention. It is not just that there is always a certain amount of preformed material, but also that there is nothing to stop the players from repeating what they have done before. What is significant, in fact, about improvisation is not that the players are constantly inventing anew but that they are free to do so when it is appropriate (one can hear this process in successive takes by Charlie Parker in his Savoy recording sessions of 1944 to 1948; it is not the size of the changes from one take to the next that reveals his power but the effectiveness of those often quite small alterations that he makes). In the West African drum ensemble the leader, or master drummer, has spent his apprentice years playing the supporting drum rhythms, and his performance consists of improvised variations on those rhythms, simple at first and then with increasing complexity, in such a way as to make the development of each out of its predecessor clear and audible to all. We must never forget that he and his colleagues are playing, not just for listeners but also for dancers, with whom they are constantly interacting; John Miller Chernoff even relates how, when he was learning his craft as a drummer among the Ewe in Ghana: 'When I played poorly for dancers, they *danced* their criticism by executing their steps in a half-hearted way, or they helped me by simplifying their steps to emphasise a more consistently responsive rhythm.'[9] The basic patterns are traditional, and thus given; it is what the drummer does with them in collaboration with the dancers that is the sign of his musicianship and of his command of the idiom. As A.M. Jones says, 'The master drummer . . . has a number of standard patterns at his disposal . . . What he does, having first established the pattern, is to play variations on it . . . Besides being able to repeat the patterns at will, he can also play them in any order and he need not play them all. It all depends on the aesthetic sense of the drummer and the fitness of the pattern to adorn the dancing of any particular dancer who happens to be dancing.'[10]

This may involve repetition of the same pattern for quite a long time. There is no need for the master drummer to be constantly inventing new rhythms; on the contrary, his task is not so much to invent as to give form and organization to what already exists, in collaboration with the other drummers, whose task in turn is to support him through the repetition of what are individually simple rhythms but which in combination build into complex and subtle, constantly developing, sound structures. He does not dominate the musicking so much as pick up in his playing and give a focus to the general sense of the occasion, to how his fellow-drummers (without whose rhythmic patterns his own would be meaningless), the dancers and even the spectators feel and move, and to allow everyone to contribute to it. 'A musician,' says Chernoff, 'can afford to take his time because of the openness of the arrangements to various interpretations. He does not have to change much because he is not trying to monopolize the possibilities. He knows he is not responsible for providing all the interest and that he can only suggest some of the potential that is there.'[11]

This brings us back to what we have seen is an important aspect of African musicking: the musician regards himself as responsible, not just for the sounds that he makes, but for the whole social progress of the event, for its success as a human encounter. The musician as he improvises responds not only to the inner necessities of the sound world he is creating but also to the dynamics of the human situation as it develops around him. It is his task to create not just a single set of sound perspectives which are to be contemplated and enjoyed by listeners, but a multiplicity of opportunities for participation along a number of different perspectives. As Chernoff says: 'The music is best considered as an arrangement of gaps where one may add a rhythm, rather than as a dense pattern of sound.'[12] And again: 'As they display style and involvement, people make their music socially effective, transforming the dynamic power of the rhythms into a focus of character and community. We are even quite close to a metaphysics of rhythm if we remember that sensing the whole in a system of multiple rhythms depends on comprehending, or "hearing", as the Africans say, the beat that is never sounded. At the convergence of essence and form stands the master drummer, not creating new rhythms but giving order and organization to those already there. Every place, a drummer once told me, has its own rhythms which give it character; going there, one must find a rhythm which fits, and improvise on it.'[13]

Here we see a social purpose in the performance of music which goes far beyond the evocation of an individual response to a sound-object such as we find in the western classical tradition; such a purpose could not possibly be served by the note-perfect reproduction of a musical entity created at another time, in another place, for another purpose, no matter how perfect in itself that entity may be or how skilled and sensitive the performance. It is only by keeping possibilities open, by modifying the performance as it goes along, that it becomes possible to pick up the sense of an occasion, to bring it into focus and enhance it for the greater social and spiritual benefit of all. The traditions of African music represent a cultural achievement of the first order in their gift to the the music maker of the materials and the idiom through which he or she can do this. It is a gift which has been passed on to the Afro-American musician.

It is of course not only in the African tradition of improvisation that one finds this carefully maintained balance between, on the one hand, existing musical material and organizational principle (one could, by analogy with spoken language, legitimately call it a syntax) and on the other the sense of what the occasion requires. The sitarist Viram Jasani, in conversation with Derek Bailey, says of Indian improvisation: 'The time that we spend with a Guru is purely spent in trying to understand the framework in which Indian music is set. And a Guru doesn't, or your teacher doesn't, really tell you how to improvise . . . What (the student) really learns from his teacher is the framework in which improvisation or performance of Indian music takes place.'[14] Or the flamenco guitarist Paco Peña: 'I'd say that within a piece you can reach certain heights because you have let yourself improvise, say, a little bit, not too much, but that little bit changes the whole character of the piece. But I certainly would not say that the whole piece is improvised — anyway in my case it never is completely improvised — but it is true that it can change according to how I feel at the moment . . . you are completely free to improvise and you also have the choice not to improvise. You can leave it as it is, simply because it feels better to leave it as it is.'[15]

To improvise, then, is to establish a different set of human relationships, a different kind of society, from that established by fully literate musicking. As we examined the relationships that are to be perceived when people come together to take part in different kinds of classical performance, let us now look at the relationships brought into being when musicians improvise in the idioms of the Afro-American tradition.

I have already made some observations concerning blues as performance; we can now look more deeply into its meaning. Once again, we find that no blues performance is invented from scratch, but consists, both poetically and musically, mainly of pre-existing material. The performer may, indeed, perform the blues exactly as he or she heard it from another singer, merely giving, perhaps, his or her own twist to the melody, a different accentuation to the words, a different shape to the instrumental 'responses'; these changes may not be premeditated or even intentional, but may arise simply from lapses of memory, or from the possession of a different kind of voice or different instrumental technique — they may be none the less effective for that in the new circumstances in which the performance is taking place. And of course a performer, having found an effective way of putting across a blues, may do it in the same way over and over again — but this does not rule out, at any time, the possibility of introducing something new. A mediocre performer may be satisfied with evolving a performance and sticking to it, and, indeed, audiences may demand that he or she do so (recording artists are constantly under pressure to perform exactly 'as on the record') but the great and questing artist will remain constantly in search of the performance which fits a given situation most completely, and will remain sensitive to the listeners' responses and adapt to them.

Solo artists, as were most of the early blues singers, have of course only their own performance and interaction with the audience to worry about; we have seen how they articulate the listeners' thoughts and emotions, drawing them closer together in an intense and mutually supportive community. When the accompaniment (if one can call it that in view of its role as second expressive voice) is played by a group, who might be playing electric guitar, piano, alto saxophone, string bass and drums, a new and more complex social situation is brought into existence. The musicians are usually not reading from written parts; their performance will probably have been roughed out and rehearsed, but invention is possible at any stage. The music of the blues, as we saw earlier, conforms to quite orthodox progressions of tonal harmony, with endless repetitions of the same twelve-bar pattern, and it is this pattern that mediates the relationships between the musicians. Because it leaves room for a greater degree of spontaneity than those literate forms we looked at earlier, and, because, too, the form and the content of the performance can be determined to a great degree by the response of the audience, performers and listeners are in a more intimate relationship than literate musicking can create. From the moment when the performance begins, performers and listeners are dynamically engaged with one another; the listeners respond, not with stillness and the formal signs of 'polite' attention, but with cries, handclaps, shouts, movement and dance — which are much better-mannered in black society than silence. Performers and listeners are bringing into existence, if only for the duration of the performance, an ideal society very different from that created by a classical performance; it confronts the values of industrial society with a celebration of the body and its movements, an affirmation of those qualities of warmth, communality and emotional honesty, which black Americans call soul.

An improvised performance, through the constant repetition that is bound to occur in the working life of a professional, or even active amateur, performer, may well become what one might call a non-literate composition; the line between them is thin. Some non-literate cultures place more value on the accurate rendition of the received text than do others; European vernacular traditions, as we have seen, place great emphasis on accuracy, and this emphasis can also be found in some aspects of the Afro-American tradition in which white culture is dominant. Thus we find that the preservation of the text is of more importance in white country music than in black blues. But regardless of whether the performance has grown out of improvisation and settled down into a routine, or whether it is a carefully worked-out arrangement, one feature that remains constant is the possibility of the creative involvement of the performing artist in the very substance of the music. Even when it is traditional material or the work of another musician that is being performed, the performance is the performer's own, and he or she is free to make changes, the permissable extent of which is determined by the idiom in which the performer works, and will be well known to all.

On the other hand, nothing the improvising artist does is completely new. His apparent freedom lies in the recognition of necessity, as represented by the idiom, to which his or her first loyalty is given; the artist is manipulating material which has been received from the idiom through prolonged immersion in it to the point where it becomes part of the performer's own nature. The apparent naturalness of even the 'primitive' blues singer of the rural American south is thus an illusion; like any other musician the singer has an idea of the effect desired and works hard to achieve it. And thus, too, paradoxically, the individual sound of each musician results from an affirmation of the strength of the tradition and of the performer's place within it. Even the most apparently revolutionary of artists, for example those who created the jazz style known as bebop in the late 1940s were seeking, not to overthrow the traditional relationships but to reaffirm their power in a new context.

Bebop is interesting, in that it represents a quite conscious regrasping of the principles of blues, in eclipse to the white-dominated bands of the swing era; its early development owed more to blues-based bands such as that of Count Basie (and most especially to their rhythm sections) than to the swing bands which were its more obvious predecessors. What the beboppers were out to do was to make the blues swing not less but more; their approach was perfectly comprehensible within the blues tradition. Bebop shares with blues the simple basis of improvisation over an endlessly repeated harmonic sequence, whether it be the blues progression itself, an elaboration of it, or the harmonies of a popular song.

Which brings us back to the passage quoted earlier from Jonathan Harvey's book on Stockhausen, in which we can see further evidence of that profound misunderstanding of the nature of improvisation which seems to be common among classical musicians today. Within that tradition, what Harvey calls functional harmony is the central technique for the creation of that surprise and drama which are essential characteristics of the music, and when he speaks of the impossibility, in group improvisation, of making 'cogent' harmony, he clearly means harmony which will fulfil its traditional function of creating tension and drama through the juxtaposition of chords in time. In this he is correct, since it is unlikely in the extreme that all members of an improvising group will all simultaneously hit on the same unexpected but dramatically apposite chord, but he can see no alternative other than the abolition of tonal functional harmony altogether.

Within the Afro-American tradition, however, effective group improvisation has remained possible because the musicians have changed the meaning of tonal harmony. Blues, as we have seen, uses simple, even banal progressions of a quite conventional kind, which are drained of dramatic content simply by repetition, so that the progression gains strength, not through surprise but through predictability. Bebop improvisation, while its harmonies are more elaborated, still repeats them in cycles of sixteen, twenty-four or thirty-two bars, the conventional lengths of the popular songs on which the improvisations are commonly based. These harmonic progressions, which might be in themselves quite elaborate (many of them are the work of those 'Broadway masters' whom I discussed in the last chapter), are the 'givens' of the performance, the underpinning which holds it together, while the real interest lies elsewhere, in the ingenious and expressive improvised patterns which the players build on that foundation. The fact that the harmonies are drained of all dramatic content means that that personal drama of the individual soul which has been the essence of a composition in the classical tradition from its seventeenth-century beginnings to the contemporary avant garde, is not a concern of the jazz or blues musician; absent also is any sense of climax and resolution, any of the drawing-on of the listener through time, through those often abrupt and even violent contrasts of volume and timbre, tempo and texture, which are essential ingredients of that drama.

We see here a crucial difference even from those great solo improvisations which so excited the listeners of Bach, Mozart and Beethoven: the performers are not trying to invent, on the spur of the moment, a composition which will compare with those which the musician, in the peace and quiet of his study, and with unlimited time in which to work it all out, can elaborate and present through the medium of notation; they are making a performance. A composition, in the classical sense of the word, is a music-object which has an existence over and above any performance of it; the processes of composition and of performance are secondary to the existence of the object, the first taking place only to bring it into being, the second in order to bring it to realization. But improvisation is all process; there is no product. What we are taking part in is, in the first case, the re-enactment of a drama that was complete and done with before a note of it was heard, while in the second we are taking part, at first rather than at second hand, in the drama of creation itself. The improvisors are playing a dangerous game; at any point many things can go wrong, just as they can in any other living relationship, and only the most skilful, quick-thinking and above all 'accommodating to the others' as Aguzzari has it, can stay the course. This is why listeners see no reason to restrain their applause until the end of the performance, for they are applauding, not one thing, but many skilful and daring acts which are being carried out by the musicians as ritual representatives of the whole community.

When Harvey tells us of the replacement in western music over the last four hundred years or so of improvised by fully-composed pieces, he is describing not, as he seems to think, an improvement but a change in attitude which is profound and which reflects the European preoccupation with things which has developed over that period of time. He is not the only musician to have been misled by the preoccupations of four hundred years of European music; the subject of his book, Stockhausen, has himself been pleased to observe: 'I think that if free jazz musicians also played "composed" new music their techniques and their sense of coherent musical entities would develop even more,'[16] while Boulez dismisses improvisation thus: '. . . with improvisations, because they are purely affective phenomena, there is not the slightest scope for anyone else to join in . . . Improvisation is a personal psychodrama and is regarded as such. Whether we are interested or not, we cannot graft our own affective, intellectual or personal structure on a base of this sort.'[17] One should not perhaps think too hardly of these eminent musicians for what is after all a lack not so much in themselves as in the tradition in which they work and in the training which they received. For the modern classical tradition (by which I mean not only the tradition of composition but also that in which performing musicians work) provides nothing in the way of idioms, models or performance situations in which an aspiring improvisor might work; without a score before him he is left with only the terrifying prospect of being free to play whatever comes to mind, with no guide for procedure, no agreed conventions, no common stock of material, no way even of knowing whether he is doing what he is doing well or badly. No wonder Boulez cannot graft his own affective structure on to such a base; no wonder Harvey, in a passage just preceding that quoted earlier, finds that group improvisation can produce only 'either boringly obvious climaxes or lulls or . . . a veneer of complexity which sounds all too obviously the unsatisfactory handiwork of chance,'[18] when from the very beginning of their musical training these musicians, like virtually every beginner, were in all probability told that 'playing by ear' is inferior to playing from the notes, that they must stick to 'the music' and not 'play about' on their instrument, and were made to play every written note exactly as written.

Let us now return to a consideration, which I broke away from earlier, of the kinds of relationship that are set up among the participants in a musical performance, the kinds of ideal societies that are brought into existence. Let us think first of a group of improvising jazz musicians. Having agreed on the tune upon which they are going to improvise, and on a tempo, they are joined together, even if they have never played together before, by the common idiom, the common stock of material and by the melody and its harmonies. But while the players are free to engage in dialogue with one another, to explore, affirm and celebrate their various identities and their relationship, in a more direct and less restrained way than when there is a score to mediate those relationships, they are still bound by the requirements of the idiom; there are ways in which they may respond to one another and ways in which they may not. They are caught in the ancient and creative paradox of all human social life: that relationships can be established between people only through the acceptance of some kind of common language, and yet the very conventions which allow for communication and interaction also structure that interaction and prevent the participants from attaining to more than a certain degree of intimacy. We have seen how the modern symphony concert is a ceremony which celebrates, among other values, the isolation of the individual in western society, and how even more domestic forms of music making, such as that of an amateur string quartet, aim for and achieve only a certain degree of intimacy in the encounter between the participants. Developments in jazz, on the other hand, at least since the bebop generation, can be seen as a search, not so much for new sounds or new rhythms, as for new kinds of relationship, unmediated by the restraints imposed by industrial society.

In the case of the original generation of beboppers, we read that many other musicians, even if they knew the harmonic changes (which were, after all, common property) were completely flummoxed by the new rhythms and new ways of phrasing and articulating; it was if someone had taken a familiar vocabulary and, by altering the syntax by means of which the relationships between the words were established, had created a new language, tantalizingly similar to the old, but one in which they were unable to converse. And since, as we noted earlier, members of a culture define themselves as much by what they are not as by what they are, this exclusion brought about a greater freedom and intimacy among those who *could* cope with the new twists of language, an intimacy that was not unconnected with the first stirrings of the modern black civil rights movement and with the fact that white musicians for a long time could not cope with the style. The new musical forms and relationships articulated and celebrated new social relationships in which the blacks, free to love one another like brothers and sisters, at the same time received the respect that was their due. It was a society held together not by power (for all are equal in the jazz group and all share equally the creative responsibility which is not delegated to any outside authority, either composer or conductor) but by love and mutual responsibility, a society which can exist only if its members are all fully realized human beings and mindful of one another's needs. That this society did not, could not, exist outside the time and space of the performance, and that it contrasted so cruelly with the actual society in which they had to live and make a living, must have induced appalling strains and have contributed to the destruction of many fine musicians of the time.

The stripping-off of the constraints of tonal harmony

(which is to say, of the constraints imposed by white society not only on the blacks but also on itself) which followed in the sixties and after, and the affirmation of values of community and autonomy can be seen in the titles of many jazz albums that were issued in the 1960s: *Spiritual Unity*, *A Love Supreme*, *This Is Our Music*, and *One Step Beyond* — very sixties preoccupations, a cynic might say, but I doubt whether that is how it would have appeared to the artists. None of them would have found in their performances anything that was incompatible with the ethic or the aesthetic of the old blues; they were as faithful to the idiom, and through the idiom to the ritual and the community, as had been the bluesmen. In renouncing harmony they were perhaps signalling a more austere rejection of the blandishments of American affluence, but then, this has always been a powerful strain in black American culture. As Lawrence Levine says: 'For large numbers of Negroes, the bulk of them at the lower end of the social and economic scale, it was possible and necessary to speak openly about a number of realities that American popular culture needed to suppress'.[19] And as far as the 1960s were concerned, it is possible to argue that the Age of Aquarius, so recently begun, with which that decade was so preoccupied, was no more than a naïve and literal interpretation (a literalness which black Americans themselves were far too experienced to fall for) of those enduring preoccupations, those truths, of which black musicking had been a ritual since the days of slavery; as we shall see, the forms that the white popular music of that time took were, in a manner of speaking, 'literal' interpretations of black American ways of musicking. It was the gift of black America to white society, which did not, and could not, understand it rightly.

The society of the jazz performance has long since been enlarged to include those white musicians and listeners who can accept its premises; the apparent exclusiveness of the original black society is always, it seems, accompanied by an implicit invitation to whites to take part as well — with the ironic proviso 'if you can'. This is the 'trap of reciprocity' of which Edwin Mason writes — a tender trap, one must add, from which both parties ultimately benefit.

We should note also the supreme importance of the

relationship of the musicians with dancers, and the importance of dance in the development of blues and jazz improvisation. In black culture, we must never forget, dancing is as subtle, as intellectual and as ritualistic an improvised art as musicking. A story from Marshall and Jean Stearns's *Jazz Dance* must serve to make the point. It dates from 1937 and comes from Leon James, one of a band of dancers who used to frequent the famous Savoy Ballroom in Harlem at that time, later turning professional and making a career in Hollywood: '"Dizzy Gillespie was featured in the brass section of Teddy Hill's screaming band. A lot of people had him pegged as a clown, but we loved him. Every time he played a crazy lick, we cut a crazy step to go with it. And he dug us and blew even crazier stuff to see if we could dance to it, a kind of game, with the musicians and the dancers challenging each other"'. The Stearns's comment: 'Great musicians inspire great dancers — and vice versa — until the combination pyramids into the greatest performances of both. "I wish jazz was played more often for dancing," said Lester "Prez" Young during his last years with the Count Basie Band. "The rhythm of the dancers comes back to you when you're playing."'[20] Such a peak of social interaction can, of course, occur only when both musicians and dancers are free, within their idiom, to respond directly to one another, that is, when they are improvising.

In his book *Improvisation* (the fact that it is to my knowledge the only book in English which deals with the subject shows the importance which it is allowed in official western music), Derek Bailey, himself a noted guitarist and improvisor, makes a distinction between what he calls 'idiomatic' and 'free' improvisation. The former is the kind of improvisation with which we have been concerned so far, in which the performer works within an idiom which provides the framework for entering into relationships with other musicians and with listeners, and which shapes and limits those relationships. As Bailey says: 'No idiomatic improvisor is concerned with improvisation as some sort of separate activity. What they are absolutely concerned for is the idiom; for them improvisation serves the idiom and is the expression of the idiom.'[21] And the idiom, as we have seen, is the ritual embodiment of the community. The 'free' improvisor, on the other hand, considers him or herself to be free of any kind of idiomatic restraint, and thus to be relating to fellow musicians and listeners directly without any mediation whatsoever, even that of a commonly agreed musical language. Here is Bailey again: 'For many people free improvisation is about playing with other people. Some of the greatest opportunities provided by free improvisation are in the exploration of relationships between people.'[22] True enough; I have found in my own experience that some of the most intense and satisfying musical experiences, both as performer and as listener, have come from just such free improvisation. It is worth giving further consideration to its nature and meaning.

Primarily, it means that the performers believe themselves to be playing without any idiomatic guide whatsoever, without any preconceptions concerning what they are going to play, without, in fact, any external guide to their actions other than what they decide on the spur of the moment to do, either as an initiative or in response to an initiative by another player. The improvisors do not feel tied even to any set units of pitch or time; there is not necessarily any scale or regular beat to which they play. Nor are they restricted to the use of orthodox western instruments, either those of the symphony orchestra or those of vernacular music; elaborate sets of *ad hoc* percussion made from whatever makes an interesting sound when struck, African drums, South American flutes and any number of home-made instruments are liable to turn up. It follows that orthodox concepts of instrumental tone or technique are also thought unimportant, and even the quality of sound in itself is secondary.

To the listener accustomed to the mellifluous sounds of classical music that must seem like a recipe for intolerable cacophony. Certainly, unless all those taking part practise the most intense discipline, cacophony will result — but the discipline is not so much that of instrumental technique as of care and mutual consideration, careful listening and considerate playing. The free improvisor, in fact, is seeking not an idiom but those universals of music which transcend idiom, and through them the universals of human relationships. Like all close human relationships, it is a risky business, of all forms of musicking the most dangerous; the musicians show themselves to one another, and to whoever is listening, technically and emotionally naked, without any outside constraints to mediate their relationship. It is often said that free improvisation is fine for the players but hell for the listeners, and while in my experience that is not true, in that when the playing is going well performers and listeners alike are caught up in an intensity of community that can only be called erotic, there is, on the other hand, no need for anyone present to be a mere listener; everyone is free to take part. Just as, ideally, there are no listeners to a conversation, so free improvisation will go best if everyone present is taking an active part in the process. At its best, free improvisation celebrates a set of informal, even loving, relationships which can be experienced by everyone present, and brings into existence, at least for the duration of the performance, a society whose closest political analogy is with anarchism — anarchism, that is, in the real rather than journalistic meaning of the word, a society in which government is not imposed from the top or from the centre, but comes from each individual, who is most fully realized in contributing to the wellbeing of the community — the polar opposite, one might say, of the symphony concert.

It is thus interesting that free improvisation is frequently a meeting-point for classical and vernacular musicians, the latter largely but by no means exclusively from a background in jazz (we should remember that few vernacular musicians allow themselves to be placed into a single category but are liable to work within a variety of styles and genres). Jazz, of course, requires a very exacting apprenticeship, and those musicians who engage in free improvisation are often those who have, as it were, gone through jazz styles and come out the other side still looking for closer contact with other musicians. Approaching them from the opposite direction have been many classically trained musicians, often fugitives from the centralized, composer-dominated avant-garde. In many cases they have made a conscious break with the social and political implications of classical music generally and of their conservatoire training in particular, from which contemporary classical music offers no escape, however technically revolutionary it may appear to have been; thus musicians from both sides of western musical culture have found themselves making common cause in the dissolution of idiom and technique, and in the quest for direct interaction.

Does the free improvisor, then, work without any rules or conventions whatsoever? The question relates to the earlier discussion in which I suggested not only that culture is a set of attitudes and assumptions which underlie conscious thought and even perception but also that, as Geertz says, 'a cultureless human being would probably turn out to be . . . a wholly mindless and consequently unworkable monstrosity.'[23] If musical performances establish relationships, no relationships can be established without the existence of commonly understood meanings, and there can be no meanings without rules. Where, then, do the rules come from which enable free improvisors to establish those vital relationships within the group and the intimacy which they seek? Clearly, not from outside constraints such as melodic, rhythmic or harmonic idioms, but rather from those universal patterns of human behaviour and response in which it is necessary for the players to believe implicitly, if not necessarily consciously, before engaging in such a risky activity. What happens in practice is that as the musicians play together they evolve a set of common understandings; they invent, as it were, their own culture — not from scratch, of which I believe the human mind to be incapable, but from the creative blending of the manner of thinking and playing of each musician (since each will bring to the performance habits of playing, favorite procedures and habitual responses) into what can only be called a new idiom. This idiom, because it is unconscious and habitual, eventually becomes as binding on the members of the group as is the flamenco idiom on the flamenco musician, or the idiom of Indian classical music on the Indian musician; to this extent, free improvisation is different from other forms not in kind (there is only one kind) but in the degree to which the musicians rely on their own experience to create the idiom, the syntax, through which they establish their relationships. There is in fact no escape from culture or from the necessary limits which it imposes on relationships; but the attempt to escape may well result in either the creation of new, or the rediscovery of very old, modes of human social response.

In most of the world's musical traditions the word 'improvisation' has little significance, since what we have been calling improvisation is just the normal way of musicking; they call it, quite simply, playing, and the idiom in which they work is, equally simply, 'the way we play'. It is only in the modern west that a separate word has become necessary for what is, after all, only the assumption by the performer of responsibility for what is played as well as for how it is played, and thus for the kind of society that is brought into existence during the performance, and for the lack of separation between the roles of composer and performer which are so clearly demarcated in the western classical tradition today. This separation, with which may be associated a rise in the status of the composer relative to that of the performer and a devaluation of improvisation, has played its part in the decline of creative energy in the classical tradition which can be seen and heard around us today. It would seem as if there is a direct relationship between the strength of, and the respect given to, a tradition of improvisation (or 'playing') and the health of the musical culture in general. Certainly the state of exuberant proliferation that has characterized Afro-American musicking in our century contrasts strongly with the increasing withdrawal of classical composers from the concerns of even the majority of classical-music lovers, let alone the overwhelming majority of westerners, who, contrary to official assumption, are perfectly capable of creating and certainly of understanding a musical performance. And even within the history of the Afro-American tradition it is possible to see an ebb and flow of creative energy in the intermittent eclipse of improvisation, generally in pursuit of a more perfect, elaborate or predictable music-object, such as occurred in jazz in the swing era, and occurs today in large and expensive performances by superstar rock groups.

NOTES

1. CARDEW, Cornelius, *Treatise Handbook*, London, Edition Peters, 1971, p xi.
2. These comments are quoted in BYRNSIDE, Ronald: 'The Performer as Creator: Jazz Improvisation' in HAMM, Charles *et al.*: *Contemporary Music and Music Cultures*, Englewood Cliffs, Prentice-Hall, 1975, p 245.
3. quoted in ROSE, Gloria: 'Aguzzari and the Improvising Orchestra', *Journal of the American Musicological Society*, Vol 18, 1963, p 389.
4. BAILEY, Derek: *Improvisation*, London, Latimer New Directions, 1979, p 42.
5. HARVEY, Jonathan: *The Music of Stockhausen*, London, Faber & Faber, 1975, p 122.
6. COLLES, H.E.: 'Extemporization or Improvisation', *Grove's Dictionary of Music and Musicians*, Vol 2, London, Macmillan, 5th edition 1954, pp 991-2.
7. *ibid.*, p 992.
8. quoted in ROBBINS LANDON, H.C.: *Beethoven*, London, Thames & Hudson, 1970, p 98.
9. CHERNOFF, John Miller: *African Rhythm and African Sensibility*, Chicago, University of Chicago Press, 1979, p 67.
10. JONES, A.M.: *Studies in African Music*, Vol 1, London, Oxford University Press, 1959, p 80.
11. CHERNOFF, John Miller: *op. cit.*, p 114.
12. *ibid.*, p 113.
13. *ibid.*, p 155.
14. BAILEY, Derek: *op. cit.*, p 16.
15. *ibid.*, p 26–27.
16. COTT, Jonathan: *Stockhausen: Conversations With the Composer*, London, Robson Books, 1974, p 199.
17. BOULEZ, Pierre: *Conversations With Célestin Deliège*, London, Eulenburg Books, 1975, p 65.
18. HARVEY, Jonathan: *op. cit.*, p 123.
19. LEVINE, Lawrence: *Black Culture and Black Consciousness: Afro-American Folk Thought from Slavery to Freedom*, New York, Oxford University Press, 1977, p 283.
20. STEARNS, Marshall and Jean: *Jazz Dance: The Story of American Vernacular Dance*, New York, Schirmer Books, 1968, p 325.
21. BAILEY, Derek: *op. cit.*, p 28.
22. *ibid.*, p 125.
23. GEERTZ, Clifford: *The Interpretation of Cultures*, London, Hutchinson, 1975, p 68.

Chapter 11

STYLES OF ENCOUNTER III: A LOT OF LOVING GOING ON

Of all the styles of Afro-American music, in so far as they can be separated out from one another, that which is known as jazz is the one with which white intellectuals and classical musicians today feel most at ease. They manage to assimilate the values and the aesthetic of jazz to those with which they were brought up, and they feel able to accord to its artists a status and a respectability denied to other Afro-American musicians, and not far beneath that accorded to classical artists. This almost classical status is illustrated neatly by the fact that the British Broadcasting Corporation devotes about four hours of a total weekly airtime of some 120 hours on its classical-music channel to jazz. Among intellectuals and classical musicians the names, and the work, of Brubeck, Basie and Beiderbecke are almost as familiar as those of Boulez, Beckett and Bergman, and there exists a literary tradition of jazz scholarship, criticism and exegesis, not shared by any other Afro-American style, going back fully fifty years to the pioneering writings of André Hodier and Hugues Panassié. All this suggests that jazz has affinities with classical music that other Afro-American styles do not have.

Of all Afro-American musicians jazzmen, and jazzwomen, have always been the most eclectic; everything they hear, from blues to symphonic music to Anglo-Celtic folksong, from gospel to opera arias to the post-war avant garde, is grist to their mill. It may even be possible to propose a definition of jazz as that aspect of Afro-American musicking that has closest links with classical music. It is not a satisfactory definition, but it does have the merit of drawing attention to the fact that a major source of creative energy for the artist in jazz has come from the tensions between European, or Euro-American, and Afro-American values.

These tensions can be perceived in a number of ways. We can see them as between, on the one hand, the literate culture of western industrial society, with all its tendency towards centralization and standardization, and on the other the orality and decentralization of black American culture. In musical terms this can be heard as, on the one hand, composition through notation, the separation of composer from performer and the authority of the written text, and, on the other, improvisation, non-literate composition and the autonomy of the performer. As we have seen, the composition-improvisation antithesis has important implications for the kinds of relationship that are brought into being by a musical performance — how close to or distant from one another the participants are, how active or passive the listeners, and so on. We have seen, too, how the classical tradition has abandoned improvisation, and it is interesting to see how whenever that tradition has become dominant in jazz the space for improvisation has become curtailed; one could use the extent to which the musicians are obliged to rely on notation as a yardstick for determining which of the two cultures is dominant at any point in the history of jazz performance.

It is important to bear in mind that these two tendencies, or orientations, are not mutually exclusive, but exist side by side in most western people, white and black. We have seen that even the most literate of western people still acquire some of their most important cultural attitudes and assumptions through the oral-aural mode, from parents, elders and peers, even if in our society the superiority of the literate mode is assumed without discussion. Conversely, it should not need to be pointed out that black Americans are just as much at home in the literate mode as are their white compatriots — but they continue to place a higher value on orality, and tend to be more proficient and imaginative with the spoken word, than whites. The fact that a literate society is a centralized and hierarchical one, which Africans and Afro-Americans have traditionally resisted, is also important.

If the fundamental concern of all music is human

relationships, the problem in group music making of all kinds, from symphony orchestras to Balinese *gamelans* to heavy-metal bands, is the establishment of workable relationships between the participants, which will allow room for the individual player to make full use of his or her musical skills and imagination to explore, affirm and celebrate an identity, while preserving that over-all order which is essential if the musicking is to generate any meaning either for performers themselves or for whoever is listening. Those relationships incarnate ideal human relationships as imagined by the participants, and both the technical problems encountered and the techniques used to solve them are metaphors for the problems, and the methods, of maintaining an acceptable social order. In a symphony orchestra those problems have been solved, once and for all, by the evolution of a hierarchical structure and centralized authority vested partly in a composer and partly in a conductor, each of whose authority in his own area is absolute — an uneasy combination at best, at least when the composer is around to make his views known. Those who have worked in or with professional symphony orchestras know that while an orchestra's power structure may, in theory, be precisely defined and static, the actual day-to-day relationships are as edgy as those in any other industrial organization, with the players constantly challenging the conductor's authority and subjecting each new piece to the most merciless scrutiny. But, grumble and smoulder as they may, they make no serious attempt to depose either authority from his (it is rarely *her*) position, not surprisingly since without a conductor and a score they would be at a complete loss for anything to play or for how to play it. In a symphony orchestra, then, as in other kinds of classical performance today, the question of order has been settled in the way most contemporary governments would like to be able to settle it. The performances that are made possible by this centralized and authoritarian order can be of an indubitable splendour and brilliance, but they are bought at the price of the players' autonomy and of creative satisfactions that ought to be commensurate with the skills and the musicality that are demanded of them. The players are rewarded for this sacrifice in other ways, with a social status and a degree of financial security that is denied to their colleagues in vernacular musicking.

That there is necessarily an antithesis between individual freedom and social order is a notion that Europeans, and those who have absorbed European and Euro-American culture, have interiorized so completely that they scarcely even notice that they are thinking in that way, still less consider the possibility of alternatives. The notion is implicit in the activities of all contemporary governments, who take it for granted that considerable sacrifices of individual freedom are necessary to preserve a social order in which it is possible to live free from the fear of rape, pillage and robbery — and of conquest by the forces of other, like-minded governments. It is implicit in the writings of some of the greatest of European thinkers; the whole line of thought that is descended from Thomas Hobbes's *Leviathan* is based on it, while even Freud, in his last writings, mused despairingly on the repression that seems to be necessary if civilization is to exist at all. It is noticeable also in the whole organizational structure and the teachings of the Christian church, even if it is less in evidence in the recorded words of its founder. But in traditional African culture such an antinomy is by no means self-evident. As the Ewe proverb has it, 'Man is man because of other men'; individual and society live, not in antagonism but in mutual dependency, the individual coming to fullest development only within the social framework, and the society flourishing only on the basis of fully realized individuals whose individuality is necessary for social health. The elaborate rituals of traditional African societies, the musicking, the dancing, the masking, the cult ceremonies, are all designed ultimately to mediate social and individual necessity, to bring them into harmony rather than merely to effect compromises between antagonists. We have seen how the Africans brought their social attitudes with them on the Middle Passage and how those attitudes became a powerful factor for survival in the terrible conditions of slavery and its aftermath, and I have suggested that Afro-American musical performances in this century, especially in blues and gospel, have been rituals that have continued to affirm and to celebrate the mutual support of individual and community.

To play jazz, for a black musician, is to go beyond such rituals into a more complex and even dangerous task; it is to move out from one's base in the community (that is, from blues and gospel music) and to engage oneself with the values and the assumptions of white society, going to meet them and to play with them, and trying on roles in symbolic fashion in relation to that culture and society through its musicking, discovering what is of use for oneself and for the community. Black jazz musicians are thus no less the ritual representatives of the community than are bluesmen and gospel singers, and their task is in many ways even more important. Conversely, when white musicians play jazz, they are in almost a complementary situation in exploring the values of the black culture. How deeply they are able to do this will depend on the extent to which they are able to submit to the social and musical values they find there; it is in a sense even more difficult for them than for their black confrères, since as members of the socially dominant culture they have more to unlearn, and more intellectual baggage to dispose of, before they can enter fully into the engagement.

But both are also engaging with that most pressing of twentieth-century problems: that of the relationship between freedom and social order, and they are empowered to do so by a style of musicking which does not assume that there is any necessary antithesis between the two. In jazz a soloist appears at his or her best (which is not the same as 'most virtuosic') when collaborating with equals, the composer realizes his or her compositions most fully when they are taken up and developed by fellow musicians, the individual realizes his or her gifts best in the company of a committed group. Thus the notion found in many histories and other studies of jazz, of the great individual artist-hero — Charlie Parker, John Coltrane, Miles Davis for instance — creating out of his own nature and genius, has to be treated with great caution.

Of course, there have been many outstanding artists over the history of jazz, but we should beware of treating them as great isolated originators, as the classical tradition today treats Beethoven, Mozart and J.S. Bach (it is strongly arguable that the way they are treated is a gross distortion of the real nature and achievement of *those* artists also) or indeed, as the world of commercial entertainment — showbiz — treats its stars. In so far as the jazz musician's world perforce overlaps with and partakes of the nature of both those worlds it is understandable that this should happen — and of course it does pay the musicians, who after all have a living to make in that world, to go along with it as far as they can — but it should never be forgotten that those who stand out as the 'great names' in histories and other studies of jazz are no more than first among equals, and owe at least a part of their eminence to the labours of many other musicians. To say this is not in any way to detract from their gifts or their achievements, but simply to point out that the nature of jazz performance requires that performers, whether famous or obscure, function in skilled and close collaboration, and that they depend on one another in everything they do.

The words 'composer' and 'composition' therefore have a very different significance in jazz from classical musicking; in jazz, as in the great age of classical music, to be a musician is primarily to be a performer, and those who compose regard composition simply as the creation of material for themselves and their colleagues to play. It is rare, though not unknown, for what is created to be a fully worked-out composition; more usually it is a springboard, which may or may not be notated, from which all the musicians may take off into collaborative creation. Many of these 'compositions', such as Thelonious Monk's *Round About Midnight*, Charles Mingus's *Goodbye Pork Pie Hat* and Charlie Parker's *Parker's Mood* are beautiful in themselves, but they reveal, and are meant to reveal, their full character only when the composer and his colleagues have played with them, in all seriousness and all fun (the two are not incompatible). The composer's gesture to his fellow musicians is one of love and trust in giving them a part of himself to make of it what they will, and it calls from those musicians a greater sense of responsibility and involvement than does the realization of a fully notated score. And in so far as there can be as many versions of the 'piece' as there are occasions of its performance, the place and the listeners also make their contribution, just as in African musicking.

All too often, of course, the place is a sleazy nightclub with a minuscule bandstand, a tinny beat-up piano and a dressing room that is no more than a cupboard next to the gents' toilet, while the listeners are a crowd of drunken businessmen and their wives on a night out, but the musicians' loyalty to one another and to their musicking can still make the performance transcend the limitations of the occasion. And when the place is suitable (not necessarily either grand or luxurious), the listeners committed and the dancing skilled (for does not dancing reveal a deeper involvement with the musicking than just sitting still and listening?) the performance, for as long as it lasts, can transform the participants into a society of mutual love and responsibility, of deep and multi-valent relationships, that reveals the poverty of the affluent European society of a concert hall.

For a jazz performance is not as much about the *rejection* of European values as about *transcending* them, and about the incorporation of the oppositions of classical music into more realistic unities. Jazz musicians have always been concerned with classical music, not as representatives of an inferior culture trying to latch on to the superior, but as natural heirs who are claiming it as their birthright — or, rather, as a part of their birthright — and building it into their own synthesis. It is a dangerous game; the musician is constantly on both a musical and a social tightrope in attempting to reconcile the two sets of values. It is for this reason that, for all the excitement that can be generated by a jazz performance, the quality most valued by the musicians themselves is 'cool' — that coolness of mind and clarity of musical judgement which together enable them to keep their balance while on the tightrope. The history of jazz is littered with, on the one hand, fine and even great musicians for whom the responsibility was too great, and, on the other, with musicians who have given in to the pull of one or the other culture.

There is a stereotype of a black jazz musician who, brilliant as he or she may be as performer, is nonetheless inadequate or worse in everyday relationships and the business of life, who is killed by drugs, alcohol and the appurtenances of high living; Charlie Parker and Billie Holiday are two often-quoted examples. They could not, we are led to believe, live out the ideal relationships which they brought into being with their music. This dissonance between the actual world and its relationships, and the ideal world which they have not just imagined but actually experienced, has always placed highly creative musicians in danger; Mozart, who died only two years older than Parker, was clearly overwhelmed by it, while even the archetypal artist-hero, Ludwig van Beethoven, managed somehow to survive twenty years more without ever coming to terms with the world in which he lived, or even being able to form a mature relationship with another human being. In the case of black artists the dissonance is intensified, only they know how deeply, by the racism of the society which they are obliged to inhabit, and for which they are creating their model of a community held together, not by coercion, but by love. The marvel is not that some succumb, but that so many survive, and survive triumphantly, with that ideal still alive, if not unscarred by their experiences. And that even those who, like Parker and Holiday, did succumb, continued to affirm their 'philosophies of beauty and ethics' for as long as they were physically able.

The relative pulls of the two cultures spanned by jazz are not symmetrical, owing to the far higher social and financial rewards which the classical culture is able to offer to most musicians. A musician who accedes to the pull of the Afro-American culture will be found playing blues or gospel, in a musical ritual of a community that remains largely isolated from the mainstream of American society, and which continues to find within itself the resources for survival. For black musicians such a step is to move back into the maternal culture, a recharging of the batteries perhaps, which many, if not most, seem to do from time to time, while for white musicians, on the other hand, it is a venture not merely into a culture that still remains exotic and mysterious, not merely an adventure, but almost also a homecoming, an acknowledgement of one's real ancestors. For the musician playing jazz, it is the pull of the European classical culture that represents the greater threat, since as the dominant and socially superior culture it has more to offer. It can co-opt musicians almost without their realizing what is happening to them — a not infrequent happening in the history of Afro-American music as a whole. For the black musician it tends to be a no-win situation, as the guardians of the classical culture are liable to pat him on the head and make it clear to him that he is getting ideas above his station. Every so often there appears on the scene a young lion who is intent in storming the classical-music citadel; I cannot help wondering whether what is in that citadel — the approbation of white middle-class audiences and critics — is really worth his effort.

The history of jazz can be seen as a struggle between the two sets of values, expressed in musical terms as a to-and-fro between solutions to the problem of freedom and order. Unlike the situation in classical music, the struggle presents us with no final solution, only with a constantly changing series of accommodations; perhaps the only conclusion to be drawn is that no conclusion is possible — something with which Africans would no doubt concur. It should, of course, not be assumed from this that relations between white and black musicians within jazz have been of hostility or even of opposition; the history of the art abounds with shining examples of amicable, even loving collaboration. But it is easy to understand that because a black musician is staking more on his musicking than a white one, it has been black musicians who have been mostly the leaders and innovators, since genuine musical innovation, as we have seen, is a matter not just of new sounds or techniques but of new forms of relationship. This has been a more urgent quest for blacks than for whites — though, God knows, the white majority is in more desperate and urgent need than it knows of what it can learn from its black compatriots. Albert Murray expresses it memorably when, writing in praise of certain white musicians, he says that they 'eagerly embrace certain Negroes not only as kindred spirits but as ancestor figures indispensible to their sense of romance, sophistication and elegance as well. Negroes like Duke Ellington, Louis Armstrong, Bessie Smith, Billie Holiday, Chick Webb, Coleman Hawkins and others too numerous to mention inspire white Americans like Woody Herman, Gerry Mulligan and countless others to their richest sense of selfhood and their highest levels of achievement.'[1]

'Ancestor figures', we notice — that is to say, models not only of music but also of values and conduct, and it can be said, not only that the most creative periods in the development of jazz have been those in which black musicians moved to throw off white domination of their art, but also that those same musicians have at those times quite consciously and deliberately chosen to re-assert the traditional social as well as musical values of their culture. At such key moments, it has been to the sources of black music, much of it outside the experience of whites, that they have turned for renewal; if, as is sometimes said, jazz should be called 'Afro-American classical music', it is in the sense that Haydn, who was well in touch with the vernacular sources of his art, would have understood, while Boulez or Cage, to whom such nourishment seems to be inaccessible, would probably not. Murray does in fact, in his book *Stomping the Blues*, refer to the major figures of such moments — Louis Armstrong, Ornette Coleman, Charlie Parker and others — as bluesmen *tout court*, which is fair enough in a way, and does enable us to recognize the vernacular roots of their art but at the same time it ignores the important factor of cultural tension, which is far stronger in jazz than in blues and is not only a principal source of its creative energy but also a key to its human importance in our time.

For jazz is not a comfortable form of musicking to live with; as Frederick Turner says: 'It is as if we hear an interior sound in jazz that prevents us from embracing it in the ways we obviously have its derivatives, pop music and rock. Jazz, we obscurely sense, is hard to take at the level of pure entertainment, because however little we may know of it, of the history that went into its sound, we know enough to feel that it cuts too deeply into some unresolved national dilemmas to be casually accepted or lived with comfortably on a daily basis. We hear in the interior sound an intensity of purpose and aspiration that fends off easy familiarity . . . Jazz is the sound of life being lived at its limits, dangerous as an element that can burn.'[2]

It is true that there is in jazz a quality of sound that is unique in western music; it is not exactly austerity, but a lean, stripped-down quality that makes no concession to conventional notions of beauty, and certainly resembles very little the smoothly blended sound of the symphony orchestra. But there is also a playful, ironically teasing quality about most jazz performances, which by no means negates their intense seriousness but has misled many, who are accustomed to the solemnity of classical performances, into dismissing it as frivolous. The tensions that fuel the performance are real enough; the humour is one way, not only of rendering them bearable, but also of subverting the values of the dominant society. It is probably for reasons such as these that jazz has been a really popular music (by which I have to mean, popular among whites, for that is where the purchasing power lies that determines popularity in today's society) for only brief periods, and it is significant that those were periods in which white cultural values were dominant, and the tensions resolved, at least for the time being.

Rather than attempting an historical survey of jazz, I intend to examine some phases of that history, to see how these accommodations between black and white values have taken place at specific points. It is proverbially difficult to say just when jazz first emerged as a recognizable style. It is possible to imagine a number of ways in which it might have taken place, and the prehistory of jazz, as of many cultural styles (style being defined precisely by Charles Keil as 'a deeply satisfying distillation of the ways a very well integrated human group likes to do things')[3] contains many such distillations, taking place in many different parts of the United States, according to the cultural mix of influences that happened to be around at the time. Ragtime was one such distillation, as we have seen, black minstrelsy and vaudeville were others, established on well-organized circuits by 1900. It is possible to see, even in the work of musicians as early as Francis Johnson, a similar cultural work taking place, while the very large number of black, and the smaller number of white wind bands in which European marches, dances and entertainment music were 'ragged', all over the United States, testify to the continuing experimentation that was taking place. In New York, for example, we know that James Reese Europe, conductor of the famous orchestra of the Clef Club, the centre for black musicians in the years before the first world war, and of the Hellfighters Band in France during the war, had a difficult task keeping his black musicians to the written notes: 'I have to call a daily rehearsal,' he wrote, 'to prevent the musicians from adding to their music more than I wish them to. Wherever possible they all embroider their parts in order to produce new, peculiar sounds. Some of these effects are excellent and some are not, and I have to be continually on the lookout to cut out the results of my musicians' originality.'[4] Despite Europe's keeping the lid firmly on the improvisational pot, the Hellfighters caused a sensation when they were sent to Paris in August 1918 to give a single concert and stayed for eight weeks. As Europe said later, 'Had we wished we might be playing there yet.' It might have been instructive, and perhaps chastening, for some of today's virtuoso conductors and orchestras to hear how the Clef Club Orchestra handled those works of the classical tradition which their repertory included as a matter of course; but, alas, no records were made of them.

But these and countless other ways of musicking, fascinating and rewarding as they were, did not add up to a single and unified way of doing things. The one exception, ragtime, paid for its undoubted coherence with a narrowness of range, too close an identification with European classical techniques, too complete a reliance on notation, too highly developed a set of technical procedures, all of which left little room for a contribution by the performer, to make it usable as a vehicle for further developments. A style is a curious affair; it is like rain, which needs, in addition to a saturation of water vapour in the air, a focal point on which the vapour can begin to condense. The 'vapour' was heavy in the air between 1900 and 1905 everywhere in the United States where there was a sizeable black population, but only in one location were there conditions where the blackest of black musicking were brought into contact with the whitest of white; that was New Orleans.

New Orleans is unique among the cities of the United States. Its French origins, its cession to the United States as part of the Louisiana Purchase of 1803, its wealth and corruption, its cosmopolitanism and devotion to pleasure and the arts at a time when other American cities were still dominated by Puritan influence, are all part of legend, and the legend, for once, is substantially true. By 1840, for example, there were three more or less full-time opera companies in the city, whose population, including blacks, was a mere one hundred thousand. These companies, moreover, were no third-rate colonial imitations of metropolitan French culture but were described by knowledgeable European visitors as the equal of all but the finest European houses, and they performed works by the greatest names of the day, from Mozart to Rossini, Donizetti and Meyerbeer, as well as by competent local composers. Blacks as well as whites attended; even slaves could sit in the amphitheatre of the opera, and we have already seen that the Negro Philharmonic Society had its own orchestra and engaged visiting soloists. And of course blacks dominated the city's bands, for which the citizens had a passion; the famous slow march to the graveside at funerals and the return, playing lively music, was a feature of the city's musical life which a visitor noted as early as 1819.

The interplay was thus two-way. As blacks heard and used white styles, so the musicking of the blacks was picked up and used by the whites; the lower classes, as we have seen, picked it up directly, while the upper classes did so through the medium of the ubiquitous minstrel shows. That was only an extension of what was taking place wherever blacks and whites encountered one another musically. But there was another factor: miscegenation. Since the days of French sovereignty, it had been a custom among the old Creole (that is, of French or Spanish descent but born in the New World) aristocracy to keep a black mistress in a separate establishment. Unlike those who were fathered by Anglo-Saxon Americans, the offspring of these unions were generally acknowledged by their fathers, and often well provided for, some even receiving a Parisian education, so that there grew up in the city a class of 'Creoles of colour', who regarded themselves as to all intents and purposes as white, and who absorbed European rather than Afro-American culture.

With the racial blacklash after Emancipation, however, the Creoles of colour found themselves, along with all who had the slightest known or visible trace of African ancestry, reclassified under the city's notorious Legislative Code 111 of 1894 as black, and subject to all the legal and social disabilities of that status. Try as they might to hold on to their European ties, they found themselves driven out of employment in white areas and forced to associate, willy-nilly, with the despised blacks. A large number of professional and semi-professional musicians, trained in some cases in Europe but anyway in the European style, found themselves forced, if they were to earn a living at all, to play in the company of Afro-American groups, with their ragged rhythms, their blues-like melodic inflections and their 'dirty' and highly individual instrumental tone. As the Creole musician Paul Dominguez said, many years later, 'They made a fiddler out of a violinist — me, I'm talking about . . . If I wanted to make a living I had to be rowdy like the other groups.'[5] It seems that it was this forced association, with all the hardship and real suffering that it caused, that brought about exactly the right combination of social and musical interaction to cause the condensation of a new style of playing among the large number of musicians who were capable of playing in any style that was asked of them.

The versatility of black and Creole musicians was another specific feature of the New Orleans scene that was a consequence of the large number of Creole musicians who, in an attempt to retain their European standards, became teachers of music. Frederick Turner tells of one Professor Jim Humphrey who would take the train out of the city once a week in the 1890s to teach talented plantation children, always in the 'correct' European style; his pupils later formed the nucleus of New Orleans' famous Eclipse Brass Band.[6] Many of the early 'greats' of New Orleans jazz passed through the hands of such teachers, having become skilled not only in playing, in the European manner, more than one instrument but also in reading and writing music; Bunk Johnson, Freddie Keppard, Louis Armstrong, Sidney Bechet and Jelly Roll Morton all had a training of this kind, or something like it. The legend of 'primitive' or 'unschooled' jazz musicians does not stand up to close examination; indeed, the nature of jazz would have been very different had they not had contact with European as well as Afro-American styles.

It seems to have been between about 1900 and 1905 that the new style crystallized. As it developed, it gradually absorbed into itself the diverse elements of other 'proto-jazz' styles, and its eventual naming as 'jass' around 1910 (the word seems to come from the same source as 'jissom', revealing a disapproving attitude to the music's assumed sexual content) showed that the dominance of the new style was recognized; as Charles Keil says: 'the very naming of musics . . . is a declaration of consolidation.' Keil goes on to describe exactly the kind of process that must have taken place in the early years: 'An exclusion principle or focus on a sharply limited set of forms marks the beginning of a style, but it grows by inclusion, assimilating to its purposes the instruments, techniques and ideas of significant other styles within earshot.'[7] To see this process at work it is instructive to examine the work of two important figures in New Orleans music between 1900 and 1905.

The cornettist Charles 'Buddy' Bolden (1877–1931) is generally regarded as the first major performer and band-leader of New Orleans jazz. He was taken to a state mental institution in 1906, in circumstances that remain obscure, and never emerged alive, so that it is not surprising that legends proliferate around his name. No recordings of him or his band exist, but he was by all accounts a phenomenally powerful player (the phrase 'five miles on a clear night' was coined to describe his carrying power) and, if not the originator, at least an early protagonist, of jazz horn sound. He is usually thought of as the archetypally rough 'gutbucket' player, and, indeed, it is clear that he could play wildly exciting blues and other black-style dance music, but, on the other hand, those who heard him attested to his ability to play very sweetly also; as one player said in later years: 'When it came to playing sweet music, waltzes, there was nobody in the country who could touch him . . . Everybody was crazy about Bolden when he'd play a waltz, schottische or old low-down blues.'[8] And he could not only read music, as could most of his sidesmen, but he could write it too. His early professional experience had been in a small band for society dances and parties where he would have had to play in a 'refined' style. As his biographer Donald Marquis says: 'Bolden played both by note and by ear, and he liked to please the audience. Having a good ear he could hear another band play and . . . was able to duplicate it by the end of the evening. As he matured musically, he would listen to a number, memorize it instrument by instrument, and then teach the part to the others.'[9] Clearly no 'primitive' cornet player, then, but a musician whose skills and imagination were considerable, and whose rough and riotous playing was the result not of unschooled technique but of self-identification and of conscious artistic decision.

Bolden's chief rival in that period of headlong development and consolidation, John Robichaux, was, as his surname suggests, a Creole of colour. He had received a formal musical training, and his band, playing always in the literate mode, had, before the advent of Legislative Code 111, been employed in some of the most elegant halls and ballrooms of the city. After they found themselves forced to associate with black musicians, Robichaux adapted his style and held the band together in the rougher environments where they had to work; some of his players even moonlighted with black street bands. And, as Marquis says, 'The two pioneers cared enough about music to recognize the skills the other possessed and the contributions each was making. Bolden was known to have used ideas from the Robichaux band; some of Buddy's fans remembered seeing Robichaux seated by himself at the back of a hall where Bolden was playing . . . And the two bands, Bolden's and Robichaux's, provided the earliest and most clear-cut examples of the two types of music, Uptown and Downtown, that simultaneously borrowed from each other and hastened the development of jazz.'[10]

The Bolden band was essentially one of improvisors, whose performances were held together by a minimum of prearranged material which may or may not have been written down, while the Robichaux band based its performances on written arrangements which allowed minimal space for improvisation. Borrow from each other they may have, but finally it was the Bolden style that expanded at the expense of Robichaux's, assimilating the latter's ideas and techniques into the kind of synthesis which the community, who were the final arbiters, required. It was Bolden's, rather than Robichaux's, solution to the problem of musical, and thus of social, order that the community wanted. But then, as far as those musical solutions were concerned, we need not imagine that the community of listeners and dancers were unaware of the problems, or of the solutions arrived at, then or later; there is a transparency about the procedures adopted by jazz musicians which make it quite clear to those who care to notice it what is going on within the performing group, both as a musical and as a social entity.

The early New Orleans bands set a pattern for musical order which was to be followed for over half a century of musicking, through the simple expedient of using the harmonies, the 'changes' of the tune being played, whether popular song, blues or original composition, as the unifying element over which each musician was able to improvise as he liked provided he observed the changes and remained faithful to the idiom, that is, to the community. As with those seventeenth-century Italian orchestral musicians whom I discussed earlier, playing 'as he liked' meant for a good musician not only performing his part with idiomatic correctness but also taking due regard both for what the other musicians were doing and for the over-all effect; despite the power of the rules and the skill of the individual players, it was, finally, mutual human care and consideration that would enable the ensemble to give a performance that would satisfy the community of listeners and dancers. Behind the wild and often dissonant interplay of melodic lines in those early New Orleans bands, there is a deeper human harmony which still appeals, an informal collaborative society whose model is more African than European. We can never recapture the atmosphere of those early jazz performances, of which present-day 'traditional' or 'Dixieland' bands give only the palest shadow; I sometimes wonder if the present-day popularity of 'Dixieland' among white audiences, especially in Britain, is not in part due to its evoking the society of that time in which blacks were kept firmly in their place and entertained the whites. Those who took part in those early jazz performances left little record of their thoughts on such matters, but it is hard to believe that performers, listeners and dancers had not, in that time of brutal repression and seemingly endless economic deprivation, given some thought to their relationship to the dominant Euro-American culture. The gaiety of the music we can still hear today is *not* mindless but that of serious and thoughtful musicians exploring their identity within the larger society and affirming and, above all, *celebrating* that identity in a way that was to make the whole world listen and dance.

The dispersion of the musical style from New Orleans took place partly through riverboat musicians on the big rivers, partly through the migration of blacks to northern cities in the years after about 1915, and partly, after 1917, through phonograph records. New Orleans, for all its French origins and relatively relaxed racial atmosphere, was still a southern city, and had its population of poor whites living close to the blacks; these would have been the first whites to absorb the new musical style and make it their own as part of everyday experience, rather than being filtered through the dance halls and brothels in a way which coloured the perceptions of those upper-class whites who heard it on their low-life excursions into the fabled Storeyville (and which continue to colour white perceptions of jazz even today). It was a band of those white musicians, mostly of Italian immigrant stock, the Original Dixieland Jass Band, who happened to be on the spot in New York when the chance to record came, and seized it. Their first two sides were an immediate success, selling over a million copies — probably as much for the animal imitations of *Livery Stable Blues* as for any genuine jazz quality.

As the first jazz band to record and to become widely known both in the United States and in Europe, the ODJB, as it has been known to succeeding generations, did much to set the climate for jazz as far as its wider, white public was concerned. In the first place, they simplified the idiom of the black musicians, substituting crude melodic formulas for their often subtle and flexible improvised melodic lines, and mechanical patterns for their vigorous rhythms. As Gunther Schuller says: 'In its rigid substitution of sheer energy for expressive power, of rigid formula for inspiration, the ODJB had found the key to mass appeal.' And, secondly, the members of the band promoted assiduously the idea that they were all untutored musicians who just played whatever came into their heads. Schuller tells us that the leaders even 'kept bombarding the public with provocative statements such as "I don't know how many pianists we tried until we found one that couldn't read music."' 'But,' says Schuller, 'their playing belied the myth of total anarchy such statements were designed to create. Contrary to being improvised, their choruses were set and rehearsed, and they were unchanged for years.'[11] The ODJB, in fact, solved the problem of order by pretending that there was no problem, and like all such solutions, it could not last; the band was defunct by 1924. But the fiction of total anarchy served its purpose for them and for their successors and imitators; even today it remains an important factor in the public perception of jazz musicians and of their mode of performance. There is a sizeable proportion of the public who sees jazzmen as jolly, irresponsible fellows, not over-intelligent, who have a good time playing the first thing that comes into their heads. The fiction continues to be encouraged especially among the musical 'establishment', serving as it does to defuse the challenge posed by jazz.

That jazz served well enough the spirit of revolt in the 1920s is clear from the electric effect that bands, both black and white, had on the young (black bands did not get to record until 1923 and did not until much later gain the amount of exposure offered to white bands, while racially mixed bands were unthinkable until the 1930s), especially on young middle-class whites and, perhaps even more explosively, on young middle-class blacks such as Edward Ellington in Washington DC, Fletcher Henderson in Georgia and James Lunceford in Fulton, Missouri. As the carrier (one might say, the embodiment, since the values were embodied in the ways in which the music was played and responded to) of values which called into question those of white American culture of past and present, jazz was the natural medium of rebellion against the standards of prosperous middle-class America which had given the young everything except what they really needed: communality, warmth and emotional honesty. James Collier describes the differences in the attitudes of black and white musicians towards jazz in that period, differences which have not completely disappeared today even if the two groups are not quite so separate as they were then: 'A black jazz musician was among his people a star, a hero, who held a place something like the place held by a basketball star today. But for the young white players, playing jazz meant entering a hidden world . . . As a result, these [white] youngsters, most of them teenagers when they started, came to jazz with the sense that they were a group of elect outsiders who had devoted themselves to a high truth.'[12]

What is implied here is that what attracted the young white musicians, and their equally young audiences, to jazz was not just new sounds and rhythms, but new relationships, those of the hitherto inaccessible culture. It does not matter too much that the whites' perceptions of black culture were coloured by a great deal of romanticism and wishful thinking (we must remember that the society that was brought into existence in a jazz performance was, for blacks no less than for whites, an ideal, a potential rather than an actual society); what people believe affects what they do no less than what actually is, and the important thing was the view that jazz seemed to offer of an alternative set of values and relationships. Their elders, who remained apparently satisfied with white America as it was, felt otherwise, and social leaders — politicians, clergymen, teachers and medical men — thundered about the mental, physical and moral damage inflicted by jazz (the fulminations against rock 'n' roll in the 1950s had a familiar ring to those who had lived through the 1920s). The vehemence of the denunciations suggests an appreciation, even if it was not fully conscious, of the challenge offered to conventional assumptions about the nature of human societies by the music and the manner of its performance, but, given the preoccupations of white culture at the time, it is not surprising that most of the alleged dangers of jazz boiled down to the usual brew of sexual and racial fears. As in the 1950s, the outrage at the flouting of familiar values was compounded by fear disguised as contempt for the mysterious foreigners in their midst, who seemed to have access to pleasures and to sources of power denied to themselves. 'The consensus of opinion of leading medical and other scientific authorities,' wrote the medical officer of a leading Philadelphia girls' school, 'is that its influence is as harmful and degrading to civilized races as it has always been among the savages from whom we borrowed it'[13].

There is a sad little story which illustrates for me the gulf that existed at that time between respectable white society and jazz. It is said that Bix Beiderbecke, who is generally regarded today as the first major white soloist in jazz, used to send proudly home to his parents, prosperous German-American merchants in Davenport, Iowa, copies of all his records as they were issued; on a visit to his home he found them all stowed away in the back of a cupboard, their postal wrappings still unbroken.

Beiderbecke spent a large part of his brief career in the big orchestra of Paul Whiteman, the self-styled 'King of Jazz'. The orchestra, excellent as it undoubtedly was, only intermittently even sounds anything like jazz as we would recognize it today. In the 1920s — notwithstanding its nickname, the 'jazz age' — not many people had even heard those artists who today figure as jazz masters of their time, since their performances were generally in small night clubs and speakeasies where relatively few people went, and their records were mostly available only on the 'race' labels aimed at the black market and sold only in ghetto shops. The high performance standards of the Whiteman orchestra were achieved at the cost of a denial of that freedom within the ensemble which had been the essence of jazz performance up to that time. Although a number of later-to-be famous musicians passed through the orchestra in its fifteen-year history, between 1920 and 1935, they were permitted only the briefest of solos, and improvisation was practically nonexistent. Authority was centralized in the arrangers, who were often brilliant by any standards, and in the conductor; the problem of freedom and order had been not so much solved as closed off. It was the first, but by no means the last, attempt to produce the sounds and rhythms of jazz through the techniques and disciplines of the symphony orchestra. The closeness of the link with contemporary symphonic music is emphasises by the use not only of 'symphonic' dramatic introductions, often leading, anticlimactically, into perfectly ordinary dance tunes, but also of harmonies and orchestral devices derived from the 'impressionist' composers of the time, notably Ravel and Delius. It is easy to sneer at the Whiteman orchestra today, but Whiteman was undoubtedly a good musician who did his best for the music as he perceived it; if his aim was, as he once put it, to 'make a lady out of jazz', and to make jazz accessible to those white Americans for whom in its undiluted form it was too alarming, then in that aim he succeeded. It was he, too, who as part of that aim commissioned *Rhapsody in Blue* in 1924 from George Gershwin, for which we can be grateful. But the fact that he should have thought it necessary in the first place to make jazz respectable has much to say about the social and cultural divisions in our society.

The tendency to drift into easy solutions, based on imposed authority, to the problem of musical order was to recur frequently in the ensuing years, and, indeed, is still with us. The temptation to do so grew greater over the 1920s as the size of bands increased in response to the need for bigger sounds to fill the ever-larger ballrooms without the aid of electronic amplification, and to the desire for a greater range and variety of instrumental colour. We see it occurring to various degrees in the big white, and some black, swing bands from Benny Goodman and Fletcher Henderson to Artie Shaw, and culminating in the relentlessly rehearsed arrangements of the Glenn Miller Band, whose ideals of instrumental blend are remarkably similar to those of the symphony orchestra, and whose working practices allowed no room for the uncertainties of improvised solos. There were other pressures on those bands, too, not only the demand by audiences in the big ballrooms and, from the 1930s, in the radio shows with which they lived symbiotically, to hear the songs 'just like on the record', but also the need of a large and expensive organization to cater for the paying white audience and its desire for comfortable and not too demanding entertainment music. This was the same audience that the Broadway Masters catered for in musicals and individual songs, and, indeed, it was the latter who wrote most of the songs which arrangers arranged and the bands played, in ballrooms and nightclubs (places into which, since the end of prohibition, respectable people could go), on radio and records and in film and stage musicals. Jazz became during the 1930s and 1940s a popular music for the first and last time; the big bands appeared regularly in Hollywood films, and bandleaders were stars whose activities, and especially their sex lives, were reported and commented on as avidly as those of film stars — or, indeed, of rock and pop stars today. Jazz and jazz musicians had been co-opted to serve the values of white society, and its challenge had been defused.

This kind of jazz survives today, in showbands and backing bands, its style changed remarkably little since the 1940s. It survives also, interestingly, in educational institutions, whose 'Jazz Ensemble', 'Jazz Band' or 'Showband', usually under the baton of the Director of Music, can form a showpiece for the school's or college's progressive image. Such ensembles, however, are generally dependent on scores, usually commercial arrangements, which leave little room for either individual or group improvisation (they sometimes include fully notated 'improvised' solos) and leave the conductor firmly in charge of everything that takes place. There is no conflict here with the values of the school, or of the centralized industrial state whose interests, as we have already noted, the school is designed to serve.

That such a solution is not inevitable even when a large number of musicians are involved can be seen from the history of jazz in the midwest and southwestern United States, especially in those blues-based bands, climaxing in the long-lived band of Count Basie, which sheltered from the Great Depression in the relative prosperity of the corrupt but freehanded Prendergast administration in Kansas City. Basie, like many of the Kansas City bandleaders of the day, led from the piano; as one commentator has said: 'He sat at the piano, smiling modestly, giving out the occasional tinkle with so little fuss that a stranger might have asked what he *did*. Yet he was the leader of a band full of brilliant, individual soloists who swung together with a unique lift and power, a rhythmic unity that seemed like second nature. And almost all of those individualists would have agreed that Basie was a great leader, though none could explain exactly why.'[14] The same writer said of the band: 'The standing repertory consisted of head arrangements worked up at rehearsals from . . . the store of sketches and rough charts. In the main the band's style depended on its collective spirit and the flow of ideas from soloists, brought about to a singular degree of unity by Basie's quiet, musicianly leadership and orchestral deployment of the piano.'[15]

The Basie band consisted of individuals each of whom was in his or her own right a musician of superb skill and musical intelligence, who realized those qualities to their fullest by placing them at the service of the common enterprise. It was a remarkable social, no less than musical, achievement, not the least of which lay in the realization that the problems can never be solved once and for all but must be solved again and again every day and require constant vigilance and diplomacy to keep the need for order and the need for freedom in harmony with each other. But the rewards were commensurate with the effort; judging from their recordings, I do not know of any of the major bands of the time, not even that of Duke Ellington himself, that could play with such power and such delicacy and with such evocation of the spirit of joy and of love as the Count Basie Orchestra. Those fifteen or so musicians, constantly free to create something new, must have felt most fully themselves when building their commonwealth of the spirit in collaboration with their listeners and dancers (we recall that it was Lester Young, the band's great tenor saxophonist of its peak years, who liked to play for dancers because 'the rhythm of the dancers comes back to you'). Even if a large proportion of those listeners were just the proverbial tired businessmen on a night out, all but the most insensitive must have perceived, however faintly, the outlines of that commonwealth and have been touched, if not fully knowing why, by its values. In its later years, it is true, the band succumbed to some extent to pressures for a more smoothly complete product and became more dependent on written arrangements, with a consequent loss of the players' improvisatory freedom, but it remained a powerful and beautiful group right up to Basie's death in 1984.

The group which perhaps shows most clearly how delicate is the balance between improvisatory freedom and audible order is that of Duke Ellington. When the orchestra began playing, in 1923, it was a co-operative group, of which Ellington gradually assumed command, more, it seems, through a talent for leadership than through his musical skills, which were at that time somewhat sketchy. The orchestra's performances initially evolved on a collaborative basis, with all the musicians making creative contributions, and as Ellington began to take control it became simply a matter of his having a veto over those suggestions and ideas as they were tried out. The conditions under which they worked from 1927 to 1933, at Harlem's Cotton Club, where they were required to provide music not just for the patrons to dance to, but also for the lavish and often fantastic floor shows, demanded a type of composition that could be co-ordinated with choreography and repeated on successive nights — which meant using notation. It was under these conditions that they developed a way of working in which ideas presented by the leader, or by one of the sidesmen, were tried over, added to and placed within a framework in such a way as to allow a considerable degree of improvising freedom to the various brilliant soloists in the orchestra. Only after this process had been gone through would the arrangement come into being and be written down — and even then it was possible for it to go on developing as it was performed. This way of working still left the soloists with considerable responsibility for the performance, and there are instances in the orchestra's recorded legacy, for example in the *Black and Tan Fantasy* where, as Gunther Schuller says, 'Through the dominance of one soloist, [the trumpeter Bubber Miley] the collective equilibrium that was such an integral part of jazz was temporarily disturbed.'[16] That such a disturbance was possible, however, shows the vitality of the idiom and its openness to whatever may happen.

We are told that Ellington was not very interested in contemporary classical music, that the 'impressionist' harmonies which abound in his orchestra's performances come not directly from Ravel, Delius or Stravinsky but rather from other black arrangers, notably Will Vodery, who was chief arranger for the Siegfeld Follies, and Will Marion Cook, as well as from the big orchestras such as that of Paul Whiteman. But although over the years the balance between improvisation and composition remained remarkably open (the orchestra was always capable of making superb improvised performances from simple 'head' arrangements) we find Ellington in later life being increasingly drawn to the kind of fully composed large-scale work for his orchestra that is usually thought more appropriate for the concert platform than for the bandstand — pieces such as *Black, Brown and Beige, Liberian Suite, Deep South Suite* and the three *Sacred Concerts* intended for performance in church. These works have been variously praised and damned, the former often by those who like to hear something they can recognize as compositions in the classical sense, the latter equally often by those who say that they are not jazz (neither verdict has much to do with their real qualities); an interesting comment is that of the critic Francis Newton in the London *New Statesman*, quoted by Schuller, that Ellington had 'solved the unbelievably difficult problem of turning a living, shifting and improvised folk music into composition without losing its spontaneity.'[17] That a musician of Ellington's kind, and his proven stature, should want to do such a thing testifies to the continuing attraction exerted by the respectability of the concert stage. He lived to perform the Sacred Concerts in London's Westminster Abbey, where English monarchs have been crowned for centuries, and one cannot get much more respectable than that; the pieces are to my ears less immediate, less involving than the less formally composed pieces, and can perhaps be heard as the work of a musician who has lived dangerously and now feels the need to relax from the tension of reconciling two sets of values. But they can also be seen as representing a victory for 'classical' respectability.

The Ellington Orchestra always stood aside from the rest of the history of jazz, paying only superficial tribute to successive styles as they came and went. I referred in a previous chapter to the renewal of the encounter between values, after the closure brought about in the era that was dominated by the big white swing bands, that took place with the style which was known as bebop in the 1940s and 1950s. As with many stylistic revolutions, the passing of time enables us to recognize the continuities as well as the breaks, and we can now see that these musicians were returning consciously to a reaffirmation, in a new and sophisticated way befitting the generation of the reopening of the civil rights struggle, of the values that had animated the older jazzmen. This continuity is emphasised by the fact that not only did many of the principal musicians of that revolution came from the midwest, where the older musical values had survived better than in the very commercial New York scene, but also that the rhythmic revolution that underlay bebop was a development of what the Kansas City bands, notably Count Basie's, had been doing for a long time.

Thus the dialogue was reopened and has continued undiminished over the subsequent years. A reaction in the 1950s towards the forms and techniques of classical music was led by a number of classically-trained white musicians, who attempted a fusion, by the use of classical forms such as fugue and of asymmetrical rhythmic patterns (Dave Brubeck's *Take Five* is a famous example) and by the cultivation of the refined atmosphere of a chamber-music concert. None of this had much lasting effect on the art itself, but, as James Collier says, 'Cool music . . . was popular for the simple reason that the European elements in it made it comprehensible to audiences raised in the European tradition . . . For the white majority, before 1950, jazz was a hobby for a handful of eccentrics; by the 1950s, especially on college campuses, it was an accepted part of the cultural scenery, something one knew about in the way that one knew about Freud, Beethoven and Van Gogh. For jazz, before rock swept everything away, the 1950s were a relatively good time.'[18]

For white musicians with a college degree, at any rate; I shall leave the reader to ponder the implications of that paragraph in the light of the earlier discussion. For the rest, things were not much different from what they had always been. The succeeding generation of musicians, coming to maturity in the 1960s, brought, as we saw in the previous chapter, a renewal of concern for the enduring resources and values of black culture, in folk music, the music of the churches, and of course the blues. This renewal was, wrongly, dubbed by certain critics 'the new thing' or 'the new jazz', since it was neither new nor a thing, but an attempt to shake off the restraints imposed by European harmony and even those of the tempered scale, using instead an interplay of melodic lines built often enough on ancient modes — an old idiom representing an old community. Those same critics also attempted to set up a rivalry along Brahms-Wagner lines between certain musicians of the time, but there was in fact no necessary antithesis, rather a different approach towards a common cultural pride and a common desire for independence of European cultural norms. Today there seems a more cautious spirit abroad, and a move towards European high culture and the avant garde — which may represent not a capitulation but simply a striving to take possession of its forms and to turn them to the musicians' own purposes. The danger of capture has never retreated, however, and is indeed perhaps even stronger than ever in the social and political climate of the 1980s. We can only, from a distance, wait and hope.

None of this, I hope, should suggest that jazz as a way of musicking, or the issues that it raises, concerns black Americans only. For generations now there have been white musicians for whom jazz is a natural way of playing, who are motivated by nothing more or less than a need to affirm, explore and celebrate values to which they feel closer than to the official ones of western society as embodied in classical music, and more profoundly than popular music permits. On the other hand, jazz will in all probability never again be a popular music; it is too uncomfortable for that. But those who are prepared to allow themselves to go with the tensions generated by that way of musicking can be rewarded with some of the most heartening musical experiences possible in western society today. Players and listeners are taking part in a process which at any point can end in disaster; the musicians have chosen to place themselves in the most delicate, subtle and dangerous relationship with their listeners, while the listeners have the responsibility of feeding back to the players the energy which they have received from them, so that when the performance is going well it resonates back and forth, to create a community in which at the same time all can feel fully realized as individuals. Contrary to what is often said, the excitement generated by a good jazz performance is not just physical, although the part played by bodily response and bodily movement must not be denied; it is the exhilaration of finding oneself, to use Albert Murray's words once more, raised 'to the richest sense of selfhood and to the highest level of achievement.' There is no product, no final solution to the problems, only the unending process of exploration, affirmation and celebration. The magic does not happen with every performance, even with the finest and most devoted performers and the most sympathetic of audiences and the most skilled of dancers; there are too many workaday pressures which militate against it, not least of which are the pressures on the musicians to produce a saleable and consistent product and to ease tension by submitting to routine. But the ideal remains, and is realized sufficiently often to make the enterprise worth while for both players and their listeners ('Once a year, if I'm lucky,' said Dizzy Gillespie.[19]).

I conclude this chapter with some remarks by musicians, all quoted in Nat Hentoff's *The Jazz Life*, which illuminate the musicians' task better than any words of mine. First, the drummer Jo Jones to a beginning professional musician: 'You're a musician. Don't ever forget that. You can do what very few other people can do. You can reach people, but to move them you have to be all open. You have to let everything in you out. And you have to be in a condition to play what you hear.'[20] Second, Charles Mingus, 'I play or write *me*, the way I feel, through jazz or whatever, whether it's hip or not. Music is the language of the emotions. If someone has been escaping reality, I don't expect him to dig my music . . . my music is alive and it's about the living and the dead, about good and evil. It's angry, and it's real because it's angry.'[21]

And, finally: 'Some years ago, a quartet had just completed a particularly exhilarating set, and its young Negro drummer came off the stand grinning with satisfaction. "You sure sounded good," said a listener. "Yeah," said the drummer, "there was a lot of loving going on up there."[22]

NOTES

1. MURRAY, Albert: *The Omni-Americans: New Perspectives on Black Experience and American Culture*, New York, Outerbridge and Dienstfrey, 1970, p 102.
2. TURNER, Frederick: *Remembering Song: Encounters with the New Orleans Jazz Tradition*, New York, The Viking Press, 1982, p 3
3. KEIL, Charles: 'People's Music Comparatively: Style and Stereotype, Class and Hegemony', *Dialectical Anthropology*, Vol. 10, 1985, p 122.
4. EUROPE, James Reese: 'A Negro Explains "Jazz" (1919)' in SOUTHERN, Eileen (ed.): *Readings in Black American Music*, New York, Norton, 1983, p 239.

5. quoted in BUERKLE, Jack V. and BARKER, Danny: *Bourbon Street Black: The New Orleans Black Jazzmen*, New York, Oxford University Press, 1973, p 10.
6. TURNER, Frederick: *op cit.*, p 70
7. KEIL, Charles: *op cit.*, p 126.
8. MARQUIS, Donald M.: *In Search of Buddy Bolden: First Man of Jazz*, New York, Da Capo Books, 1978, p 100.
9. *ibid.*, p 47.
10. *ibid.*, p 81-82.
11. SCHULLER, Gunther: *Early Jazz: Its Roots and Musical Development*, New York, Oxford University Press, 1968, p 180.
12. COLLIER, James Lincoln: *The Making of Jazz: A Comprehensive History*, London, Granada Publishing, 1978, p 127.
13. quoted in LEONARD, Neil: *Jazz and the White Americans: The Acceptance of a New Art Form*, Chicago, University of Chicago Press, 1962, p 39.
14. RUSSELL, Ross: *Jazz Style in Kansas City and the Southwest*, Berkeley, University of California Press, 1971, p 258.
15. *ibid.*, p 135.
16. SCHULLER, Gunther: *op cit.*, p 350.
17. *ibid.*, p 350.
18. COLLIER, James Lincoln: *op cit.*, p 436.
19. quoted in WILLS, Geoff: 'Under Pressure', *International Musician*, October 1984, p 46.
20. HENTOFF, Nat: *The Jazz Life*, New York, Da Capo Press, 1978, p 24.
21. *ibid.*, p 45.
22. *ibid.*, p 74.

Chapter 12

ON THE DECLINE OF A MUSIC

We have now reached the point where we need to confront directly what has so far been looked at only obliquely and indirectly: the condition of the classical-music tradition in Europe and America today. Classical music in the present century has exhibited a decline in creative energy, in openness to fertilizing outside influences, and, above all, in usefulness for the social and individual concerns of those who in the past formed the constituency for creative musicians, which is in striking contrast to the riotous expansion and proliferation of Afro-American music. The decline has occurred in its most precipitous form in the years since the first world war (which seems to have been a watershed for the self-confidence of the western middle classes), but it is only the culmination of processes which have been going on for the last two hundred years or so. That it should have thus accelerated at a time when the skills of individual musicians, the virtuosity of orchestras, the splendour of great concert halls, and the production standards of opera houses, are considered to have reached new peaks is a paradox which I shall attempt to explain.

No hint of this decline is given in the many books claiming to be histories of twentieth-century music that have appeared over the last thirty years or so. They tell their story as if it were a mere continuation of those older histories of which I spoke earlier, mostly confining their attention without comment to the European classical tradition and dealing with compositions and their composers, arranged in as neat an order of influencer and influenced, cause and effect, as can be managed with limited hindsight. The story relates how traditional tonal harmony came to the end of its resources, to be replaced by other, notably serial, means of pitch organization, how new tonal material and new means of sound production came into play, how a new emancipation of sounds and rhythms took place, how composers began looking for inspiration to other cultures and how some composers succeeded in obtaining further mileage from the resources of tonal harmony by sheer force of will and with the aid of the folk musics of their respective homelands. They tell also of the survival, often in new guises, of traditional forms such as the symphony, the concerto and opera, of the politicization of some composers (politicization seems always to mean left-wing, a right-wing orientation or one that simply acquiesces in the status quo being apparently invisible); it tells, too, of composers' tireless experimentation to find new sources of sound and new ways of organizing and notating these sounds, of their making use of the most sophisticated resources of modern technology where they have been available, and, finally, of their questioning the very basis of western music itself in order to purify and renew it.

The writers of these histories are at pains, while stressing the novelty of what has happened, to assure their readers at the same time of the legitimacy of the classical music of this century, by stressing its continuity with that of the European past. Here, for instance, is a paragraph from a widely-read *Introduction to Contemporary Music*, aimed explicitly at leading uncommitted non-professional listeners into the world of twentieth-century music: 'At three points in the history of music — as it happens, they were equally distant from one another — the forces of change were so much in the ascendant that the word *new* became a battle cry. Around the year 1300 progressive composers were referred to as *moderni* and their art designated as *ars nova*, 'New Art'. The breakthrough of this modernism produced new rhythmic and harmonic principles as well as basic reforms in notation. The year 1600 is another such landmark. The contemporaries of Monteverdi raised the banner of *le nuove musiche*, 'The New Music'; expressive melody and the dramatic concept of opera challenged the tradition of religious choral music. Similarly, around 1900 there emerged the New Music, with an explosiveness that gave rise to many a bitter battle . . . Contemporary music, so rich in its diversity, so excitingly tuned to the spirit of the twentieth century, is the latest — and consequently the most vivid — chapter in man's age-old attempt to impose his artistic intuition on the elusive stuff of sound: that majestic five-thousand-year-old attempt to shape the sonorous material into form possessing logic and continuity, expressive meaning and nourishing beauty.'[1]

Apart from his curious idea of dating the origin of music at five thousand years ago, and the ethnocentricity of the reason for musicking given in the final sentence, the author fails to tell us of four critical disjunctions in the classical music of this century which not only set it apart from that of previous centuries but also suggest a process not of continuing advance but of retreat. These disjunctions are: between creator and performer, between producer and consumer, between classical and vernacular traditions and between composer and his potential audience (the last I believe to be a consequence of the other three). It is hard to say which has proved the most disastrous. None of the four is entirely new to our time, but each is the end result of processes that have been going on over the whole history of the tradition; they are, in fact, implicit in the very social and aesthetic assumptions on which it rests. An examination of those assumptions and of that history must wait for a later work; here I propose looking at the disjunctions themselves as they have affected the way in which musicking in the classical tradition has taken place during the present century.

The break between composers and performers I dealt with at some length in Chapter 10, and need not elaborate further, except to note the disastrous consequences of the retreat by performers from the creative act. They are many-layered. On one level, there is the impossibility of composing, and thus of performing, anything that cannot be notated; the resultant complexity of notation, often to the despair of performers who might otherwise be willing to embrace the composers' expressions, frequently conceals simplicity if not downright poverty of invention. On another level it concerns the reduction of the performer to an instrument of the composer's will, while deepest of all is the impoverishment of the relationships and of the society that are created during a performance, since if a performer has no creative role to play, then still less have his listeners.

There have been attempts within concert-hall music since about 1945 to involve players in the creative process, usually without much success: this is either because the players, as I pointed out earlier, are unprepared either by training or by basic assumptions for such an activity, or because of their feeling, in my opinion not without some justice, that composition is the composer's job and that he should do it. Such attempts as are made are usually called 'indeterminacy', which is defined in John Vinton's *Dictionary of 20th Century Music* by reference to 'musical material that is unpredictable before a performance.' The writer of the article goes on: 'The composer using indeterminacy may specify any degree of performer choice from arranging totally notated elements to extensive improvisation. He may ask that the performer work out all or part of a score ahead of performance (perhaps by chance operations) from materials and instructions he provides. He may also ask the performer to respond during the performance to instructions and diagrams, to actions and situations, either real or imagined. Free improvisation may be asked for in indeterminate scores, but this is a subordinate technique and not a compositional means.'[2] Clearly under these conditions the work remains the composer's (the final sentence gives the game away); the performers are allowed their improvisatory head only when it does not affect the composer's over-all control. Whatever the performers do (so long as they do not play *Sweet Adeline* or *O Rest In The Lord* as mischievous orchestral players have been known to do) will serve his conception, and there is no way in which they can transcend it — not at all the same kind of situation as that partnership between composer and performers which we noted in jazz and even in early Baroque performance. This is clear from some remarks of Stockhausen; when asked in an interview why players should need a composer at all he replied in characteristic style: 'Why does a spiritual group need a guru? Why has an atom a nucleus? Why in the whole universe is there nothing that doesn't have a centre? Why are there not only moons? Why is every planet not a sun? The composer has to fulfil the role of gathering together those people who are good interpreters but by nature are not original sources. Why are there fountains in the world and why doesn't the water come from everywhere? I mean, I can't answer you. You would have to ask the spirit of the cosmos'[3] — who clearly has no experience of either African or Afro-American musicking. In the same interview he described the measure of independence that he allowed to the performers as 'like taking an element from its context and letting it run like a strip of sounds until I stop it again.'

Another user of indeterminate methods, who has assimilated them into an elaborate and very influential aesthetic doctrine incorporating elements of eastern philosophy, is John Cage. His avowed intention is to abolish intention: 'One may give up the desire to control sound, clear his mind of music and set about discovering means to let the sounds be themselves rather than vehicles of man-made theories or expressions of human sentiments.'[4] That, of course, is itself the expression of a man-made theory: the old Hobbesian doctrine that there is a necessary antithesis between social and individual interests. But, in any case, Cage's approach in practice, whatever he may say in his extensive writings, creates a situation in which he *appears* to let go of control while remaining very firmly in charge; in claiming to have no intention he creates a social situation such as Kafka might have invented, in which nothing that performers or listeners can do will release them from his (non-)intention. His concern for sounds seems greater than his concern for the human beings who make or listen to them. Nor does he seem to have noticed that there is nothing of any significance in his theories which does not appear, without anyone theorizing about it, in the practice of Afro-American musicians since the beginning of the present century. The procedures of these two musicians, and of others like them, might have been designed in order to prevent the creation of a society in which performers and listeners can act as autonomous, responsible human beings; if we can find a social analogue with them it might be what Marcuse calls the 'repressive tolerance' of modern industrial society.

The fact that I am able to use the words 'producer' and 'consumer' with regard to music is significant of the nature of the second disjunction in the present-day classical music scene. These terms imply that at the centre of music is a product, which is the *raison d'être* for all musical processes that take place. The concept of art as product in fact pervades the whole of our culture today, from the inflated sums of money paid for old-master paintings to the consumer-guide function of critics' writings. It shows itself even in the title of a recent authoritative book on the sociology of art, called without apology or explanation *The Social Production of Art*[5], while in every book I have seen on musical aesthetics the starting point and the limitation is the notion of music as objects whose existence and whose characteristics, even their effect on listeners and their social function, stem from their nature as objects. Music is product, made by a composer (producer) for the listener (consumer) and marketed like any other commodity; the possible effects of mediation in performance are scarcely mentioned, nor is any other possible form of human interaction, other than the one-dimensional transaction between producer and consumer, even discussed.

We have seen how the listeners' function as consumers of music is celebrated in the ceremony of the symphony concert, in which it is made clear to them that they have no more control over, or even access to, the process of production than they have over the design and production of their car or their breakfast cereal. Their only active role — and even that is more apparent than real — lies in the power to make a choice between competing brands.

The producer-consumer relationship in classical music, like most other relationships in industrial society, is a closed one. The producers form an exclusive group, whose skills and whose status are certified by the state after a process of selection, training and examination which ensures, certainly, that all are of a certain level of skill, but ensures also that all are of the same kind and that all have submitted to the state's values. Consumers have no access to the world of the producers, of which they are afforded glimpses in the pages of glossy magazines and festival brochures and in television arts programmes; it is never suggested that they might wish, or be able, to take an active part in that world. The exclusion of the consumer is completed by the professionalization of the art;

the amateur musician (the very word has become a term of ridicule) scarcely ever gets the chance to perform in public.

Everything about the modern classical concert, as we have seen, serves to emphasise the separation of performer from listener, and to emphasise the pyramidal model of the distribution of musical ability. It is hard to say who suffer most damage from acceptance of that model: composers, who are encouraged to take an unwarrantedly exalted view of their own musical and social importance, but who suffer private agonies through their apparent inability to reach those for whom they are supposed to be creating; or performers, who are the objects of much social admiration but are condemned in perpetuity to play music without ever being able to acknowledge in public a single musical idea as their own; or 'music lovers' whose role is simply that of consumers of what others have produced; or the 'unmusical' majority, on whom that label is hung regardless of the extent to which they may participate in other, less socially elevated, forms of musicking, and who are obliged, whether they like it or not, to contribute through taxation and through the price of commodities to the support of the structure that weighs upon them.

The third disjunction, between classical and vernacular traditions of music, is in our time so taken for granted that it tends to be thought of as universal and God-given; it is of course neither. This does not mean that there was in the past no distinction between the two traditions, but they overlapped with, drew upon and nourished each other. That climactic period in the history of the classical tradition that is called the Viennese classical period recognized this; not only were the melodic and harmonic styles of Haydn, Mozart, Beethoven and, especially, Schubert, as well as of their contemporaries, based upon Austrian folksong but their music fed back into it. Any one of those masters could, and did, create music for dancing (which today we listen to, still and silent, in concert halls — the masters themselves would not know whether to laugh or to cry were they to see us) without any compromise of their standards of inspiration or craftsmanship. If dance music was wanted, then it would be the best dance music, no less than the best mass, concerto or opera. In each case the musician considered his audience and composed for it and for the occasion of its performance. Mozart wanted his music to be popular, and why not? since popularity meant financial security and he was an ambitious man with a special skill and a family to support, and with a touchy pride in the knowledge that he was the best in the business. He was delighted when his music pleased the audience for whom it was composed (the words 'pleased' and 'failed to please' occur again and again in his letters). Here he is writing to a friend from Prague in 1788 after a performance of the very successful production there of *The Marriage of Figaro*; he described how he went to a ball but, being too tired to dance (he must have been very tired indeed, for he was a skilled and enthusiastic dancer) he sat and watched: 'I looked on with the greatest pleasure while all those people flew about in sheer delight to the music of my *Figaro* arranged as quadrilles and waltzes. For here they talk of nothing but *Figaro*. Nothing is played, sung or whistled but *Figaro*. No opera is drawing like *Figaro*. Nothing, nothing but *Figaro*. Certainly a great honour for me!.'[6] Mozart's melodies, like those of many other 'classical' musicians, became part of the vernacular tradition, not only played by village bands and café orchestras, not only eaten to, danced to and sung the length and breadth of Europe but also without doubt having their influence on vernacular musicians and on their musicking.

The nineteenth century saw a drawing apart of the two traditions. The cyclic movement of earlier centuries was reduced to a one-way traffic only, as classical composers drew upon the musical vernacular in support of a political and cultural consciousness that was essentially middle-class; for the peasants and the lower orders the creation of the new nation-states of Europe was just another cross they had to bear. Very little of the 'nationalist' music of the nineteenth century struck any answering chord among vernacular musicians; in any case Smetana, Dvorak, Mussorgsky, Rimsky-Korsakov, Borodin and Grieg were drawing upon vernacular traditions which even in their time must have been in full retreat in the face of industrialism (it is a curious fact that none of the classical music of the time shows the slightest awareness of the fact that the whole of Europe, not excepting Russia, was industrializing explosively throughout the nineteenth century). By the early twentieth century the new generation of nationalists — Kodaly, Bartok, Vaughan Williams, the young Stravinsky, and even, in their own ways, Ives, Copland and Villa-Lobos — were drawing on rural traditions that were dead or dying, their existence continuing for the most part (it is where both Stravinsky and Vaughan Williams obtained most of their folk material) in the pages of published collections. One might see this exploitation of the old cultural forms of a peasantry whose way of life was being brutally transformed by rural industrialisation as signs of a middle-class nostalgia for an ancient and stable European social order which never did exist — the same social order, in fact, as that which we see presented on the stage in innumerable nineteenth- and twentieth-century 'folk' operas.

As the mine of European musics became exhausted, many recent composers have turned to new sources of new sounds to revitalize their inspiration, in particular to the musical cultures of the Orient, as well as to the Afro-American tradition; if African music has so far escaped their attentions, it is probably in part because of the aura of 'primitiveness' that still in most European minds surrounds Africa and in part because of the difficulty of dealing with African polyrhythmic concepts. There is little sign in contemporary western classical music of any genuine understanding of Oriental music, that is to say as modes of performance involving people rather than as abstract systems of sounds, as musicking rather than as music. Stripped of the verbiage which so often accompanies the performance of such works (its shallowness is revealed in two famous photographs from the 1960s, one of Cage sitting at the feet of a Zen master, the other of Stockhausen with a group of Japanese Nō-play actors, both wearing identical solemn expressions of inadequately concealed incomprehension), these quarryings of exotic musical styles without regard for their social content have been at best as frivolous as the attempts made earlier in this century by western visual artists to use the forms of African sculpture, in complete ignorance of its social and ritual meanings. At worst they can be seen as a mode of further western exploitation of the whole world, of that Orientalism of which Edward Said says: '*is*, rather than expresses, a certain *will* or *intention* to understand, in some cases to control, manipulate, even incorporate, what is manifestly a different (or alternative and novel) world.'[7] There is, and indeed can be, in these essays in Orientalism no genuine attempt to enter into and accommodate to that world in a way that might make for genuine comprehension and learning; all is brought back, like the spoils of earlier forays which fill the ethnographic museums of the west, to be exhibited proudly in those musical museums which are concert halls.

Nor does the classical tradition's response to Afro-American music show any more genuine attempt to understand it on its own terms. Afro-American music has in fact been colonized, and serves as raw material for exploitation, a novel flavour to be used when the composer feels like it. I have already commented on Stravinsky's uncomprehendng attempt to exploit ragtime; Aaron Copland's remark concerning his own jazz-tinged Piano Concerto of 1926, that he had 'done all he could within the limited emotional scope of jazz', quoted with clear approval in a recent talk on the BBC's classical-music channel, sums up as well as anything the prevailing attitude amongst classical musicians. The one notable work which does to my ears sound like a genuine attempt to come to terms with jazz's cultural premises (sounding in places remarkably like a thirty-year anticipation of the 'cool' jazz of the 1950s) is Darius Milhaud's ballet *La Création du Monde*, of 1923. It had no successors, since, as William Austin says, 'By 1926, when Milhaud next visited America, his interest in jazz was exhausted.'[8] George Gershwin is a different case altogether, for despite the classical training which he underwent in common with many of the other 'Broadway masters' of the time, he came as a practising musician to classical composition only after considerable experience in Afro-American music; the small number of concert pieces he created before his premature death in 1937, and especially his opera *Porgy and Bess*, give a hint of a genuinely popular concert and theatre music, of a kind that Mozart would have understood. In general, however, the attitude of classical musicians towards the Afro-American tradition has been at best of incomprehension and condescension, at worst of violent antagonism.

A remarkable attempt to bring about an understanding

between vernacular and concert musicking, to create in effect a vernacular concert music, was made after the second world war by a group of Greek musicians (that it should have come from a society that was most tragically riven by violent conflict is perhaps not without significance) of whom the best known are Mikis Theodorakis and Manos Hadjidakis. These musicians worked in the low-class *rebetiko* style, from the bars and dives of Athens and Piraeus, whose favoured instrument is the bazouki, refining and elaborating it as the basis of a popular concert, dance and especially theatre music. Hadjidakis in particular pioneered a musical form which is a kind of suite, of up to twenty short pieces, all popular in style and each quite simple, which cumulatively build to a powerful and beautiful, often tragic, totality, of a kind which orthodox classical music in our time seems unable to achieve; the finest of these which I know is *Lilacs Out of the Dead Land*. Despite the popular success of many of their works throughout Europe (aided no doubt by Theodorakis's well-publicized stand against the Greek Colonels), or even perhaps because of it, the international classical-music establishment has not wanted to know about them; neither of those musicians is mentioned in any of the histories of twentieth-century music that I have seen, and neither rates an entry under his own name in the *Dictionary of 20th Century Music*; nor have I heard a note of their music on the BBC's classical-music channel.

Understandably, any idea that the classical tradition might feed back into the vernacular is well in the past. About the only fragments of classical music from this century that have become established in the vernacular in Britain have been vehicles for crude patriotic or right-wing sentiment: *Land of Hope and Glory* to Elgar's first *Pomp and Circumstance March*, Parry's setting of William Blake's *Jerusalem* (what Blake would have had to say about the hijacking of his poem by the British Conservative Party is a matter for conjecture) and an odious patriotic hymn, much sung in British schools, whose words I shall spare the reader; it is set to the big 'Jupiter' tune from *The Planets* of Gustav Holst.

Today the disjunction is complete; with very few exceptions, all of them relegated to the fringes of concert life, contemporary composers of classical music have cut themselves off from those vernacular sources which nourished the inspiration of their predecessors. The two cultures are not only separate but also mutually antipathetic. But while the cutting-off has been bad for the whole of western music making, it has been disastrous for classical music; just as it is arguable that the explosive growth of western technology has been a response more to scarcity than to plenty, so it is possible to view the large number of disparate styles in present-day concert music as evidence more of a desperate search for that common idiom which comes naturally when classical and vernacular musicians are able to interact freely than it is of any real creative vitality. The technical revolution which followed the 'exhaustion' of tonal harmony (it is alive and well elsewhere) has undoubtedly given rise to sonic structures of great interest and sometimes even beauty, but those glittering and ingenious sound-objects remain, for want of a clear understanding of the meaning of the act of performing them, only ever more gorgeously-coloured and intricate toys for the diversion of ever more frivolous audiences. Those audiences cannot be anything other than frivolous, for they are never permitted to be more than spectators of the musical act; being denied any active role in that creative gesture which is a musical performance, they can have no part either in the creation of that society which the performance brings into existence. That society which has been created for them has been called the Society of the Spectacle, of which Guy Debord says: 'The spectacle presents itself as something enormously positive, indisputable and inaccessible . . . The attitude which it demands in principle is passive acceptance which in fact it has already obtained by its manner of appearance without reply.'[9] Although Debord's comments refer to the wider society of the industrial state, they fit that of the modern concert hall with remarkable exactness.

If audiences are powerless to affect performances, that powerlessness is in proportion to the arrogance of composers, an arrogance which mirrors that of scientists, upon whom, rather than the poets of the nineteenth century, they model themselves and their activities; Edgard Varèse once said 'Scientists are the poets of today' — a silly remark which is nonetheless indicative of a state of mind. Just as do scientists, composers present us with the result of their researches, ready-made and unasked-for; take it and like it, we are told from the subsidized eyrie, it is good for you. The arrogance, I hasten to add, is as much institutional as it is personal; composers, like scientists, are in the main decent enough men and women. But in present-day concert life not only the publicity and the media attention but also the very nature of the relationship with players and audience turn every performance of a composer's work, willy-nilly, into a monstrous ego-trip, which seems to have led some composers, at least, to believe their own publicity and to take an exaggerated view of their own importance in the world.

For all its technical sophistication, there is nothing new in the view of the world and of human relationships offered by 'the new music', since all the relationships of the concert hall reproduce in if anything intensified form those of the industrial state. Indeed, there is something impoverished about the human values embodied in the performance of most contemporary music (a parallel again to the values held by their models, the physical scientists); the wheels spin most ingeniously but do not engage with any real social or emotional load.

The impression of social naivety is, for this listener, always given most intensely in the performance of those musical works whose composer has attempted to engage explicitly with social concerns, and most especially when the composer strikes left-wing or populist political attitudes: the stage works of Henze and Nono, Berio's anti-capitalist and anti-bourgeois pieces, Stockhausen's essays in cultural ecumenicism, as well as works such as Pousseur's 1968 orchestral piece *Couleurs Croisées*, in which the song *We Shall Overcome* serves, as the composer himself says, 'as a matrix from which the whole composition is strictly derived . . . In particular, it is projected through a whole system of melodic-harmonic fields, beginning with a disjunct, chromatic expressionist musical reality and ending . . . in a diatonic state which is relatively, hypothetically, at peace'[10] and Frederick Rzewski's *Attica* and *Coming Together* of 1972, in which the words of inmates involved in an American prison riot are used with (again quoting the composer) an 'attempt to heighten them by underscoring them with music. There is therefore a certain ambiguity between the personal, emotional and meditative aspects of the texts, which is enhanced by cumulative repetition, and their wider political implications. I believe that this ambiguity can be either a strength or a weakness in performance, depending on the degree with which the performer identifies personally with the revolutionary struggle taking place in America's prisons and the world at large.'[11] It would have been interesting to hear the reaction of George Jackson or of Martin Luther King to a performance in a concert hall of these pieces.

The naivety of such posturings is cruelly exposed when they are compared with the streetwise sophistication of black American musicians and their musicking. It is a dangerous and irresponsible naivety, which conceals from the composer — and his audience — the fact that he is serving the values, and thus the interests, of those to whose advantage the modern state is organized; no matter what message the composer may *think* he is conveying, the act of performance within the structure and the conventions of the concert hall or opera house carries its own message. It is not that the medium *is* the message, or even that the medium conveys a message that can swamp that which is intended; rather, it is that anyone who genuinely desired social change would not subject his message to such an conservative medium as the concert hall. For those who are happy to serve the values of the modern state, there is of course no problem, but I wonder if those who seek to use the concert hall and the opera house for the expression of revolutionary or populist sentiments really understand what it is they are doing. For in order to gain entry to that culture which is incarnated in the buildings and in the events that take place within them, it is necessary, whether one realizes it or not, to submit to the values which they were built to celebrate. That is the price exacted for the subsidy given by states and wealthy organizations to classical musicking: that the performance celebrate those values which legitimize the position of the privileged of the state. It is a trap into which not many vernacular musicians, whose noses are being constantly rubbed in the realities of power and of money, are likely to fall

— not, at any rate, without being aware of what they are doing.

Perhaps it does not matter too much, for this is where the fourth disjunction comes into play; what contemporary composers, and those who perform their music, do, would appear to relate to the concerns of only a small minority of even that minority of the population who enjoy the ceremonies of the concert hall and opera house, or who buy records of the music that is performed there. I have already remarked that most concert goers shun the offerings of contemporary composers, preferring to hear pieces that are the work of dead, and usually long-dead, musicians; we need now to investigate more fully this phenomenon and the reasons for it. Certainly little has been added since about 1920 to the repertory of pieces that are regularly played in concert halls and opera houses, and nothing that has been added has attained to anything like the popularity, as measured by frequency of performance, of the 'immortal masterpieces' of Beethoven, Brahms or Chaikovski, or of Verdi, Wagner or Puccini. It is not possible to invoke any 'inevitable timelag' which is supposed to be required for the assimilation of new works; the composers I have mentioned did not have to wait for anything like the length of time which has already elapsed since the first performances of such critically acclaimed works of the twentieth century as Schoenberg's *Pierrot Lunaire* (1912), Varèse's *Arcana* (1927), Berg's *Chamber Concerto* (1925), or even Boulez's *Le Marteau sans Maître* (thirty years old in 1984) and Messaien's *Chronochromie* (coming up to 25). Those who champion 'the new music' await its assimilation into the repertory much as the early Christians awaited the Second Coming, greeting each new performance as the first rays of a new dawn. But in fact the only music composed since World War I which has found anything like general acceptance with concert goers is that which, like the later works of Rachmaninov and Sibelius (and even the latter are a bit modern for some) shows an obvious affinity with the world of nineteenth-century romanticism.

The virtual freezing of the repertory has had the consequence that a concert very rarely furnishes any new musical experience at all. The number of composers whose work is regularly played in orchestral and chamber-music programmes is not large, around fifty at most, with a few others represented by perhaps one or two, often immensely popular works; Bruch's First Violin Concerto and *Scottish Fantasia* and Dukas' *Sorcerer's Apprentice* come to mind. It can be, and often is, pointed out that there are always generations of young people for whom these composers and their works are new; this is undoubtedly so, but hardly seems to justify giving over the whole of modern concert life to them. As Arthur Loesser says: 'Programs consisting largely of twice-sifted masterpieces may, of course, appeal more readily to people of wider culture and greater discrimination than those that dwell mostly in the froth of fashion. Nevertheless, too persistent a preoccupation with the past, even with its glories, is an elderly posture, one of diminishing hope. Old music could seem new to the ever-resurgent generations who had not heard it before; still, on the whole, what a "classical" program gains in "taste" it loses in living force.'[12]

The human need for novelty, however, remains, and is met, first, by the researches of musicologists into ever more obscure corners of the past repertory, exhuming works and even composers who served their times and their occasions and might have been happier to be allowed to rest in peace. The rediscovery of the Baroque in the 1930s and 1940s must have been, at least in part, the first major response to the freezing of the repertory, while today, one after another, the works of old musicians, previously just names in history books, are being brought out of the libraries and restored to the consciousness of classical-music lovers. But such quarrying of the past for the semblance of new musical experiences must come, as with all strictly non-renewable fossil resources, eventually to an end; although possibly still containing untapped fields for exploitation they are not inexhaustible, and already musicologists are reduced to the rediscovery of forgotten English cathedral organists and German kapellmeisters (mercilessly mocked in Peter Schickele's P.D.Q. Bach, 'history's most justly neglected composer') and even to making notional completions of incomplete or mutilated works which up to now have stood as they are, for example Mahler's Tenth symphony and even Schubert's Eighth, known to generations as *The Unfinished*. Anything will do that is new to the ears of audiences but bears the reassuring stamp of the familiar musical language and gestures. Another means of meeting the quest for novelty lies in the reassessment and reworking of familiar masterpieces with a view to restoring 'authenticity' (a chimera if ever there was one) with the use of period instruments, or copies of them, and scrupulous research into performance style (style, that is, viewed narrowly as the realization in sound of the composer's notations) and elaborate care taken to recreate the piece exactly as the composer intended — in all but its most vital aspect: the purpose and the kind of occasion for which it was composed.

All this activity is fed happily by record companies, so that record collectors who have just completed buying their boxed sets of all 104 symphonies of Josef Haydn find themselves faced with having to buy them all over again on CD with authentic instruments. It is all good for business, but it would seem to reveal a massive ebbing of confidence. No music, it seems, will ever be as good or as satisfying again as it was up to the time of the first world war; the book of creation, if not exactly closed, is being filled with writings that are either unintelligible or repellent or both. We are forced to ask whether a culture able to take full advantage of present creativity would feel obliged in this way to nit-pick at its past, and to try to discover what might be the reason for such a state of affairs, which contrasts so sharply with the ceaseless creative activity, and the ceaseless demand for new experiences, in the other western musical culture with which the classical tradition coexists so uneasily.

If we accept that musicking is a ritual activity in which the identity and the values of the members of a group are explored, affirmed and celebrated, then a symphony concert is a ritual which performs this function for the members of the middle and upper classes of industrial society; many social surveys taken in a number of countries have shown that the overwhelming majority of both performers and listeners who take part in symphony concerts qualify in terms of income, formal education and social attitudes for membership of those classes, today fused in a single elite whose social and artistic leadership is not allowed to be questioned. As a ritual, it is, to use the ideas introduced in Chapter 2, a celebration of the 'sacred history' of those classes, and an affirmation of faith in their values as the universal and abiding stuff of living. As these values, and those of industrial society in general, come increasingly under attack both from social critics and from the pressure of events, so the concert becomes more important as a way of affirming a belief in stability in an unstable world. The lives and the personalities of 'the great composers', their sufferings, their triumphs and their defeats, their loves and their hates, all embodied quasi-autobiographically in those psychodramas which are symphonies, concertos, sonatas and tone poems, are paradigms for that belief, which is reaffirmed every time their music is played before a paying audience in a concert hall. Beethoven's triumph over his disability, the death- and work-obsessed Protestantism of Sebastian Bach, the warm rational Enlightenment optimism of Haydn, Vaughan Williams's vision of a pastoral England that probably never was, Schubert's insouciant but doomed bohemian existence, Elgar's espousal of the uneasy imperialist extravagance of Edwardian England (comforting to an England presently in disastrous decline) and, perhaps most significant of all to the late twentieth century, Mahler's outward success and inner alienation and misery — these and other past musicians are models for the values and the experience of their audiences.

The 'history of music' as perceived by the average music lover is a mythological landscape, peopled with heroes and their adversaries, tasks to be accomplished, tricks of fate to be overcome, destinies to be fulfilled. However rationally musicologists may present that history, however obsessively they may order and date them, in the catalogues of Köchel, Longo, Deutsch and Hoboken, the works of the classical tradition remain obstinately, in the minds of most music lovers, outside historical time; no other assumption could induce a moment's credence for the idea commonly held that these are 'immortal masterpieces' that will last as long as time. The violence of many music lovers' reaction to the mere suggestion that the works of Bach and Beethoven may not be in the literal sense immortal, but will one day cease to have meaning for performers and listeners and will simply disappear, testifies to the power of the myth. Nor can the ritual of stability afford heroes who are alive in the present; like Theseus, Maui, Arthur, Gilgamesh and other civilizing heroes, 'the great composers' belong in the time of myth, and their works must live for ever.

Even the much-trumpeted 'raising of performance standards' (that is, the insistence on ever-greater precision in the execution of the notations and the development of ever-greater digital dexterity to meet its demands) over the last few decades speaks of an obsessional need for accurate performance of the ritual, in default of which the whole ceremony is rendered invalid. The obsession is understandable; as our grasp of present events becomes more precarious, so we tighten our grip on the past with a magical ceremony to keep things as they have been (or as we *imagine* them to have been) and avert the catastrophic changes we fear. The quest for 'authenticity' in performance can be seen in the same light; the 'sacred history' of the culture which, as Eliade has said, 'must be carefully preserved and transmitted intact,'[13] has become fixed and rigid, in a way it does not seem to become in non-literate cultures, leaving little room for creative development. The urge to fix and to preserve intact has an ally in the gramophone; Stravinsky, for example, tried to capture his own performance of every one of his works on disc so that future generations could know exactly how they should be played. What Haydn would have thought of that we can only speculate. For the most part, musicians and listeners in other cultures, including the Afro-American, don't give a damn about preservation, being much too busy with the present process of creation; if pieces survive, well and good, but it does not matter too much. If they were to think about the matter at all (and there is no particular reason why they should) they would probably feel that there was plenty more where that came from.

That it was no part of the intention of, say, Beethoven that his great symphonies should become part of a ritual of the twentieth-century industrial state is obvious. Seated in the regimented comfort of the modern concert hall, it is difficult to imagine these works, and others from the past that are performed there, as having been heard in any other kind of setting or as serving any other purpose, but the fact is that all but the most recent have been wrenched out of the social context for which they were intended, and the varied and complex social meanings of their performance have been reduced to a single meaning to serve the values of the powerful in present-day society. Musicians, of course, have always tended to gravitate towards centres of power — after all, that is where the money is — and to celebrate the values of the powerful, but in the past those centres of power were not centralized or unified, nor were the events of which the performance formed a part of one kind only. Music which today is heard in the bland — but *not* neutral — conditions of the concert hall might have been originally heard in a medieval church as part of its liturgy, in an eighteenth-century German bourgeois household during a wedding festivity, in a sixteenth-century French academy open only to members, in the drapers' hall of a nineteenth-century German city, in a sixteenth-century English cathedral, as a background to elegant conversation and eating in an eighteenth-century German court, as an ornament to the river trip of an eighteenth-century English king, as part of a gathering of friends in the apartment of an obscure nineteenth-century Viennese musician, as part of the coronation festivities of a Holy Roman Emperor, as accompaniment to the dancers in a nineteenth-century Viennese ballroom, as part of the solemn Good Friday obsequies in a provincial German church, at a fashionable aristocratic salon in Paris or a rival *haute-bourgeoise* soirée just before the first world war. None of these events took place in a space that was purpose-built for the performance of music, in none of them was music the primary object of the coming-together of musicians and listeners, in few of them would the performing musicians have been all professionals, and to none of them could one gain admission by the purchase of a ticket. With the hijacking of these, and countless other forms of musical encounter, to the modern concert hall, an enormous number and variety of social meanings has been reduced to one — and that meaning, as I have suggested, is one of defence, of holding on to what one has, rather than of enterprise and the exploration of new territories of the spirit which was embodied in the original performances, and which has animated Afro-American musicking in the present century.

It is even possible that those superb concert halls and opera houses of which most large cities in the wealthy west are so proud, built generally with no expense spared and often at the leading edge of new building technology, as well as those superbly disciplined organizations that are orchestras, chamber-music ensembles and opera companies, can themselves be seen as symptoms of the decline in creative energy. We can obtain a clue to this from Northcote Parkinson's jokey but fascinating book *Parkinson's Law*. In the chapter 'Plans and Plants', he describes a visit to a kind of business organization common enough today, which is housed in a magnificent building: 'from behind closed doors will come the subdued noise of an ordered activity. A minute later and you are ankle deep in the director's carpet, plodding sturdily towards his distant, tidy desk. Hypnotized by the chief's unwavering stare, cowed by the Matisse hung upon his wall, you will feel you have found real efficiency at last.

'In point of fact you will have discovered nothing of the sort. It is now known that *perfection of planned layout is achieved only by institutions on the point of collapse* . . . During a period of exciting discovery or progress there is no time to plan the perfect headquarters. The time for that comes later, when all the important work has been done. Perfection, we know, is finality; and finality is death'[14] (My italics). There can be no doubt that the great concert halls, and the organization that is necessary to run them, impose a particular character on everything that happens within them, creating in particular severe limitations on innovation; it is not surprising that the most interesting and innovative musicking of today should be taking place, as probably it always did, in unsuitable places with such facilities as they possess impoverished and probably inadequate. With such places Monteverdi and Buddy Bolden must have been familiar; it is there that it is possible for musicians, listeners and dancers to hammer out new musical styles, and new social relationships, together.

The flattening-out of the social function of classical music has meant that composers who work for the concert hall have for the most part abandoned the music of popular entertainment, of popular theatre, films and television, of popular dance and of social occasions in general, either to vernacular musicians or else to specialist colleagues who are prepared to weather the contempt of the high-art world for the sake of the financial rewards and of the wide exposure their music will receive. It is interesting, for example, that Max Steiner and Erich Korngold, two of the most prolific and, through the Hollywood films with which they were associated, probably most heard orchestral composers of the twentieth century, receive no mention at all in most histories of twentieth-century music. It all looks like a calculated retreat from any attempt either to make music of any kind of direct social usefulness or to woo and win an audience, the esteem in which a composer of 'new music' is held by the critical establishment being in something like inverse ratio to the extent to which he makes the attempt. That Mozart and Haydn would not have dared, even if the idea had occurred to them, to ride roughshod over their audiences' preferences is obvious; they simply would not have eaten.

There is an audience to be won, though a small one, a minority within a minority, which is apparently able to use performances of 'new music' in the service of its self-definition, and for whose members such performances are capable of constructing social relationships which satisfy some ideal that they hold. It is a seductive ideal that is celebrated, of a highly rational, centralized society, a society in fact, of the technological fix, but it is fundamentally no more than a naive celebration of technique which does not require or even consider any change in social relationships; what such musicking does is place both performers and listeners in an even more subservient position than before to the will of the composer, even more completely relegated to the role of spectators at processes they do not, and are not expected to, understand — a model, in fact, of political processes in contemporary societies, not least in those which call themselves democratic. The audience is necessarily small, since it defines itself in terms of exclusion of even the majority of classical-music lovers, for whom the all-purpose term of abuse, 'bourgeoisie', is used. Tom Wolfe, in his study of the modern movement in architecture, describes the exclusion thus: 'Composers, artists or architects in a compound began to have the instincts of the medieval clergy, much of whose activity was devoted exclusively to separating itself from the mob. For mob, substitute bourgeois — and here you have the spirit of avant-gardism in the twentieth century. Once inside the compound, an artist became part of the clerisy, to use an old term for an intelligentsia with clerical presumptions.'[15]

Wolfe's proposition, that contemporary classical musicians, like their colleagues in the other arts, have, in collusion with their audience and with those who hold the pursestrings, built themselves into a compound within which they can regard themselves as 'having access to the godhead, which in this case was Creativity,'[16] deserves some attention. What is not widely understood today is, first, that what we today call 'classical music' is a conflation of ways of musicking that were affirmations of identity for a large number of different social groups at different historical times; practically the only thing they had in common is that they were literate and that they were associated in some way with contemporary centres of power in European society. And, second, that those groups have always had an element of exclusiveness about them, even if some were more exclusive than others. It was only with the spread of music publishing in the eighteenth century, of public concerts in the nineteenth, and of records in the twentieth, that the music first heard in the *châteaux* and *Schlossen* of the aristocracy, and in the salons of the rising bourgeoisie, became more widely available; up to that time, if one were to attend the performances at which the music was heard one had to belong to that social circle.

There is nothing extraordinary about this, since musical performance has always been a way in which members of social groups have affirmed their identity, and exclusion has always been an element of that identity. But with the spread of what we can crudely call bourgeois ideals and their cognate, industrialism, across the whole world, and with the takeover of the entire history of literate European music, and its conflation into what we equally crudely call classical music, to serve the value system of industrial society and of those who benefit from it, the differentiations and exclusivities which were still present even in the nineteenth century (for example, the two rival traditions, that popular tradition which emphasised improvisation and virtuosity, as represented by Liszt, Thalberg, Meyerbeer and Rossini and that of 'serious' composition as represented by Schumann, Wagner and Brahms) have been merged into an amorphous corpus of 'great music'. Anyone today who possesses the price of a concert ticket or of a gramophone record can gain admission to the 'World of the Great Composers', as the record-club advertisements so picturesquely put it. Exclusiveness has to be gained by other means, and it is appropriate that those who consider themselves intellectuals should define themselves by references to musical performances that are too 'difficult' and complex for the ordinary music lover (it parallels in a way the aristocratic practice of self-definition through eating game meats in so rotten a state that the fastidious middle classes will not touch them) — and then that they should insist that this way of musicking is the natural and inevitable successor of that of 'difficult' composers such as Beethoven and Mozart who, the story goes (it is quite untrue) were also understood in their own times only by a small coterie of intellectuals.

How this collusion between composers, sponsors and audience came about is an interesting history. It climaxed in a brilliantly successful takeover by a group of aggressive and ambitious young composers of the summer school at Darmstadt, in West Germany, which was founded in 1947 with funds provided by the city and by the American occupying forces and was aimed to restore the continuity of German classical music with that of the rest of Europe after the disruption caused by twelve years of Nazism. That aim was rudely thrust aside and Darmstadt became a showcase for the work of those young composers and their like-minded friends. Other more conservative musicians were left stranded like beached whales by the rapidity and the completeness of the takeover; even the august Stravinsky was obliged, in order to retain his credibility, to adopt the young lions' compositional methods and pay his tribute to their idol, Anton Webern, an eccentric, fastidious master who had been conveniently killed just after the end of the war and could not protest at the unwarranted weight placed upon his beautiful but fragile music.

The key to their success lay in their gaining not only access to, but virtual monopoly of, the sources of subsidy, which in this case were West German Radio, the Donaueschingen Festival (a lavish annual affair financed by a music-loving family of aristocrats and Southwest German Radio) and, later, broadcasting networks and academic institutions in Europe and America, most of which were dragooned into lending support by the fear of seeming antiquated and out of touch. Once they had invested in 'the new music' they were naturally enough interested in protecting their investment and were happy to act as propagandists for it. The way in which the takeover was managed in the first place is not clear, but it shows clearly the coincidence in values between subsidizer and subsidized which we noted in an earlier chapter. There would not be too much significance for the rest of us in this coincidence, if the money was the sponsor's own and the musicking was sponsored for his own pleasure and that of his friends; but when the money is public, and is being used to support public musicking, then the question of values does become publicly important. There is no space here to investigate the number of unexamined assumptions that underlie the subsidizing of contemporary composers and of those who play their music, but we note that subsidy does make it possible for musicians to sustain a posture of intellectual independence and artistic commitment which, to put it no more strongly, does not always accord with the facts. Successful contemporary composers are able to insist on the musical and social necessity of writing as they do, at the same time pointing out the personal and private nature of their inspiration, considerations against which the need to please an audience is at best secondary, and this is the result of their having persuaded those who hold the pursestrings that theirs is an activity which supports the sponsors' values — which, of course, both parties may sincerely believe are true values.

I venture these comments on present-day classical music not simply as what advertisements call 'knocking copy', in order to make the product I am selling look better by comparison, but in order to set the record straight, in that those who practise, listen to and sponsor classical music in our time are in the habit of presenting it as the one significant 'serious' musical culture of the west. It is this claim that must be exposed if we are to perceive where the true human centre of western musicking today lies. For the fact is that the classical tradition, which over the past sixty years or so has produced works of undoubted ingenuity and even occasionally beauty, has failed signally to articulate values or to create a community that is of use to more than a relative handful of people today. Its failure has lain, not in musical technique, but in those human relationships which are brought into existence whenever music is performed, and that is a grievous failure indeed. For music is, first and foremost, performance, which is a collaboration between performers and whoever is listening, and maybe dancing; those human relationships which the performance brings into existence are inescapable, and if we ignore them in our quest for ever more ingenious and elaborate objects, then they will become distorted and sterile, just as they do in the wider society of which the performance is a model.

This is what I believe has happened in the classical tradition today. In the first place, we have a sizeable audience (still, however, a small minority of the population) which concerns itself with the performance and the contemplation of a number of sound-objects bequeathed to us from the past, and an extensive quasi-industrial apparatus to provide them with those objects; there is no taste for adventure there, only a retreat from new experience and a fear of change. And in the second, we have musicians driven by a kind of technological imperative to create ever more complex and esoteric works whose performance creates a model of centralized power and authority. Together they present us with the twin faces of the industrial state today, its fears and its drives, and, above all, the poverty of its relationships. There does not seem to be any way out; composers cannot abdicate their authority, or they would no longer be composers, and in any case performers would be unable to play without them, having never learnt how to become autonomous musicians able to take responsibility for what they play, and having nobody to show them how.

The whole massive apparatus is kept alive through injections of subsidy, so that the majority, who have no interest in any of it, are obliged to pay for the support of the musicians, as well as for the buildings and institutions with which they are associated; even the money that is given by Ford, Eastern Airlines and Texaco, among others, comes not from nowhere but from the price of cars, airline tickets and petrol — and from those tax deductions for which the taxpayer ultimately foots the bill. Take away that subsidy and most of the structure would collapse, for it has little genuine base in human lives. What remained — probably mostly amateur, which is to say, people making their own experiences — might be the healthier for it; in the greatest period of the classical tradition, after all, the majority of the musicking, both public or private, was carried out by amateurs, with professionals functioning as leaders and pacemakers in the common task. But perhaps that time can never come again — not, at any rate, in such a way as to preserve the relationships that are embodied in present-day classical musicking.

The one thing that the vernacular musician cannot forget is his relationship with his audience; it is ironic that for that he is despised as 'commercial' by the classical-music establishment. Conversely, that audience expects to be able to relate directly, on a personal level, with its musicians. This direct relationship, however distorted by the forces of commercialism, however over-eagerly it may sometimes be sought by musicians, however insincere, even hypocritical, it can on occasion become (hypocrisy being the tribute paid by vice to virtue), can nevertheless come genuinely into existence for the duration of a performance and provide a vision, however fleeting and partial, of a society whose values are a genuine alternative to the present destructive and dehumanizing society of the industrial state. The presence of those alternative values in western music today can almost always be traced to the musicking of black people in the Americas; in the next chapter we shall see once again this presence in action.

NOTES

1. MACHLIS, Joseph: *Introduction to Contemporary Music*, London, J.M. Dent & Sons Ltd, 1963, p 3.
2. VINTON, John (ed): *Dictionary of Twentieth-Century Music*, London, Thames & Hudson, 1974, p 336.
3. quoted in 'Spiritual Dimensions: Peter Heyworth Talks to Karlheinz Stockhausen', *Music and Musicians*, May 1971, p 34.
4. CAGE, John: *Silence*, Cambridge, Mass, The MIT Press, 1966, p 10.
5. WOLFF, Janet: *The Social Production of Art*, London, Macmillan, 1981.
6. BLOM, Eric (ed): *Mozart's Letters* (transl. by Emily Anderson), Harmondsworth, Penguin Books, 1956, p 221.
7. SAID, Edward: *Orientalism*, London, Routledge & Kegan Paul, 1978, p 12.
8. AUSTIN, William W.: *Music in the 20th Century from Debussy through Stravinsky*, London, J.M. Dent & Sons Ltd, 1966, p 482.
9. DEBORD, Guy: *The Society of the Spectacle*, Detroit, Red & Black, revised edition 1977, paragraph 12.
10. quoted in GRIFFITHS, Paul: *A Concise History of Modern Music from Debussy to Boulez*, London, Thames & Hudson, 1978, p 195.
11. quoted *ibid.*, p 194.
12. LOESSER, Arthur: *Men, Women and Pianos: A Social History*, New York, Simon and Schuster, 1954, p 423.
13. ELIADE, Mercea: *Rites and Symbols of Initiation*, New York, Harper & Row, 1965, p ix.
14. PARKINSON, C. Northcote: *Parkinson's Law, or the Pursuit of Progress*, London, John Murray, 1957, pp 84–85.
15. WOLFE, Tom: *From Bauhaus to Our House*, London, Jonathan Cape, 1982, p 18.
16. *ibid.* p 19.

Chapter 13

STYLES AND RITUALS: WANTING TO BE PART OF THAT MUSIC

The eruption of rock'n'roll into popular music in the mid-1950s took most white people by surprise; it seemed as if this extraordinary raucous but exciting music had suddenly come from nowhere to displace the familiar strains to which they had been accustomed as a background for social events and for decorous dancing. That it was in fact a product of the long evolution which I have been describing in this book, and that it had strong links with other contemporary styles of Afro-American musicking was not at that time clear to many people, and indeed it is still largely obscured by an imposed taxomony which tends to conceal its true origins. In this chapter I intend to show the strength of those links by tracing the main lines of its development both backwards into its past and forward to the present forms of popular music.

One of the major difficulties in discussing the great four-dimensional jigsaw puzzle that is Afro-American music, and in showing how the various elements articulate one with another, lies in the necessity of using the literary medium, which is obstinately sequential, to represent a process in which so many interlinked things have been going on at the same time. Performers and listeners alike have resisted the pigeonholing that both entrepreneurs, trying to make money out of the musicians' activities, and scholars, trying to make a tidy and manageable order out of what is essentially an untidy and unmanageable activity, have tried to impose on them. The record industry, which has of course been intimately involved with the development of all kinds of western musicking since at least the turn of the century, has always been keen to pigeonhole its artists and its publics; built as it is on music as a commodity for sale, it finds that this practice makes for greater ease of packaging and marketing, as well as making it possible to direct sales efforts towards specific markets and from time to time to produce the illusion of having something new to sell. There can be no doubt that this packaging of artists for a particular market has had its effect on the history of western music in this century, not excepting classical music, and has played a large part in the erection of what are often quite artificial categories in Afro-American music. In real life, however, musicians have always been willing to work in as wide a variety of styles and milieux as their skills will permit (the two musicians described by Titon in Chapter 7 are by no means exceptional), while on the other hand audiences have on the whole not cared to confine their listening to one musical style only; this need not surprise us since identity is a complex, dynamic and many-layered affair. The categories that are commonly used are at best convenient approximations, at worst commercial and even political fictions, and trying to establish the boundaries between them is like trying to put fences between the colours of the rainbow.

That is not to say that giving names to styles of Afro-American music, or any other music for that matter, has no basis in reality. Styles do crystallize and become dominant, and musicians as they play, listeners as they listen and dancers as they dance, do group themselves together, bound by common values and identities; such groups frequently adopt names for the purpose of self-identification. The fact that the power to name is also the power to define is of great importance in musicking, concerned as it crucially is with identity, and we need to look very carefully always at how a name is given, who gives it, and whose power of definition it reflects. The need becomes more pressing when the musicking under discussion is concerned with the self-definition of large numbers of people, as is that modern popular Afro-American music known as rock, or pop.

The most notable instance in this century of self-definition on a mass scale through music occurred in the mid-1950s, with the coming of rock'n'roll, perhaps the most profound and enduring reshaping of a dominant musical style to have taken place since the Renaissance. An astonishing feature of that reshaping, in an age of mass communications (that is, one-way communication), is that it took place initially without the mediation of the controllers of mass communication, the major record companies and the radio and television networks. How it took place is a much-told tale, but it needs retelling here, since the way in which the story is told and has become accepted is itself a significant part of that history.

According to the conventional history, up to the early 1950s the popular music that was most widely known to the majority (that is to say, the white) audience across the industrialized world was the literate, usually 32-bar, popular song which we encountered in Chapter 9. The great majority of the artists, like the audience, were white, and the music was cast in the form of the two most popular dances of the time, the foxtrot and the quickstep, with an occasional waltz. Those few black artists who did make hit records, such as Nat 'King' Cole and the Ink Spots, did so by making themselves sound as 'white' as possible and by conforming to popular-song conventions (though the Ink Spots, like the earlier Mills Brothers, were drawing all unbeknownst to their audience on the male gospel-quartet tradition); but they were few indeed. Every now and then a hint of another culture would emerge and cross over into the popular-music field; in hits like Count Basie's *One O'Clock Jump* of 1941 and a few other 'jump' (that is, rhythm-and-blues under another name) records, notably by the great Louis Jordan, those of us who were in our teens at the time felt a whiff of something stronger than the offerings of Bing Crosby, Vera Lynn and Glenn Miller, although we had no idea where it came from. On the whole, however, the melodies and the rhythms, like the artists, were firmly European in origin, with just a hint of jazz-blues inflection. The record market itself was dominated by six 'major' companies, which had control not only of the artists and the repertoire, but also of recording facilities, production and marketing. It was, as we noted earlier, essentially a music that was aimed at adult tastes and experience; adolescents (there was no such creature as a teenager until the 1950s) accepted the music and its curiously stylized lyrics as part of their environment. Jazz, and especially blues, were esoteric, acquired tastes, the latter in any case not widely available outside the black ghettos of the United States.

We have seen how blues was transformed in the late 1940s by the new mood and expectations of black Americans; it was also transformed musically by a greater emphasis on the dancing beat, as well as by the application of electrical amplification to the guitar, giving it not only new bite and penetration but also greatly increased sustaining power. Dance has always been an important part of the function of the blues, but, as the rhythm sections of blues bands became more powerful and emphatic, the character of the music changed, gaining for it, according to the conventional account, the name of 'rhythm-and-blues'. This was a music still made more or less exclusively by and for black people. It was hardly at all recorded by the major record companies and mostly ignored by the radio networks, but there were individual radio stations that played it, and even some that specialized in it, and more adventurous white listeners, bored with the offerings of the networks, would turn the knobs of their radio sets and pick up this music, which was the antithesis of the networks' staple; it was loud, often crudely produced and recorded, with a powerful dance beat and the harsh but vibrant voices of such now legendary figures as Muddy Waters, Howlin' Wolf and Joe Turner — and it was, above all, exciting.

The conventional account tells also how the real expansion of interest in this music among white audiences came when a Cleveland disc jockey named Alan Freed launched it, first in his radio programme and then in a series of monster live shows in Cleveland and, later, New

York, coining the term 'rock'n'roll' in an attempt to render the music more acceptable to the white majority audience. These shows presented in the flesh for the first time to that audience such artists as Chuck Berry, Fats Domino, Joe Turner and The Drifters, the last-named being one of the many black vocal groups whose singing, often called doo-wop after the sounds made by the backing singers, was based on the gospel tradition. Recordings of these, and other artists, were made not by the major companies, who regarded the whole thing as a fad and beneath their notice, but by a number of smaller companies that had grown up in the space they had left vacant: Chess in Chicago, Sun in Memphis, King in Cincinatti and a host of others that came and went almost overnight. In the absence of those large-scale resources for the production, promotion and marketing of records which the majors had at their disposal, it was some time before rock'n'roll became a dominant music — not, in fact, until the majors woke up to its commercial possibilities.

Before that could happen there needed to be an injection from white American music, notably, the story goes, from country music. Enter, stage left, a country band called The Saddlemen, to be transformed by Milt Gabler, who happened to have also been Louis Jordan's record producer, into Bill Haley and the Comets, the first *real* rock'n'roll band. They brought a dash of country style of instrumental performance to what was basically rhythm-and-blues, as well as a spectacular stage show in which Haley pranced about the stage, played the sax while lying on his back with his legs in the air, and generally set the style for subsequent rock'n'roll performance. Enter, stage right, a young man who in the summer of 1954 had walked into Sam Phillips' Sun studio in Memphis, legend has it to make a birthday record for his mother. Phillips, who had recorded a number of successful rhythm-and-blues performers on his Sun label, had developed a unique recorded sound, and, after a number of false starts, a record of Elvis Presley was issued in July 1954, with on one side a black blues and on the other a white country song. It was an astonishing debut, assured, even arrogant, and it initially puzzled listeners as to whether the singer was black or white — an important question in those segregated days. It was the first of five discs by Presley that were issued on the Sun label before Phillips sold his contract to RCA in December 1955; it was then with all the resources of a big record company behind him, that he began the historic career that opened with *Heartbreak Hotel* and continued with a string of huge successes that aroused the young to ecstasy and their elders to fury. But from that point on it was downhill all the way to the sordid moment in 1977 when, fat and stuffed with drugs, he died in his Memphis mansion at the age of forty-two.

The synthesis brought about by Presley and Haley between white country and black blues styles was followed up by a number of white artists — Jerry Lee Lewis, Charlie Rich, Carl Perkins and many others — which crystallized into a moment that was given the picturesque name of Rockabilly before it was recognized, simply, as rock'n'roll. The blues form is clearly recognizable in much of this music, but its subject matter is far removed from the blues's traditional concerns. Carl Perkins's *Blue Suede Shoes*, later recorded by Presley, is typical; it is a twelve-bar blues, but the words, delivered in the nasal voice and southern accent of the country singer, speak of a new hedonism and narcissism previously unknown in traditional blues, black or white.

The conventional account of subsequent development can be quickly summarized. As was inevitable, once the major companies had recognized the commercial potential of the new music (newly affluent teenagers of the postwar boom years were discovering the delights of independent purchasing power) they were quick to enter the field and take it over. First they issued cover versions, by their own contracted artists, of records originally made by rock-'n'roll artists (Pat Boone covered Little Richard's *Long Tall Sally* and the Flamingos' *I'll Be Home*, while a white group, the Crew Cuts, covered The Chords' *Sh-Boom* and The Penguins' *Earth Angel*), then by creating white stars of their own. A series of unrelated events — Presley's induction into the army for two years, Chuck Berry's conviction under the Mann Act in 1959, the deaths of Buddy Holly and Eddie Cochran in 1959 and 1960, in plane and car crashes, the British scandal concerning Jerry Lee Lewis's marriage to his thirteen-year-old cousin — removed some of the major artists of the first generation from the scene, creating a vacuum that the record companies were only too happy to fill. The names of their instant stars of the later 1950s read like caricatures, record executives' notions of teenage fantasies: Bobby Vee, Frankie Avalon, Fabian, while the names' owners were often chosen more for their photogenic qualities in the centrefolds of fan magazines than for any real musical ability. Britain endured the same thing around the same time, with Johnny Gentle, Marty Wilde, Billy Fury and Tommy Steele; a few singers in both countries survived their rechristening to show real ability and staying power. The effect, however, was to dilute the revolution wrought by the earlier artists of rock'n'roll and reduce the music to pop pulp. Rock'n'roll, as Charlie Gillett observed, was rechristened 'rock and roll'. 'The industry, with typical sleight of hand, killed off the music but kept the name, so that virtually all popular music (with the exception of what came to be called "easy listening") was branded rock and roll. The abolition of the apostrophe was significant — the term looked more respectable but sounded the same. Perfect. Upon a younger generation than that which had discovered and insisted upon the original rock'n'roll was palmed off a softer substitute which carried nearly the same name'.[1] And to that younger generation by 1960, at least in white America, the names of Chuck Berry, of Carl Perkins and Jerry Lee Lewis, and of other heroes of rock'n'roll meant little or nothing. The only artist of the group who was still consistently producing hit records was Elvis Presley, but he was by now only a shadow of his former self.

Black music was, of course, by no means extinct in the United States at that time; it continued to develop and, more importantly, to break down the barriers of segregation that had been breached with rock'n'roll. Rhythm-and-blues continued popular with black audiences through the 1950s, and in 1960 Tamla Motown, the first black-owned-and-operated record company to achieve international success, began its lucrative and influential career with artists who were able to draw on the resources of rhythm-and-blues and of gospel. They aimed unashamedly at the larger commercial market, and they won it. What they achieved for black America also was a new image of glamour and success before white audiences as well as black, using the full resources of theatre — careful visual presentation, with choreography and costume playing an important part — in a way that, rather than denying their own tradition, as many black artists before them had been obliged to do, drew upon it.

With rock and roll in the doldrums in America, a new impetus was to come, unexpectedly, from Britain, whose own popular music had since the invasion by ragtime and jazz between 1910 and 1920 been a mere province of the American. Rock'n'roll had established itself there in the early 1950s, mainly as a working-class music, unlike in the United States (British middle-class youth listened to New Orleans revival jazz and despised rock'n'roll — a whiff of class still hangs around rock'n'roll in Britain) and was linked indissolubly in the anxious public mind with the Teddy-boy cult and with violence. This association was 'proved' by incidents, made much of by the press, during screenings of the film *Rock Around the Clock*, in which Bill Haley and the Comets starred, when youngsters, excited by the music but prohibited from getting up and dancing to it, took to ripping up the seats instead. Such home-grown rock'n'roll stars as existed were pale imitations of the Americans. But British rock'n'roll did spawn one important, if short-lived music: skiffle, a kind of simplified rock'n'roll played on home-made instruments, generally washboard and tea-chest bass, with only an acoustic guitar as melody instrument. It was a way of musicking that broke through the barriers of formal skill and freed many youngsters, who would otherwise have remained musically impotent, to take an active part. When the craze faded, around 1959, many groups continued to play and these provided a reservoir not only of, admittedly somewhat elementary, skill but also, more important, of self-confidence and experience, the feeling that there was something that they could do.

Rhythm-and-blues did not form part of the received tradition for British musicians, but still it is less surprising than it might at first appear that British musicians should have been enthusiastic about it when their white American contemporaries had all but forgotten about it. To them at that time, in the early 1960s, race was not an issue, and rhythm-and-blues was exotic and exciting, so that when The Beatles served their apprenticeship, clad in leather, in rough Hamburg bars, it was on the records of Chuck Berry and Muddy Waters, of the early rock'n'rollers and the Motown artists that they based their performances — as did their contemporaries from London, The Rolling Stones, whose very name comes from a Muddy Waters song, and as did countless others in British pubs and clubs. And when The Beatles and The Stones arrived in New York in 1964, they were in fact bringing rock'n'roll back to white America, along with elements that were specifically British, notably the tendency towards pentatonicism and the modality of Anglo-Celtic folk song.

This development out of the spirit of rock'n'roll became known simply as rock, and it has not only gone out through the whole world but has also been in a constant state of development, change, and, in particular, synthesis. Rock melded with the already powerful American folk-music revival to produce folk-rock; it enlivened the seemingly moribund rock'n'roll style, still around in places, to produce 'rock revival' or 'heavy metal'; in the drug culture of 1960s California, it became 'psychedelic' or 'acid' rock; it became part of the literature and mythology of political protest; it entered the new discotheques of the 1960s, where little mattered except a pounding, dancing beat, to become disco music; and it fused with one wing of jazz to become jazz-rock or 'fusion'. Its heroic age was undoubtedly the 1960s, and its association with the hippie ethos and the revolutionary youth movements of that decade, with its love-ins and its mammoth rock festivals, is well known. At the time it all seemed like a breath of fresh air, a tremendous new liberating art of community in which everyone could join, a final throwing-off of the industrial ethic, a revolution through music that would be quite painless except perhaps for the effect of too many decibels on tortured eardrums. What was hardly noticed at the time was that the music, the festivals and even the love-ins were as much dependent on high technology as were the weapons which were at that time being used in Vietnam, and that commercial interests had very early on staked a claim to the counter-culture. From the vantage point of the cynical 1980s, it all seems incredibly naive and self-indulgent; nevertheless, the music remains, a testimony to a remarkable explosion of creative energy, even if the new society which it was to introduce has proved only an even more depressing version of the old, and it continues to absorb the energy of countless musicians and listeners.

This is the conventional history of the popular music of the last thirty years or so; I have before me a copy of a book written by a respectable American academic, and intended for use in schools, which gives exactly this version. At the same time popular music and the industry it supports have been extensively researched by sociologists, psychologists and journalists, as well as by Marxist historians and aestheticians seeking evidence either of the collapse of capitalism or of its continuing malign power; it has been researched as commodity, as industry, as business, as racket, as provider of role models for young people, as corruptor of young morals, as opium of the people, as magic ceremony, as counter-culture, as career, as educational problem and as educational challenge. Studies of these and other kinds are doubtless important in helping people to come to terms, from their own point of view, with the music, and many have resulted in valuable insights, especially into the relations between music (rarely *musicking*) and society. My own reservations concerning practically all of them are twofold: first, like the history I have just summarized, they ignore and even obscure the music's continuing nature as *act* rather than as thing, by concentrating their attention on what is on record, and, secondly, they tend to view today's popular music as an isolated phenomenon rather than as part of the great Afro-American tradition which we have been studying in this book. What most histories of the popular music of the last thirty years or so describe, is in fact the history, not so much of the musicking and of those who took part in it, as of recordings and of the attempts by record companies, radio networks and others to control a form of musicking that began as a spontaneous affirmation of identity by members of an underdog group in society.

Let us look at what these reservations imply. The ubiquity of records, and indeed of recording artists, suggests to the casual observer that the whole of popular music is to be found in the grooves of vinyl discs or in electro-magnetic impulses on tape, and that, therefore, total control is exerted over the content of popular music by those who control the record industry, or, to put the matter more mildly, that control is a tug-of-war between the record industry which offers the commodity, music, for sale, and those who exercise their choice, greatly influenced, it is assumed, by advertising and by peer pressure, of either buying or not buying what is on offer. Therefore, we find that much attention is given to relations between producers (the record companies) and consumers (those who buy the records and concert tickets), to the ways in which the producers try to control the consumers' buying behaviour, to the uses (not always those which the producers intended) made by consumers of the records, and to the effects of the records on the customers. Little attention is paid to the act of musicking itself in the popular tradition, to the effect the musicking has on the performers, or to the relations between performers and listeners. History is written mainly in terms of those musicians who have been recorded and of their recordings, while critical commentary and musical analysis are based entirely on what can be heard from the record grooves.

This is natural enough, since what is in those grooves is all the audible evidence we have of past performances, but it is quite unjustifiable to treat those artefacts, simply because they are all that *remains*, as if they were all that there ever *was*, or to draw conclusions concerning the music process or about the genesis of musical styles solely on the evidence of records. In the first place, those who actually get to record are only a small proportion of the musicians who are actually playing at any time in the history of that particular music; in the second, the act of recording imposes limits on the musicians' performance and changes it, often considerably; and in the third, and perhaps most important, those who make commercial recordings are not necessarily the most active, innovative or even representative performers. Concentrating on the product only, in fact, diverts attention from what has been a major premise of this book: that the meaning of music is to be found not in the music object but in the act of musicking, which, we recall, involves listeners no less than performers. This is not, of course, to say that records and recording are not vitally important elements in present-day musical culture the world over, but to give attention solely to records and to the music and musicians that are recorded is to impose a seriously one-sided view of both the history and the meaning of music of all kinds, and popular music in particular.

Popular music is popular not only because it is accessible to all listeners, without the need for formal training or classes in musical appreciation, but also because it is accessible to all performers. This means, not that no skills are required, but rather that there are no institutional barriers to the acquisition of skills; anyone with a mind to do so can engage in performance, just as anyone can acquire the skills of language and engage in conversation. And anyone is capable of making a creative contribution to the development of his or her own chosen musical style. This means that in cities, towns and villages of the industrial world there are thousands upon thousands of people engaging in musicking at every possible level of skill in an enormous variety of popular styles, from polka bands to steelbands to jug bands to rock groups to folk singers. The great majority are using an instrumentation which derives from that of blues or rock'n'roll bands — electric guitars, drumkit and possibly saxophone and keyboards — and they will be playing in a way which owes at least something to the blues. There would be many more were it not, as I suggested earlier, that so many people accept the label 'unmusical' that is hung on them in school music classes.

I have already mentioned the thousand or more rock groups that in 1983 were reported as active in Liverpool. Another well-documented scene is that of San Francisco in the 1960s, when groups such as Jefferson Airplane, The Grateful Dead, Big Brother and the Holding Company, and Creedence Clearwater Revival, came to the attention of the public. These bands, and others like them, grew out of a spontaneously erupting social scene to which musicking was central as an act of self-definition. The fact that many of those who formed the early bands around 1964 were, to put it mildly, minimal in terms of musical skill was no barrier to that self-definition, but indeed formed an element of it, since, initially at least, the fantasy of being a musician was as important as actually being one. It was only later that the latent musicality and the skills of some of the performers emerged under the pressure of nightly professional performances — the reverse of what is generally assumed to occur. The history of one of the first San Francisco groups is instructive.

The Charlatans were formed in the spring of 1964 by one George Hunter, who recalled later: 'A style emerged, a musical and visual concept. It had to do with simply seeing what style was already there and picking up all the good pieces of it, bringing them together. It was the blues guitar of Wilhelm; baby-faced Olsen the kid from Chicago; an old-time piano player who looked like he'd just stepped out of a saloon. Together it had a certain connotation. It was set against what was going on in society at the time, with everyone getting tired of a plastic world. It seemed like a good assemblage and people were ready for it.'[2] Having auditioned successfully for a job in a saloon in Virginia City, Nevada, when everyone present was so tripped-out on LSD (still legal at that time) that they didn't know what was going on, they found themselves playing, in Hunter's words, 'four sets a night, five nights a week for a hundred dollars a week apiece along with bed and board, as we were really getting good' with what was described as 'an increasingly tight repertoire of rollicking rock'n'roll.'[3] The band's career came abruptly, if appropriately, to an end when they were all busted for drugs, but by the autumn of

1964 a number of similar groups had been formed from the emerging San Francisco hip scene.

As these groups found themselves working as professional musicians so they became more professional, while retaining, the best of them at least, something of the cheerful anything-goes amateurism of the early days, as well as a healthy distrust of record companies and professional managements and entrepreneurs. The record companies were obliged to make concessions to what the bands saw as their integrity; one of the comic spectacles of the late 1960s was that of record executives growing their hair and moustaches and adopting hippy dress and speech mannerisms. It is true that the whole San Francisco scene, and its innumerable spinoffs throughout the industrialized world, can be seen as the self-indulgence of well-heeled white youth in a well-heeled society, but it is equally true that through its musicking the particular community that congregated in the Bay Area in the 1960s did contribute to the formation of a sense of identity in those who, like the Kent State University students and those at the 1968 Chicago Democratic Convention, as well as just across the Bay in Berkeley, were confronting the industrial society and its troops head-on. The assumption implicit in the whole hippie ethos of which San Francisco was a centre, that revolution can be fun, may seem naive and self-indulgent today, but the fact remains, equally, that the reclaiming of fun as part of the serious business of human life is the most subversive and revolutionary aim of all. The sixties have left, still, a large number of unexploded bombs in our society.

The genesis of the musical culture of the Bay Area in a hip community whose tool for the affirmation, exploration and celebration of identity it was, and the resistance of that culture to being taken over as a commodity for sale, has been well documented, because for the most part those who took part were white, broadly middle-class, and thus literate, educated and listened-to. All accounts of the musicking of that place and time show that it arose out of a community whose musicians and audiences shared a set of values, and that the musicians developed their techniques, sometimes based on conventionally-acquired skills, sometimes not, over a period of time, to articulate those values — not necessarily a conscious process. Like all musicians, of course, they were not averse to any access of fame or fortune, but their attitude to such matters seems to have been casual, even careless, and they adopted a distinctly take-it-or-leave-it stance towards the record companies. That the dozen or so bands who made names as recording artists were only a tiny fraction of those who were active at the time is shown by a list compiled by Ralph J. Gleason, one of the editors of *Rolling Stone* magazine, of over four hundred bands in San Francisco in 1969. 'It is,' remark Gene Sculatti and Davin Seay, 'perhaps the only time such groups as Black Shit Puppy Farm, The Drongos and Hofmann's Bicycle ever saw their names in print.'[4]

These, then, were young, white, mostly middle-class and formally-educated people who found that their questioning of the values in which they had been brought up was inseparable from their questioning of the musical values of their society, and that that musical questioning did give them tools for the affirmation and celebration of an identity which did not depend, at least not wholly, on those values. In adopting musical techniques, that is to say, ways of going about the making of music, that were based firmly on the blues, and in using the instrumentation and performance style which had been developed by black musicians, they adopted also values, and an identity, which served to replace the nine-to-five mentality which their upbringing and education had prepared for them: the values and the identity of black Americans, viewed no doubt through the same lens of romanticism and wishful thinking that their predecessors, forty years before, had used when approaching jazz, but no less potent for that. The hip stance (the very word comes from black culture) of cool, knowing self-possession, the hip vocabulary, the use of marijuana as favoured drug rather than alcohol, the accent on total style, and the central position of musicking in the definition of that style — all these came from black culture, as did the models for instrumental and vocal sound production (listen to Janis Joplin), for rhythmic structure and even the subject matter of the lyrics, and as did, and still do, the models for relationships among performers, between performers and listeners and among listeners. There is nothing in traditional European music, whether 'folk' or 'classical', that offers either a model or a parallel for relationships of that kind. It is in fact blues that is the consistent thread, the *only* consistent thread, that runs through this and through the whole of modern popular music; in no matter how attenuated or distant a form, no matter how distorted by commercialism, it is always there.

We have, then, to understand two important things: first, that the vast majority of the musicking going on in western society today is what is known, curiously, as 'live', that is to say, in an environment where performers and listeners are directly face to face; records, however dominant they may appear, have rarely been the source of significant musical innovation or invigoration, but have ridden on what has already been generated collaboratively between performers, listeners and, generally, dancers, in those face-to-face situations. This is true even in the post-*Sergeant Pepper* era of the record producer and of multi-track recording. And, second, that innovation and invigoration have, almost without exception, come from black musicians or through their influence; it is to their enduring ideals of community and sociability no less than to their ways of performing, which we have encountered over and over again in this book, that modern popular musicians, no matter how 'commercial', and their audiences owe their musical models and their concept of identity. These two facts are linked by the assumption made in black culture, and validated by nearly four hundred years of black musicking in the Americas, that the act of musical creation is open to everyone, and that, just as with words, the resources for musical creation lie within the community and the culture for everyone to use. If I place those two facts against what is the obvious commercialism and exploitativeness of the modern popular-music scene, it is in order to justify the claim that within popular musicking lies the potential, at least partly realized, for its use as a tool for self-definition and autonomy in opposition to the official values and the imposed identities of industrial society. We need therefore to look again, somewhat more carefully, at the history of that music in order to correct certain misconceptions which have been propagated, not necessarily deliberately, in conventional accounts, and which have had the effect of writing black musicians out of their central role in that history.

It will be recalled from Chapter 7 that blues and other black ways of musicking were, at the time of the first recordings, kept well segregated from what at the time was regarded as the main stream of American popular music, by the simple expedient of issuing the records of that music on separate labels (the 'race' labels) which were available only in the black ghettos or on mail order. This accorded with the rigidly segregated nature of American society at that time. By the late 1940s black musicians were beginning, in line with their new social and political expectations, to show resentment at this musical segregation, which cut them off from their proper rewards and allowed white musicians to win fame and fortune using their techniques and often even their songs and performances. It was due to their pressure that when, around 1948, black music began to cross over into the main stream of popular music, the industry and the trade papers abandoned the term 'race music' and adopted the term 'rhythm-and-blues' instead. The formation at that time of a new performing-rights organization, BMI, which was more interested in black music than the older ASCAP, was an important factor in that crossover. Rhythm-and-blues was in fact a code term which, while it happened to suit the changing nature of blues itself, did nothing to abolish the segregation, since the code was well known to all concerned.

It was radio, by its nature a desegregated medium, at least for its listeners (since no control can be exercised over who listens to which programme), that was responsible for the wider dissemination of rhythm-and-blues; the conventional history is accurate enough on that point. The role of Alan Freed in popularizing the name 'rock'n'roll' is clear also (he called his 1954 New York radio show, the first to play rhythm-and-blues on a white-oriented station, the 'Rock'n'Roll Show') but he did not coin the term, which had been in currency among black Americans for a long time; his motive was also clear enough, since he was trying to widen the appeal of rhythm-and-blues by playing down its black associations. But Freed was under no illusion that rock'n'roll was a new music or any kind of black-white fusion; to him it was still black blues, and he regarded it and its makers highly. In later years he wrote in the journal *Down Beat*: 'To me, this campaign against Rock and Roll smells of discrimination of the worst kind against the great and accomplished Negro songwriters, musicians and singers who are responsible for this outstanding contribution to American music.'[5]

The conventional version of history, that rock'n'roll was born out of a marriage between black blues and white country music, does not stand up, even at this stage. The records which were played by Freed, and, very soon after, by numerous imitators on other local stations, were made by black artists such as Little Richard, Fats Domino, Chuck Berry, Muddy Waters and Little Esther; thirty years and more later they still sound fresh, vital and earthy, and are suffused with a sexy human warmth which must have been overwhelming in the 1950s, in the America of Eisenhower and HUAC. It was on the success of those musicians that Bill Haley, leader of a country band, made several attempts to capitalize before hitting the jackpot in 1956 with a cover of a rhythm-and-blues song, *Rock Around the Clock*, that had been recorded the previous year by a black artist called Sonny Dae. Its success was in fact fortuitous, in that it was used on the soundtrack of the hugely successful film *The Blackboard Jungle*, and from there it reached the big radio networks and television, which still at that time would not touch black artists. Thus it was that white America as a whole got its first taste of rhythm-and-blues, rechristened rock'n'roll, from Haley's not very skilful imitations of black musicians, notably of Louis Jordan, imitations which extended to the on-stage behaviour which I mentioned earlier. The sensational success of Elvis Presley's first nationwide hit, *Heartbreak Hotel*, followed in the next year, and was confirmed by his appearances on television, to which black artists had little access.

There is no doubt that Elvis was a superb performer from the moment of his first recordings, and he did bring together elements from both black and white music — not surprisingly since both, as we have already seen, were part of his everyday culture. It is a puzzle, listening to those early records today, that anyone could have thought he sounded like a black singer; he himself never thought so, and he would not in all probability have liked the thought. His own comment was 'I don't sing like nobody'; but his art owed more to black musicians than just the blues which formed part of his early repertoire. And he was one of a kind: *as a singer* he had no successors. *As a success*, however, he did, and those white rockabilly musicians mentioned earlier got their chance from his breakthrough; as he retreated into the softer side of country music, with only occasional flashes of his old brilliance (after the early period his lifestyle, down to his stage costume, remained that of the country singer), they too retreated back into what was their natural style, from which they had been tempted by the promise of fame. Only Jerry Lee Lewis, another superb unclassifiable, has stayed, if somewhat erratically, the course.

The truth is that, for all his brilliance as a performer, Elvis's overwhelming success was really a creation of the media, in particular television whose darling he was from the moment of his first, from-the-waist-upwards only, appearance on the Ed Sullivan Show. Even as late as 1957, at the height of his fame, his records were still being outsold by those of Little Richard — but Little Richard, despite being an even more electrifying performer (one journalist described him as having 'a bounce and flash that made even Elvis look slow and a voice with more speed than a runaway express train')[6] was black, and although he took rock'n'roll, or rhythm-and-blues, to new heights of controlled excitement, he never received the kind of treatment from press or television which was accorded to 'The King', and which served to define rock'n'roll as a separate music, created by white artists from a fusion of black and white elements. This enabled black artists to be written out of the presumed evolutionary process, leaving them stranded in the role of predecessors and forerunners, of historical interest only — and of course once again denied the rewards that accrue to the winners in the game. It is a process that has occurred more than once in the history of Afro-American music.

As with many acts of racial exclusion, it is hard to know just how deliberate it was, and how much it was simply the consequence of those assumptions that white people, in Britain and Europe no less than in the United States, make unthinkingly about blacks. But John Lennon, for one, was under no illusions; in an interview given as late as 1982 he was forthright: 'The only white I ever listened to was Elvis Presley on his early music records and he was doing black music. I don't blame him for wanting to be part of that music. I wanted to be like that. I copied all those people and the other Beatles did, and so did the others until we developed a style of our own. Black music started this whole change of style, that was started by rock and roll, and rock and roll is black. I appreciate it, and I'll never stop acknowledging it.'[7]

'Wanting to be part of that music' is the key to the subsequent history of modern popular music. If the term 'rock'n'roll' has any meaning at all apart from rhythm-and-blues, it could be used for the musicking of white musicians trying to come to terms with, and to catch something of the joyous sexy spirit of, black blues, as did Buddy Holly, Eddie Cochran, the songwriting and producing team of Lieber and Stoller, and countless others. This is in itself an entirely honourable, not to mention sensible, thing to do, the more so in that blues offers itself and accommodates itself in a truly human and courteous way to so many local styles of musicking, and provides, from Liverpool to Wellington to Tokyo, an idiom, which is to say a community, for those who wish to take back to themselves the power of self-definition through music. The muddying of values that occurs when the pure spirit of the musical act (the 'redemptive three-minute flash'[8] as one commentator called it) encounters the commercialism of the professional music world is another matter; the basic impulse behind the attempt by white musicians (an attempt which has resulted in kinds of musicking that have their own power and urgency) to assimilate to black music lies, as it always has lain, in the search for those values, and for that community, real or imagined, which is brought into existence whenever the music is performed. No matter how diluted, no matter how distorted or attenuated by that commercialism which, one might say in a sour moment, is Europe's and Euro-America's gift to the music, it is the spirit of the blues, and, further back, of the black churches and even the spirituals, that lies behind every popular performer today.

I quoted in an earlier chapter Albert Murray's comment on certain white jazz musicians; one might adapt it to say that modern white popular musicians see 'certain Negroes not just as kindred spirits but as ancestor figures indispensable to their sense of romance, sophistication and elegance as well. Negroes like Chuck Berry, Muddy Waters, Louis Jordan, Little Richard, B.B. King, Smokey Robinson and others too numerous to mention inspire white musicians like John Lennon, Janis Joplin, Eric Clapton and countless others to their richest sense of selfhood and their highest levels of achievement.' It doesn't quite work in a literal way, but there is a truth there: the ancestor figures of modern popular music, as of modern popular dance, the models of romance, sophistication and elegance to which all musicians and all dancers aspire, are not European but Afro-American, and ultimately African.

The other important matter I have already discussed briefly: that records and the record industry, and even the world of the professional musician, are not the whole of that process of self-definition which is modern popular music, and quite possibly do not even represent its most inventive or creative phases. For this reason it is probably impossible ever to write a true history of popular music, since the only hard evidence of what the music has been like is on record and tape — and they are just as unreliable, or at least as incomplete, as indicators of what really happened when the musicians played as are scores of the true history of classical music. Certainly, to write a history of popular music, or indeed to make any kind of study of it, in terms of recorded performances and performers alone is to explore a picture which, while interesting and even valuable, is very partial indeed; one might go so far as to say that to work in that fashion is to reduce the history to a downmarket version of that of classical music, with rock stars substituted for The Great Composers. Similarly, to study the present-day meaning of the music only in terms of the relationship between the record industry and the buying public is not only to acquiesce in the rigid producer-consumer dichotomy which we have seen afflicts classical music today but also to ignore the complex reasons why musicians — and I do not mean professionals only — make music; by ignoring those reasons we leave room for a tacit assumption to creep in, the pervasive economist's assumption about human activities, that they are only doing it for the money. People make music, of course, for a variety of reasons, of which making money is one (that applies no less to the classical than to the vernacular musician), but there are easier ways to make money, and the *pure* motive of financial gain is probably not common among musicians, even those who cheerfully admit to having sold out; certainly it is rarer than among, say, stockbrokers.

It is no doubt true that for most listeners the majority of music they hear comes through the media of records, radio and TV, but that is to look at the matter from a narrowly consumerist point of view. If we look at the music act, the performance, itself, we see that notwithstanding the growth of those electronic media the vast majority of musicking that takes place today still involves 'live' musicians and 'live' audiences. A record, after all, still represents only one performance, even though it may duplicate that performance millions of times. The point is not a trivial one, but is important to an understanding of the nature of popular music today; most musicians, even if they ever see the inside of a commercial recording studio (and more do not than do) still spend more time playing outside it than in it. That is not to say that the record industry has not had a profound effect on the history of popular music; it clearly has, but what takes place in recording studios represents only a small part of the musicking that is going on at any one time, and, further, it is to a large extent parasitic on, or at most symbiotic with, the activities of the very large number of musicians who never get to make a commercial recording. Behind every artist who makes a record stands an untold number of musicians of whose musicking his or her own represents at best a synthesis. One only has to consider the number of black musicians whose musical activities created the music which we hear today on blues records, and the number of young people in the late 1950s whose performances on guitar, washboard and tea-chest bass contributed to the remarkable recapturing of British popular music from the Americans, and indeed the four hundred or so groups listed as active in San Francisco in the mid-1960s — and those only the groups offering themselves for professional employment (how many more just played for their own benefit and for that of friends?) The surfacing of rap in the last few years as a powerful new form of musical expression provides us with an outstanding contemporary example of the same thing.

Rap is not new at all, of course, but stems from the perennial admiration given in black culture to the possessor of highly developed speech skills. As David Toop observes:

> 'With the coming of the new American music called Rap in 1979, people all over the world began to be aware of it — thinking of it as a description of rhythmic talking over a funk beat. The first so-called rap records were in fact the tip of the iceberg — under the surface was a movement called hip hop, a Bronx-based subculture, and beneath that was a vast expanse of sources reaching back to West Africa. The praise singing, social satires and boasting of savannah griots that appeared to reincarnate in groups like Grandmaster Flash and the Furious Five, Afrika Bambaataa and Cosmic Force, The Treacherous Three and Funky Four Plus One More, had all been present in black music over the past eighty years.'[9]

Like the breakdancing with which it is associated, it is essentially a street culture, what Toop calls 'the sophisticated cross-cultural fusions which meld the oldest traditions with the freshest of musical technologies, or, at the other pole and clinging for life, the bottom line of street survival.'[10]

From an interview with David Toop by the Harlem record producer Bobby Robinson we learn of the spontaneous origins of rap, compared by him to that gospel-inspired, group vocal harmony music, called doo-wop, which in groups like The Orioles, The Chords and The Penguins, formed an important element of rock'n'roll in the 1950s. Both musical styles were, it is clear, fully developed long before the first record company A & R man ever got wind of them:

> 'Doo-wop originally started out as the black teenage expression of the '50s and rap emerged as the black teenage ghetto expression of the '70s. Same identical thing that started it — the doo-wop groups down the street, in hallways, in alleys and on the corner. They'd gather anywhere, and, you know, doo-wop doo wah da da da da.

> You'd hear it everywhere. So the same thing with rap groups around '76 or so. All of a sudden, everywhere you turned you'd have these kids rapping. In the summertime they'd have these little parties in the park. They used to go out and play in the park. They used to go out and play at night and kids would be out there dancing. All of a sudden, all you would hear was, hip hop, hit the top don't stop. It's kids — to a great extent mixed-up and confused — reaching out to express themselves. They were forcefully trying to express themselves and they made up in fantasy what they missed in reality.'[11]

Finally, Toop emphasises the function of rap for young people trying to work out who they are in a society that bombards them ceaselessly with self-serving stimuli, and shows it to be simply a new aspect of the continuing struggle for survival:

> '. . . the mythological tricksters and heroes are replaced by electronic-age superheroes recruited from kung-fu, karate, science fiction, and blaxploitation movies, re-run television series, video games, comic books and advertising. The central heroes, of course, are the rappers themselves, aggressively claiming respect (as a means of finding self-respect) with the same expertise in verbal expression as that wielded by streetcorner orators, standup comics, testifying preachers and vernacular poets for generations.'[12]

It is not possible to make a commercial takeover of something unless that something already exists; behind every kind of recorded music, even the most relentlessly trivialized such as can be heard on top 40 radio, stands a huge crowd of musicians, amateur and professional and all stages in between, who, while they themselves may, and do, draw upon the work of recorded artists, are not bound by any musical market other than that transaction which involves themselves and their listeners directly. The musicians and their audiences are jointly, and in however confused a way, working to explore, affirm and celebrate their identity; the techniques may often be crude, even rudimentary, but the message they bring is always clear: *This is who we are*. And, further, the language, the idiom, of that affirmation and celebration is, at some remove or other, derived from those idioms which black people in the Americas have forged and used through the generations in order, not just to survive, but to make survival worth fighting for.

Modern popular music is not just the creation of commercial interests, but is part of an historical continuity that stretches back to the first encounters between Africans and Europeans when African slaves were first shipped to America in the early years of the sixteenth century. The ruthless commercialism that pervades it today is the creation, not of the musicians themselves, but of those who stand to profit from their work; that some in each generation allow themselves to be taken over and used in return for the not inconsiderable rewards of their capitulation is of course no news, but for every musician, every band, that gives in to the ceaseless pressures which commercial interests apply to those trying to make a living from their art, there are many more who engage in constant negotiation with those interests, and try to retain control of their own performances. It is that process of negotiation which we must now examine.

NOTES

1. GILLETT, Charlie: *The Sound of the City: The Rise of Rock and Roll*, London, Souvenir Press, 2nd edition 1983, p 168.
2. SCULATTI, Gene and SEAY, Davin: *San Francisco Nights: The Psychedelic Music Trip, 1965–1968*, London, Sidgwick & Jackson, 1985, p 28.
3. *ibid.*, p 35.
4. *ibid.*, p 168
5. quoted in REDD, Lawrence N.: 'Rock! It's Still Rhythm and Blues', *The Black Perspective in Music*, Vol 13, No 1, p 38.
6. quoted in ELSON, Howard: *Early Rockers*, London, Proteus (Publishing) Ltd., 1982, p 92.
7. quoted in REDD, Lawrence N.: *op. cit.*, p 43.
8. FULWELL, Pete: *Dancing in the Rubble*, feature broadcast on BBC Radio 4, 9 January, 1983.
9. TOOP, David: *The Rap Attack: African Jive to New York Hip Hop*, London, Pluto Press, 1984, p 8.
10. *ibid.*, p 12.
11. quoted *ibid.*, p 84.
12. *ibid.*, p 28.

Chapter 14

ON RECORDS AND REWARDS

I suggested in the preceding chapter that to judge modern popular music solely from recordings is to gain a very partial and even distorted view of it. Records, and the recording industry, have clearly had a profound influence on the history of all western musical performance in this century, and the Afro-American tradition is no exception, but it cannot be said either that they have entirely determined what happened in any part of that tradition, or that what can be heard on records gives a complete picture of it. In this chapter I wish to examine some of the effects of recording, and the role the music industry has played in Afro-American musicking.

To this end, I intend making what seems to me a reasonable assumption, that the nature of recorded music and, in particular, its function in human life, remains the same as that of 'live' musicking; to put it briefly, it remains a performance, in which the relationships which go to make up the participants' sense of identity are explored, affirmed and celebrated. This would appear to go against the nature of a gramophone record, which is indisputably an object, but in fact nothing essential has changed from live performance. We have first to ask what recording does to a performance, by interposing between performers and listeners a process of electronic transformation of the sound vibrations into ripples in a groove or into electromagnetic impulses in a tape. We shall leave aside for the moment the commercial aspects of the operation, which, important as they have become, are not intrinsic to it.

In the first place, recording does not capture the whole performance as we have observed it; only the sounds made by the performers are reproduced, leaving all other aspects of the performance to the imagination of the listener. Those sounds are extended by the recording as far as is desired in both time and space; they are made available to those who cannot be present either for geographical or for temporal reasons — or, indeed, for social reasons, since they are made available also to those who are unwilling or frightened to go into the place of the actual performance (this of course applies as much to classical performances as to low-down blues or punk rock). If the sounds are to be recreated as a performance in the mind of the listener, that is to say, if listeners are to be able to construct from them that set of social relationships which we have seen to be the real function of a musical performance, imaginative work has to be done on them. It is for this reason that we cannot obtain the complete meaning of a record from its audible content only, any more than we can from the sound-content alone of any other performance, or indeed from a score.

Let us look at it first from the performer's point of view. To record the sounds of a performance is to fix them in a way never before known in the history of human musicking; not even the fixing that occurs in the pages of a score is so complete. This means that the performers have to decide much more carefully than for live performance which part of their repertoire, and which of the large number of possible ways of performing it, best represents them, and they are thus obliged to engage in a greater degree of premeditation and preparation. Musicians and their listeners seem to have accepted over the years of recording that some sacrifice of spontaneity and excitement is necessary in order to obtain the cleanest and most polished performance, one that will stand up to repeated playings. The fixing is coupled with the limitations of duration that the medium imposes. For the classical musician, accustomed to the pre-existing limits of the score, and to the predictable length that this implies, the durational limits of recording are no great problem; the relation between the duration intended by the composer and that permitted by the recording is easily worked out in advance, and breaks made where necessary in the performance. But for the Afro-American musician, to the extent that the performance is normally improvised, and depends for its duration on such factors as audience response, the limits of even the LP record, let alone the earlier three-minute, 78-rpm disc (the limits of the CD medium have yet to be explored) can be a Procrustes' bed. As a remarkable account by William Ferris Jr has shown, blues performance in its original habitat — a gathering of a few friends at home over cans of beer — is a freewheeling affair, interspersed with stories and jokes and lasting continuously through the evening: 'Throughout the evening there is a constant flow of verbal interplay between the singer . . . and his audience . . . the role of 'performer' shifts repeatedly from the singer to his audience and back to the singer.'[1]

The actual blues sung in Ferris's transcription were all taken from records, confirming the idea of Harold Courlander which I quoted earlier, of 'feedback' from records to 'folk' performance and back again, but the blues sung here were fragmentary, frequently elided and combined freely with one another. On records, on the other hand, the performer has to make his or her point within the brief timespan (the three-minute convention seems to have outlived the limit imposed by 78-rpm records), and therefore has to move at a speed quite different from the leisurely build up that is possible under live conditions of that kind. The three-minute format was standard for all kinds of Afro-American musicking up to the coming of the LP record, and for a long time after that it was only jazz musicians who took advantage of the twenty or so minutes permitted by the LP to expand and take their time. The favoured type of record for rock'n'roll remained the 7-inch, 45-rpm single; it was the free-form improvisation favoured by San Francisco musicians that first made use of the potential of LPs in the rock field.

It is common today to find a popular song issued in at least three recorded forms: a three-minute 7-inch, 45-rpm single for home listening and for jukeboxes, a somewhat longer track on an LP, and a twelve-inch, 45-rpm version which extends the performance to ten or fifteen minutes and was developed for use in discotheques, where dancers like to hear the music over a longer timespan. These different versions are not made during the recording sessions, where, indeed, it is likely that they have never existed at all, but by permutating during the editing process the material that is on the tapes. The fact that these different versions can be made emphasises the music's nature as being essentially performance, and the expansion and contraction of that performance to suit the needs of different kinds of occasion is entirely in accordance with the procedures of improvising musicians in the Afro-American tradition.

Another factor that changes the musicians' performance in the recording studio is the need to imagine rather than experience their relationship with an audience; without that response they often feel they are playing into a void that gives them no help at all. Many performances, of course, are put together in the editing process, piece by piece, much as a film is constructed, and many musicians do not, or have learnt not to, mind too much the lack of direct communication. But there is always a loss of excitement and 'lift' that no amount of studio technology can conceal, and what is to be heard on record with some musicians does nothing like justice to their live performance. The practice of making recordings in front of an audience, sometimes in the studio itself, can ameliorate this situation, but it has its difficulties also. For practically all artists making a record is a matter of balancing spontaneity against accuracy and clarity.

For the listener, on the other hand, the sounds heard when a record is played have to be fleshed out by the imagination before the illusion can be created of a performance that has any meaning; somehow the ideal society has to be created, in no matter how imaginary a form, if any emotional experience is to be gained. Again, this is not difficult for the classical-music listener, for not only are the relationships of the concert hall already formal and distant because the listener in the hall is in any case alone with the sounds, but also he or she needs to do a good deal of imaginative work before the impersonal surroundings can be transformed into the composers' imaginary Iberias and Vltavas, and the prosaic-looking musicians who are impassively bowing, blowing and banging on the platform can become Don Juans, Romeos and Juliets and Polovtsian dancers or the heroes and heroines of those abstract dramas which are symphonies and concertos. All that the listener requires of the record, therefore, is that it preserve unchanged, or possibly enhanced, the sound-relationships of the concert hall or opera house (I have more than once heard listeners who, having got used to the sound of a symphony orchestra on modern recordings, have expressed disappointment at the way it sounds on first hearing it in the concert hall). And of course, as audiences are used to sitting still and being passive, having never considered the possibility of influencing a performance or experiencing the mutual stimulation of performers and audience, they do not miss these things on the record.

The society brought into existence by a performance in the Afro-American tradition, on the other hand, is made with the active collaboration of both parties, and it is an important part of the business of every performer to establish a relationship with the listeners that is close, warm and, above all, personal (the fact that in many cases this closeness and warmth are not genuine but are faked does not diminish the strength of this ideal but rather pays tribute to it). The very uniqueness of vocal and instrumental tone cultivated by Afro-American performers has contributed to this personal feeling, even more so since the days when records were made by shouting into an acoustic collector horn, giving what was probably the initially accidental effect, produced by the necessary disposition of the musicians in relation to the horn, of having the singer's voice sound closer than the instrumentalists. With the flexibility bestowed by the microphone, and, later, by multiple microphones and multi-track recording, it has become possible to play with the perspective of the sounds, placing some close up and some at a distance, in a way that would be impossible in a live situation; the art of crooning, practised with such success by Bing Crosby and the young Frank Sinatra, was an early example of creating the illusion of physical presence in this way. Modern recording techniques can bring into existence, by manipulation of the sound-perspectives, a whole theatre of the imagination in which the listener can imagine a drama played out by him or herself with the artists, generally of course the lead singer, the physicality and individuality of whose vocal presence (what Roland Barthes called the 'grain' of the voice) invites a response which may be completely independent of what the artist is singing about. It is not only a singer that can evoke such responses;

great instrumentalists like Lester Young (who insisted that his solos 'tell a story'), Charlie Parker, Jimi Hendrix or Jerry Lee Lewis can equally create the illusion of presence and direct communication with the listener even though they are separated not only by space and time but also by a complex technological process.

It was, and is, a technique; it does not happen naturally, that trick of creating the illusion of physical presence in a medium that is not naturally sympathetic to it. It seems to have been mastered first by black blues artists, who grasped very quickly the fact that the physicality of the performance, which is necessary if the listener is to extract any meaning from it, must be simulated in the recording process. There is, clearly, nothing wrong with such simulation, any more than there is in the simulation of the concert hall or the opera house on a classical record; it is simply a way of making it possible for the social relationships of the live performance to be recreated in the listener's imagination. The listener is of course not bound to do simply this, but is free to use the imagination in any way he or she likes; thus it is possible to imagine oneself on the podium of a great concert hall, conducting the Berlin Philharmonic Orchestra, or lying in bed next to the singer who is singing to oneself alone. The more private the listening the more possible it is to indulge in such solipsism, to create a world in which only the singer and the listener exist. Alternatively, it is possible to bring into existence new kinds of community, such as that described by Paul Willis, in which leather-clad bike boys cement their culture and community in transport caffs with jukebox-played records of 1950s rock 'n' roll (it has to be on seven-inch singles — LP transcriptions will not do); as Willis says: 'For them the loud strident tones of the music symbolically held and generated all the important values — movement, noise, confidence. The very air was fuller and more homely to breathe, vibrated by *their* music.'[2]

On the whole, however, listening to records is not a particularly sociable activity, but tends to be done either solitarily or in small groups (it can cement a society of two, as would-be seducers know well). The sight of a roomful of people sitting and staring into space while a symphonic work is played on a record player seems somehow irresistably funny, a caricature of all the intrinsic oddness of the concert-hall ritual. The tendency for larger groups of people to use recorded music simply as a background for social intercourse (itself a valuable social function of music, and not to be despised) is not a result of corruption by Muzak; on the contrary, Muzak owes its ubiquity to the lack of social focus which is inherent in the performance of recorded music. Perhaps this is why the habit has grown up in British pubs of having the record player or jukebox turned up so loud that everyone has to shout at full voice to make themselves heard above it.

The one type of social activity for which recorded music can and does act very successfully as focus is dancing. It is interesting that early advertisements for the gramophone and for records made much of this function, and, more specifically, that it was much used among rural black Americans, of whom, in the 1920s, 'between 10 and 20 per cent had phonographs, and a larger proportion had records.'[3] Their records, virtually all made by black musicians, were greatly treasured in families that often had little else to treasure, both as an expression of racial pride in the artists and as a source of music for dance. The communal function of recorded music is discussed by Titon:

> '. . . 19 per cent of the black homes in Macon and Green Counties, Georgia, had phonographs early in the 1920s. The families listened and danced to records made by black blues singers, jazz musicians, preachers and gospel singers, which were aimed directly at the black buying market. Neighbors without phonographs bought records and played them on their friends' machines. Since the record players were actuated by spring motors, the small models could be taken outside to picnics, parties and other social affairs, where music was popular and local singers were unattainable.'[4]

Dancing is itself a powerful tool for the affirmation and celebration of common values, and can thus reinforce the relatively weak society created by a recorded performance. The most intense contemporary use of recorded music in this way is in discotheques, 'focal points, contained environments,' say the authors of a book on New York's discos, 'with a common music, where people gather together to do whatever people do in places where they come together to dance and celebrate, to entertain and be entertained . . . As you enter, electricity shoots through the air in all directions. The energy flows from the music and the lights and the crowd, from inside yourself . . . Perhaps you are excited knowing that you are dressed in a certain way, in a way that you have chosen to present youself to the world that is this particular disco . . . The music and mix are constantly changing. A deejay tries to sense and physically see what brings the crowds, what keeps them shifting and continually building on the dance floor . . . Each night there is a peak of disco experience, a peak of excitement when the music is most stimulating . . . The peak is like a sexual climax when everything and everyone flow together, a moment when time seems erased. Before this peak, there may be lesser crests and dips, oscillations in energy and excitement. After the peak, the most chaotic, individualistic and generally frenzied moments of the disco night tend to happen. The moment itself is indistinguishable while you are experiencing it.'[5]

There is clearly more to the task of the disco deejay than simply putting on records and ensuring a continuous flow of sound; to take the inanimate objects that are gramophone records and combine them in improvised sequence in such a way as to take hold of a crowd of strangers and turn them into a unified group, to catch the mood of the occasion, to enhance and reinforce it, as an art that partakes of the nature of musical creation. The way that certain black disco deejays in Harlem and The Bronx, as well as certain Jamaican sound-system men, developed this art further and in a highly unexpected manner is the story of rap and of toasting, the first of which I have already discussed; apparently independent in their origins but now intertwining in the discos of New York and London, the two arts are manifestations of the black genius for humanizing the mechanical in surprising ways, a genius that can be seen, too, in the spray-painted designs on the cars of the New York subway trains.

It will thus be clear that, whatever changes the recording of musical sounds has brought about, it has not changed the fundamental nature or social function of the musical act. The gramophone record or recording tape is an inanimate object containing coded information which can be turned into sounds by putting it into movement on the appropriate apparatus, but to turn those sounds into music, which is to say a performance, requires imaginative work on the part of the listener; it is this that ensures that musical meaning resides not in the recording alone but in the interplay between the sounds coming from it and the listener's imagination. Thus the meaning of a record is not determined, any more than is the meaning of a musical composition; there is always room for creative response on the listener's part which can turn the most banal of recorded sounds into a significant experience. In this respect a record has much in common with other vernacular art-objects. A greeting card, for example, may in itself, by high-art standards, be banal and tasteless, but the act of sending and receiving it can be moving and beautiful. It will of course be more moving if it is the most beautiful card the sender can find — but still it is the act of choice that is treasured; the card is only the instrument of that choice. As in all human life, things themselves are important only in so far as they facilitate or obstruct desired actions; the opposite belief is the prevailing heresy of modern industrial society and thus, of course, of its art.

Records have a dual nature, in that, while they are undoubtedly things, and things with a saleable value, they are bought in order to turn them back into actions, that is to say performances, and for most people they are valued only so long as the performance they carry is itself valued; only the archivist values them as things in themselves. The high turnover rate in popular music as a whole means that there is a high rate of discard of old records, while in the classical field, and, to a lesser extent, jazz (reflecting perhaps the closer relation which we have noted it bears to classical music) there is a tendency to hold on to them. This is in line with the presumed permanent value of works of classical music and with the tendency to historicism which we have noted. The attitude of the classical-music enthusiast towards recording is encapsulated in an enthusiastic comment by the American historian Jacques Barzun:

> 'This mechanical civilization of ours has performed a miracle for which I for one cannot be too grateful: it has, by mechanical means, brought back to life the whole repertory of Western music — not to speak of acquainting us with musics of the East. Formerly, a fashion could bury the whole musical past except for a few dozen works arbitrarily selected . . . [Today] neglected or lesser composers come into their own and keep their place. In short the whole literature of one of the arts has sprung into being — it is like the Renaissance rediscovering the ancient classics and holding them fast by means of the printing press. It marks an epoch in Western intellectual history.'[6]

I shall not comment on this passage, other than to suggest that the epoch which the writer hails may be one of decline rather than of development: the phrase 'holding them fast' seems to sum up the enterprise. In any case, the average buyer of Afro-American music — and indeed the average Afro-American musician — would probably find in it little point of contact with his or her experience and interests. For such a musician, or record buyer, records are a way of extending the performance in space rather than in time. The past is gone, and posterity can look after itself; what matters, what has always mattered, in Afro-American musicking, is the validity of the present experience.

Up to now I have been writing as if records were made only to serve the purposes of the musicians who play for them and the listeners who listen to them. But it is of course impossible today to ignore the third party to the transaction: the record company and others who stand to make money from the manufacture and sale of records. There are many excellent accounts of the ways in which the financial structure of the record industry affects what musicians play and what listeners get to hear, and I do not intend to duplicate them here, but some comments are necessary. It is significant that most stories about the horrendous practices of record companies are confined to the popular field; we read much of the way in which recording groups such as The Monkees, The Bay City Rollers, and, more recently, Frankie Goes to Hollywood, were put together by record companies or producers without regard for musical criteria in order to extract the pocket money of teenagers, who are assumed to be so bemused and brainwashed by the publicity that they are incapable of distinguishing good from bad, but little is said of similar practices in the classical field. An account of the role played by Decca Records and by the publishing firm of Boosey and Hawkes in the career of Benjamin Britten, or by Deutsche Grammophon in those of Dietrich Fischer-Dieskau and Herbert von Karajan would make equally interesting reading.

If the practices of record companies in classical music are less outrageous than in Afro-American, it is largely because in classical music, which accounts for less than one-tenth of record sales over-all, there is less money at stake. But there is another factor; although the classical-music market is small by comparison with the huge sales of popular records, the recording industry's control over that market is much more assured, and we need not imagine that the record companies are not aware that there is an extensive, if informal, propaganda machine at work on their behalf, staffed by critics, schoolteachers and classical-music radio executives, both affirming the social prestige (a classic advertising ploy) of classical music and inculcating the idea that there are certain works (eg the symphonies of Beethoven, the concertos of Mozart) which every 'serious' music lover ought to have in his collection of records. There is thus a market which may be small in comparison with that for, say, David Bowie, but it is steady; further, each work can be sold over and over again, not only in new interpretations (often by the same artist) but also as new technological resources become available; first, electrical recording, then LP, then stereo, quad and finally (so far) CD. New 'authentic' performances on period instruments, a bonus from the musicologists, whose labours are often financed by record companies, are also good for business.

Classical records are advertised and marketed like any other commodity. Here, in an unguarded moment, speaks the advertising sales manager of a British commercial television company: 'The British public is not ignorant or effete in its taste. It's just not well enough advised. People don't want to be embarrassed by going into a specialist record shop and not knowing what to buy. TV is a natural to give that advice . . . The emphasis at first is of course on the music and not on the artists — although certain classical artists would go down very well indeed. Then in time people become fussy — look at confectionery and the amount of advertising (and consumption) now of relatively sophisticated products like After Eight [chocolates]. Television also reaches the immense A/B, C1 market, and that's a very important one for classical records.'[7]

A musician, of whatever kind or persuasion, who wants to make a career in his art is bound at some point to do business with the record industry; since the early 1950s records have replaced publication as the dominant mode of dissemination of musical compositions, and it is the representatives of the record industry who control musicians' access to a wider public. Because of the clear-cut division of labour in classical music, and because the musical work to be recorded is already in existence, the classical artist finds himself speaking the same language as the record executive; contracts are drawn up and fees paid according to a system, and with the protection of a copyright law, that has precisely this situation in mind.

A vernacular artist, on the other hand, especially one working in the potentially lucrative field of popular music, is from the moment of entering the record executive's office in a vulnerable position. Not only is the division of labour by no means clear-cut, not only is there a good deal of traffic in material of which nobody is sure who (if anyone) is the owner, but in many cases the musical work comes into existence only in the recording studio or the cutting room; further, the record company may insist on assigning to an artist or a group one of its staff producers who may completely remake the performance. As many people have to be paid, all this contributes to the artists' being ripped off; they may well find that they have signed a contract which makes them responsible for the expenses of a recording session, or that they are to be paid a flat fee only, with no access to royalties no matter how successful the record they make; composers of songs are liable to be paid little or nothing for songs made successful by major recording artists (the black bluesman Arthur Crudup received no royalties at all for *That's All Right Mama*, Elvis Presley's first record). The original recording artist, who is often black, may have to sit by and watch another, often white, musician make money and reputation by covering his or her songs and even sometimes his or her very style of performance. Here, for instance, is the experience of two major black musicians in the recording industry on which they are forced to rely for the dissemination of their performances. First, Billie Holiday: 'My friends are always telling me, "You should be rich, Lady, I just paid ten bucks for a couple of your LPs." I always say, I'm grateful you like my songs — even those of twenty years ago. I have to tell them it ain't going to bring me a quarter. I made over 270 songs between 1933 and 1944, but I didn't get a cent of royalties in any of them.'[8] And, second, Ornette Coleman: 'Ornette made eight more records, a total [in 1966] of ten, but as yet he says he has never received a royalty cheque large enough to pay his phone bill. In fact, one company informed him that he owed *them* money . . . A reputable critic has said that one record of Ornette's was reissued three times, and had a gross sale of 25,000 copies.'[9]

Even the most commercially successful artists receive only a small proportion of what their talents and hard work have earned: 'Frank Sinatra kept only 6.66 per cent of the $11 million he earned between 1941 and 1946 . . . Even The Beatles got only 8 per cent of the profit of LP sales as performers, while EMI got 40 per cent and the retailers 26 per cent. On singles, the artists earned only 2 per cent!'[10] Not even The Beatles could buck that system. It is in fact possible to propose a rule of thumb, that if an artist or group makes a lot of money it is only after a lot of other people have made a lot more money first. Thus, Elvis Presley may have become a millionaire, but 'the sale of Presley's records soon accounted for nearly 25% of Victor's overall sales, and carried the company through the latter part of the fifties, much as The Beatles were to carry Capitol [*with their US sales alone!*] in later years.'[11]

I say this, not merely to show how badly record companies can treat popular artists, given the chance — that has all been well documented elsewhere — but to absolve the artists from necessary complicity in the system that abuses them and their talents. They have to expect to be ripped off; the best that they can hope for is, first, that sales will be sufficient to provide, out of the small proportion that comes back to them, a reasonable sum, and, second, they will attain a strong enough position vis-à-vis the record company to gain a measure of control over what they play, how they play and how their records are presented to the public. Musicians of all persuasions, of course, enter the profession for a wide variety of reasons, ranging from, at one extreme, a pure desire to make money (music, like sport, can form an avenue of escape from poverty), or the wish to enter the charmed world — mostly fictitious — of the famous and glamorous, or to enjoy power, to, at the other extreme, the pure desire to make music in a particular way and to have it disseminated as widely as possible. Most musicians' reasons are a mixture of any or all of these; few are averse to making money from their art but most are just as concerned as other people to make a decent living, as well as to do the job as they think it ought to be done. The motives of record executives, on the other hand, are a mixture of cupidity, cynicism, racism, assumptions and prejudices about popular music, with genuine enthusiasm, knowledge and even love of the music. What is finally released to the public is the result of negotiation between these factors.

There is, however, no need to assume that such negotiation will result in a mere compromise between the opposing forces of 'art' as represented by the musicians, and of 'commerce' as represented by the management. It is, after all, not inconceivable that both parties might have an interest in producing something that is as good as possible, even if they do not always agree on what the word 'good' means. The assumption that there is a necessary opposition, commonly made by highbrow critics (and especially by Marxist critics, of whom Theodor Adorno was the worst but by no means the only offender), is based on a further assumption which equates popular taste with debased taste, portraying 'the masses' as bemused victims of the ruthless publicity machines of record companies and others, and as zeroing in unerringly on all that is worst in their products. The worse it is, they assume, the better it will sell. Here, for instance, is one of Britain's best-known high-culture salesmen writing in the London *Times*: 'If enough people are fed for long enough on a diet of bread and milk — and, moreover, mass-produced sliced bread and sour milk — they will cease to believe that there is more robust fare available, quite apart from the danger that their teeth will fall out, thus making it impossible for them to eat the meat even if they could be persuaded to try it. I could, of course, declare that since *I* know the difference between art and rubbish I don't care how many people are unaware of it; but I do not like to think that all that yelling and lies and public relations and salesmanship and fiddling and puffing are making it impossible, or at least very difficult, for millions to reach out for art who might otherwise do so.'[12] For this writer, 'art', as the remainder of his article makes clear, means the symphonies of Mozart.

I have no doubt that record company executives frequently wish that the high-culture demonographers' nightmare *were* true, that the entire world of popular music *were* inhabited by a single taste public conditioned to accept anything that they cared to foist upon it. But even though such ideas form the basis of the music policies of the British Broadcasting Corporation, of which I shall have more to say later, and of the Arts Council of Great Britain, not to mention the educational system, the very statistics show their absurdity. The record companies themselves base their calculations on the assumption that only about one record in ten will ever make any money, while, according to Simon Frith, one writer has calculated that 'more than sixty per cent of all singles released are never played by anyone.'[13] It would appear that the marketing strategies adopted by record companies, from radio interviews to payola, from personal appearances and tours to promo copies, are responses more to failure than to success in controlling the musical tastes of the majority of record buyers.

The trouble, from the record companies' point of view, is that the popular-music public is not monolithic at all, but consists of a very extensive network of overlapping publics of differing tastes, each based on a shared sense of identity which itself may be subtle, and unexpected to the lover of classical music (it is not necessarily even class-linked), which interlock and overlap in often surprising ways, as well as changing rapidly over time (it is, after all, in the musical sense a non-literate public); all of this renders it highly unpredictable. Further, musicians themselves have as a rule a clear sense of their own identity and that of those to whom they want or expect to appeal, and while they like to think their records will sell a large number of copies their commitment to that is not quite of the same order as that of the companies themselves (I supppose that is what 'selling out' really means to a musician: the exchange of one's own sense of identity for that of the company), who don't give a damn who they sell to as long as they sell. Thus, while the final aim, or at least dream, of the big record companies is of a single unified world-wide public taste, musicians know instinctively, and probably not even consciously, that this is not only not desirable but not even possible; the nearest thing to it is the public for classical music, but that is another matter.

That this should be so is not surprising, for, regardless of the technological and commercial processes which intervene between performer and listener when a performance is recorded, the fundamental motivation for participating in a musical act remains the same as it has always been: to affirm, explore and celebrate the participants' sense of who they are. That professional musicians have always had to negotiate a position between their own values and those of whoever is paying them is a matter which I discussed earlier, and nothing in the recording process changes that; since the beginning of civilization money has been an element in that negotiation, and today, when society as a whole is governed as never before by money values, and who you are is to a great extent how rich you are, it is not surprising if money is built into the identities of many musicians, both classical and vernacular. While the love of wealth is not necessarily an amiable character trait, it is one that is today greatly encouraged by the leaders of our society, and at least in many popular musicians it is fully integrated into the public personality; it is upfront, as they say, and not hidden behind a mask of disinterested devotion to art. This integration means that art and commerce are not necessarily in opposition; it is noticeable how many of today's popular musicians, even those who, as they are quite willing to tell us, devote themselves single-mindedly to the pursuit of fame and money, manage to do so through songs and performances that are well-crafted, at worst competent and at best memorable. There is, after all, nothing new in this; many of what are today regarded as great masterpieces of western music (Mozart's *Requiem* is only the first that comes to mind) were made strictly and explicitly for money. That highbrow critics should today damn popular music because it is made for money is special pleading which rests on the security of an art that is insulated from the brute realities of survival by state and private subsidy, as well as on the assumption that those who pay for their own musicking are unable to distinguish good from bad. It is not a mistake that is made by vernacular musicians themselves; those who do make the mistake of despising their audiences, to the point of deciding that anything will do for them, very quickly learn to their cost that it will not.

It all means, in the end, that vernacular musicians today, even the most 'commercial' of them, make music for the same reasons as musicians have always done, and that, furthermore, they maintain their identity, as musicians have always done, in a process of negotiation with those who pay them. Unlike the classical musician, whose ultimate source of support is the state, or those close to the centres of state power, the vernacular musician is paid, finally, by those who want to hear him or her; the power of record companies, as of radio networks, publishers, entrepreneurs, managers and promoters, lies in their ability to bring about or prevent, and to influence the manner of, the encounter between performers and listeners. But only performers and listeners, between them, can realize that encounter, and that is the source of *their* power.

It is interesting to consider two ways in which record companies, as well as radio networks and other interested parties, do attempt to impose some order on the situation; these are the star system and the imposition of categories onto the endless variety of vernacular musicking. Both of these devices involve manipulation of musicians' and listeners' sense of identity in a particular way and both are, up to a point, successful.

A star, of course, is not just a good player or singer; rather, it is an artist who has the ability to project a kind of personality, which is usually simplified and two-dimensional, and onto which a large number of those watching and listening can project their own personalities, their desires and their aspirations. From the point of view of the purveyor of music as product, the 'star system' means ease of marketing, with an easily recognizable and stable product, no matter whether the star's name is Michael Jackson, John Coltrane, James Galway or Herbert von Karajan. The buyers know what to expect and the company knows what its market is. This is the rationale behind those cover versions of rock'n'roll records which were made in the mid-1950s by members of the major American record companies' stable of contract artists; Pat Boone's version of *Long Tall Sally* might have been a pale shadow of Little Richard's, but it was stable, predictable and controllable, unlike the unnerving and unpredictable volcano which was the original.

For the fans, a star is a means to another end, a tool in the development of their sense of who they are, to be used for as long as he or she is useful for this purpose. One writer, describing her teenage experiences as a fan of the Bay City Rollers, a British group of the early 1970s (one reference book calls them 'the epitome of a mediocre pop group turned into superstars by astute management')[14], said: 'Our real obsession was with ourselves; in the end, the actual men behind the posters had very little to do with it all.'[15] The rock critic Dave Rimmer, commenting on this, says, 'In the classic model, of which both the Rollers and Duran Duran are examples, what the actual men behind the posters *do* have to do with it involves a convoluted process of both desire and identification. Sure, the fans drool over the man of the dream. But as long as he's a cut-out-and-keep graven image rather than an actual flesh and blood presence, in their dreams is precisely where he remains. This distance is undoubtedly part of the attraction. It's safe. It allows an outlet for all the fans' newly-discovered sexual energy while at the same time allowing them to cling a little longer to an ideal of romance and true love. Sooner or later the stark realities of burgeoning adulthood will come creeping in, but for the time being, a poster does fine.'[16]

There is much that is questionable in such easy assurance, not the least of which is the assumption that the star will be male and the fan female. The author does, however, make it clear that the fan is actively involved in his or her own fanship, making what he or she wants of the image that is presented, a point that is made also by Simon Frith: 'The usual theory is that the star is an extraordinary fellow who brings excitement and glamour into the lives of his fans, ordinary people, but the process works the other way around too; stars, dull professionals, are made glamorous by the imagination and wit and excitement of their fans.'[17]

The trouble is that the star system imposes severe limitations on the potential for growth of both stars and fans, not only reducing their interaction to a small number of stylized gestures, and distancing fans from the realization of their own creative potential, but also requiring that the image projected by the star be stable enough over a period of time to permit full exploitation of that identification. An abrupt change of style, which is a natural event in human growth, or a change which is not immediately comprehensible, can lead to rejection — a fact which has posed problems for many stars who want to move on to new creative fields, and not only in music. Bob Dylan, for example, encountered the wrath of fans in 1965 when he switched during a Newport Folk Festival concert from acoustic to electric guitar, with all the change of identity that that implied, while, more recently, Boy George, when he cut his hair and tried to modify his cosy drag-star image, found himself simply abandoned by the fans who had previously taken him to their hearts. What is at stake here is not the absolute right of the artist to follow the dictates of artistic impulse — outside the subsidized sector that has always been a matter for negotiation — but, rather, a matter of permitting those natural processes of development and change which we all undergo to take place.

The star system also has wider social and political implications, characterized by Guy Debord as a prime manifestation of the Society of the Spectacle: 'Under the shimmering diversions of the spectacle, *banalization* dominates modern society the world over . . . The celebrity, the spectacular representation of a living human being, embodies this banality by embodying this image of a possible role. Being a star means specializing in the *seemingly lived*; the star is the object of identification with the shallow seeming life that has to compensate for the fragmented productive specializations which are actually lived. Celebrities exist to act out various styles of living and viewing society — unfettered, free to express themselves *globally*. They embody the accessible product of social *labor* by dramatizing its by-products magically projected above it as its goal: *power* and *vacations*.'[18]

The star system, in fact, completely dominates the arts of western industrial societies; it functions effectively to distance the majority of people from their own creativity by using talented people to act out fantasies of creativity, as well as of 'power and vacations'. The star, in fact, as Debord suggests, is chosen to do the living on behalf of his or her fans. The image of success is as shallow as the whole business is fraudulent; the star's life, simply by reason of his or her stardom, is in its own way as narrow, as confined and anxiety-ridden as that of any fan. To turn a musician into a star is thus to defuse any challenge his or her musicking may pose to conventional values; the star is removed to another plane of existence, a fantasy world, where nothing that is done or said has any bearing on the real world. Only the image is real. Once a vernacular musician achieves any kind of success, the temptation to allow oneself to be thus co-opted is constant and insidious, and very rarely able to be resisted completely; we may be practically sure than any musician who achieves fame has made some compromises with the system, and will be obliged to do so every day of his or her professional life. For the classical concert artist or composer, on the other hand, the tensions involved in being a star are not so acute, since, as I have already pointed out, that person already has made an accommodation with the prevailing power system, to the point of internalizing its values, before ever stepping on to the concert stage.

Erecting categories and confining musicians in them also makes for easier marketing; we may consider it as a kind of obverse of the star system. The practice is as old as recording; Caruso and Melba, both of whom started recording in the first decade of the present century, were probably the earliest whose image was as important a part of their appeal as what they actually sang. Similarly, in the 1920s, the 'race' labels advertised their stars like so many known commodities: 'Don't miss this latest hit by Ida Cox and the famous Blues Serenaders;'[19] 'Now you'll get a kick out of this new Paramount "Lockstep Blues". It has good words and a good tune, one of Blind Lemon Jefferson's best,'[20] and so on. Under the system of classification, Melba and Caruso sang opera (Caruso, in an interesting and surely calculated extension of his image, later extended into Neapolitan song and even the songs of George M. Cohan), Ida Cox and Lemon Jefferson sang blues, Boy George the New Pop, Dylan folk songs, and each was expected to remain within the image and the category. It might be good for marketing to keep the image of the star steady, the categories clear, but it is limiting for musicians, confining them in a way quite unlike that in which they operate in real-life performance. In each generation there is a handful of artists, such as Miles Davis, David Bowie and the pack-joker Malcolm McLaren, who manage (or are given permission?) to avoid typing and becoming trapped in an image — if, indeed, their shape-shifting does not become, as Bowie's seems sometimes in danger of doing, an image in itself and marketed as such.

The recording process, then, is perceived differently by the three parties to it. Musicians see it primarily as a means by which their performances can be made available to a large number of people, for reasons which vary from pure delight in making music to pure delight in making money, with any mixture of these and other motives. Those two aims are not, as we have seen, necessarily incompatible with each other, and coexist in most musicians. Musicians will try to extract as much satisfaction (that is to say, affirmation of identity) from the performances as possible, while trying to make them as attractive as possible to listeners, and while it is the second that will make them their living, we should remember also that the desire to engage with an audience is an essential part of the makeup of every musician. This desire stems not from exhibitionism or sycophancy but from a genuine need for identification; what Charles Keil says of the urban bluesman, that 'his first obligation is to his public rather than to a private muse,'[21] is probably true, in their heart of hearts, of all musicians, deny it as they may. Musicians will, in fact, use whatever situation in which they find themselves to do what gives them most satisfaction, and that satisfaction comes ultimately from establishing a satisfactory relationship with their audience. The interpolation of the apparatus of recording, production and marketing of records in order to widen the circle of that relationship exacts its price as well as making the relationship much harder to assess, since sales of records, the final criterion, are very much after the event; there is no immediate feedback. Nevertheless, it is unlikely that without the desire to build a relationship with listeners, however alloyed it may be with the desire for money and for the trappings of fame, any musician or group of musicians can ever attain more than a momentary success. This applies both to concerts and to the recording studio; those who buy tickets and records are also searching for, and quickly recognize the absence of, that relationship. As with all human musicking, 'good' tunes, 'good' arrangements and so on are only the material on which a good *performance* can be built, and a good performance is one in which performers and listeners together can explore, affirm and celebrate their feelings of who they are. Recording changes nothing in that respect.

Record companies, for their part, share with musicians an interest in making records that will appeal to as many people as possible, but their executives are inclined to think of records as so many 'units' to be sold, and of musicians as workers whose labour and ideas are unfortunately necessary in order to give those units value. It is they who control the musicians' access to the audience of record buyers and thus to their main source of income; while outstandingly successful musicians may gain considerable negotiating power and even control, not only over their performances but also over production and marketing, the ultimate power over what gets recorded, how it is recorded and how it is presented to its potential audience lies with the company. That said, the fact remains that the company has no power either to generate or to command the use of performances; that lies with the musicians and with the audience. It is at best a middleman, a facilitator.

The role of the third party, the listener and record buyer, is ambiguous. To the record company, and to some extent the musicians, he is simply a member of 'the public', that fickle monster which exists in order to buy records, fan magazines, posters, T-shirts and other appurtenances of the star system, to attend concerts on promotion tours, and to respond to the musicians' often outsize egos, and which must be placated and manipulated in its power to make and destroy careers. It is this public that the highbrow critic perceives as stupid, monolithic and willing to buy whatever rubbish musicians and record companies, in sinister collusion, care to foist upon them. But for the individual listener, on the other hand, the purchase of a record or of concert tickets is a matter of deliberate and careful choice, often highly informed and discriminating, and the response to the musicians' personality and style, only a part of which can be inferred from the sounds which are coming from the record grooves, is a matter to which he or she gives a good deal of attention. Opinions on music and musicians among enthusiasts, once past the teenybopper stage, are likely to be at least as judicious and as shrewd as among classical concertgoers and generally stop short of the kind of undiscriminating adulation given, often by those whom one would expect to know better, to say, James Galway, the Amadeus Quartet or the King's Singers.

It is clear that the control exercised by the record companies, despite their central position in the recording process, is precarious, to say the least. It is a testimony to the creativity of so many musicians and listeners that under these conditions so much valuable musicking does take place. The system takes a heavy toll, however. It is not just that only a small proportion of the $2.5 billion that the record industry was reputedly worth in 1983 finds its way back to the musicians on whose activities it is all based, but also that owing to the star system the distribution of rewards is extremely uneven.

This unevenness bears particularly heavily on black musicians. It has been a major argument of this book that the vernacular-music tradition which has come to be the principal form of musicking in western society in our century is black American in origin and in essence. It is not only that the whole tradition has grown out of those two powerful trunks, blues and black religious music (themselves the outcome of a synthesis made by blacks of African and European ways of musicking) but, further, nearly every major style of twentieth-century vernacular music and dance owes its origin to initiatives by black musicians and dancers, most of them unknown to history. As we have seen, many white artists warmly acknowledge those black ancestor-figures, but the fact is that the skills and the inventiveness of black musicians and dancers have never been properly recognized, either in terms of public appreciation or in terms of financial reward in proportion to their achievements. To the public at large, the Kings of Swing were Benny Goodman and Glenn Miller, not Count Basie or Duke Ellington, the greatest tapdancers were Fred Astaire and Gene Kelly, not Bill Robinson or Honi Coles, the first important musicians of rock'n'roll (I have it on the authority of a serious history intended for use in schools) were Elvis Presley and Bill Haley, while Little Richard and Chuck Berry were mere r-and-b singers who rode on their coattails to fame. One could multiply examples over and over — there are others to be found in this book — without in any way wishing to detract from the achievements of many fine white artists which, considerable as they are, do not only owe much to black creativity but would have been unthinkable without it.

The inability to see the power of black creativity, and the insistence on perceiving blacks simply as entertainers but nothing more is deeply ingrained in European and Euro-American society. It is an aspect of those attitudes which seem to have developed out of the continuing need to justify slavery, a hundred or more years after its formal ending, so deeply is its unacknowledged guilt burned into the European soul, which go under the name of racism. One need not postulate any conspiracy to keep blacks from gaining their proper recognition; it is quite sufficient that whites as a whole have learnt to perceive blacks even in the most favourable light as emotionally and spiritually underdeveloped — in a word, as childlike — and not to be taken seriously either as people or as artists. It makes no difference in practical terms if this underdevelopment is attributed to persistent 'primitive' African traits (the colonialist position) or to the brutalizing effect of slavery which is supposed to have destroyed all traces of the blacks' former culture (the liberal position); either way blacks are simply not regarded as capable of engaging in serious human, let alone artistic, activity. Whites do not think this; we *know* it, as we know the colour of our hair and the sphericity of the earth, having absorbed rather than consciously learnt it from a thousand words, stories and gestures of peers and elders, from books, films, television and newspapers alike. I do not believe that any white European or Euro-American can have escaped this conditioning; it is a fact which any white person who wishes to enter seriously into a discourse with Afro-Americans and their culture (something which for our own sakes we need to do) must face, as the alcoholic must face the fact of his or her alcoholism. The most damaging forms of racism are those which do not recognize themselves for what they are. Damaging, of course, to whites as well as to blacks, for what whites are denying is not only an important means of exploring, affirming and celebrating who we are, but also a crucial aspect of our intellectual and cultural heritage, which as long as it remains unacknowledged leaves us helpless in the face of our own destructive myths. 'Repressed gods,' says Ean Begg, 'take their captors captive.'[22]

Those who control the access of musicians to any but their most intimate audiences — record companies, radio networks, promoters and managements, even historians and scholars — bear a heavy responsibility in the denial of the centrality of the black contribution, not only to modern vernacular musicking, but to modern consciousness itself. They would not, however, have been so successful in their denial were the white majority not so willing to be deceived. I have argued earlier that this willingness is the result, not of any inbuilt quality of the human soul (racism, especially in view of what black people have endured over the centuries, is remarkable for its absence in their attitudes — a fact which is confirmed by the whole nature and history of black musicking) but of the particular circumstances in which Europeans, and especially British, people encountered Africans for the first time on a large scale in the sixteenth and seventeenth centuries. These circumstances have been admirably desribed by Winthrop Jordan[23] and I need not go into them here, but it is possible to see in present-day musical and scholarly practices, many of them in themselves trivial, the way in which the downgrading of blacks operates. A few examples must suffice.

At a recent broadcast by a well-known wind quintet on the BBC's classical-music channel, after the 'serious' fare of the concert an encore, Scott Joplin's *The Entertainer*, was played, to a clearly delighted studio audience, at breakneck speed which destroyed all its elegance and subtlety, and in flat disregard of its composer's instruction on the score: 'Not fast — it is *never* right to play ragtime fast.' There is an assertion by a premier scholar in the field, James Pullen Jackson, that blacks could not possibly have developed spirituals from their own resources but must have cribbed them from whites. Look at the conventional account of rock'n'roll which writes black musicians out of their central role in its development. Or the use of the term 'serious music' for western classical music. Or look at the redefinition of bebop by some writers as over-intellectual and out of touch with its origins (the opposite was true) and the insinuation made by many critics and jazz historians that the musicians were getting too big for their intellectual boots — which happened precisely at the point in history when black artists, like other black Americans, were demanding recognition as serious human beings. Then the virtual absence from British television and radio of programmes in which Afro-American music is treated as an important part of contemporary experience, and the almost universal presentation of Afro-American music in a featureless, eventless perpetual present which by depriving it of both history and context renders it trivial and devoid of positive social content.

The last two examples remind us how we can be misled by high-culture critics concerning Afro-American music. It is not that record companies and radio stations are foisting a load of trivial and pernicious rubbish on to a helpless public, but rather that those gatekeepers, through their manner of presentation, are trivializing a way of musicking which, for musicians and listeners alike, is a powerful means of affirming and celebrating identity, in a society whose tendency is increasingly to render the majority of its members powerless and faceless. The trivialization serves another purpose also.

We have seen how the musicking of the slaves incarnated the values of a culture which was very attractive to those white Americans and English who encountered it in the eighteenth and nineteenth centuries, and how that attraction could be neutralized and rendered safe through the process which has been called minstrelization. It is possible to see that process at work today, not necessarily any more consciously now than then, as those who have a large stake in the industrial values of Europe and America perceive the attraction and at the same time the danger which Afro-American culture, through its musicking, presents. Since those who exercise control over the contact between musicians and audiences have a considerable stake in those industrial values, we can see a circular process at work which would, if it were not for one factor, result in the relegation of Afro-American musicking to the fringes of western musical activity. That factor is the profitability of the music for concert promoters and managements, record companies and radio networks, as well as for T-shirt manufacturers, souvenir sellers, fan-magazine publishers and other hangers-on who for the most part have no interest in the social, political or spiritual content of a performance, and do not care how subversive it may be to the values which support their own prosperity, so long as, in the short run, it makes money for them. This is the Achilles' heel of the system which Afro-American musicians have always been prepared to exploit as they themselves are exploited by it. Unlike classical performance, in which the ideological circle, as we have seen, is closed, keeping the culture safe from 'pollution' but also closing it off from life, the control over the content of Afro-American musicking, as well as over its accessibility to both performers and listeners, is never complete.

Jimmy Cliff expresses this from the viewpoint of the black reggae musician:

> 'I see the music industry as just another industry within the Babylon system. The Babylon law is a jungle law — the fittest of the fit survive. The music industry happens to be the one I'm involved in — but the whole system is a jungle of vampires, parasites, ticks . . . lice. The only way is to study and understand how the system works, then you can start to do something about it. When you are naive, when you come

> with honesty in your heart, you find the world isn't so — it's really a matter of studying. I've had a lot of hard experiences in my career, not only with the film [*The Harder They Come*, in which he starred] but with records. These mistakes can't be made again. The whole system's a vampire, everybody's out to dig you out or rip you off — you have to learn or you'll get burnt . . . They can rip you off, but they can't take everything . . . I don't see it's wise to go to extremes and kill your life . . . I don't see it's wise to lock myself away either. But intertwine and learn.'[24]

We are thus faced with the paradox that, on the one hand, the musicians and their musicking are downgraded by the representatives of the official musical culture and some of the most creative and innovative musicians of our time are thrown onto the mercies of the most rapacious sector of society and denied the proper reward, either in terms of social esteem or financial gain, of their creativity, skills and hard work, while on the other hand it is that same outsider position and low status that enable them to evade the kind of ideological control to which musicians in the classical tradition, apparently without even noticing it, are submitting. The moral panics, scandals and clean-up campaigns which erupt every few years around popular music, especially in times of political reaction, are indicators not only of the fear felt by the representatives of the official culture for those human values of which Afro-American musicking has been the vehicle for more than two hundred years, but also of their failure to cast out the simultaneously disturbing and liberating outsiders or even to keep them under control. If those panics and scandals tend to centre on one aspect of the musicians' expression, that of sexuality, that tells us more about the guardians' principal preoccupation than of what is actually embodied in the musicking, and should not blind us to the fact that its subversive liberating force penetrates every aspect of human identity.

NOTES

1. FERRIS, William, Jr: *Blues From the Delta*, London, Studio Vista, 1970, pp 64–83.
2. WILLIS, Paul: *Profane Culture*, London, Routledge & Kegan Paul, 1978, p 36.
3. TITON, Jeff Todd: *Early Downhome Blues: A Musical and Cultural Analysis*, Urbana, University of Illinois Press, 1977, p 23.
4. *ibid.*, p 23.
5. MIEZITIS, Vita and BERNSTEIN, Bill: *Nightdancin'*, New York, Ballantine Books, 1980, pp xix–xx.
6. quoted in GELATT, Roland: *The Fabulous Phonograph*, London, Cassell, 2nd edition 1977, p 301.
7. RENNIE, Peter, quoted in ASHMAN, Mike: 'Mining Gold from the Classics', *Classical Music*, 23 December, 1978, p 6.
8. HOLIDAY, Billie, with William Dufty: *Lady Sings the Blues*, New York, Lancer Books, 1956, p 166.
9. SPELLMAN, A.B.: *Four Lives in the Bebop Business*, New York, Random House, 1966, p 129.
10. HARKER, Dave: *One For the Money: Politics and Popular Song*, London, Hutchinson, 1980, p 105.
11. CHAPPLE, Steve and GAROFALO, Reebee: *Rock and Roll Is Here To Pay: The History and Politics of the Rock Industry*, Chicago, Nelson-Hall, 1977, p 43.
12. LEVIN, Bernard: 'A Classic Case of Over-Statement', *The Times*, Thursday 27 September, 1984.
13. FRITH, Simon: *Sound Effects: Youth, Leisure and the Politics of Rock'n'Roll*, London, Constable, 1983, p 147.
14. CLIFFORD, Mike (ed): *The Illustrated Rock Handbook*, London, Salamander Books Ltd, 1983, p 17.
15. RIMMER, Dave: *Like Punk Never Happened: Culture Club and the New Pop*, London, Faber & Faber, 1985, p 109.
16. *ibid.*, p 110.
17. FRITH, Simon, *op. cit.*, p 264.
18. DEBORD, Guy: *The Society of the Spectacle*, Detroit, Red and Black, revised edition 1977, paragraphs 59 and 60.
19. TITON, Jeff Todd: *op. cit.*, Fig. 109.
20. *ibid.*, Fig. 128.
21. KEIL, Charles: *Urban Blues*, Chicago, University of Chicago Press, 1966, p 154.
22. BEGG, Ean: *The Cult of the Black Virgin*, London, Routledge & Kegan Paul, 1985, p 37.
23. JORDAN, Winthrop: *The White Man's Burden: Historical Origins of Racism in the United States*, New York, Oxford University Press, 1974.
24. quoted in WALLIS, Roger and MALM, Krister: *Big Sounds from Small Peoples: The Music Industry in Small Countries*, London, Constable, 1984, p 287.

Chapter 15

STYLES OF ENCOUNTER IV: A VERY SATISFACTORY BLACK-MUSIC CIRCLE

In writing this book I have been obliged to keep reminding myself of what I intend it to be, and, just as importantly, what I do not intend it to be, since books, like their readers, define themselves as much by what they are not as by what they are. I do not intend it as a complete survey of Afro-American styles of musicking; such a task would be quite beyond my resources and, in any case, it would almost certainly cause my real aim to be swamped beneath a mass of historical and musical detail. That aim is not only to pay what tribute I can to the musical and social power of untold musicians, both famous and unknown, who have created a way of musicking that can embody the most precious of human values, but also to show the consistency and the essential unity of the various forms which that musicking has taken over the past three centuries. Here, surely, is the central musical culture of the west in our time, which despite the commercialism and the star-making inflicted upon it remains a music of participation rather than of spectacle, in which all are invited to join, and through which even the most downtrodden members of industrial societies can come to define themselves rather than have definition thrust upon them.

To show more clearly how this has taken place I have concentrated my study on the musicking as it has taken place in the United States, not only so as to keep the amount of material under control, but also because it is the United States which has been the place of origin of most of the music as it is today experienced across the world. We need not, however, imagine that the Afro-American tradition in the United States has been entirely autonomous or uninfluenced by what has been going on elsewhere. It is in fact possible to see the United States as a focus on which have converged a number of musical cultures from all over the world, but most especially from South and Central America and the Caribbean, where they have been assimilated and then disseminated once more, sometimes to be re-assimilated in their place of origin; this process may have been repeated many times, a sign not only of the commercial dominance of what has become known as the music industry in the United States but also of the creativity and adaptability of poor people, both black and white, in the Americas and wherever the sounds of the music have been heard and absorbed into the culture.

In this chapter I shall examine a few of those external interactions, not with any intention of completeness but simply to show some of the ways in which Afro-American ways of musicking have resonated, and continue to resonate, around the world. In particular, we see them crossing and recrossing the Atlantic Ocean, which today may be thought of, in terms of music power, as a lake of the African diaspora.

The present dominance of the United States in the Americas, and its sharp differences, as an effectively Anglo-Saxon Protestant country, from its southern neighbours whose dominant culture is Iberian and Catholic, obscure the fact that in the colonial period there was more affinity and even political unity between the southern North American colonies and the West Indies than there was between them and the northern colonies. It was not just that both societies were based on slavery, or even that colonization in the two areas was planned and financed in much the same way by the metropolitan powers of France, Spain and England, but also, as Dena Epstein points out: 'the two areas shared close commercial ties and a constant interchange of population, both black and white. In the seventeenth and eighteenth centuries both Britain and France regarded all their colonies in the New World as part of the same colonial structure, regardless of where they were located. Barbados and South Carolina, the French Antilles and Louisiana, were closer in their interests, their plantation system and their exchanges of population, than, say, Massachusetts and South Carolina.'[1] Furthermore, in the colonial period it was the West Indies in which both the British and French governments were principally interested, 'for the most elementary of financial reasons: enormous fortunes were to be made from sugar.'[2]

Leaving aside the city of New Orleans, which still remains today, as one writer has said, 'in effect a Caribbean island beached on the US mainland,'[3] there were two major differences between the Caribbean islands and the North American slave colonies. In the first place, the mainland was colonized principally by surplus population from the British Isles (among whom the black slaves were initially intended only as ancillary labour and were always in a minority) and that population was there, for better or for worse, to stay; they were committed to America. The Caribbean islands, on the other hand, especially those of Britain and France, were run as enormous sugar factories by a large number of slaves supervised by a small number of whites, few of whom had any commitment to the islands other than as places to make their fortune — and fortunes *were* made, as the eighteenth-century saying 'rich as a West Indian' reveals; West Indian sugar magnates returning to England and France were a byword for ostentatious wealth. In the islands slaves outnumbered masters many times and masters took little interest in the slaves' lives as long as they did what was required of them. Hence the slaves had relatively little contact with European culture, and African ways were able to survive — and continue to survive today — much longer than on the mainland.

The second major difference was that, apart from the British possessions (and in those there still remain today traces of prior Spanish occupation) the culture into which the Africans were thrust was not Anglo-Celtic and Protestant but Iberian and Catholic. The Iberian peninsula, of course, has long had closer links with Africa than has the rest of Europe, not only through the centuries-long occupation by North Africans which finally ended in the very year in which Columbus crossed the Atlantic, but also through an earlier slave trade which had resulted in the presence of a sizeable black population in Portugal by the middle of the fifteenth century, and which according to W.E.B. DuBois affected even the genes of the royal family: 'The royal family became more Negro than white. John IV was Negroid, and the wife of the

French Ambassador described John VI as having Negro hair, nose, lips, colour.'[4] To what extent this facilitated cultural contact in the New World it is hard to say, but it must have facilitated a convergence of musical styles in what is now Brazil.

But there were other features of the encounter in Central and South America, and in the Latin Caribbean, that were to have an effect on the Afro-American culture that developed there. First, there was the balance of population; in Spain and Portugal there was, unlike in England, a chronic population shortage so that there was less reason to export people to America; as a result blacks and mulattos have always formed a larger proportion of the population than in North America, even in the slave colonies. Second, there was the retention, as a matter of deliberate policy by the Spanish and Portuguese colonial governments, of African ethnic groupings, and the encouragement of institutions such as *batuques*, or black dance clubs, which embodied the distinctions between them, in order to ensure the continuance of traditional enmities that had existed in the African homeland, 'to renew,' in the words of a Brazilian official, 'those feelings of mutual aversion that they have taken for granted since birth, but tend gradually to vanish in the general atmosphere of degradation which is their common lot. Now such sentiments of mutual hostility may be regarded as the most powerful guarantee which the major cities of Brazil enjoy today.'[5] To what extent the black 'nations' within Latin American countries today represent a genuine survival of African tribal or ethnic groups is uncertain, since black society there has had its own dynamic, and the more powerful groups — the Yoruba for one — have tended to absorb weaker ones; but they have been powerful forces in the conservation of African cultural traits. Roger Bastide tells us, for example, of the public masked processions in the streets of Havana at Carnival and Epiphany, where 'the masks were faithfully copied from those in use in African societies . . . the musical instruments which accompanied them were just the same as we find employed in Africa; and . . . the names given to characters in the dance were those of gods or spirits.'[6]

A crucial influence on the style of the encounter was Catholicism itself, at least as it manifested itself in the

Americas. We have seen how slaves in the North American colonies, and, later, states, were converted to Christianity mainly through the efforts of Protestant, especially Nonconformist, groups, in particular during the waves of religious revivalism that swept the United States in the eighteenth and nineteenth centuries. The blacks were obliged to undergo instruction, and to be catechized, before being baptized and received into the church; this meant that the concepts of nonconformist Christianity were taught to them with some care. Their worship, too, was watched over carefully by the white clergy to ensure that decorum, as they saw it, was preserved, leading to the rapid elimination of specifically African forms of worship. What remained of African beliefs and worship in North America has been called a 'reinterpretation' of Christian doctrine 'in the light,' says Bastide, 'of his own mentality, sentiments and affective needs; what emerged was a Negro rather than an African brand of Christianity.'[7]

The Catholic Church, on the other hand, first because it regards the sacraments as something to be experienced rather than intellectually understood, and second because it was in the New World what Bastide calls 'a social rather than a mystical phenomenon',[8] was more casual in its attitude to doctrinal instruction. Baptism was often carried out *en masse* at the port of embarkation, or on arrival, on the slave's learning a few prayers and ritual gestures. Besides, there have never been enough priests in Latin America to cater for all the souls in their charge, even in the cities; in the country the blacks have been left largely to themselves. The massive black migration to the cities during this century has not changed things much; in the *favelas*, or *barrios*, that surround the great cities such as Lima, Caracas and Rio, where as we have seen the civil authorities' law hardly ventures, the grip of the Catholic Church is very loose indeed. As a result, the Church has had to wink its eye at both the introduction of African elements into its rituals and at the existence of a number of syncretistic religious cults that were derived extensively from the doctrines, the imagery and the pantheon of Christianity and blended with African deities and their observances.

But there was not, in South America any more than in

North, any clinging to the forms of the past; what occurred was the dynamic response of a highly creative people to the need not only to survive but also to make survival worth fighting for, to preserve identity, community and a sense of human dignity. Even after Emancipation, which occurred at various times in the nineteenth century (the last was Brazil, in 1888), and despite official denials of racism in countries such as Brazil and Colombia, blacks in those countries remain mostly at the bottom of the social system. There is no 'official' dividing line which, as in the United States and Britain, marks anyone with the slightest trace of African ancestry as 'black' and thus inferior, but there is a finely developed sense of hue which ensures that the darker a person's skin colour the more disadvantaged he or she will be. As one Brazilian musician said to Jeremy Marre, 'They say there is no racism — only discrimination.'[9]

In this situation, very different from that in Anglo-Saxon North America (and one to which the surviving Indians have made a significant contribution, both genetic and cultural) we find a much greater survival of African cultural forms. Into the religious space left by the Catholic Church have moved a number of genuinely syncretistic religions which draw equally on Christianity and on memories of Africa (kept alive in the present century by much traffic with West Africa) such as Brazilian *Candomblé*, Haitian *Voudou* (by no means the sinister cult beloved of B-movie makers but a sophisticated and morally elevated religion), Cuban *Lucumbi*, and Puerto Rican *Santaria*. If one finds in these and other religions such (to European eyes) bizarre features as the giving of names of Christian saints to *Voudou* gods, and the uttering of Catholic prayers before *Voudou* ceremonies to bring a blessing on the participants, or the attending of Mass to give thanks for the successful initiation of a new devotee to the *Candomblé*, we can find some explanation in the words of Bastide:

> 'Syncretism by correspondence between the gods and saints . . . can be explained in historical terms by the slaves' need, during the colonial period, to conceal their pagan ceremonies from European eyes. They therefore danced before a Catholic altar, and though their masters found this

> somewhat bizarre, it never occurred to them that these Negro dances, with their prominently displayed lithographs and statuettes of saints, were in fact addressed to African divinities. Even today, the priests and priestesses of Brazil recognize that syncretism is simply a mask put over the black gods for the white man's benefit. At the same time, it can be justified, theologically, in the eyes of the faithful. In essence, the argument runs, there is only one universal religion, which acknowledges the existence of one unique God and Creator. However, this God is too remote from mankind for the latter to enter into direct contact with him; therefore, "intermediaries" are necessary — Catholic saints and the angels of the Old Testament for Europeans, *Orisha* and *Vodun* for the Negroes. Though this universal religion takes on local forms, varying according to race and ethnic group, the variations are not fundamental. In any case, one can always "translate" one religion into another by assimilating some African divinity to a special saint, or to some local variant of the Virgin.'[10].

Without doubting for a moment the necessity for concealment, one may see at the same time something even more positive in this religious double vision: that ability of Africans, not only to tolerate but actively to make use of and to enjoy multiple identities.

We need not be surprised, given the intricate ways in which religion is woven into the texture of Afro-American life, to find that such multiple identities are to be found in musicking also. The ceremonies of *Candomblé* are accompanied, West African style, by a trio of drums with double bell by means of which the gods are summoned to possess the bodies of celebrants as they dance; the *samba da rodé*, rural ancestor of the urban samba of the Rio carnival, is a circle dance accompanied by call-and-response singing, drumming and handclaps, in which each participant in turn dances a solo in the centre of the circle, while the *capoeira*, a form of martial arts disguised as dance, is accompanied by *berimbau*, a single-string bow with gourd resonator struck with a stick. All these represent much more explicit African survivals than anything to be found in North America, and they have filtered into the Portuguese-inflected popular music, even inflecting the music and the dancing of the white bourgeoisie. Dances of Brazil, like the samba, the carioca and maxixe, can all exist in a number of forms, from those that are acceptable in bourgeois society to those uninhibited and physical dances such as may be found in the *favelas* of Rio de Janeiro.

If the musicking of the Afro-Hispanic fusion, in those South American countries which were Spanish colonies — Panama, Ecuador, Colombia and Venezuela in particular — appears to contain fewer Africanisms, this may be, as John Storm Roberts points out, because both Spanish music and Central and West African music favour complicated driving rhythms with steady pulsating patterns. 'This,' says Roberts, 'is true of the Spanish music best known to non-Spaniards, *flamenco*, and also much other Spanish folk music, especially that of the south. The similarity between Spanish and African approaches extends to the occurrence in much Spanish music of combinations of duple and triple rhythms, though not simultaneous. Many Spanish rhythmic patterns are quite near enough to African patterns for African techniques (cross-rhythms, the overlaying of triple and duple rhythm, and so on) to fit them perfectly. And the rhythmic improvisation which is such a feature of some African drumming — the approach of the lead drummer in many areas — is not alien to the Spanish'.[11]

This affinity of rhythmic style is summed up in the rhythmic pattern known throughout Latin America and the Caribbean as *clavé*, a recurrent two-bar scheme with three accented beats in the first bar and two in the second; counting eight semiquaver beats in each of two two-four bars, a typical clavé would be ONE-two-three-FOUR-five-six-SEVEN-eight, one-two-THREE-four-FIVE-six-seven-eight (lovers of rock'n'roll will recognize that as something very like the 'hambone' or 'Bo Diddley' beat, which is of ancient provenance in black North American music, pointing perhaps to early cultural traffics). Billy Bergman calls clavé a 'truce' which is 'the true genius of the Latin American tradition; polyrhythms fit neatly between bar lines.'[12] The polyrhythms of Africa, he says, are 'caged but not tamed' and so become usable for popular dance music. We have already seen, in our discussion of ragtime, how this unequal division of an eight-beat pattern is the Afro-American accommodation between African and

European concepts of rhythm (Bergman's use of the word 'truce' is thus very apt), and the clavé is another version of the kind of pattern we found in ragtime melodies. In Latin music, however, the basic European two-four beat is not sounded as it is in ragtime; instead it is the clavé itself that is the rhythmic foundation of the whole musical structure, and players do not think of a two-four against it at all, but rather choose to superimpose any number of other patterns, in ever-increasing layers of fascinating and delicious rhythmic complexity, upon it.

It is not only the more or less universal rhythmic basis of Latin American music, but it is also long-established. The American pianist Louis Moreau Gottschalk travelled widely throughout Latin America and the Caribbean in the 1850s and 1860s, spending from 1856 to 1862 in the Caribbean, where, as he tells us in his memoirs, he wandered at random, 'indolently permitting myself to be carried away by chance, giving a concert wherever I found a piano, sleeping wherever night overtook me — on the grass of the savannah, or under the palm-leaf roof of a *veguero* with whom I partook of a tortilla, coffee and bananas . . . When I became tired of the same horizon, I crossed an arm of the sea and landed on a neighbouring isle, or on the Spanish Main. In this manner I have successively visited the Spanish, French, English, Dutch, Swedish and Danish Antilles, the Guianas and the shores of Pará.'[13] Gottschalk was of course no ethnomusicologist — there was no such creature in his day — but a musician of wide social and cultural sympathies and a keen ear, and he composed a large number of pieces for piano and for orchestra in which he incorporated (one might say, celebrated) the rhythms that he heard; the various inflections of the clavé can be heard in these pieces, often flowing seamlessly out of and into rhythms of contradance, schottische, polka and waltz which the Europeans had brought. Gottschalk, who had worked in Paris with Berlioz, organized in February 1860 a giant music festival in Havana with an orchestra which according to his own account numbered 560 players (seventy violins alone!). He is reported to have scoured the countryside around Havana and Santiago for native players of the *bamboula* and other drums to take part in his Symphony No 1, subtitled

Nuit des Tropiques, the second of whose two movements is probably the first samba ever composed for a European symphony orchestra. The picture of all those musicians, plus singers, all 'bellowing and blowing', in the composer's own words, 'to see who could scream the loudest'[14] (where *could* they have all come from?) in an orchestra alongside some fifty drummers from surrounding villages, gives a fascinating and tantalizing vignette from cultural history, and reminds us of the multiplicity of sources from which has come the present-day identity and music of the peoples of the Caribbean.

The influence of South American music on that of the United States has been intermittent and localized, consisting mostly of dance crazes which have captured white American dancers, mostly in watered-down versions, ever since the late years of the last century. The Argentinian tango, the Brazilian maxixe, samba, la conga and bossa nova are among the many which have surfaced briefly and disappeared, surviving today rather weirdly as an element of identity among white ballroom-dancing enthusiasts. It is from the Caribbean and from Mexico that the most enduring influences have come, for reasons which probably have to do partly with their geographical closeness to the United States, partly with the amazing mobility of Caribbean people and partly with the fact that the Caribbean has for centuries been the forum for the encounter between many different kinds of identity. Their history has been extremely complex, with successive waves of European masters following the initial Spanish colonization, the major powers being Britain and France but with the Dutch, Swedish and Danish also represented, and waves of forced migration from different parts of West and Central Africa. In all this history the central part played by the blacks themselves in the development of the islands and of their culture has been consistently left out of account. As Eric Williams says, writing about the economic and political crisis of slavery in the early nineteenth century:

> 'the most dynamic and powerful social force in the colonies was the slave himself. This aspect of the West Indian problem has been studiously ignored, as if the slaves, when they became instruments of production, passed for men

> only in the catalogue. The planter looked upon slavery as eternal, ordained by God, and went to great lengths to justify it by scriptural quotation. There was no reason why the slave should think the same. He took the same scriptures and adapted them to his own purpose. To coercion and punishment, he responded with indolence, sabotage and revolt. Most of the time he merely was as idle as possible. That was his usual form of resistance — passive. The docility of Negro slaves is a myth. The maroons of Jamaica and the Bush Negroes of British Guiana were runaway slaves who had extracted treaties from the British Government and lived independently in their mountain fastnesses or jungle retreats. They were standing examples to the slaves of the British West Indies of one road to freedom. The successful slave revolt in Saint Domingue was a landmark in the history of slavery in the New World, and after 1804, when the independent republic of Haiti was established, every white slave-owner, in Jamaica, Cuba or Texas, lived in dread of another Toussaint L'Ouverture. It is inconceivable *a priori* that the economic dislocation and the vast agitations which shook millions in Britain could have passed without effect on the slaves. Pressure on the sugar planters from the capitalists in Britain was aggravated by pressure from the slaves in the colonies. In communities like the West Indies, as the governor of Barbados wrote, "the public mind is ever tremblingly alive to the danger of insurrection."'[15]

With the ending of slavery, at various times over the nineteenth century (a result less of the efforts of humanitarians than of the collapse of the West Indian sugar economy with the import into Europe of cheaper sugar from India and the East Indies), the islands and their populations, which had created for the 'mother countries' such vast wealth, were treated by them with cynical disdain. 'Jamaica to the bottom of the sea!,' said one British Member of Parliament in 1844. 'These "barren colonies" had been the "most fatal appendages" of the British Empire, and if they were to be blotted out from the face of the earth Britain would lose "not one jot of her strength, one penny of her wealth, one instrument of her power."'[16] The islands had even to learn how to feed themselves; in the heyday of sugar, land had been too profitable to be given over to such mundane commodities as food, livestock and the like, all of which had been imported from the American mainland; hence the seemingly bizarre liking of present-day Jamaicans for dried and salted North Atlantic cod. The general neglect was interrupted from time to time when the mother countries found themselves in need of fighting men or cheap labour; otherwise they were left to rot.

It is this ruthless economic exploitation coupled with neglect that is at the root of the image of picturesque decay, of indolence, superstition and ignorance, summed up in the words 'Creole decadence', which lingers in the European mind today — not an altogether erroneous image so far as the surviving remnants of the planter class are concerned, but completely belied by the cultural vigour of the slaves' descendants as well as of those who were, at various times over the nineteenth century, brought in as indentured labour in ill-conceived attempts to revive the island economies (the problem was not shortage of labour but rather shortage of investment, which the mother countries were never willing to provide): East Indians, Syrians, Indians, Chinese and even Africans, mostly from present-day Zaire. These latter-day immigrations were complicated by the mobility of the islanders themselves; Cubans and Jamaicans have commuted between each other's islands for two hundred years and more, and thousands of Jamaicans emigrated in the 1920s and 1930s to the United States and Canada (they were particularly active in the 'Harlem Renaissance' of the 1930s), while it was mainly people from the British West Indies who built the Panama Canal. It is this mobility and penchant for island-hopping that have brought about some surprising phenomena, such as the spectacle of English-speaking inhabitants of the hispanophone Dominican Republic parading in the streets of San Pedro at Christmas dressed in colourful costumes and reciting garbled versions of medieval English mummers' plays to the accompaniment of a drum-and-fife band which plays a mixture of British military music and African dance music. Perhaps nowhere else in the world — certainly nowhere else in the western world — have there been in historical times such vigorous surges and counter-surges of societies and cultures.

In most of the Caribbean islands people of at least partly

African descent are in a majority — certainly they are in a majority over-all. In most, too, owing to a pernicious combination of neglect by the dominant powers in the area and negative interference from the moment they try to do something for themselves, the economies are in a ramshackle condition, despite the presence in most of a small well-off middle class. Instead of the blanket racism of the United States and Europe which assigns anyone with any visible trace of African descent automatically to an inferior position, the colonial powers fostered, through their control of employment prospects, a more subtle and very divisive system of discrimination based on skin tone, which is slowly dying out as the islands have gained at least the legal forms of independence; this has affected the self-perception of the islanders, who see themselves very differently from a racial and cultural point of view from the way in which Americans and Europeans see them. There is, at least within most of the islands, no white majority who hold the economic power and who are able to co-opt black musicians and their musicking to their own purposes, so that the culture is more autonomous than the black culture of the United States and, today, of Britain. The music remains within the community and in touch with its origins — which, in those mainly rural societies, are generally in the villages and small towns.

There is in the rural areas an unending source of new ways of musicking and of dancing; virtually every community has its own variants which identify whose who practice them as being from this or that village or town. These are ideolects within the dialect of their country or island, which is in turn a part of that common language of music and dance which is recognizable as Afro-Caribbean. Those styles generally remain within the community from which they sprang, but every now and then, perhaps through the activities of an unusually gifted or ambitious musician, one will spread to the towns to become a popular dance style throughout a region or an island, being possibly recorded for local labels and moving socially upwards as part of the music and dance of the middle and upper classes, such social barriers as are erected against the invasion of this lower-class music being almost always eventually swept aside. Such styles may be ephemeral, or may remain permanent features of the local scene, but they will retain contact with their rural origins; as Kenneth Bilby says: 'the various Caribbean popular musical styles, like their rural predecessors, have maintained their strong family resemblance; they are, after all, extensions of the same creative process of blending that has been shaping Caribbean musical life for centuries.'[17] These styles will invariably be non-literate in origin, becoming literate probably at some point on their ascent up the social scale; the rapid succession of one style by another points not only to the cultural vigour of Caribbean peoples but also to the speed of change and development that we noted earlier, which is a characteristice of non-literate cultures.

Roberto Nodal gives an account of just such development, of the Afro-Cuban *són* in the second decade of the present century. He tells us that in the nineteenth century there was much European music played, for example by touring opera companies, who could rely on picking up their orchestras on the island, as well as in churches and at the 'elegant receptions given by the plantation owners.'[18] These orchestras comprised mostly black musicians (we have here the answer to our earlier question of how Gottschalk could have found 650-odd musicians for his mammoth orchestra in Havana); just as in the United States, black musicians had no difficulty in becoming competent in European styles, and they also played for white dancing — *contradanzas*, derived from a French eighteenth-century courtly dance, and Spanish *zapateados*, which they gradually Africanized as *danzas* and *danzóns*, whose characteristic clavé-based rhythms we today recognize in the habanera. Those Africanizations were much condemned; Nodal quotes a Havana newspaper of around 1840: 'We think that the *danza* and the *danzón*, though born in Cuba, are of African origin . . . The music of these dances contains something of the wanton voluptuousness which characterizes the meek indigenous peoples of hottest Africa.'[19] It would appear that white Cubans found the same half-guilty fascination in black culture that we have seen in the whites of North America. Earlier opinions, says Nodal, were reversed after Cuba obtained independence from Spain in 1902, and musicologists claimed to hear in the *danza* and *danzón*, now become respectable, an 'example of white Cuban creativity with no black influence, or else traced their origins to fictitious Indian influences.'[20] For the blacks, it would seem, there was no winning either way.

The government of the new Cuban republic, imbued with Europeanizing fervour, embarked on the impossible task of eliminating all trace of African presence from the island, going to greater lengths in their measures against black culture than at any time during the colonial period. 'A "culturally whitened" black minority supported the government's campaigns to de-Africanize customs . . . Black religions were persecuted and the use of African drums forbidden.'[21] But 'despite the legal restraints, the African drums survived and kept their mighty sounds echoing through the republic.'[22]

It was under these conditions that the *són* arose, in the easternmost part of the island, and slowly gained in popularity. It was heavily dependent on complex clavé-based rhythms beaten on hand drums such as bongo and conga, and on maracas, claves, guiros and timbales — the first Cuban popular music to use such a powerful battery of percussion, and a forceful affirmation of identity by the Afro-Cubans in the face of the attempt to destroy, or at least suppress, their culture. Not surprisingly, it aroused considerable opposition among the white upper classes and the authorities, but it became immensely popular in the slums of Havana, and, in the way of such things (not unconnected with both the fascination exerted on the whites by black culture and that exerted on the upper classes by the lower — factors which have been perennially important in the diffusion of Afro-American musical styles) it was soon played and danced to in upper-class salons also. As it moved upwards it changed, becoming smoother, less 'African', so that we find there were several versions of the *són*: a rural version, a lower-class urban version and an upper-class version. Common to them all, however, was the use of the heavy battery of hand-beaten drums and the complex clavé polyrhythms. The *són* was taken to the United States by travelling Cuban musicians possibly as early as 1910, but it was in the form known as the *rumba*, in the early 1930s, that it became really popular there, and with it the whole range of Afro-Cuban percussion that is nowadays taken for granted as part of the instrumentation of Afro-American music.

To white North Americans, Latin America is a romantic place, where the writ of the Protestant Ethic and Anglo-Saxon puritanism, under which they themselves are obliged to live, does not run. They picture it as inhabited by indolent, picturesque, easy-going people much given to fiestas, revenge and violent politics; among the stereotypes whose power is not diminished today are those of the heavily-moustachio'd Mexican lying under his sombrero in the sun and murmuring 'Mañana' (an image assiduously fostered in the United States ever since the Mexican War of 1846–48 when Mexico was relieved of the present-day states of California, Texas, Arizona, New Mexico, Colorado and Utah), the sultry Creole lady whose favours are difficult but gratifying to obtain, and the Caribbean black, flashing white teeth in a beguiling smile but given to taking part in bloodcurdling nocturnal ceremonies. It would seem to have been designed by a benevolent Providence as a playground for romantically-minded North Americans — and for their unromantic business interests. Reinforced by stage musicals and by Hollywood movies with titles like *Flying Down to Rio*, *Saludos Amigos*, and *Caribbean Carnival*, not to mention the *Speedy Gonzalez* animated films, these and similar images have dominated northern perceptions of Latin Americans and Caribbeans for a century or more; northerners, including northern Europeans (as Britain's 1982 adventure in the South Atlantic demonstrated), simply do not take the people or their culture seriously.

Latin and Caribbean musicians, who, naturally enough, have long looked to the wealthy United States as a focus for their ambitions, have found themselves faced with these attitudes and have been obliged to tailor their musicking to them; Latin music is not just 'fun' but even slightly absurd — the image of Carmen Miranda and her banana-topped headgear comes irresistibly to mind — and in order to reach the wider white audience the music has been smoothed out and tidied up to suit its perceptions. Many Latin musicians have made a good living, both in North America and in Europe, by playing what is esentially American popular dance music with a Latin sauce.

But for two hundred years or more the response of black Americans to Latin music has been of another kind. We have already seen that there was in the colonial period a good deal of traffic between, in particular, southern North America and the Caribbean, and, as is usual, with the traffic went the music. The whites' romantic and frivolous images of Latin America have never taken hold of the black American imagination (romanticism being in any case a luxury most blacks could not afford), and blacks have been able to find in the complex Afro-Latin rhythms a way of escaping from the ubiquitous four-square four-four and two-four time that could be seen as a metaphor for their oppression by a Northern-European-descended majority. Latin clavé-based polyrhythms are after all closer to African complexity than anything in indigenous North American black music, and while strictly African polyrhythms have long since disappeared a liking for polyrhythms remains in all New World black people. Such rhythms would no doubt provide a strong reinforcement for black feelings of common identity with their South American and Caribbean fellows, and there is no doubt that black musicians, unlike the majority of whites, have always taken them very seriously indeed. As John Storm Roberts says: 'Latin rhythms have been absorbed into black American styles far more consistently than in white popular music, despite Latin's popularity among whites.'[23]

Such absorption can be seen, for example, in the rhythmic patterns of ragtime melodies, with their predominantly 3-3-2 accentuation; many of them would seem perfectly natural if placed over a habanera bass instead of the steady one-two (there are in fact a few rags by Joplin where that actually happens). It can be seen, too, in much early jazz, in which Jelly Roll Morton noticed, and himself used, what he called 'the Latin tinge'; indeed, Roberts suggests that the blending of the habanera rhythm into black music may have been 'part of what freed black music from ragtime's European bass.'[24] He quotes an anecdote from W.C. Handy's autobiography which tells how, around 1906, Handy introduced a habanera rhythm into the dance music at a black carnival in Memphis, observing in the dancers a 'sudden proud and graceful reaction to the rhythm'.[25] The use of both Latin percussion and Latin rhythms has been a persistent feature of jazz throughout its history; the collaboration between Dizzy Gillespie and the Afro-Cuban conga drummer Chano Pozo is only the best-known of many.

Latin and Caribbean rhythms, then, have long been a natural and expected element of black North American music. But their wider diffusion came with the major influx into mainland United States of Puerto Ricans after they had been accorded full US citizenship in 1917 (the island had been taken from Spain after the Spanish-American war of 1898 but for reasons of *realpolitik* had not, like Cuba, been granted independence). They were followed by Cubans, the first wave in the 1930s and 1940s and the second in the 1960s after Castro's revolution. The influx of Spanish-speaking immigrants, not only from the Caribbean but also, mostly illegally, from Mexico, has meant that today nearly one person in five in the United States is hispanophone; in New York estimates put it between one in three and one in two. This large 'Hispanic' presence (itself a genetic mix that ranges from pure Southern European through Oriental to African) has meant that there is in the United States today a large socially disadvantaged minority for whom Caribbean and Latin music is a major element in their sense of identity. That means, in turn, that a Latin musician has a considerable constituency today, if a mainly poor one, for his art. It also means that, as the new generation of Spanish speakers grows up in the United States, the individual identities of Cubans, Puerto Ricans and others tend to become fused in a composite 'Hispanic' identity, just as, three centuries and more earlier, the separate identities of the various African peoples in the North American colonies became fused into a single 'Afro-American' identity.

The musical style that gives expression to that sense of identity more than any other has been christened salsa, a term which means, simply, 'sauce'. Mario Bauza, a pioneer Cuban musician from the 1930s, told John Storm Roberts: 'What they call salsa is really nothing new. When Cuban music was really in demand the kids didn't go for it. Now they call it salsa and they think it belongs to them. It's good as a gimmick.'[26] Whatever the origin of the term, salsa is an exciting and joyous affirmation, exploration and celebration of the identity of Hispanic Americans which draws not only on Caribbean Latin styles of musicking but also on black American styles, especially rhythm-and-blues and jazz — thus bringing about a meeting, from different directions, of two African descendants — and spreading out once more into r-and-b and rock, where the influence of Latin percussion, in particular, has been pervasive, and into disco music. As with all street musics that move upwards, salsa has been taken up by record companies, with sometimes disastrous results, but also with many fine and committed recorded performances; as with other forms of Afro-American musicking, what gets recorded represents only a tiny fraction of the total. A young Newyorican community leader, Felipe Luciano, told Jeremy Marre: 'Here in New York we are among the most oppressed people. You've seen the dancers and what I call the cultural priests — the musicians. You've seen the joy, the very life, the pulsating rhythms which are our community. But all that belies our political reality. You can see the musicians playing three gigs a night, high on coke, for something like 30 or 40 dollars a night, their lips down to their knees, exhausted, trying to support their families . . . Every one of those musicians playing on the streets of New York is in his own way a keeper of tradition. There's not one musician playing conga or trumpet, whether Puerto Rican, Cuban or 'hispanic', who does not understand what the roots of his culture are. Ours will be the music of the Americas in the 1980s and 1990s. It's the street music that will survive, because there are more street people, poor people. It's the music of the people because it is their conscience. That's what salsa is.'[27]

This statement reveals in Latin American musicking, just as in that of black North Americans, that although the specific musical techniques of Africa may not have survived in the Americas, the fundamental African attitude to the act of musicking continues to flourish. If the ways of musicking of African descendants took different paths in the two Americas and the Caribbean through contact with two European cultures that were about as different from each other as one could imagine — the Anglo-Celtic and the Iberian — the two trajectories have not only met and interacted vitally over the years but also show the signs of their common origin. Any African musician would recognize the force of what Felipe Luciano says, and would recognize as well, in Afro-American musicking, no matter where it comes from, that endless process of exploration and celebration of self and of community, that loving (and often challenging) interaction between musicians, listeners and dancers, that ceaseless search for human meanings, which is also the stuff of his musicking. Such musicking becomes the more necessary for spiritual survival when the world appears to be ruled by the ruthlessly rational god whose name is Mammon, and whose rationality is always hostile to human life and conviviality. And since that search, that interaction, that celebration, is not the exclusive concern of people of the African diaspora (even though it is on them that the rational god has weighed most heavily), it is not surprising that whites no less than blacks have felt that Afro-American musicking in all its forms addresses them directly as well, in their inmost sense of who they are.

The fact that Afro-American music has spread across the world to affect the sensibilities of virtually all people — Viennese jazz orchestras, Thai pop stars, Japanese reggae bands (complete with permanent-waved dreadlocks), Czech and Russian rock groups, even Indian film musicians, are only a few of its manifestations — has often been cited as evidence of its destructive power, in league with big-business interests, on indigenous cultures. But, in the first place, no-one, not even with the backing of the most sophisticated apparatus of advertising and marketing, can persuade people to enjoy musical performances that have no relevance to their lives, their feelings or their identity. It is not Afro-American music that is destroying the ancient communities and cultures of the world, but Mammon, and his instrument the industrial society. Afro-American music, as we have seen, has been from its beginnings the weapon of a people in the struggle to preserve identity and community, and its presence the world over, in however diluted or skewed a form, testifies to a similar need in peoples the world over as they are torn from their traditional communities by the demands of the rational god. Even the simulacrum of community offered by the most commercial of pop concerts or top twenty record programmes clearly feeds a real hunger, just as the classical concert or record feeds the sense of identity of those who have benefited most from the god's destructive activities.

And in the second place, what is to be heard on record or seen on TV and in pop concerts is only a small fraction of the musical activity that is going on at any time; it is just not possible to develop a commercial popular-music industry unless there is a great deal of musicking going on unregarded in the lower reaches of the society. One may take it as axiomatic that the real work of Afro-American musicking — of all vernacular musicking, in fact — is done out of sight and hearing of middle-class observers; what is to be heard in public is only that part of it which someone reckons will appeal to a public beyond the community in which it originated, and make him some money. It will quite possibly not be the musicking that is most valued within that community, and may not even be representative of it. What is also axiomatic is that the more widespread the practice of musical performance the more discriminating and demanding its audience will be.

This may explain, at least in part, one of the most remarkable developments in Afro-American music in the present century, namely the return of the music to Africa, to give expression to traditional African social and personal values at a time when those values, and the social structures they support, have been subjected to intense and destructive pressure from outside. Here has occurred another turn of the creative spiral, as Caribbean, and in particular Cuban, rhythms have blended with existing West and Central African idioms to produce a series of dance styles which have swept the dancehalls of Accra, Lagos, Kinshasa, Nairobi and other African cities, each new style accompanied by a chorus of complaints that it was killing older styles. But each, in Roberts's words, would 'give way to another new fad, leaving only a few useful stylistic traits behind. Meanwhile, the local music goes on, at every moment seemingly about to be swept aside, but always surviving.'[28] From highlife to juju, musicians have always remained mindful of traditional ways of musicking and in particular of their traditional task in African communities; as Roberts says of I.K. Nairo, who is credited with the dissemination of juju beyond the Yoruba among whom it originated: 'He has produced music that is new but asserts its newness in a framework of the past, thus supplying both novelty and continuity to a people who value both.'[29] Continuity and novelty are also to be found in the bands who play this music, using as they do both the newest in electronic technology and traditional instruments — not only drums and other percussion but also xylophones, various stringed instruments and the mbira — as well as traditional vocal styles. In the swirling mix of styles can be detected also the sounds of European military bands, missionary hymns, and British, French and American pop music; influences as diverse as those of The Ink Spots, James Brown, the British danceband leader Joe Loss and muted trumpeter Eddie Calvert have all been noted by Roberts.

The ways in which Afro-American music returned to Africa have been well documented and recorded, and fall outside the scope of this book. There is, however, one feature which does bear comment in the light of our discussion, the tendency of West and Central Africans to favour Afro-Caribbean, and especially Cuban, styles whereas black South Africans have tended to be more interested in jazz. John Storm Roberts has an explanation for this: 'There is no mystery why different Afro-American styles were influential in different parts of Africa. In West Africa and the Congo, Cuban music was returning with interest something that largely came from there anyway, so that there is the most natural of affinities. South African music is quite different from West African and Congo-Angolan. As a generalization, it tends towards rhythmic complexity of singing voices over a regular beat; its polyrhythms come from the voices, which vary their accentuation relative to the basic rhythm. This is remarkably like jazz, especially the 1930s and 1940s music of Count Basie and others who riffed and soloed against a rock-steady four-four beat.'[30]

This is fair enough, but I cannot help being struck by the fact that in neither West Africa nor the Caribbean have black people been obliged, in recent times at least, to come to terms with a dominant white culture within their own country, while both black North Americans and black South Africans have. Jazz, as I suggested in Chapter 12, can be seen as a way in which black Americans have worked out their identity in relation to the dominant Euro-American culture; perhaps black South Africans are engaged in a similar enterprise. If there is any substance to this idea, then musical developments in South Africa over the next few years should be as interesting as the political.

In any case, Roberts's conclusion is that 'the root of all African pop styles is a blend of reinterpreted traditional — or at least local — elements with any foreign ingredients that may enhance them . . . In practice, these foreign elements are almost all Afro-American — even many of the apparently non-Afro-American influences have themselves been influenced by black music. Therefore, modern African pop music is a good deal more than a simply 'Westernized' — hence presumably neocolonialist — music would be. In fact, it contains a high degree of Africanism, direct and indirect, and completes a very satisfactory black-music circle binding together the Old World and the New.'[31]

The circle may be complete but it is by no means closed. Those African musicians have themselves been on the move, to the United States and to Europe, bringing their music with them to enliven further every aspect of Afro-American musicking. South African exiles have brought to American and European jazz an emotional intensity and rhythmic concentration that must relate to the new society that is today being born with such agony in their homeland, while West African juju musicians, now a familiar part of the concert, dance-hall and disco scene, have brought their characteristic African blend of intense seriousness and heartlifting gaiety. In addition, the multicoloured balloon of the New Pop has descended upon Africa, sailing away with rhythms and riffs, as it has done indiscriminately with 'well, you name it: soul (in all its forms), jazz (ditto), African (likewise), British, Irish and American folk, Latin, Euro-disco, rhythm and blues, rock and roll, avant-garde classical, reggae, ska, hip-hop, Chinese, Japanese, Indian and God knows what else, including, of course, an indigenous pop tradition that was in any case based initially on a variety of black musics.'[32] Exploitative such music undoubtedly is, but its ecleticism gives it a vivid flash-in-the-pan vitality that, for all its unashamed commercialism — or perhaps even because of it — is somehow endearing. All of it is serious, even the most frivolous, for it is all concerned with the most serious of all human concerns, the quest for identity.

I have left to the last the most succesful and influential of all musical styles to have emerged from the Caribbean in recent years, since it does reveal the intimate relationship between the emergence of a musical style and the development of a sense of communal identity. The crystallization of a new musical style by means of which black Jamaicans have been able to affirm, to explore and to celebrate a new way of relating to the world, to bring into existence a new kind of musical society, took place at a particular moment in the mid-1960s, when a number of social forces in Jamaica, making for the emergence of a new identity, came to operate together. It is worth looking more closely at those forces, and also at the factors which made it possible for that new identity to be recognized and empathized with by a large number of people beyond that small and impoverished Caribbean island.

When, in 1955, Jamaica celebrated, if that is the word, three hundred years of British colonial rule, with a fine show of loyalty to the 'Mother Country', the old colonial states of mind were already disintegrating. Since the abolition of slavery in 1838, black Jamaicans, especially the members of the small middle class, had learnt to despise their African cultural inheritance, and to look to Europe, and especially Britain, as the source of all cultural values and benefits. Children prepared for the Cambridge Local examinations, the boys in the flannel trousers, blazers and straw boaters of the English grammar-school boy, their sisters in navy-blue serge gymslips and black woollen stockings, imported if possible from England. They entered, or tried to enter, a civil service that was based on Whitehall, and they went to England to study and to fight for the Mother Country in two world wars. As we have already noted, there was only a minute white overclass on the island, but there was an elaborate system of social stratification based on skin tone which could vitally affect one's career prospects in banks, civil service, large overseas firms and the tourist industry. Three hundred years of British rule had been highly successful, especially in dividing the colonial population against itself. At the same time there was a fair degree of quite genuine acculturation to European high culture; leading church choirs in Kingston were used to giving fine performances of masterpieces of the European choral tradition from *Elijah* to the *Saint Matthew Passion*. And if a proportion of the choristers had learnt their parts by rote rather than by note, who can say that the performances were the worse or the less committed for that?

On a lower social level, Jamaicans absorbed the harmonies of British hymn tunes and sea shanties, the rhythms of waltz and quadrille, the instrumentation of military and drum-and-fife bands, and blended them with African elements in a rich variety of Afro-Christian religious rituals, an African-style three-drum ensemble called *burru*, as well as a four-square dance called *mento*, with heavy bass, a strong fourth beat and often bawdy social-commentary lyrics which were not unlike Trinidadian calypso in social function if not in form. In 1955 these and other syncretistic forms were emerging from the shadow of the European culture and were highly visible, and audible, in the tricentenary celebrations; the African inheritance was ceasing to be an embarrassment and begining to become a source of pride. By 1962, when independence was granted, along with desperate economic and social problems which included massive unemployment and an agriculture in ruins owing to three hundred years of colonial exploitation and mismanagement, the colonial mentality was in full retreat.

One of the signs of this retreat was, paradoxically, a decline in interest in older folk musics among the younger people, especially those who flocked to Kingston looking for work and who found themselves consigned to the same kind of *barrio*, in West Kingston, that we have already noted on the outskirts of other Third World cities. For most of those youngsters, the 'rude boys' or 'rudies', there were only two possible ways out of the *barrio* — through crime and through music. Crime was only too easy to get into, especially as the currency adopted by American drug dealers for paying the *ganja* (marijuana) growers was guns and ammunition rather than money, while music meant initially a Jamaican version of the rhythm-and-blues that could be heard from AM radio stations on the US mainland (Jamaican local radio was, naturally, modelled on the BBC, and did not broadcast such music). R-and-b, it will be recalled, was the euphemistic name given by the record industry to black blues which had been transformed by the new demands black Americans were beginning to make on US society after fifty years or more of intense repression. It is hard to resist the idea that it was the exuberantly black musicking of Louis Jordan, Fats Domino, Little Richard, Chuck Berry and others which appealed also to those Jamaicans who had come from a variety of ethnic backgrounds but who shared the common desire of that time to shake off the hegemony, both cultural and material, of the colonial power. The older, syncretistic culture of Jamaica must have been associated with an identity that had for too long been static and supine under British dominance; rhythm-and-blues was the music of a people who were, at last, on the move.

The trouble was that in the late 1950s the whole r-and-b style ran into the sand; when about 1964, the music that we know today as rock emerged, it had become transformed in a way that no longer appealed to Jamaicans, who liked their musicking hard, vigorous and black (the emergence of rock was of course a sign that whites had regained control of popular music). There was nothing for it but to make their own — a notable gesture of independence, since one of the characteristic states of mind that is inculcated by colonial rule is the belief, which does not have to be explicitly stated, that nothing indigenous is any good until it has been validated by the guardians of the metropolitan culture. As those guardians are never going to say it is good enough (for that would render the colonial as good as the master, and undo the very basis of colonialism), the colonial is kept in a constant cycle of self-negation which can be broken only by a massive gesture of assertion such as occurred at this time in Jamaica.

There were already a few small record studios in Kingston in the late 1950s, mostly making mento records for the tourists, and the owners of those portable sound systems which had become a feature of Jamaican musical and social life started to make their own r-and-b records, using local talent. (The minimum equipment for this highly competitive profession was a small truck or van, twin decks, amplifiers and the biggest speakers possible, ready to be set up in a hall or open space on a Saturday night. Each sound-system man kept the titles of his discs very secret, even scratching off the labels, and battles between rivals not infrequently came to the point of legendary shoot-outs.) The records they made were at first not for sale, but in single copies for their own use. Using the usual r-and-b instrumental line-up of horns, guitars, and rhythm section, they attempted to make their own r-and-b records — which came out, inescapably, with a Jamaican accent. Mento might have been repudiated in the mind, but it was in the blood, and those would-be r-and-b performances came out bass-heavy, with tricky bass lines and a powerful back-beat.

Naming, as we have seen, is a vital stage in the growth of a new identity, and the moment when it became recognized that what was being played was not unsuccessful rhythm-and-blues but a new kind of music occurred when the style was christened — by whom, who knows? — ska. Ska had other ingredients also, welling up from deep down in the subconsciousness of Jamaicans: the sounds of church hymns, of brass bands, of other Latin and Caribbean musics, even of jazz and the religious music of the Revival and Pocomania cults — and of Rastafarianism.

There is no space here to discuss the origins and history of this remarkable religious faith, but two comments are relevant to our discussion. The first is that Rastafari is the first religious faith to be constructed consciously and deliberately on an identity as exiled Africans and to look to Africa for its sources; it was thus very much in tune with other Jamaican currents of feeling at the time. And, second, that like early Christianity it is a faith which supplies an identity for poor people. As one writer has said: 'In Jamaica today the Brotherhood of Rastafari is not just a millenarian sect waiting to go back to Africa but an alternative spiritual nationality that supplies a mass cultural identity for thousands of young Jamaicans stranded between their school years and an endless cycle of demeaning labour and unemployment. For the estimated 75,000 Rastas in Jamaica the beliefs and rituals of Rastafari resolve all the killing ironies of a white man's god in a brutalized colonial society. Rasta asceticism allows poor people to make their way through the mechanical detritus of the twentieth century with dignity instead of shame and envy.'[33] It is not only a religion of the unemployed, however; many of Jamaica's finest artists — poets, sculptors, painters, actors and dancers as well as musicians — are Rastas. The same writers quote a young Jamaican engineer as saying that 'Rastas have contributed *more* to Jamaican culture than any other group. In time, they've become the conscience of the country. We feel we need them more than they need us.'[34]

The developments in Jamaican life and politics, themselves quite complex, which led to the transformation of ska, first into rock-steady around 1967 and then into reggae in the early 1970s, need not concern us. Those were years of violence, which are not yet over, and they were the years in which the new identity of the Rastas and of the Rude Boys (often finding themselves on the same, wrong, side of the law, especially the drugs law) was being hammered out in opposition to the traditional colonial values, their identities often being confused by the ordinary Jamaicans who found themselves caught in the crossfire. Both Rastas and Rude boys, often recruited for a single recording session, paid a few dollars and thrown out in the street again, had important roles in the development of rock-steady and reggae as at the same time both good-time musics and vehicles of often bitter and vehement social and political comment; nor did the Rasta musicians, despite their intense seriousness and their penchant for apocalyptic imagery, have any monopoly of the latter.

In musical terms, one can perceive in reggae, not an Africanization in the sense of the deliberate adoption of specifically African techniques, but rather a re-integration of scattered African elements from both Jamaican and American popular music: the return to a percussive approach throughout the whole musical texture, even on instruments not commonly thought of as percussive like the electric guitar and organ; the deliberate over-and-over repetition of small melodic and rhythmic figures; the simultaneous use of two or more pulse rates in the drumming; and of course the uniquely powerful emphasis on the backbeat, to the point that beats one and three virtually disappear, with two and four emphasised by the choppy *(um)-chaka-(um)-chaka* pattern, completely reversing that of strong first and third and weak second and fourth beat which is otherwise virtually universal in western music. All of these techniques, that is, these ways of going about the making of music, show in themselves the emergence of a new identity which says, unmistakably, Here we are, this is how we are, and you can like it. It is a point which is emphasised by the musicians' on-stage demeanour: cool, elegant, with a hint of arrogance which proclaims that they are making no concessions to the world, and certainly none to the audience.

Reggae is also different in another way from other Caribbean and Latin musics. We have seen how Latin and Caribbean musicians, if they were to gain a reputation that extended beyond the local or regional, had been obliged to 'make it' in the United States; those who controlled the means of dissemination there controlled access to the rest of the world. Reggae was the first musical style to break that hold, the first musician to do so being Bob Marley; he had tried, and failed, to succeed in the States and returned home to make his first successful records. This was partly because of the incredibly rapid development of recording skills and technology in Kingston studios, partly because of the initial monopoly possessed by Jamaican rhythm sections of the definite and precise, even finicky rhythms and basslines of reggae. But none of this would have been decisive had it not been for the appeal of its languid, casually elegant rhythms which turn the European rhythmic order upside-down, its combination of good-time sounds and sharp social commentary, and the stance of contained self-possession adopted by the musicians, with which dispossessed people everywhere found they were able to identify.

Another turn of the creative wheel came with the migration of large numbers of people from the British Caribbean — not only Jamaica but also Trinidad, Barbados, St Lucia, Dominica, Grenada — to Britain after the second world war in response to urgent supplications from the British Government and large firms, as well as from organizations like London Transport. Having been encouraged in school, as we have seen, to believe themselves British, and indeed having been granted full British citizenship by act of Parliament in 1948, they came to the Mother Country, to bitter disappointment in employment (despite the desperate shortage in Britain at that time of skilled workers, and despite the fact that over half of them were skilled, often highly skilled, they found themselves for the most part having to settle for the jobs that no-one else would do) and above all to the chronic hypocritical racism of the British, a racism which only intensified when the immigrants did what people everywhere are apt to do: they married and had children. Those children had the misfortune of coming to adulthood in the late 1970s, when unemployment was beginning to reappear on a large scale in Britain, intensified by the policies of the Thatcher administrations of 1979 and 1983, which believed in confrontation and repression, rather than dialogue and collaboration, as the way to solve the attendant problems.

The style of musicking that was to become reggae had travelled to Britain with the Jamaicans.

> 'Not smuggled in like contraband under false-bottomed suitcases and grips, nor was it absentmindedly left in the trouser pockets of those loose fitting two-piece suits in which the West Indies took the plunge into British society. It was even more insidious than that; it was under the skin, shapeless, formless and nameless, like an invisible implant whose carrier doesn't notice its presence on his person. The transitory Jamaicans weren't consciously aware that it had travelled with them, because it was an integral part of their make-up which there was little reason to isolate, examine or investigate. This was . . . Jamaica on the move, at the head of a Caribbean exodus, invitations in hand, to the colonial motherland, where the children were to be greeted with inferior living conditions and treated with hostility and suspicion. And the spirit of reggae settled down to incubate in boarding houses, nourished on sweat and toil and subjected to immense pressure.
>
> 'Strictly speaking, although the name reggae hadn't yet come into existence, the road to its development was well underway, because at this time Jamaica had begun to break out of its dependence on imported American R & B records, as the staple food for its dancehalls. The frenetic tempo of

> ska had emerged as the indigenous sound of the day. This mood was in turn transmitted to England where the Caribbean community enjoyed music as a means of relief and insulation as much as anything else. There was privacy in the illicit shebeens and basements where nightstalkers converged to drink, socialize and do the new dance.'[35]

It was, initially, then a private way of musicking which was used to support the reality of the displaced West Indians. But its qualities and its sharp power of definition were too obvious for it to remain for long unnoticed by the indigenous young. 'Ska,' says Dick Hebdige, 'obviously fulfilled the needs which mainstream pop music could no longer supply. It was a subterranean sound which had escaped commercial exploitation at a national level and was still "owned" by the subcultures which had originally championed it. It also hit below the belt in the pleasantest way imaginable and spoke of the simplicities of sex and violence in a language which was immediately intelligible to the quasi-delinquent adolescent fringe of working-class culture.'[36]

By 1970 the transformation of ska into rock-steady and then into reggae was complete. It is curious that the white group that was most enthusiastic about the new sound was the skinheads, themselves very much an out-group, subjects of those moral panics which periodically sweep over the English, and with a reputation for robbing old ladies and beating up coloured immigrants. They would attend the same reggae clubs as the young blacks, dancing to the music and imitating as best they could the latters' studied cool elegance. It did not, could not, last; the chasm between the groups was too wide, but for a brief period in the early 1970s it seemed possible that a real rapprochement might occur between the two social out-groups; it is a testament to the way in which people can use musicking and dancing as a way of trying-on an identity, without necessarily being committed to it, that things went as far as they did. The skinheads clearly felt something that appealed to them about the identity of the young blacks and about their style, which was for a time able to overcome the endemic racism of British society, but it was not strong enough to negate it permanently.

Reggae, while attractive to many white people, has still remained the 'property' of blacks in Britain to a surprising extent. It has been largely resistant to the siren calls of commercial success (the Rasta asceticism of many of the groups has contributed to this) and it forms a focus of identity for black British youth. It has taken over from and displaced the musical forms of other Caribbean islands, notably Trinidadian calypso and its offshoots (without, however, ousting them completely — soca is a definite presence in Britain also), much as salsa has among Hispanic New Yorkers. The relationship between British reggae and its Jamaican origins is ambivalent; the two have clearly developed in different ways over the last twenty years or so, even though there continues to be a great deal of overlap as musicians from opposite ends of the Atlantic frequently work together and appear on the same bills. Arguments about 'authenticity', though common enough, are pointless; as we have seen throughout this book, Afro-American musicians have never troubled themselves about such matters unless scholars and experts troubled them, and the only authenticity that matters is truth to the participants' experience, and power to serve their sense of who they are. As far as young black British are concerned, that identity seems to be becoming 'blacker' (clearly such a generalization is dangerous) as they find themselves increasingly isolated, through no fault or desire of their own, from the society into which they were born; it is today not uncommon to meet young black men and women in London or Birmingham who, having passed their school-days speaking local working-class English, now talk broad Jamaican patois, and some who even deny being English at all. There is at the same time, naturally enough, a fringe of musicians who court wider acceptance by moving towards the pop mainstream, but it does not often happen that a black reggae artist or group makes it in pop in a big way; a few years back a poll of fans chose the white reggae-influenced rock group, The Police, as 'best reggae group'.

The spread of reggae influence into the mainstream of pop, while it does little to enrich those who play the music in Kingston, London or Birmingham, does speak once more of that feeling in white people which we have noted over and over in the history of Afro-American music, which amounts to a subconscious admiration, even envy, of blacks and an empathy, which can cross the lines drawn by racial prejudice, with the values of their culture. The empathy became explicit for a while in Britain in the 1970s with a number of groups, themselves generally ethnically mixed, who made music in cross-cultural styles. Interestingly enough, The Specials, the best-known of these '2-Tone' groups, had found themselves initially unable to carry out their intention of combining reggae and punk in such a way as to get blacks and whites on to the dance floor together, and were forced back into ska for a fusion with which both groups could identify. The members of those groups well understood that a real rapprochement, even a fusion, must happen within the musicking itself; solemn exhortatory lyrics were worse than useless. 'Behind the fusion of rock and reggae lay the hope that the humour, wit and style of working-class kids from Britain's black and white communities could find a common voice in 2-Tone; that a new, hybrid cultural identity could emerge along with the new music . . . The 2-Tone bands were more interested in harmonizing the form and lyrics, the sound and the sense, so that, without being obtrusive, the multi-racial message could be *inferred* by a broadly sympathetic audience. They were giving shape to a sensibility rather than to a political programme.'[37] But they were going against the grain of British society, whose racism was being pandered to by populist right-wing politicians and mendacious national newspapers, and at the end of 1981, after a series of nasty racial incidents, The Specials quit. Nonetheless, the very existence of 2-Tone brought some comfort to those who hope eventually to see a genuinely multi-cultural Britain, even if their demise suggests equally that we are unlikely to see it in the near future.

In the meantime, reggae functions for the beleaguered black community in Britain in much the same way as blues did for American blacks in the early years of this century, as a tool for survival and for the preservation of community in a situation that must be endured, while at the same time functioning for a minority of whites as a 'model for romance, sophistication and elegance.' It is true that the poetry of reggae is more aggressive and explicit in its articulation of discontents than was the blues — or at least the blues we have on record, which may not be completely representative — and the activities of dub poets such as Linton Kwesi Johnson and Benjamin Zephaniah (Johnson testifies to having been moved to write poetry after reading W.E.B. DuBois's *The Souls of Black Folk*) have shown, even if the outbursts of violence in British cities in 1981 and 1985 had not proved it, that the spirit of resistance is by no means dead. And, again as with blues, there are many, both in Britain and in America, not to mention the rest of the world, to whom reggae speaks clearly and unmistakenly of a human identity in the midst of the 'mechanical detritus of the twentieth century' through which we are all, white as well as black and any other colour, increasingly having to find our way.

NOTES

1. EPSTEIN, Dena J.: *Sinful Tunes and Spirituals: Black Folk Music to the Civil War*, Urbana, University of Illinois Press, 1977, p 22.
2. *ibid.*, p 23.
3. BERGMAN, Billy et al: *Hot Sauces: Caribbean and Latin Pop*, New York, Quarto Books, 1985, p 74.
4. DU BOIS, W.E. Burghardt: *The World and Africa: An Inquiry into the Part which Africa Has Played in World History*, New York, International Publishers, new edition 1965, p 47.
5. BASTIDE, Roger: *African Civilizations in the New World*, transl. by Peter Green, London, C. Hurst & Co., 1971, p 91.
6. *ibid.*, p 94.
7. *ibid.*, p 154.
8. *ibid.*, p 153.
9. MARRE, Jeremy and CHARLTON, Hannah: *Beats of the Heart: Popular Music of the World*, London, Pluto Press, 1985, p 222.
10. BASTIDE, Roger: *op. cit.*, p 156.
11. ROBERTS, John Storm (1): *Black Music of Two Worlds*, London, Allen Lane, 1973, p 83.
12. BERGMAN, Billy: *op. cit.*, p 11.
13. GOTTSCHALK, Louis Moreau: *Notes of a Pianist*, New York, Alfred A. Knopf, 1964, p 39–40.
14. *ibid.*, p 26.
15. WILLIAMS, Eric: *Capitalism and Slavery*, London, Andre Deutsch, 1964, p 202.
16. *ibid.*, p 144.

17. BILBY, Kenneth: 'Caribbean Crucible', in HAYDON, Geoffrey and MARKS, Dennis (eds): *Repercussions: A Celebration of African-American Music*, London, Century Publishing, 1985, p 148.
18. NODAL, Roberto: 'The Social Evolution of the Afro-Cuban Drum', *The Black Perspective in Music*, Vol 11, No 2, Fall 1983, p 158.
19. *ibid.*, p 159.
20. *ibid.*, p 160.
21. *ibid.*, p 160.
22. *ibid.*, p 161.
23. ROBERTS, John Storm (2): *The Latin Tinge: The Impact of Latin American Music on the United States*, New York, Oxford University Press, 1979, p 40.
24. *ibid.*, p 40.
25. quoted *ibid.*, p 40.
26. quoted *ibid.*, p 188.
27. quoted in MARRE, Jeremy and CHARLTON, Hannah: *op. cit.*, pp 82-83.
28. ROBERTS, John Storm: *op. cit.*, (1), p 250.
29. *ibid.*, p 251.
30. *ibid.*, p 245.
31. *ibid.*, p 260.
32. RIMMER, Dave: *Like Punk Never Happened: Culture Club and the New Pop*, London, Faber & Faber, 1985, p 82.
33. DAVIS, Stephen and SIMON, Peter: *Reggae Bloodlines: In Search of the Music and Culture of Jamaica*, New York, Doubleday Anchor, 1977, p 63.
34. *ibid.*, p 65.
35. KAMBA, Mark: 'The Growth of British Reggae from Ska to Smiley', Programme Booklet to *Reggae Sunsplash*, Selhurst Park, London, June 29 1985.
36. HEBDIGE, Dick: 'Reggae, Rastas & Rudies', in HALL, Stuart and JEFFERSON, Tony (eds): *Resistance Through Rituals: Youth Subcultures in Post-War Britain*, London, Hutchinson, 1975, p 148.
37. DAVIS, Stephen and SIMON, Peter: *Reggae International*, London, Thames & Hudson, 1983, p 160.

Chapter 16

CONFRONTING THE RATIONAL GOD

It is common among white people, not only among those who admit to being racist, to think of black people as somehow simpler, 'closer to nature', more instinctively musical (especially when it comes to rhythm), and certainly less 'serious' than people of entirely European descent. The liberal may explain those qualities as not of black people's making (after all, the terrible system of slavery brutalized them and destroyed every vestige of culture they may once have possessed, did it not?) but nevertheless such liberals are as deeply in error as the most unredeemed of racists; none of the above notions will stand up to the most superficial acquaintance with black people or to the most cursory study of black history or culture. The fact is that Afro-American culture as it has developed over the last five hundred years is a strategy which has been evolved by a highly creative and socially sophisticated people, using remembered, and indeed consciously and carefully transmitted, African ways of thought and perception as well as whatever elements of European and Euro-American culture came to hand, in order to make life worth living in a situation that was at best difficult and at worst desperate.

It should be understood that those Africans, and their descendants, who were enslaved in the New World were the first of the world's peoples to experience the full dehumanizing impact of modern industrialism. The system of chattel slavery as practised in the Americas (a very different system, as we have seen, from that of Africa — or indeed of medieval Europe) was in every aspect save one a fully-formed industrial system, the only difference from that to which European peasants were later subjected being that the actual mechanical technology did not yet exist. It was the slaves themselves who were required, not just to serve machines, but actually to *be* machines; as far as the slavemasters were concerned all the slaves' human attributes were nothing more than a nuisance, and only their labour power was of value. It was on the plantations of the Americas that the new capitalists not only accumulated the wealth that made European industrialism possible but also learnt the techniques of industrial organization that they were later, as the technology became available, to transfer to the factories of Europe and of North America, and they applied them in a most ruthless and thoroughgoing way, which far exceeded anything they dare impose later in Europe. That they were able to do to the Africans what they could not do to European peasants and artisans was due to the successful implantation in European minds of the idea of the formers' innate inferiority. The development in recent decades of machines that are as intelligent as the slaves were required to be in their work seems likely to prove the final fulfilment of the capitalist dream of an intelligent and wholly submissive workforce; this is surely the real industrial revolution to which the man-machine pair that has existed in the factories of the last two hundred years has been only an unsatisfactory prelude. It does not require too perverse a reading of history to see the eventual failure of American slavery as having provided the impetus for the development of machines to do the slaves' work; and the reason for slavery's failure in the long run to deliver the goods as planned lay in the obstinate humanity of the slaves themselves, expressed in rebellion and flight when possible, and as passive resistance, sabotage and affected stupidity when they were not.

In the struggle not only to survive but also to make survival worth fighting for (the indigenous populations of South America and the Caribbean apparently thought it was not) the slaves possessed powerful psychological weapons, not dependent on material objects, which they inherited from their African forebears: a firm but flexible identity based on community, the ability to adapt and to improvise, a sense of the sacredness of life which permeates all aspects of living, and, not least, the great performance art of music and dance by means of which that sense of who they were could be affirmed, explored, and, yes, still, celebrated. It was, and remains, that strong sense of identity which has, for example, enabled black people in the Americas not only to face the need both to dissemble before the master, and, later, 'The Man', and to remain at the same time true to the community, not being torn apart by the contradiction, but also to search out and take from the American environment what was needed for living, and to blend it with what was remembered of the old.

The various phases of Afro-American musicking, as outlined in this book, show that that great performance art is no mere entertainment, but a vital tool in the building and the maintenance of identity. It is a weapon for the imagination in bringing to being, at least for the duration of a performance, a society which is richer and less coercive than that which today we know in reality, where individual and community enhance and complement, rather than oppose, each other. We need not look for the survival in Afro-American musicking of specific African techniques, but we need be in no doubt that the attitudes that lie behind the musicking derive from Africa. The culture itself has greatly changed over the centuries of the encounter with Europe, but the style of its change and adaptation is itself unchanging. The strength of any culture lies, not in any resistance to change, but in the ability to adapt to new conditions while always enabling individuals to say, This is who I am, and This is where I belong, against those who would say, That is who you are, and That is where you belong. It is the combination of a specific kind of cultural inheritance with a situation which ensured that that inheritance was selected (in a sense that is quite analogous to Darwinian natural selection) as an aid to survival which has formed Afro-American music as we know it today. It is neither 'simple' nor 'natural' in any of its phases but the complex and sophisticated art of a people caught in a particular historical situation. That the response to that historical situation has been, even at times of the most ruthless oppression, not a withdrawal from, but a reaching-out to, and engagement with, the dominant Euro-American culture must be recognized as an achievement of the first magnitude.

Let us briefly recapitulate some of the characteristics of

Afro-American music as we have seen them in our investigation; they are generalities only, to which any number of exceptions can be found, but they do nevertheless represent the main tendencies of the ways in which Afro-American musicians work. In the first place, it is not exclusive; the gift of musicking is open to all. It is not necessary for aspiring musicians to undergo any extended process of formal instruction, let alone to be examined or certified, before they can begin to make a contribution; they simply start with what they can do, just as in the arts of speech (also much cultivated among black Americans), and build upon it. In this the imitation of admired masters and mistresses of the art plays a major part. We need make no mistake, however; Afro-American musicians work just as hard at their art as do those of the European classical tradition, even if not so much time is spent in solitary practising. Groups spend rather more time cultivating that empathy and instantaneous response which are essential when not all the information required for a performance is available from a score; in any case, there is not much point in practising alone what can only be done in a group, and Afro-American musicking is essentially a communal occupation. Technical virtuosity for its own sake is not much sought after; it is what the performer does with what he or she has that is valued.

Secondly, all performance carries within it an element of original creation, however modest; it is not just the recreation of another person's composition. If the final music-object should turn out to be less complex and developed than a work of classical music that is not really significant, since, as John Blacking points out, 'apparent simplicity of sound produced may conceal complex processes of generation.'[1] Even more important, the relations that are established between the participants during a performance in which 'thinking and performing music simultaneously' takes place are much richer and more complex than those established when a player is realizing a score, since the listeners (and the dancers, should there be any) are not mere witnesses at a spectacle but active participants in that human encounter which is the performance. It is thus silly, on the one hand, to ask what the Afro-American tradition can offer to match the splendour of

Bach's *B Minor Mass* or Beethoven's Ninth Symphony, and equally silly, on the other, to try to set up John Lennon and Paul McCartney, as did one injudicious music critic in the 1960s, as the greatest songwriters since Schubert. It is not just that both concentrate on the sound-object, which in Afro-American music is relatively unimportant (even a record represents no more than a stage in the development of a performance), but also, they depend on the assumption, derived from classical music, that music originates from the top downwards, being handed down from Great Composers (or Great Songwriters) via Great Performers to the ordinary music lover. In Afro-American music, as we have seen many times — it is without doubt its greatest strength — new musical styles originate at the bottom of society and work their way upwards, reaching the ears of the middle and upper classes, generally through the medium of records, and often in diluted form, quite possibly around the same time as their anonymous creators (anonymous to us maybe, but not to their community) are abandoning them for something new.

Thirdly, relationships between the participants in a performance are not hierarchical; the performers do not dominate the audience, nor are they dominated by any outside person such as a composer or conductor. Nor is the performance dominated, or the relationships mediated, by a written score; where notation is used it tends to function more as a guide or a set of promptings to performance than as a set of prescriptive instructions. Performance itself is more concerned with the exploration of relationships between the participants than it is with the feelings or spiritual adventure of any individual, more concerned with being than with becoming, with present enjoyment than with either the past or the future. The question often asked by lovers of classical music: 'Yes, but will it stand the test of time?' is another silly question (I believe it to be an equally silly question to ask of classical pieces); if the performance serves the moment and the participants' sense of who they are, what more ought one to ask of it?

As a tool for self-definition and for the building of community, Afro-American musicking is an activity of profound seriousness and significance, even at its most frivolous and lighthearted. But that leaves us with the question posed in the Introduction to this book: why is it that it has reached out beyond an underdog population in the Americas to become an important element in the self-definition of so many millions of people, most of whom have no contact with the experience of black people in America or elsewhere, and has transformed the ways in which they make and respond to music? After all, there are many such underdog populations throughout the world, and virtually all of them cultivate their own styles of musicking, by means of which they affirm and celebrate their sense of who they are to themselves and to anyone else who will listen, but mostly those styles remain just that, little known outside the communities that gave them birth, exotic oddities at best and appreciated among outsiders only by enthusiasts and musicologists. In the United States alone, every ethnic minority has its own music, which may well serve for its people something of the same function as that which we have noted for Afro-Americans; many of these musics are exciting and beautiful, yet they remain minority tastes. And even they have been infiltrated by Afro-American styles; I heard in Buffalo a fine Polish-American dance band whose front-line players embellished their polka music with exuberant blues licks.

There are also the rich and complex musical styles of non-industrial countries such as those of India, Bali and even of traditional Africa, all of which celebrate values which are not those of the industrial state; they have been the objects of many attempts,none of which has 'taken', to graft them on to western music. What was it, then, that caused the musicking of this initially enslaved and still despised and underprivileged people to spread out, first through the Americas and then across the world, to become what is clearly the major music of our time? There can be no doubt that it is the *majority* form of musicking of the west today; if the European classical tradition numbers its adherents in millions, mainly in those societies that have a large enough and wealthy enough middle and upper class to support the expensive apparatus of symphony orchestras, concert halls and so on which the creation and performance of this music requires, the Afro-American tradition numbers its own in tens, if not hundreds of millions, extending from the poorest inhabitants of Africa, South and Central America, the Caribbean and Asia, to the poorer members of the wealthy societies and even into their middle and upper classes.

There would of course be no need to state the antithesis thus baldly if the two cultures were in a state of peaceable coexistence and collaboration, with each accorded equal status and importance within our society. But we know that this is very far from being so; the devotees of the European classical tradition assume at every turn the inherent superiority of their art, regarding it as the highest achievement of the human race in the art of sound and as the norm and ideal of all musical experience, while the overwhelming weight of state and private subsidy goes towards the support of those who make that music, as well as of those who teach it, research it, criticize it and act as its guardians. The devotee of classical music is of course inclined to disregard statistical criteria as irrelevant; if the mass of people, despite all the efforts made to educate them, still do not recognize the evident superiority of classical music, so much the worse for them. In any case, privately, he is inclined to believe that the music is not and never has been a matter for the masses; this attitude has the support of no less a figure than Arnold Schoenberg, who has written: 'If it is art, it is not for all, and if it is for all, it is not art.'[2]

The appeal of Afro-American music, despite its 'obvious' inferiority, has to be explained somehow, and it is generally attributed to the effect on a bemused and ignorant populace, whose ability to judge quality has atrophied during two centuries of proletarianization, of the machinations of cynical and unscrupulous media operators, especially record companies and radio and television networks. One need not follow the arguments through the maze of contradictions which rest on the assumption that most people are incapable of telling 'good' from 'bad' music without the aid of professional critics, and even that the masses have a kind of homing instinct for all that is worst (an assumption which is remarkably similar to that made by the guardians of public morals, who, like the critic quoted in Chapter 14, exempt themselves from the general incapacity). This means that the worse a musical performance, on or off record, the more successful it will be and the more it will profit those bogeymen, the record companies and the entrepreneurs. Marxist critics, at the head of whom is Theodor Adorno, have their own variant on this thesis: that the whole of Afro-American music is a gigantic capitalist conspiracy to keep the proletariat in a state of passive acceptance of its lot; jazz, in Adorno's world, is especially singled out for condemnation for its ability to make 'the inescapable easier to bear' and to encourage the listener to 'develop a taste for' the attitudes of subordination required of them in ordinary life. That such views can be quoted, straight-faced, in an authoritative survey of Marxist aesthetics published in 1984[3] shows the continuing hegemony of European high-cultural assumptions and of racism over those who would change society; indeed, the dominance of such assumptions over both the author of the book and those whose views she discusses engenders serious doubts concerning the clarity of their thinking on other matters.

While one cannot but agree that there are those who seek to use the musicians and their musicking for their own purposes, including political ones, or that the quality (which is to say, the human value) of the musicking has suffered from their manipulation, we still have to confront the basic question. The fascination that black culture, and especially black music, has exerted over white people in the Americas since early colonial times, and the mixture of attraction and fear it has engendered in them, has too long a history to admit of such lazy and self-serving explanations as those which the high-culture critics, whether Marxists or double-dyed political conservatives, in remarkable unanimity offer us.

We can see this mixure of attraction and fear in white people as far back as the beginnings of the encounter between the two peoples in the Americas. We see it in the genuine empathy which seems to have existed between slaves and poor whites as fellow-sufferers under a colonial aristocracy, which brought about the beginnings of a fusion of cultures; we see it in the minstrel show, which defused fears of the very attractive black culture and of its subversive potential by presenting it as laughable; we see it in the commitment to jazz of many young middle-class whites in the 1920s and in the panic-stricken response to it of the guardians of public morals and public music; we see it in the similar response in the 1950s to the advent of rhythm-and-blues under the name of rock'n'roll; we see it in the way in which rock musicians are treated by passport and customs officials when moving from one country to another; we see it in the attitude of educational institutions to Afro-American music and in their efforts to control it when they cannot exclude it; we see it in the persecution of rock musicians in totalitarian countries. The list could go on, but the pattern is too clear and consistent to be accidental. The greater the commitment to the values of industrial society and its associated high culture, the greater is the fear of Afro-American culture and Afro-American music. The pattern of that commitment *tends* to lie, as many social surveys show, along class lines, but it is by no means thus determined; it can be found at all social, economic and educational levels, as can its absence. Where the division between the two attitudes does *not* seem to lie to any great extent, is along a line drawn between left-wing and right-wing political orientations; the commitment to high culture is as common among the former as among the latter — which seems to me to point to some serious conceptual weaknesses on the left.

The history of individual musical styles in the Afro-American tradition shows generally an upward social drift, from a beginning in poor black or white communities, and acceptance in the lower reaches of society through performance in places that are generally nót frequented by 'respectable' people (as we have seen, the empathy between groups at the bottom of the social heap can sometimes transcend the hostilities of racism). At any point in its history a style may reach the limits of its acceptance and remain purely local or communal; this must be an everyday occurrence which passes unrecorded, in both senses of the word. A musician who is skilled enough, ambitious enough and lucky enough to catch the eye and ear of an astute manager or an influential tastemaker can carry it into the wider society, often at first the hip demi-monde, and get it recorded. If it attracts enough attention (again the help of influential people is needed at all stages), it will be taken up by white musicians, whose motives will be either genuine enthusiasm for the music or the desire to get on a bandwaggon — or, as usually happens, a mixture of both. Genuine enthusiasm will inspire some other musicians to play it regardless of rewards, most likely bringing their own playing habits to the performance and changing it in subtle ways which they themselves may not even recognize, adding a new turn to the creative spiral. The bandwaggon effect will bring even greater changes, mostly in the direction of European values, generally diluting the style to make it more acceptable to those for whom Afro-American values are too subversive, too disturbing. All of this activity will bring about a number of variants to the style, most of which will be recorded by either large or small record companies (the larger tend to use the smaller ones, which are more flexible in their response and have their ears closer to the ground, as scouts for new talent or a new style, snapping up the style as it becomes popular). A glance through the bins in any large record shop will suggest that there is someone who is prepared to issue a record of practically anything, no matter how unlikely it may appear. But, as our glance at the San Francisco scene showed, even this quantity and range represents only a small proportion of the musicking that is going on at any one time.

By the time the new style reaches the consciousness of the broad public, and in particular of middle-class 'music lovers', it is likely to have become considerably diluted, and indeed it is interesting to see how often the latter, when 'slumming' among Afro-American music, will zero in on innocuous or even tasteless versions of the music; in the case of jazz, for example, they are likely to favour versions by The King's Singers, The Swingle Singers, Jacques Loussier, even Yehudi Menuhin in duet with Stéphane Grappelli — anything to avoid the direct confrontation with those issues which jazz raises, and the dangers it presents to comfortable feelings of superiority.

For the majority of people, the principal medium for the encounter with Afro-American music is the radio. It is not altogether surprising that middle-class lovers of classical music should find their worst preconceptions confirmed when listening to a pop radio station, since not only is the choice of what is played there extremely limited (one might compare it to a classical station which played an endless diet of ballets by Delibes and Massenet, operas by Gounod and Donizetti and piano music by Hummel and Mendelssohn, with a few warhorse concertos thrown in) but also it is presented in such a relentlessly mindless atmosphere of asocial and ahistorical triviality that even the most genuinely inquisitive may be put off. The BBC's pop radio channel, Radio One, which blankets the whole of the British Isles, was recently described in a newspaper article as 'a vital promotional outlet for the record companies, an imperturbable daytime sedative, and forever terrified of saying or doing anything that might galvanize a cortex or bring a blush to the cheeks'.[4] The fault lies neither in the musicians nor in their musicking but in the way in which radio broadcasting is organized. It is difficult to perceive in the record industry, which is simply interested in short-term profits, anything that would give support to conspiracy theories such as that proposed by Adorno; as Simon Frith says, 'All A & R [artist and repertoire — who plays and what they play] decisions are basically financial and the calculations have to be precisely made . . . The answers depend on one single consideration: How much is the act going to earn?'[5] In the structure of radio programming, on the other hand, it is possible to perceive, if not a conspiracy, at least the operation of a number of self-serving assumptions on the part of the guardians of the official culture to bring about a defusing of the challenge presented by Afro-American music. It is worth a digression to show how those assumptions and values operate in Britain to determine what is allowed to be broadcast on radio, and how it militates against a true picture being presented of what musicians are really doing.

The first public broadcasts in Britain, twice-daily half-hour transmissions begun by Marconi in 1919, were quickly banned by the Government of the time, in accordance with the obsessive distrust of their own people held by successive British governments at least since the beginning of the nineteenth century. Acts of Parliament in 1922 and 1925 established the British Broadcasting Corporation and gave it a monopoly of the airwaves; no-one else was allowed to broadcast. The BBC was from the beginning run by an oligarchy appointed by the government in the same way as was, twenty years later, the Arts Council of Great Britain. Its motto, inscribed on the walls of Broadcasting House in London, was 'Nation Shall Speak Peace Unto Nation', which expresses better perhaps than they knew the priorities of its creators, since the idea of abstractions speaking to abstractions has been the source of many of the vices as well as the undoubted virtues of the BBC. In any case, the people have rarely had the chance to speak peace, or anything else, to the people, the BBC having operated from its origins on the assumption that it knew best what the people ought to have spoken to them.

As we have seen in the case of the Arts Council, the important consequence for music of that top-downwards distribution of power which pervades all the political institutions of Britain, has been that middle-class tastes and, equally important, middle-class assumptions about lower-class tastes, dominate the BBC's music programming. Initially the BBC broadcast on one channel only, a single programme that by 1930 was covering the country; this was later augmented to two, called, cosily but significantly, the 'Home Service' and the 'Light Programme', the former broadcasting a mixture of news, features, documentaries, plays and classical music, the latter playing 'light' music, which was a compromise between what the BBC management thought the populace wanted (their notional listeners were housewives over the kitchen sink and workers on the production line) and what it thought they ought to hear. Such slumming could only be disastrous for vernacular-music broadcasting in Britain, allowing only the most mediocre of performances to be broadcast; it was even more disastrous for the state of British popular music generally between the wars, especially for those musicians, of whom there was a considerable number, who were genuinely interested and skilled in Afro-American styles (there were also in Britain between the wars many fine West Indian musicians who might have brought a new vitality to British music had they ever been given a chance). 'Needle-time' agreements with the Musicians' Union resulted in severe restrictions on the broadcasting of records, so that little American music reached the ears of British listeners; jazz was represented by the staid all-British band of Henry Hall, and the airtime was filled out with cinema organs, palm court orchestras and showbands. Even in the rock'n'roll era, as Charlie Gillett observes, 'most of the music shows were family-oriented request programmes, which invariably concluded with a presumably educative extract from a classical music composition.'[6] It is not clear what happened in the 1950s to requests, which must have been sent in, for Elvis Presley or Little Richard, but they were not to be heard on the BBC's Light Programme. The BBC's monopoly was partly circumvented by commercial stations whose offices and studios were in London but whose transmitters were on the continent; the principal stations were Radio Luxemburg and Radio Normandie, which lived on revenue from British advertisers, largely the major record companies. Their coverage was, however, limited, as was their repertoire, the latter being dominated, predictably, by the majors' own offerings.

During the second world war, a third radio channel was established by the BBC to cater for the devotees of minority high culture, with a diet of classical music, highbrow plays, talks and discussions. Within its narrow compass it was excellent (today, as Radio Three, it has degenerated into a cosy middle-class club) but the channel's managers, either at that time or later, have never regarded Afro-American music as sufficiently 'serious' to warrant the attention of its listeners, with the exception of a few hours a week of jazz in ghetto slots. Up to 1961, then, there was no way in which British listeners could hear played on British radio what had become the dominant form of popular music, let alone other kinds of Afro-American music.

The vacuum was bound to be filled sooner or later, and in 1961 the first 'pirate' broadcasts began from a ship anchored outside the twelve-mile limit, followed by a fleet of others surrounding the British Isles. The best-known of these, Radio Caroline, anchored in the North Sea, claimed to have a full million listeners only three weeks after starting broadcasting. It was pop music, of course, that was played, a wildly eclectic selection from the music of the day, whose choice was dictated simply by the tastes of the disc jockeys who introduced the programmes. The quality of the programmes was variable, but they were personal, and there was a human identity behind them that could be sensed by the listeners. Commercial they certainly were; dull they were not, and certainly not as dull as the BBC Light Programme. Action was finally taken against the pirates (the very word tells us that the official mind was never in doubt who had the right to control the ether) which were run off the air by mid-1967. At exactly the same time, coincidentally, the BBC reorganized its services into four channels, of which Radio One was the popular-music programme, complete with some of the disc jockeys who had been thrown out of work by the demise of the pirates; up to that point the BBC had had announcers, who made no attempt to identify with their working-class listeners, but patronized them in plummy voices, in a way which to my colonial ears seemed to verge on the offensive. These are still to be heard on Radio Two, which has inherited the mantle of the old Light Programme; to listen to Radio Two today is to imagine oneself caught in a time-warp at around 1947.

Radio One had, and still has, a difficult if not impossible brief; as one writer has put it: 'It had to stave off all the moans and groans of the pop kinds left in the lurch by the crushing of the popular pirates, capture the Luxembourg listeners, suck in and flirt with the housewives, and provide a steady stream of hits, flim-flam, time checks and ninety-second news spots for factory and other workers.'[7] The writer continues: 'In order to maximize Radio One's audiences, few risks were taken; the aim was to serve "the centre of the market", at the expense of minority tastes. *It didn't matter if a consensus fun-loving middle group didn't actually exist*'[8] (My italics). Quite so; in trying to capture the whole audience for vernacular music the BBC ended up by not actually representing anyone. Only a member of a middle-class bureaucracy such as that which runs the BBC would have failed to recognize that, in using the word 'pop' as a blanket label for the whole of modern vernacular music, he is ignorantly conflating a large number of different ways of musicking, a large number of levels of seriousness, all of them valid for different social purposes, into one monolithic figment of his imagination. Trying to cater for the entire popular-music public at once is doubly impossible, first through the very real diversity of identities and tastes which it represents, and secondly through the impossibility of any member of the management bureaucracy of a radio network knowing what those identities and tastes are, or even what is going on among the musicians, especially in view of the new developments that are always taking place. The addition, in the mid-1970s, of local commercial radio stations, authorized by the businessmen's government of the day, has added little; in their attempt to deliver as many listeners as possible to the advertisers, to whom commercial stations owe their first responsibility, they follow virtually identical policies to Radio One, forcing both into absurd and destructive ratings battles.

In these battles the choice of records is thought to be too important to leave to the deejays who actually introduce and play them, and this task is carried out by a committee of network executives who meet periodically, listen to all likely-seeming new records and decide which may be played on the air and which may not. Their criteria relate not only to what they think listeners are likely to enjoy but also to what might be too disturbing, too politically subversive, too sexually explicit and so on, and from these meetings emerges a 'playlist' of acceptable records. As Simon Frith points out, there is a good deal of circular argument in the compiling of playlists, since a record that does not get on to it is likely to be severely handicapped in the struggle for popularity and sales:

> 'Radio moulds as well as responds to public taste, and record companies respond to as well as mould the playlist. Field promoters may not be able to persuade programme directors to use airplay deliberately to benefit their company, but they can persuade them that their company is producing the sort of records that are *a means to the programme director's own ends*. The plugger's task is to convince a radio station that a record is right for its shows, *fits its ideology of entertainment*, meets the needs of its audience; and even if record companies have no direct control over the "gatekeepers" of the airwaves, their guesses at the pass-words are, nevertheless, well informed and routinely accurate'[9] (My italics).

We notice that in this process, not only are neither musicians nor listeners consulted, but also that decisions are made on what is played on the basis of criteria that seem to have little to do with the actual quality of the performances on the records. In the circumstances it is remarkable how much good music does get played on pop radio, even if one has to listen past the endless stream of mindless prattle, silly jokes and pointless phone-in competitions that are the deejay's stock in trade. It is scarcely surprising, considering that they have no say in the choice of records, to learn that most deejays have come to think of the records as mere interludes between episodes of their own self-presentation; in any case, they have probably learned to regard the job as only a stepping-stone on the way to the more glamorous task of hosting television shows. Only on obscure late-night programmes is one likely to encounter anything that sounds as if it is the result of genuine enthusiasm for the music itself, or any evidence of musical taste, of whatever kind, as opposed to guesses concerning the likely popularity of a record.

The effect of this has been to vitiate that social transaction which, as I have maintained throughout this book, is the real function of the musical act. It is not the musical performances themselves that are bad — on the contrary, it is surprising how often one's ears are caught by striking and often intense performances when one really listens to pop radio — but that there has been introduced into the transaction a third person, the deejay, whose relentless self-presentation, just as in a conversation, constantly gets in the way of the establishment of any real relationships, and of any exploration of values or of identity. The deejay's world is ahistorical, eventless except for rock concerts, sporting fixtures and the premieres of films and musicals, and populated by 'the stars' and their doings; it is impossible for human encounters of any significance to take place, or for social or political values to be expressed other than the most conventional of majority prejudices. It is a free-floating world, with no anchor in the real stuff of living — or of musicking — and it functions effectively to cancel out any reality in the encounter between the listeners and the records played. What official radio in Britain has done to the musical performances it presents is much like what the British food industry has done to the products it purveys: it has removed anything that might make the encounter with them either nourishing or truly pleasurable, and in the attempt to make them look good has added elements that are actively detrimental in effect.

In this circular way, Afro-American musicking has been trivialized and rendered innocuous, its subversive potential defused, and even turned, as have the works of the older classical tradition in today's concert halls, to the service of the values of the modern state. Those who have assumed control of the airwaves, either for purposes of profit or because they believe it to be the state's right and duty to do so, have created a self-validating system to neutralize the fear with which those with a stake in the values of European industrialism and high culture regard Afro-American music. They call it 'giving the people what they want' but in fact it is a matter of giving the people all they are thought to deserve. It is not what they want but, rather, like convenience foods and denatured bread, it is all there is on offer; like those products, it still does offer something, even if it is only a relief to the tedium of a day's employment, or unemployment, and the counterfeit of community to soothe the loneliness of the citizen in the modern industrial state.

That it is not what people really want can be seen from the extensive musical culture, or, rather, network of cultures, that thrive without recourse to radio at all, but through the passing of news by word of mouth. As will be obvious, only a small proportion of the records that are issued are played on the radio; the Top Twenty, or Thirty, or Forty, production line which dominates the airwaves represents only a small segment of the total number of performances on record. Whole genres and styles, each representing a community and a set of values, are unrepresented, misrepresented, or only minimally represented, and the fact that among these can be found some of the best-selling records of their time testifies to the existence of an extensive network of enthusiasts, whose nature even the record companies' own distribution organizations do not fully understand.

When the music lovers themselves do take control of the airwaves the quality of the broadcasts is transformed. The development of new technology in the last few years has meant that a VHF (FM) transmitter of reasonable power and quality can be bought for less than two hundred pounds, and need be no larger than a suitcase; this has meant that a new generation of pirates, operating very cheaply indeed with portable equipment from council flats and the roofs of high buildings, have braved the severe penalties for unauthorized broadcasting laid down by three acts of Parliament since 1948, in order to transmit programmes of their own choice. The official argument for such penalties, that too many stations will disrupt the workings of the emergency services, will not wash; in New York City alone there are over one hundred legal stations, seventy of them on FM. Those who engage in pirate broadcasting risk, at the very least, confiscation of their equipment; one community station in London had its transmitter confiscated thirty times in fifteen months, while another was raided nine times in five months. It requires a high level of commitment to continue broadcasting under such circumstances, and the motives of the broadcasters are various. Purely commercial motivation is rare, except among those who operate offshore stations, where the possibility of raids and shutdowns, which might deter possible advertisers, is remote; more common are the desires to broadcast alternative political viewpoints, to provide something for immigrant and foreign-language communities, or even to cock a snook at authority, but by far the commonest is enthusiasm for musical styles that are neglected or misrepresented by official radio. Most of the enthusiasts are broadcasting one form or another of Afro-American music — jazz, funk, reggae and associated styles, soul, soca, juju and hip hop — and they do it mostly without thought for profit. One such enthusiast describes the beginnings of their South London station thus: 'I loved the music and joined up with Tony from there. In the early days pirate radio was a lot different from now. There was no advertising and we all had a whip around of about 50 pence per week. We did it because we enjoyed doing it and liked entertaining people — there was no profit motive.'[10] There is, of course, no such thing as pure, contentless 'entertainment'; identity and values are always involved, even in the most mindless of television quiz shows, and the extent of the commitment of this and other groups to the values affirmed by the broadcasting of their music shows through accounts of raids, arrests, fines, and confiscations of equipment, not to mention the hazards that are inherent in running a station on a shoestring. The operator I have just quoted added a significant comment, which shows how the action of the authorities serves to perpetuate the situation the pirates are trying to break: 'I feel the station went downhill when we started to take adverts in the late 1970s, *but we had to because we were being raided more often*.'[11] (My italics).

There was a freshness and a vitality about those stations after listening to conventional BBC or commercial radio which transformed the whole experience of radio listening; while their presentation was, given the conditions, mostly surprisingly professional there was an amateur enthusiasm which showed through whatever was broadcast, and they introduced this listener, at least, to new kinds and styles of music. While some of the exhilaration must have come from the pressures of working without proper technical backup on ramshackle equipment, not to mention the constant anticipation of the bang on the door, the principal pleasure came from hearing the recorded performances in a context that did not reduce them all to homogenized pap. But perhaps the main value of the pirate stations has been to enable a culture to speak to itself and for itself, rather than being spoken to and about, to say, This is who we really are, and not who you tell us, through official radio, that we are.

The struggle for the control of music radio is thus an aspect of a larger struggle in which all the media of information are involved; it is for the right to define oneself rather than to be defined, to speak for oneself rather than to be spoken about. That is the most basic of civil rights, from which all others stem, and it is that with which Afro-American musicking has been concerned from the moment whan an enslaved African first made a song in the new homeland. It is, of course, a question which is of concern not to black people only; we are all, black and white alike, coming under pressure from a state which is increasingly given to the imposition of identity upon its citizens, increasingly given to disrupting human relationships, increasingly able to impose its values on us. These are ordeals which black people have been enduring for centuries, and the manner of their resistance has a liberating lesson for us all.

Those brought up in European and Euro-American culture find difficulty in particular with two of the fundamental assumptions of African culture which I mentioned in the first chapter: first, the idea that what Davidson calls 'the art of social happiness' is the supreme human art, to which all other arts, and the sciences also, must contribute, and secondly, the idea that the arts, and especially that great performance art of music-dance-drama-masking-costume for which we lack a name, are vital means by which human identities and relationships are explored, affirmed and celebrated, and human societies criticized. From the first of these two major ideas flow others: in particular, first, the unity, rather than the opposition, between the natural world and human life and action, that unity which unites opposites without the need for dialectical struggle, and, secondly, the importance of the community not just as a forum for individual striving but as the very origin and essential nourishment of individual identity and development and as the point of origin of all political power. Such ideas, were they to take root in Europe and America, or indeed anywhere else, would result in the dismantling of the great superstructures of power and their supporting structures of abstract knowledge and relentless competitive individualism; they thus present us with a powerful alternative to the values which support the modern state and which militate so grievously against the social happiness of most of the world's population. The second assumption, of course, is not unique to Africa, but it is without doubt there that it is most highly developed and best understood; it is the unique and precious contribution of Africans to human culture.

But African societies, though they have endured the depredations of the slavers and the ravages of colonialism, and finally the imposition by the retiring colonial powers of nation-state divisions that may have suited the latters' own convenience but have little to do with indigenous social realities, have not been subjected to the rigid disciplines of industrial development — except in the Republic of South

Africa, where, once they regain control of their country and of their lives, Africans may yet amaze the world. There is for that reason no way in which the musicking of Africans, even though in all its variety it presents such vivid images of community, of unity in opposites and of reciprocity, can engage with the concepts and concerns of the industrial state, its hierarchies, its rigid time sense, its competitiveness, its loneliness, its conformism and its denial of the body.

On the other hand, the people of the African diaspora have been intimately acquainted with the rational god for nearly five hundred years, far longer, as we have seen, than any other of the world's peoples, and their musicking and their dancing have been tools by means of which they have learned to confront the god and his monstrous system, and to survive. The history of musical development that I have sketched out in this book is the history of a people who have not merely attempted to preserve ancestral values but have engaged constantly with that system and its associated culture to find what they could use of it and what they could not. The answers to their probing, through the media of music and dance, have never been final or absolute, but always adapted to the time and to the situation, changing as circumstances changed, always in some degree oppositional (for total acquiescence meant spiritual death) and always based to some irreducible degree on African values and ways of musicking and of dancing. It would seem as if every single member of the African diaspora must work out his or her own accommodation to the dominant white industrial culture, and that accommodation can never be final or complete, but must be improvised day by day, like a musical performance, following the rules of the African inheritance. Many white people find that power of improvisation, and that inheritance, in life as in music, enviable.

We can now, finally, arrive at an answer to the question posed earlier, concerning the appeal possessed by this music of an underdog people which could make it reach out and span the world. The answer which I offer is that black people in the Americas, North and South, and in the Caribbean, have found ways of engaging, through their musicking and their dancing, with fundamental human questions of identity and community which, as industrial states in our time become more oppressive, have become the vital questions which all of us must confront if we are to keep our power to say, This is who we are, and to explore, affirm and celebrate our sense of who we are, in relationships with our fellow humans that are not just the crude instrumental and exploitative relationships of industrialism. The tradition of western classical music, whatever it might once have been, can no longer serve us in this task, for its values have become completely identified with those of the state, and its musicians have become dependent for their livelihood on the very institutions which their art ought to criticize. Nor can the folk traditions of Europe or America, even those of the urban working class, provide the tools for the encounter with those great concerns of our time, for they are either ignorant of industrialism or else are so absorbed in its values that they can point to no alternatives but only protest, even if eloquently, at the injustices of the status quo.

We can see also the reason for the mixture of attraction and fear which each Afro-American musical style has in turn inspired in many white people, as well as for the love and joy it has inspired in countless others who have accepted the music's values and have been content to allow, as Albert Murray says, black American musicians to become 'models and ancestor figures'. Even those who have no direct contact with black people or comprehension of black experience have been able to find in the music an idiom and a set of values which they can encounter directly, without intermediaries. If the very openness and inclusiveness of the music has sometimes proved its undoing, rendering it, like the musicians who play it, liable to ruthless commercial exploitation, if some have grown rich and famous through abusing its values and offering to their listeners a mere counterfeit of the community which it celebrates, and if it even looks to some as if the whole tradition is submerged in money and in corruption, one can only point out, first, that no part of our society today is free from corruption (certainly not the classical tradition) and, second, that all the commercial activity, so visible, and audible, to the onlooker, in fact represents only a tiny fraction of the musicking that is going on at any time, not only in record studios but in cafés, bars, living rooms, nightclubs, draughty garages, open spaces, dance halls, prisons, churches, by musicians professional and amateur, skilled and unskilled, formally trained and unschooled, famous and obscure, rich and poor, all working to bring into existence, in collaboration with their listeners, that ideal society, those relations between human beings, that can enable each one to feel, in a literal sense, in tune with all the others and with the world, to know the presence of a supporting community without which survival is not only not possible but not worth fighting for. Afro-American musicking is, in a word, about surviving; it may well be needed by all of us in the years that are to come.

NOTES

1. BLACKING, John: *How Musical Is Man?*, London, Faber & Faber, 1976, p 113.
2. SCHOENBERG, Arnold: 'New Music, Outmoded Music, Style and Idea', in STEIN, Leonard (ed): *Style and Idea: Selected Writings of Arnold Schoenberg*, transl. by Leo Black, London, Faber & Faber, 1975, p 124.
3. quoted in JOHNSON, Pauline: *Marxist Aesthetics: The Foundations Within Everyday Life for an Emancipated Consciousness* London, Routledge & Kegan Paul, 1984, p 91.
4. SWEETING, Adam: 'The Longest Players of Them All', *The Guardian*, Saturday, 18 January, 1986, p 13.
5. FRITH, Simon: *Sound Effects: Youth, Leisure and the Politics of Rock'n'Roll*, London, Constable, 1983, p 104.
6. GILLETT, Charlie: *The Sound of the City: The Rise of Rock and Roll*, London, Souvenir Press, revised edition 1983, p 153.
7. HIND, John and MOSCO, Stephen: *Rebel Radio: The Full Story of British Pirate Radio*, London, Pluto Press, 1985, p 15.
8. *ibid.*, p 16.
9. FRITH, Simon: *op. cit.*, p 120.
10. HIND, John and MOSCO, Stephen: *op. cit.*, p 22.
11. *ibid.*, p 22.

INDEX

CHRISTOPHER SMALL is the author of *Music, Society, Education* (Wesleyan, 1996), *Musicking* (Wesleyan, 1998), and *Schoenberg* (1978). He was Senior Lecturer at Ealing College of Higher Education in London until 1986. He lives in Sitges, Spain.

LIBRARY OF CONGRESS CATALOGING-IN-PUBLICATION DATA
Small, Christopher, 1927–
Music of the common tongue : survival and celebration in African American music / Christopher Small.
p. cm. — (Music/culture)
Originally published: London: J. Calder; New York: Riverrun Press, 1987. With new pref.
"Wesleyan University Press."
Includes bibliographical references and index.
ISBN 0–8195–6357–9 (pbk.: alk. paper)
1. Afro-Americans—Music—History and criticism. 2. Music—United States—History and criticism. 3. Music and society. I. Title. II. Series.
ML3556.S65 1998
780'.89'96073—dc21 98–23578